NATIVE PEOPLE, NATIVE LANDS

Canadian Indians, Inuit and Metis

NATIVE PEOPLE, NATIVE LANDS

Canadian Indians, Inuit and Metis

Edited by
Bruce Alden Cox

Carleton Library Series No. 142

Carleton University Press
Ottawa, Canada
1992

Acknowledgements
Carleton University Press gratefully acknowledges the support extended to its publishing programme by the Canada Council and the Ontario Arts Council.

ISBN 0-88629-062-7

Printed and bound in Canada.
Second printing 1988, revised
Third printing 1991
Fourth printing 1992

Canadian Cataloguing in Publication Data

Main entry under title:

Native people, native lands : Canadian Indians, Inuit and Métis

(The Carleton library ; 142)
Bibliography: p.
ISBN 0-88629-062-7

1. Indians of North America—Canada. 2. Inuit—Canada. 3. Métis. I. Cox, Bruce (Bruce Alden) II. Series.

E78.C2N38 1987 971'.00497 C87-090284-9

Distributed by:
Oxford University Press Canada
70 Wynford Drive,
DON MILLS, Ontario, Canada, M3C 1J9.
(416) 441-2941

Cover: Chris Jackson

Table of Contents

List of Tables and Figures

Introduction

For A.W.C.

How are we to understand the economic life of indigenous peoples? The answer might fill volumes and still not satisfy everyone. There is, nevertheless, much to be said for the Marxian notion of the relations of production. In an earlier publication, I argued for the utility of this concept in understanding the social relations of non-industrial peoples.

> Marx maintained that men enter into "relations of production" appropriate to their "material forces of production"—that is, their technologies. These relations make up the social organizations within which individuals produce. He saw relations of production as the "real foundation" on which arises "a legal and political superstructure" and to which certain forms of "social consciousness"—that is, ideology—correspond. Hence ideology . . . and social organization are seen as part of the process by which men (and women) gain their subsistence.[1]

I argued there that the Marxian notion of foundation and superstructure offered a workable strategy for cultural ecology since it brought ideology and polity into the purview of students of adaptation. I now wish to pursue the implications of this claim, something I neglected in the earlier volume. Here I make no claims to, nor demands on, philosophical expertise, but simply hope to show that the Marxian strategy is preferable to other attempts to explain indigenous adaptations.

Let us return to base and superstructure. Causality might seem to run in a single direction, as in this early essay:

> The technological and economical aspects of culture change more readily and more rapidly than its social and religious aspects. Inevitably this brings about a discontinuity between the two which, when it reaches a certain magnitude, results in abrupt readjustive changes in social and religious institutions.[2]

Thus, technology changes first and fastest, and sweeps ideology and social relations along with it. This view, however plausible, lacks any sense of a system in operation. All causality comes from one place and flows in one direction. No role is assigned to ideology, social relations, or political organization save that of playing follow-the-leader. There is also no consideration of stability. Not everything changes all the time. What keeps a social system operating with some measure of continuity? Marxist (and neo-Marxist) scholars argue that ideology plays an important role in social continuity. In the neo-Marxist view, ideology serves to justify the relations of production, helping workers accept their position in the productive process. Usually that is said about exploitive relations of production, but it applies equally to societies with egalitarian social relations. Godelier, for example, argues that religious behaviour plays a crucial role in the continuity of the productive process among the Mbuti pygmies. On the Mbuti *molimo* rite Godelier writes:

> Religious activity broadens and exalts all positive aspects of social relations and at the same time allows the maximum attenuation, the temporary putting aside, of all the contradictions contained within these social relations. Religious activity therefore is a form of genuine *labour*. . . . Far from having nothing to do with material culture and mode of production, as some idealists would wish, religious observance is both a material and political function of production.[3]

Another example of the role of religious ideology in sustaining the relations of production among foragers comes from the Mistassini band Cree hunters, and is described by Adrian Tanner in Part II of this volume. Among the Mistassini, the right to hunt in certain areas is said to be "owned" by the leaders of hunting groups. (Feit calls these men "stewards".) Furthermore, such elderly leaders are said to enjoy "friendships" among various game species. Tanner writes:

> The concern of other hunters for the loss of the spiritual power of an old person is noticeable when such a person dies. A watch is kept at the grave for the first few nights following the burial, and the non-appearance of a member of the species which had been the old man's "friend" is taken to mean that the animal is sad at the death of his friend and will therefore leave the area. In practice, any unusual behaviour of such an animal during this period, not only at the graveside, is taken as a hopeful sign. If it is made clear that the animal will stay, the reason sometimes given is that the friendship relationship with the animal *has been taken over by another member of the hunting group, usually the man's son.* [author's italics].

Tanner describes the role of religious belief in reproducing the relations within which production is carried out in a hunting society even more clearly:

> Given that Mistassini are concerned with the inheritance of the spiritual power of the old men, can such ideas be seen as a model for the way the inheritance of rights to animal resources is conducted? In cases of spiritual power the inheritor appears always to be a co-resident, and is on warm terms with the deceased. Often he is a son . . . the explicit ideal.

In these passages religious activity is indeed seen as a "form of genuine labour" which is crucial to the reproduction of the foraging mode of production, as Godelier also argues. We must not neglect connections of the sort traced by Godelier, Tanner and others, even though they seem to stray from what is usually considered economic life. It is tempting to lose patience with scholars who trace the intricate strands of relations between religious ideology and productive labour. The following passage, reviewing an early study by Tanner, shows just how tempting it is.

> The bulk of Tanner's account of Mistassini ethno-ecology revolves about their cosmological conceptions of land, animals, spiritual forces and man's place in this scheme. . . Ethno-ecology here verged on becoming theological ecology.[4]

If this is theological ecology, let us make the most of it! When Indians report on their concepts of land, animals, spiritual forces, and mankind's relations with all of these, it is folly to suppose that these subjects have nothing to do with the organization of production. The approach taken by Tanner, and this volume, are not the same as technological determinism. Our approach focusses on the relations of production, and not the material forces of production. This is not a matter of splitting hairs. The distinction has important consequences for our understanding of the adaptations of Canadian native peoples.

Hierarchical Relations of Production

Not all who use foragers' technology share in their mode of production. If social relations define the foraging mode, then there is nothing to say that some foragers may not develop hierarchical relations of production. Legros shows that this occurred among the Tutchone of the Yukon Territory. The Tutchone consisted, in the 1800s, of "low people," slaves and "high people." According to Legros, the "high people" dominated and exploited the others.[5]

Better known cases come from the North Pacific coast, where social hierarchies, chiefly prerogatives, and slavery are well attested. Lee maintains that these societies did not take part in the foraging mode of production even though they subsisted on the products of field, forest, stream and tide.[6] Production among the Nootka, Tshimshian, Kwakiutl and their neighbours was not organized in an egalitarian manner. Leland Donald, for example, reconstructs Nootkan relations of production, showing them under the direction of the titled "owners" of the fishing sites. Chiefly "owners" brought sufficient labour power to bear by mobilizing commoners and slaves. Slavery is well attested here, and elsewhere, on the Pacific coast, but many scholars have argued that their labour power was not crucial to native production. Donald believes otherwise.

> Is there enough assignable labour power available to have a real impact on Nuu-chah-nulth-aht [Nootkan] descent group's capacity to preserve and store food? . . . [They were] about one-fourth titleholders, one-half commoner and one-fourth slave . . . [thus] clearly there was enough slave labour to make a real difference to Nuu-chah-nulth-aht production.[7]

Donald argues that much of what is distinctive about the societies of the North Pacific coast stems from the use of slaves in production, that these were, to some extent, "slave" societies.

> In a slave society everyone is affected [infected] by slavery: slave, master, and ordinary citizen. The Greek literature makes this clear [although the Greeks were not self-conscious about slavery]. The literature on the Nuu-chah-nulth-aht is much less rich on the subject, but nothing I have read contradicts this view and the violence so common in early accounts of Nuu-chah-nulth-aht life is certainly appropriate to a slave society.[8]

Where the foraging mode of production rests on food sharing and egalitarianism in political life, the societies of the North Pacific coast clearly organized their production in other terms. In that sense they remain outside the foraging mode of production, although they remain foragers in their subsistence base. We will return to the anomalous position of the societies of the Pacific coast in Section IV.

Technology of Production

The foraging mode of production cannot be defined by the technology employed in it. Relations of production comprise the defining characteristic, in our perspective, of the foraging mode. Can foragers use skidoos, boats with kickers, or bush planes to reach their hunting grounds? Likely they can, and still remain foragers, if their relations of production remain unaffected. Further, as Legros argues convincingly,[9] more than one mode of production may be contained in a single social formation. Thus there is more room for manoeuvering than the techno-determinists might suppose. Hunters can take on new technology without changing the way in which production is organized. Richard Lee, on what is crucial in foraging social organization, comments:

> What, then, is the key to the Foraging Mode of Production? I would argue that the essence is the fact of sharing and egalitarianism. . . . Hunting and gathering as productive forces are important; but they are not the primary factors in themselves.[10]

And:

> Quite central to the Foraging Mode of Production is a strong emphasis on sharing and egalitarianism. . . . Food is widely shared, and land is collectively owned and utilized.[11]

While such equitable and egalitarian relations continue, the foraging mode of production remains in force. This is more than an academic exercise; an important trial, *Kanatewat vs. The James Bay Development Corporation*, revolved on this very issue. The Corporation had attempted to prove that the James Bay natives were so changed by wages and imported technology that the proposed hydroelectric project would not significantly affect them. The Cree and Inuit did admit that they attended schools and clinics, that most bought "sugar, flour, tea, . . . tobacco, clothes, oil, gasoline, fire-arms, ammunition, fishing, hunting and trapping equipment"[12] and that they made some use of motor boats. Mr. Justice Malouf in commenting on this line of evidence, states:

> I note that many witnesses produced by respondents [The Corporation] confirm the testimony of petitioners that a great number of Cree Indians and Inuit still hunt, trap and fish. The fact that they purchase certain foods from the stores to supplement their diet does not mean that they are not dependent on the land. . . . These pursuits are still of great importance to them and *constitute a way of life* for a great number of them.[13] [author's italics]

Further, Mr. Justice Malouf's judgement came close to a concept of a foraging mode of production. In summing up, he concluded:

> They have a unique concept of the land, make use of all its fruits and produce including all animal life therein and any interference therewith compromises their very existence as a people.[14]

Notes

1. Bruce Cox, *Cultural Ecology: Readings on the Canadian Indians and Eskimos* (Toronto: Macmillan Company of Canada Ltd., 1978), 12.
2. Dominique Legros, "Chance, Necessity, and Mode of Production: A Marxist Critique of Cultural Evolutionism," *American Anthropologist*, vol. 79, no.1 (1977): 27.
3. Maurice Godelier, *Perspectives in Marxist Anthropology*, translated by Robert Brain (Cambridge: Cambridge University Press, 1977), 60.

4. Rolf Knight, "Grey Owl's Return," *Reviews in Anthropology*, vol. 1 (1974): 355.
5. Dominique Legros, "Reflexion sur l'origine des inégalités sociales à partir du cas des Athapaskan tutchone," *Culture*, vol. 2, no. 3 (1982): 65.
6. Richard B. Lee, "Is There a Foraging Mode of Production?" *Canadian Journal of Anthropology*, vol. 2, no. 1 (1981): 17–18.
7. Leland Donald, "Was Nuu-chah-nulth-aht (Nootka) Society Based on Slave Labour?" in *The Development of Political Organization in Native North America; 1979 Proceedings of the American Ethnology Society*, ed. Elizabeth Tooker (Washington, D.C.: American Ethnological Society, 1983).
8. *Ibid.*, 116.
9. Legros, "Chance, Necessity, and Mode of Production," 30–31.
10. Lee, "Is There a Foraging Mode of Production?" 17.
11. *Ibid.*, 15.
12. [1974] R.P. 38 Le chef max (One-Onti) Gros-Louis et autres C. La Société de developement de la Baie James et autres.
13. *Ibid.*
14. *Ibid.*

Part I
The Great Lakes — St. Lawrence Region

Writing early in the nineteenth century, U.S. Chief Justice Marshall commented on the position of the natives of the St. Lawrence region during the eighteenth century:

> The peculiar situation of the Indians . . . occupying a country claimed by Great Britain, and yet too powerful and brave not to be dreaded as formidable enemies, required, that means should be adopted for the preservation of peace; and that their friendship should be secured by quieting their alarms for property.[1]

In Marshall's judgement on *Johnson v. M'Intosh* (1823), "Too powerful and brave not to be dreaded,"[22] sums up the mixed feelings with which Americans and Canadians then regarded the Indians of the St. Lawrence region. Also to be found in the passage is the notion of military reputation as an aspect of inter-group relations. This was by no means a small point, particularly early on. Indeed, three of the four essays in Part I take up war and reputation as aspects of inter-group relations. Sue Johnston's contribution investigates the losses resulting from epidemics of European origin as a factor contributing to warfare during the eighteenth century. (The losses were likely greater than currently accepted estimates.) Brian Given's chapter concerning what the native wars of that period were *not* about, complements this nicely. Evidently the wars were not caused by anyone's anxiety to corner all the trade muskets, as earlier scholars, such as Hunt, had argued.

> A tribe whose enemies had weapons which it lacked had few alternatives, and all of them were unpleasant. It inevitably made war upon the competitor.[3]

In this, we run the risk of reading early warfare accounts in terms of twentieth century perceptions. The phrase, "European firearm," for example, may bring to mind a modern, breech-loading repeating rifle, loading brass percussion cartridges and modern propellants. Given dispels this notion by describing the use of muskets in Indian warfare of the period, and how poorly muskets actually performed in reality. Well into the nineteenth century, trade muskets differed in every material respect from the modern image. They were single-shot, smooth-bore, muzzle-loading, flintlocks which used black powder to propel ball shot. A common trade musket was fitted with a 3 foot barrel, weighing some 10½ pounds, and even longer guns were used in trade. It was a heavy, clumsy, fallible object—but it was still better than the seventeenth century muskets which Given tested.

Bartels carries on the theme of inter-group relations. Here, however, we deal with rumours of war, and not with war itself. Bartels argues that present-day relations between Micmacs and other Newfoundlanders are poisoned by what he calls the "Micmac mercenary myth." This is a widely-held belief that in the sixteenth and seventeenth centuries, French colonial authorities brought

Micmacs from Cape Breton and paid a bounty for every Beothuck that the Micmacs killed. It was, in Leslie Upton's words, "A very comforting explanation,"[4] as it relegated the English to a minor role in finishing off what others had begun. Thus, the demise of the Beothucks rid the Newfoundlanders of two sorts of native title, that of the Beothucks themselves, and that of the Micmacs. Or so the provincial government hoped. In the result, things have fallen out rather differently, since the Micmacs have gained federal recognition of their standing as aboriginal Newfoundlanders.

The fourth essay in Part I takes up another sort of inter-group relations. This is Harriet Gorham's, "Families of Mixed Descent in the Western Great Lakes Regions." In this essay we stray a little outside Canada's current borders. No apologies are needed for this, since it breaks away from an unhealthy parochialism. Price castigates the "narrow nationalism that is pervasive in native studies."[5] The ethnic relations described by Harriet Gorham do not stop short at the international border, unlike the weather map on U.S. television stations! Her contribution deals with the people of mixed descent in Michigan Territory of the United States during the early part of the nineteenth century and before. Her subjects are fur traders and Roman Catholics who were often francophones. Although elsewhere that mix of attributes led to the formation of a "New Nation," such as the Red River Colony, here it did not. We are apt to forget that only rarely, and in special circumstances, will new ethnic groups form. "Ethnogenesis" is as rare a process as the mixing of gene pools is common. In Part III, Jennifer Brown suggests terminology to deal with this fact.

> Written with a small "m" and italicized, *métis* is used here in the general French sense for all people of dual Amerindian-White ancestry. Capitalized, "Métis" is therefore not a generic term for all persons of this biracial descent; it refers [only] to those people who are agreed to possess a distinctive socio-cultural heritage and *a sense of ethnic self-identification* [author's italics].

Thus, when Peterson writes of the people of Indian-White ancestry in the Western Great Lakes regions as "a people in the process of becoming,"[6] we are perhaps dealing with *métis*, but certainly not "Métis." We shall return to *métis* and the Métis in Part III.

Notes

1. Justice A. MacLean (1970), "Calder et al. v. Attorney-General of British Columbia," *Dominion Law Reports* 13 (3rd series): 103.
2. Cited in *ibid.*
3. George T. Hunt, *The Wars of the Iroquois: A Study in Intertribal Relations* (Madison: University of Wisconsin Press, 1940), 19.
4. Leslie Upton, "The Extermination of the Beothuks," *Canadian Historical Review*, vol. 57, no. 3 (1977): 147.
5. John A. Price, "An Overview of Recent Books and Graduate Theses in Canadian Native Studies" (Paper presented at the Canadian Ethnology Society Meeting, University of Toronto, May 10-12, 1985): 7.
6. Jacqueline Peterson, "Ethnogenesis and the Growth of a 'New People'," *American Indian Culture and Research Journal*, vol. 6., no. 2 (1982): 25.

Chapter 1
The Iroquois Wars and Native Firearms

Brian J. Given

Between 1648 and 1652, the Iroquois, by waging war on an apparently unprecedented scale, succeeded in dispersing the Huron nation, their traditional enemies. Most authors who have attempted to understand these events have sought their explanation in the socio-economic impact of the White man's trade. More specifically, these authors suggest that many native groups such as the Iroquois rapidly became so dependent upon Euorpean trade that it "instantly divided the tribes into highly competitive groups . . . [such that by 1640 this] trade had become a social and economic necessity to them, their position . . . [having] life or death as alternatives."[1]

These changes would naturally have given rise to alterations in the pattern and scale of native alliance and warfare. An example of this line of thought is *Wars of the Iroquois* by George Hunt. In this now classic work, Hunt advances an economic theory to explain Iroquois aggression, which culminated in the destruction or dispersal, after 1648, of a number of tribes including the Huron, Neutrals, Petun, and Ottawas. Hunt argued that the Iroquois attempted to usurp the Huron position as middlemen between the Europeans and the fur-producing tribes to the northwest, and that the Iroquois felt that this drastic large-scale action was necessitated by the depletion of their own beaver population as the result of intensive overhunting.

Many scholars have based some of their own work upon Hunt's theory. Clearly, if we are to posit native trade-dependence both as an implicit premise and a motivational variable, as do Hunt, Trigger, Tooker and Goldstein,[2] we must demonstrate that such dependence actually existed during the period under discussion. It is necessary to go beyond vague notions of "trade-complex" to specify which items comprised most of it, and to discover which of these became loci of dependency. Thus, we need studies which investigate the extent of acquisition and use of specific types of trade items during given time periods. This paper summarises a project focussing upon the trade in firearms prior to 1652.

The firearm is the item of trade most commonly mentioned by Hunt, Trigger, and Tooker who are proponents of the dependency hypothesis as the major factor in such dependency.[3] The premise that the European harquebuses of the seventeenth century were vastly superior to aboriginal projectile weapons is pervasive in the literature. For example Quimby is able to state that the balance of power between the Huron and the Iroquois was maintained until 1642 when the Iroquois were able to obtain more guns from the Dutch. According to Quimby, Otterbein, Tooker, and Trigger, the Iroquois, thus armed, were able to overcome the Huron in large-scale wars, which Schlesier claims could never have been fought.[4]

In concert with Quimby, Hunt argues that the French preference for sending soldiers to protect native allies, rather than arming them, led to their defeat at the hands of the well-armed Iroquois. Goldstein (incorrectly attributing the quote to Hunt)[5] rehashes Parkman's notion that "the supply of firearms and ammunition afforded by the Dutch provoked passion for conquest and aggrandisement among the Iroquois."[6] Although Hunt does not in fact agree with Parkman's analysis of Iroquois motivation, he does assume that they required guns and ammunition to maintain their military position, and, by implication, presumes the superiority of these weapons: "The Iroquese, being unprovided with Beaver-skins to be given the exchange for guns, powder, ball, and nets would be starved to death, or at least obliged to leave their county."[7] Hunt also writes, "a tribe whose enemies had weapons which it lacked had few alternatives, and all of them were unpleasant. It inevitably made war upon the competitor."[8]

Other theorists make even more explicit assumptions. Goldstein states that with their introduction in the 1500s, guns and ammunition quickly replaced bows and arrows. Osgood asserts that "the Dutch supply of guns and ammunition explains the triumph of the Iroquois in warfare,"[9] and Otterbein attributes their victories to changing battle tactics as a function of these advances in weapons technology.[10] Tooker, agreeing with Hunt, describes the transition from a traditional Iroquois-Huron blood feud into a full-scale war.[11] In the course of this "national war", the Iroquois, who were able to secure more guns than were their rivals, gradually gained the upper hand, a position with which Trigger concurs.[12] In a more recent work, Trigger even chides Hunt for his conservatism in suggesting that Iroquois weapons superiority may not have been as great as others had supposed.[13]

The presumed Iroquois dependence upon European weaponry prior to the war against the Huron (1648–1652) would appear, then, to be a logical place to begin an examination of the general question of native trade-dependence in the seventeenth century.

The paucity of information relating specifically to the acquisition and use of muskets by the Iroquois before the war of 1648–1652 leaves us little alternative but to combine a straightforward historical approach with a deductive one. Thus we will ask first, whether the Indians *could* have obtained the weapons; second, whether it would appear that they did so; and third, whether such acquisition would have conferred any advantage. To address these issues, several basic questions were asked:

(1) Would the colonists have been able to trade before 1648 large numbers of firearms of a type which would have been useful in Indian-style warfare? And would they have been willing to do so?

(2) Did the Iroquois, their allies, or their enemies, prior to the dispersal of the Huron acquire a significant number of guns? What types of guns did they acquire? And is there evidence that these weapons gave them any advantage over their enemies?

(3) Did the gun, in fact, offer concrete advantages over native weapons in the tactical context in which it was used? And in what ways did the operational parameters of the musket differ from those of the bow?

The first two groups of questions are addressed through reference to the archival record. The third group is investigated through the use of both historical sources and "experimental archaeology."[14]

The matchlock harquebuses with which all of the early colonists were armed were heavy and cumbersome, and required a rest to support the barrel during firing. These weapons were awkward and slow to fire, and even more so to reload. Because they were difficult to aim, they were inaccurate, especially when used against moving targets[15]. With only one exception (Otterbein),[16] writers concerned with this period (Hunt, Trigger, Russell,)[17] have recognized that matchlock weapons would have been of no use to native people in their style of warfare.

The flintlock gun, on the other hand, at least in theory, could be loaded and readied to fire in as little as 30 seconds. It could be carried with the cock in the "half bent" position; the user needed only to move it back to full cock and pull the trigger to fire.

This weapon was the first and only firearm of the period which could have been useful to the natives, and which they, recognizing this, were willing to purchase.[18] Therefore, whenever we discuss the European fire-arm as a locus of trade-dependence,[19] or as an explanation for the victory of one tribe over another,[20] we are primarily concerned with the flintlock gun.[21] Thus, we must attempt to determine whether the colonists were in a position to provide this type of weapon to their Indian trading partners before the Iroquois defeat of the Huron between the years 1648–1652.

It is beyond the scope of so short a paper as this one to examine in detail the stocks of firearms of all the colonies from whom the Iroquois might have obtained weapons.[22] By way of example, however, let us look at Dutch armament during and after the period in which they supposedly supplied the Iroquois with modern flintlocks.

The Dutch

The Dutch colonists, like their French and English counterparts, arrived in North America carrying swords and matchlock guns, and wearing armour. At least in the beginning, there is no evidence at all that they had wheel-lock or flintlock guns. For example, in 1609, Henry Hudson and his men are reported to have fared badly in an encounter with Indians when all their matches were extinguished by rain.[23]

Whereas by 1620 some flintlock guns were to be found among the English colonists,[24] it is likely that the Dutch lagged somewhat behind. They faced a supply problem much worse than that of their fellow colonists, owing to the Thirty Years War. The Netherlands was exporting military matchlock guns to other

European countries as quickly as they could produce them, and were not motivated to innovate. The manufacture of flintlock weapons began in the Netherlands about 20 or 30 years later than in France.[25] It follows that relatively few of these weapons would find their way to the American colony. Such weapons were not imported in quantity from other European sources.[26]

In 1656 the colonial administration even tried to ban the importation of flintlock guns, permitting the settlers to bring only matchlocks into New Holland. Had the matchlock been considered obsolete, and the conversion to flintlock guns fairly complete, such legislation would have made no sense.

Further evidence that the Dutch had by no means replaced their own matchlocks until well after the destruction of Huronia between 1648 and 1652 may be found in the following armament lists. These supplies were considered necessary for the 150-man force which was to march in 1656, against the Swedes on the Delaware River in New Netherland:

75 muskets (matchlocks)
75 firelocks or snaphaunces
75 bandoleers
75 cartridge boxes
75 swords
75 hangers
75 sword belts
75 sabre belts
2,000 lb. powder
600 lb. lead
400 lb. musket balls[27]

This was a military operation against a hostile European colony. Consequently it is likely that this represents optimal armament for a force which was expected to encounter difficulty, rather than an average for the settlements. Similarly, in 1660, the Dutch list, "Return of Goods for the Colonies on the Delaware River", shows that both the matchlock musket and flint snaphaunce were in use:

800 lb. powder
600 lb. musket and snaphaunce bullets
    [N.B. Musket as opposed to flint gun]
40 snaphaunces
    [Worms, priming brushes and flints in proportion]
8 snaphaunces moulds
40 cartridge boxes
3 iron ladies to melt lead

It is clear that by the mid-seventeenth century, the snaphaunce and flintlock were perceived by the European colonists to be the most desirable military weapons. This design completely replaced the matchlock in military use by 1700 or so.[29] Further, in consideration of the much higher cost of the flintgun, the decision by 1656 to include a sizable proportion of these weapons as basic equipment is indicative of Dutch esteem for the design. Yet from the above examples it is evident that even as late as 1660, the Dutch, oft-vaunted as the Mohawks' main armourers, had by no means completed their own conversion to the use of those weapons which Tooker, Trigger, and Otterbein say they traded to the Indians.[30]

Fully eight years after the major Iroquois attacks began against Huronia (in 1648), the Dutch were arming only half of an important force with snaphaunces. It cannot be determined whether even that modest goal was achieved. Surely we must reconsider the suggestion whether during the 1640s the Dutch were able, let alone willing, to trade a significant number of flint guns to native people.

Throughout most of the seventeenth century, the colonists of all nationalities were barely able to arm their own populations with flint guns. Leach suggests that the matchlock was predominant until 1675.[31] Where the colonies were apparently at pains to acquire a reasonable proportion of flintlock guns for their own defensive forces, it seems unlikely that the sale of such weapons outside the community to potential enemies was possible or would have been permitted.

Iroquois Guns

The trade in muskets to native people did not get its start until after 1640.[32] Because the colonists had few flint guns for their own use, it is probable that any guns traded during this decade were matchlocks.

It would seem that the Iroquois got their first firearms from the English.[33] This could explain why in 1604 they ignored the Dutch and carried their furs to the English traders along the Connecticut River. Tooker suggests that the Mohawks' favourable trading position, which allowed them to play English and Dutch against each other, gave them the buying power to acquire, at a reasonable price goods which had become necessities, "especially guns."[35]

The Dutch were presumably convinced that in order to attract the Indian trade it would be necessary to equal the English willingness to sell guns. In all likelihood, the English only dabbled in the arms trade, for they were more settlers than traders, and would have feared an armed native population. It would appear that the Iroquois attempted unsuccessfully to convince the French to enter their "arms race." In 1641, about 350 Iroquois built two forts on the St. Lawrence as bases from which to negotiate. The French were asked for 30 muskets to add to the 36 the Iroquois had already obtained from the English and Dutch.[36] As far as we can tell, these guns were all the Iroquois possessed before 1643.

"The 400 Guns of the Mohawk"

The figure most often cited with regard to Iroquois armament is that of 300 to 400 muskets acquired from the Dutch by 1643[37]. This number echoes through the archival and ethno-historical literature.

The Jesuits tell us that by June 1643, the Mohawk had nearly 300 guns.[38] The board of accounts in Holland reported that the Mohawk had guns and ammunition to supply 400 men although sales to other Indians still were strictly forbidden.[39] This trade was probably legitimized by Arent Van Curler's treaty between the Dutch and the Mohawk negotiated in 1643, which preceded a further agreement of 1645.[40] This estimate does not alter greatly with time.

In 1648, the English heard that the Narragansetts, who were close allies of the Mohawk,[43] were preparing for war against the colonists. In August, about 1,000 Indians were reported to have gathered in Connecticut with 300 guns among them. This group included "mercenary Mohawks [who] were said to be about 400 in number, all armed with guns and three pound of powder for every man."[41]

After urgent diplomacy on the part of the English, "Wussoonkquassin gave *peag* to the Mohawks to retreat. It seems they are (Switzer-like) mercenary, were hired on and off."[42] It would seem likely that *John Winthrop* was referring to these same Mohawk when he reports that in 1648 it was rumoured that the Narragansetts and Niantics had hired a number of outside Indians: "about one thousand Indians armed, three hundred or more having guns, powder and bullets."[43]

One might, of course, argue that the above figure of 300 to 400 Mohawk guns is merely the result of speculation by the European colonists. While this may be the case, the fact that Dutch, French and English sources refer to similar numbers of guns lends credence to the estimate.

Apparently the Iroquois were able to buy guns legally until 1645, and probably illegally thereafter. The Jesuit Relation for this year suggests that Dutch firearms had enabled the Mohawk to gain superiority over all their enemies.[44]

Trigger, Otterbein, and Tooker rely upon the assumption that a large volume of illegal trade permitted the Iroquois to build massive stocks of muskets by the time of their 1648 attack on Huronia.[45]

In fact, after 1643, we have no reliable information regarding the number of guns traded to these particular Indians. My general survey of the Colonial-Indian gun trade[46] has led me to the conclusion that the only tribes to acquire a significant number of guns prior to the 1650s were the Mohawk and Huron, and even they received relatively few weapons. The weapons trade did not begin to escalate to a significant level until the second half of the seventeenth century. A ready explanation may be found in the greater availability of flintlock guns. By the time of King Philip's War (1675-76) perhaps 10 percent of the Wampanoag and Narragansett warriors had firearms.[47]

This estimate is not difficult to reconcile with reports of an extensive illicit trade. For example, the New Englanders bemoaned the extensive gun trade of the Dutch and the French from whom they were geographically and culturally far removed. Erickson has also suggested that the New Englanders needed enemies to articulate their communal boundaries. He describes a series of historical events during which these same informants saw heretic Antinomians, demonic Quakers and over 200 witches at their own doorstep.[48] These same English Puritans saw the Jesuits as the embodiment of "vile popery"[49] and naturally believed that they were arming the Indians who, of course, worshipped the devil. The French Jesuits were similarly hostile toward the Puritans, and blamed them, not entirely unfairly, for arming their native enemies.[50]

In fact, all the colonies engaged in the gun trade and each blamed the others for it. Because the trade was for the most part illegal, we cannot rely on the colonists' estimates of the trade for which they themselves were responsible. And we should give even less credence to their statements about that of other colonies.

Second, without very thorough regular cleaning, it is unlikely that a black-powder gun would last longer than three years.[51] I would be surprised if a musket used outdoors and stored in native villages and hunting camps would survive intact for even two years.

If we generously suppose that the average gun was in service for three years, and that 10 percent of all warriors of the Iroquois, Huron, Ottawa, Wampanoag, Narragansett, and Mohegan had firearms, we can generate some interesting speculations. These tribes and their close allies could surely have fielded more than 10,000 warriors (the accuracy of this figure is of minimal importance—I use it for illustration only). Given 10,000 warriors, 1,000 guns would be required to arm 10 percent of them.

Simply to maintain this level of armament, more than 300 guns would have to be acquired each year. If one in five warriors wished to maintain a gun between 1665 and 1675, for example, 6,600 weapons would have to be acquired, or an average of 660 per year. In suggesting that by 1665 every native had a gun we are assuming (given our starting figures) that 31,000 guns were acquired (or rebuilt) during the decade before 1675.

I wish to make clear that I present the particulars of this argument only to illustrate the fact that, even if we knew how many guns were sold each year by each colony, we could not simply add up the numbers. We have inadequate data on which to base precise estimates. Illegal gun-traders left few records, and, those colonists who did leave them, fearfully saw an Indian behind every tree and a gun in the hands of every Indian.

Even by 1675 there is little evidence to support the contention that any native groups had acquired so many guns that they could have considered themselves to be militarily dependent upon them. In addition, even at this late date, projectile weapons were not decisive in Indian warfare. Whether or not guns or bows were used, most battles were won through hand-to-hand combat.

The weapons trade only began in earnest during the 1650s. It is gratuitous to suggest that after eight years at most of this trade (i.e., by 1648) any group of natives was well provided with flintlocks, when this was certainly not the case even 27 years later.[52]

The Operational Parameters of the Seventeenth Century Musket

We might reasonably ask whether even a few firearms could have given the Iroquois an enormous advantage over their enemies who possessed only the bow and arrow. Hunt, Otterbein, Tooker, Goldstein, and others presume that the gun was vastly superior to aboriginal projectile weapons in terms of its concrete effectiveness.[53]

This assumption has never been adequately argued, and so I set out to determine the operational parameters of the seventeenth century musket. The results of months of range-testing are reported in detail elsewhere[54] but will be summarized briefly here. Five muskets of various bore sizes and barrel lengths were tested for reliability, range, rate of fire, and accuracy at a rifle range in the Ottawa area.

Accuracy

The absolute accuracy potential of the weapons was ascertained through the use of a modern sighting stand in which the weapons were clamped. Modern target sights were used to aim the weapons. Next, the weapons were fired under various field conditions using a cartridge-loading hunting rifle as a control.

I used a target consisting of a wooden door measuring two feet by six feet. This represents something of an ideal with reference to typical combat targets.

I found that the maximum range at which one might expect to hit a stationary 2′ × 6′ target is around 50 to 75 yards under ideal conditions. At a distance of 100 yards, less than 25 percent of shots fired from a rest (not the sighting stand) are likely to hit this idealized human target.

Neither I nor any helpers I could recruit were able to load and fire a musket in less than one minute if we used seventeenth century techniques and equipment. Even this time represents a parade-ground ideal. Needless to say, loading is very difficult if one cannot stand fully erect.

Held reported that the native self-bow can be "fired" at least six times as rapidly as the gun,[55] and can be reloaded while kneeling behind cover. Nor does such a weapon lack range or accuracy. The self-bow used by North American natives had a range of at least 100 yards, and equipped with native-made copper or European iron arrowheads, it was extremely lethal and could even penetrate armour. When compared to the musket, the bow is extremely accurate, and it is reasonable to assume that the average experienced native archer could shoot more accurately than even the finest of musketmen. Bows never blow up and seldom misfire; the musket does both. A 20 to 50 percent misfire rate is usual in good weather under field conditions. In the lightest of rains the flint-lock becomes virtually useless, where the performance of the bow is little affected. Additionally, the archer is not tied to suppliers outside of his immediate tribal group, such that cost and availability are beyond his control. While the bow could be replaced or repaired easily, the repair of the delicate snaphaunce required a technology which was not available to the natives until after the destruction of Huronia.

In conclusion, there exists little evidence to support the assumption that any native group acquired, or could have acquired, large numbers of firearms prior to the Iroquois/Huron war. In terms of accuracy, rate of fire, reliability, availability, and repairability, the native self-bow was a weapon superior to the seventeenth century musket. Because of its superior rate of fire alone, the bow is capable of six times the number of hits that are possible with a gun in the same period of time. Excepting possible psychological utility, it is unlikely that European firearms conferred any advantage whatsoever upon native users. Nor is it likely that the psychological impact of the gun contributed to Iroquois victory. While it is true that some tribes, the Eries for example,[56] used guns only against enemies who were unfamiliar with them,[57] the Huron were certainly not in this category. In fact the Huron, along with the Ottawas, had themselves used guns to frighten the Sioux in 1657.[58] The Sioux even by 1670 still had no firearms. They did, however, appreciate the weaknesses of these weapons. Armed only with stone weapons, they were able to drive off and terrorize the Ottawa and Huron, although these latter possessed not only contemporary French guns but also metal knives and tomahawks.[59]

It is not reasonable to suggest that, while good French flintlocks gave the Huron and Ottawa little advantage over the Sioux in 1670, inferior Dutch snaphaunces (even presuming the Iroquois had flintlock guns) assured Iroquois victory over the Huron in 1645-52. Further, it is clear that the Iroquois could not have acquired large numbers of militarily useful muskets prior to the dispersal of the Huron.

Notes

Source: *Papers from the Sixth Annual Congress, 1979, Canadian Ethnology Society*, Canadian Ethnology Service, No. 78, by permission of the National Museum of Man.

1. George T. Hunt, *The Wars of the Iroquois: A Study in Intertribal Relations* (Madison: University of Wisconsin Press, 1972), 18.
2. Hunt, *Wars of the Iroquois*; Bruce G. Trigger, *The Impact of Europeans on Huronia* (Toronto: Copp, Clark, 1969); Bruce G. Trigger, *The Children of Aataentsic: A History of the Huron People to 1660* (Montreal: McGill-Queens, 1976); Elizabeth Tooker, "The Iroquois Defeat of the Huron: A Review of Causes," *Pennsylvania Archaeology* 33 (1963); R. Goldstein, *French-Iroquois Diplomatic and Military Relations, 1609–1701* The Hague: Mouton & Co., 1969).
3. Hunt, *Wars of the Iroquois*; Trigger, *Children of Aataentsic*; Tooker, "Iroquois Defeat."
4. George Quimby, *Indian Cultures and Indian Trade Goods* (Madison: University of Wisconsin Press, 1966); K. Otterbein, "Why the Iroquois Won—An Analysis of Military Tactics," *Ethnohistory* 2 (1965); Tooker, "Iroquois Defeat"; Trigger, *Impact of Europeans*; Trigger, *Children of the Aataentsic*; and K. Schlesier, "Die Irokesenkriege und die Grosse Vertreibung, 1609–1656," *Zeitschrift fr Ethnologie* (1975).
5. Goldstein, *Diplomatic and Military Relations*, 45.
6. F. Parkman, *The Jesuits in North America in the Seventeenth Century* (Boston: Little Brown & Co., 1867); F. Parkman, *La Salle and the Discovery of the Great West* (Boston: Little Brown & Co., 1897).
7. Hunt, *Wars of the Iroquois*, 35, citing Baron de Lahontan .

8. *Ibid.*, 19.
9. H. Osgoode, *The American Colonies in the Seventeenth Century*, 3 vols. (New York, 1907).
10. Otterbein, "Why the Iroquois Won."
11. Tooker, "Iroquois Defeat of the Huron"; Hunt, *Wars of the Iroquois.*
12. Tooker, "Iroquois Defeat of the Huron," 117, 122-23; Trigger, *Impact of Europeans.*
13. Trigger, *Children of Aataentsic*, 629.
14. John Coles, *Archaeology by Experiment* (London: Hutchinson University Library, 1973).
15. Robert Held, *The Age of Firearms* (Northfield: The Gun Digest Co., 1957).
16. Otterbein, "Why the Iroquois Won."
17. Hunt, *The Wars of the Iroquois*; Trigger, *Children of Aataentsic*; Carl H. Russell, *Guns on the Early Frontiers* (Berkeley: University of California Press, 1962).
18. Trigger, *Children of the Aataentsic*, 431.
19. Hunt, *Wars of the Iroquois*; Tooker, "Iroquois Defeat of the Huron."
20. Tooker, "Iroquois Defeat of the Huron"; Otterbein, "Why the Iroquois Won."
21. Russell, *Guns*. In fact the flint type firearm was undergoing rapid and significant evolution during the period of interest to us. I have reviewed this development process elsewhere (Brian J. Given, "A Study of European Weapons Technology as a Locus of Native Trade Dependence Prior to the Iroquois Defeat of the Huron, 1648–52" (M.A. thesis, Ottawa, Carleton University, 1979)) and have arrived at the following conclusions. First, the only type of firearm which would have been useful to Native people was the "French flintlock" or "true flintlock"; other types were much inferior. Second, it is most unlikely that significant numbers of true flintlocks could have been traded to Native peoples by the 1640s.
22. Given, "European Weapons Technology," 10–30.
23. J. Franklin, ed., *Narratives of New Netherlands 1609–1664* (1909; reprint, New York: Barnes & Noble, 1959), 19.
24. Wm. Bradford and E. Winslow, *Mourt's Relation or Journal of the Plantation at Plymouth* (1622; reprint, New York; Garret Press, 1969).
25. Given, "European Weapons Technology," Appendix One, 25.
26. *Ibid.*, 44.
27. F. O'Callaghan, *Documents Relating to the Colonial History of the State of New York*, vol. I (Albany: Weed, Parsons & Co., 1849), 645.
28. *Ibid.*, vol. II, 185.
29. Harold L. Peterson, *Arms and Armour in Colonial America* (Harrisburg, PA: The Stackpole Co., 1956); Alexander Brown, *The Genesis of the United States*, vol. II (Boston, 1890), 19–20; N. Bouton *et al.*, *New Hampshire State Papers*, vol. III (Manchester, NH, 1867–1941), 178; Nicholas Boone, *Military Discipline* (Boston, 1701), 73; William P. Palmer and H.W. Flournoy, eds., *Calendar of Virginia State Papers and Other Manuscripts*, vol. I (Richmond, 1875–93), 80, 81.
30. Tooker, "Iroquois Defeat of the Huron"; Trigger, *Impact of Europeans*; Trigger, *Children of Aataentsic*; Otterbein, "Why the Iroquois Won."
31. Douglas Edward Leach, *Flintlock and Tomahawk: New England in King Philip's War* (New York: Macmillan Co., 1958).
32. Given, "European Weapons Technology," Appendix Two.
33. Franklin, *Narratives of New Netherland*, 274.
34. Van Laer, *New York Historical Manuscripts* (Albany: New York State Archives, 1908), 483–84; Trigger, *Children of the Aataentsic*, 631.
35. Tooker, *Impact of Europeans*, 116.
36. R.G. Thwaites, ed., *The Jesuit Relations and Allied Documents: Travels and Explorations of the Jesuit Missionaries of New France*, 1610–1791 (New York, 1896–1906).

37. George E. Hyde, *Indians of the Woodlands, from Prehistoric Times to 1725* (Norman: University of Oklahoma Press, 1962), 120; Hunt, *Wars of the Iroquois.*
38. Thwaites, *Jesuit Relations.*
39. Francis Jennings, *The Invasion of America: Indians, Colonialism and the Cant of Conquest* (Chapel Hill: University of North Carolina Press, 1975), 24, 29.
40. O'Callaghan, *Colonial History of New York.*
41. Increase Mather, *A Brief History of the War with the Indians of New England* (Plymouth, 1676), 66.
42. Roger Williams, letter dated 10 August 1648.
43. John Winthrop, *Journal* edited by James K. Hosmer, vol. 2 (New York: Charles Scribner's Sons, 1908), 348; H.M. Ward, *The United Colonies of New England* (New York: Vantage Press, 1961), 127.
44. Thwaites, *Jesuit Relations.*
45. Trigger, *Impact of Europeans*; Trigger, *Children of Aataentsic*; Otterbein, "Why the Iroquois Won"; Tooker, "Iroquois Defeat of the Huron."
46. Given, "European Weapons Technology."
47. *Ibid.*, Appendix Three.
48. Kai T. Erickson, *Wayward Puritans: A Study in the Sociology of Deviance* (New York: John Wiley & Sons, 1966).
49. Cotton Mather, *Magnalia* (1572); Trigger, *Children of the Aataentsic*, 628.
50. Trigger, *Children of Aataentsic*, 628.
51. Personal communications between John Chown and author, 1976–77.
52. See Given, "European Weapons Technology," Appendix Three, for a more detailed account.
53. Hunt, *Wars of the Iroquois*; Otterbein, "Why the Iroquois Won"; Tooker, "Iroquois Defeat of the Huron"; Goldstein, *Diplomatic and Military Relations.*
54. Given, "European Weapons Technology," 73–105.
55. Held, *Age of Firearms.*
56. Thwaites, *Jesuit Relations.*
57. S.J. Gooding, *The Canadian Gunsmiths, 1608–1900* (West Hill, Ont.: Museum Restoration Service, 1962), 27; W. Vernon Kinietz, *The Indians of the Western Great Lakes, 1615–1760* (Ann Arbor: University of Michigan Press, 1965).
58. Hyde, *Indians of the Woodlands*, 137.
59. *Ibid.*

Chapter 2
Epidemics: The Forgotten Factor in Seventeenth Century Native Warfare in the St. Lawrence Region

Susan Johnston

In recent years, increasing attention has been paid to the virgin soil epidemics which occurred at first contact in many parts of the world. Studies suggest that some of the changes formerly attributed to culture contact, especially to trade, may have resulted instead from demographic and attitudinal changes caused by the epidemic experience, an experience which influenced political, economic, social and cultural institutions. As a result, there were changes to marriage rules, lineage relationships, religious practices, and beliefs about sorcery, as well as various changes aimed at increasing population, such as a decrease in infanticide and in the killing of dead warriors' wives, an increase in captives being adopted rather than tortured, and the ecouragement of immigration.[1] It has become clear that the effects of an epidemic are far-reaching and complex, and go far beyond the immediate depopulation.[2]

Analysis of the virgin soil epidemics and their aftermath in the St. Lawrence–eastern Great Lakes region in the mid-seventeenth century suggests that what Hunt termed "the wars of the Iroquois"[3]—the intense warfare that resulted in demographic and territorial upheavals—represented a response to the epidemics experienced in the area.

Successive epidemics of European-originated infections circulated in the 1630s and 1640s among the groups known to Jesuit missionaries. These groups were both Iroquoian and Algonkian peoples[4] including the Montagnais near the St. Lawrence, the Algonkin near the Ottawa River and Lake Nipissing, the horticultural Huron, Neutral, and Petun in the area between Lake Huron, Lake Erie and Lake Ontario, and the related Iroquois south and east of Lake Ontario.

By the 1640s, not only had warfare increased, but its nature had changed. Until the 1630s the native groups had maintained allied or bloodfeud relationships with each other. This type of warfare, similar to blood-feud raiding in many other parts of the world, appears to have consisted mainly of small seasonal raids and counter-raids near each other's villages, or attacks on war or hunting parties. However, after 1640, raiding parties increased in size and number, and operated year-round rather than just seasonally. Villages and camps were attacked, and the inhabitants were killed or captured, or fled to neighbouring settlements. By the 1650s, many groups known to the French had dispersed and their territories became largely uninhabited. An exception were the Iroquois who not only had maintained their cultural cohesion, but had augmented their population with individual captives and the remnants of dispersed groups.

Various hypotheses have been developed to explain this escalation of hostilities and the depopulation of the area, but the generally accepted view—the one currently accepted in most archaeological and ethnographic analyses—is that these groups were competing for control, or the products, of the fur trade. According to this explanation, they had become dependent on or greatly desirous of European goods. Thus the Iroquois, who are perceived to have instigated the increased warfare after beaver had disappeared from their own territory,[5] no longer raided for blood-feud reasons. Now they attacked to acquire furs or European goods,[6] or to force groups with furs to trade with them.[7] It has also been suggested that the Iroquois attacked the Huron to disperse them and thus acquire their hunting territories or a safe passage by which to raid the beaver-rich Algonkins to the north and west.[8] It was this trade-oriented motive which led to the destruction of villages and the dispersal of their inhabitants. Apart from depopulation, the effects of the virgin soil epidemics, which occurred just before and during the period of increased hostilities, are not recognized or regarded as very consequential in most currently accepted explanations of events. Even the Jesuit estimates of depopulation among the Huron are suspected by some scholars to have been exaggerated.[9]

A close examination of the annual reports from Huronia and Quebec throughout this period reveals a lack of evidence for the trade-war hypothesis. Although this alone does not disprove that interpretation, these reports do include extensive descriptions of events and behaviour—those related to the epidemics and which reflect far-reaching and unprecedented demographic and attitudinal changes—which have not been acknowledged as important in analyses of this period. The epidemics and the associated famine and depopulation were unprecedented in the losses sustained; moreover, they were perceived as unprecedented in their consequences. This on-going disaster influenced beliefs, cultural confidence, and world view.

An awareness of the ways in which the epidemics were experienced, and of how the survivors perceived the post-epidemic world, is essential to our understanding of subsequent events.

The Epidemics

Of the epidemics of various European diseases circulating among the Indian groups between 1634 and 1646, we have the most information on those in Huronia and it is mainly these that will be described here. However, the evidence suggests that all groups experienced the epidemics and reacted in much the same way.

The Huron had at least three epidemics in seven years. The first lasted from autumn 1634 until spring 1635. Incidence was high everywhere: "the majority of the Montagnais at Three Rivers" and "almost all the traders" contracted it; it "affected almost all the savages." "It has been so universal among Savages of our acquaintance that I do not know if one had escaped its attacks." In Huronia, "whole villages were prostrated" and the sick were "very numerous." However, as the Jesuits observed this epidemic only in the part of the country in which they were living, it is not certain that the epidemic spread throughout Huronia,[10] although it seems likely.

Although the disease cannot be identified with any degree of certainty, it probably was measles. "This sickness began with a violent fever, which was followed by a sort of measles or smallpox, different however from that common in France, accompanied in several cases by blindness for some days, or by dimness of sight, and terminated at length by diarrhoea." In the St. Lawrence region it was described as "a sort of measles, and an oppression of the stomach." Father Brebeuf reported in May that the epidemic had "carried off many and is still bringing some to the grave" and that "very many were destroyed."[11]

In the autumn of 1636, another infection was introduced which spread throughout Huronia and "spared hardly any one." The Petun Indians who lived to the west reported that it was "causing so great ravages in their country," and the Cheveux-Relevée, from even farther west, sent three different emissaries to the Jesuits in spring and summer, asking to know the remedy. In the summer of 1637, almost a year after it began, the disease flared again to epidemic proportions in Huronia and among the groups living between there and the St. Lawrence region. Some suggest that a different infection may have followed the one endured during the winter of 1637.[12] The symptoms were high fever, lack of appetite, weakness, prostration, convulsions, unconsciousness, and nosebleeds. Trigger suggests that it was influenza.[13] A Huron trader at the St. Lawrence said, "they are all dying, in our villages and along the way." By the end of June, the "mortality prevailed everywhere" in Huronia. In the village in which the Jesuits lived, Ihonataria, most cabins had "a considerable number of deaths" and, by June, most of the elders of the village council had died. The village was described as "almost entirely ruined." One individual was described by the Jesuits as having "lost a great many of his relatives and above all the last of his children."[14]

Two years passed between the end of this epidemic and the start of the next, but many were ill in the interim—some probably with secondary infections, but also some with primary infections. Many died during this period. In addition, remnants of another group, the Wenro—who had lost many to disease and whom the Neutral would no longer protect from the Iroquois—asked if they could move to Huronia. Six hundred came, most of them women and children, and those not sick when they arrived fell ill soon after. As a result, some Huron contracted the infection. Since many do not seem to have been affected, it can be asssumed that the infection was one already experienced by the Huron. The Wenro moved into Huron longhouses left half-empty by the numerous deaths resulting from the previous epidemics.

The next epidemic, which was evidently smallpox, began in the fall of 1639. It "spared neither age nor sex" and "put everything into desolation." The Jesuits described the largest village of the Rock nation as "a woeful hospital," and reported that mortality was "ravaging the whole country." By the following spring, the Jesuits had completed a census and reported that the Huron, who they estimated had originally numbered 30,000, had been reduced to 10,000 persons.[15]

These epidemics of European infections caused far greater severity of symptoms and mortality in North America because the inhabitants were virgin soil populations with no immunity to these diseases. In such epidemics, because there is usually no notion of quarantine, incidence is frequently 100 percent. Moreover, two or three different infections are often introduced at once, or in quick succession, which would increase mortality. Secondary infections are more frequent and often fatal. There is often no one to provide care, food, or water, or even to keep the fire going. Modern medical treatment, including hygiene and nutrition, would, of course, be unknown. Traditional cures do not work, and the unprecedented incidence and mortality is traumatic. A fatalistic attitude often results, and the sick are neglected or abandoned.

Space does not permit a full description of the Huron epidemics, but a few details, as noted by the Jesuits, gives some indication of the appalling conditions: a very ill Huron being regarded as though already dead and therefore virtually ignored; a man, being ill for months and very poorly nourished; a little girl convulsing almost all night; an old grandmother, coping with three sick grandchildren (the mother having died), losing her sight and strength, and becoming too ill to grind corn or get firewood; a sick woman convulsing all alone in her cabin; a pregnant woman delivering her premature baby in the hot sun and then dying; an abandoned baby dying out in a field; and a very ill girl without a mat to lie on or a fire to keep her warm, and without sufficient covering.[16]

Famine accompanied the disease. Drought probably caused some of it, but the interruption of subsistence activities during the epidemics undoubtedly affected food supplies. The scarcity of food probably killed many of the ill. Likewise, if the healthy had to search for food, care of the ill would have decreased.

Not only did the usual cures not work, they made matters worse. The well, processing through longhouses, mingled with the sick (for whom they were processing), and both were present while dancing, singing, and drumming went on all night. The noise, the activity, the shock of the temperature extremes associated with the sweat bath cure, and the blood-letting performed by the French (which had killed many in Europe during smallpox epidemics)[17] weakened the patients, and undoubtedly killed many.[18]

How many Huron died? The Jesuits' report that two-thirds died,—reducing the population from 30,000 to 10,000—is the only contemporary estimate that we have. Trigger and Heidenreich suggest, however, on the basis of archaeological and other evidence, that the population may only have been around 20,000 originally. Trigger estimated a mortality rate of 50 percent, on the basis of smallpox epidemics elsewhere.[19] However, more recent archaeological evidence suggests that the Jesuits' estimate of an original population of 30,000 was probably more accurate.[20] Moreover, Trigger's estimate of a 50 percent mortality rate is low for two reasons: first, horticultural groups, living in large villages, with many individuals living in each house, have smallpox mortality rates higher than the 50 percent reported for smaller, hunter gatherer-groups; second, Trigger omitted from his calculations mortality resulting from the first two epidemics.

Since we don't know how the Jesuits arrived at their pre-epidemic figure of 30,000, their estimate requires corroboration. It is unknown whether they included in the 1640 census the immigrants from other groups, such as the Wenro, or how accurate their head count was for a population in which males, and sometimes females, were seasonally mobile. Other methods of estimating depopulation are therefore required against which the Jesuit figures can be tested. One method is to estimate the depopulation from each of the epidemics on the basis of known mortality rates from the same infections in other virgin soil epidemics. However, this kind of estimate is not without difficulties. The positive identification of disease, except for the last, of which the French seemed quite confident, seems to be impossible with the data which exists. The Jesuits' diagnoses are not reliable; not only was their knowledge limited to their own personal experience, but, because of the presence of secondary and concurrent infections and the greater debilitation of patients, symptoms exhibited by virgin soil populations differ from and are more severe than those of Europeans.

A second difficulty is that incidence rates are unknown. Although the last two epidemics spread everywhere in Huronia, it is not known if the first did. It is usually assumed that infection during contact epidemics spreads further than reported—that is, further than observed—but we cannot know for certain.

In addition, the mortality rates from these tentatively identified diseases are difficult to estimate. Projecting mortality rates from one epidemic to another is hazardous; the rates vary considerably according to the nature of the infection, the strain or variety of the infection, settlement and visiting patterns, native treatments, degree of fatalism, mobility, mortuary practices, nutrition, standard of hygiene, environmental factors, degree of coincidence of illnesses, presence and virulence of concurrent diseases, and the number and timing of successive epidemics. Another problem in comparing mortality rates is that carefully monitored epidemics, for which rates would be reliable, are usually those epidemics for which help, such as medicine, food, water and fuel, was available. Even the presence of the last three of these are known to have decreased mortality.[21] The Huron epidemics are thus more comparable to unobserved epidemics for which the incidence and mortality rates are unknown and of questionable accuracy. However, the method used here does permit an educated guess for depopulation from all three epidemics, and attempts have been made to keep the estimates on the conservative side. Incidence is not assumed beyond Jesuit observation and the post-epidemic population estimates have not been adjusted for the Wenro and for other immigrants.

It is not certain what the first infection was, but it shall be assumed here that it was measles. The incidence and mortality rates for virgin soil epidemics of measles are shown in Table 2-1. As reported by the Jesuits in Huronia, incidence seems to be almost universal. The Bear Nation, which they observed during the first epidemic, was the largest Huron nation, occupying half the seats on the confederation council. We shall therefore assume that it included half of the Hurons, and since incidence in the other nations is unknown, the infection rate for this first epidemic will be estimated at 50 percent.

Mortality rates vary. The one numerical estimate we have for an untreated epidemic was 26.8 percent of cases, in Brazil. Evidently, many died in Huronia. Considering it better to err on the side of caution, a lower figure of 20 percent case mortality will be used here, giving a depopulation rate for Huronia of 10 percent.

Table 2-1 Incidence and Mortality Rates from Virgin Soil Epidemics of Measles

Location of Epidemic	Incidence	Mortality
The Yanomama, South America, 1968	Almost 100%	8.8% case fatalities, some medical care provided
Fiji, late 19th century	Very high	Great mortality
Ungava Bay, Canadian Arctic, 1952	99%	7% some modern medicine
Yukon Territory, 1942	95%	
Caddoans, Texas		
1759		Took its toll of lives
1803		Considerable
Western Greenland		15 times greater than in non-virgin soil epidemics, despite good medical care
Interior of Western Canada, 1830-50		Highest mortality of all diseases, except smallpox
Brazil, 1954		Case fatalities — with care 0.6%; without care 26.8%

Sources: J.V. Neek, W.R. Centerwall, N.A. Chagnon, and H.L. Casey, "Notes on the Effect of Measles and Measles Vaccine in a Virgin-Soil Population of South American Indians," *American Journal of Epidemiology*, vol. 91, no. 4 (1970); A.W. Crosby, "Virgin Soil Epidemics as a Factor in the Aboriginal Depopulation in America," *William and Mary Quarterly* 33 (1976):293; J.F. Marchand, "Tribal Epidemics in the Yukon," *Journal of the American Medical Association* 123 (1943):1019; J.C. Ewers, "The Influence of Epidemics on the Indian Populations and Cultures of Texas," *Plains Anthropology* 18 (1973):108; F.L. Black, F.De Pinheiro, W.J. Hierholzer, and R.V. Lee, "Epidemiology of Infectious Disease: The Example of Measles," *CIBA Foundation Symposium* 49, new series (1976); A.J. Ray, "Diffusion of Diseases in the Western Interior of Canada, 1830–1850," *Geographical Review*, vol. 66, no. 2 (n.d.):154.

With less evidence, but for want of a better identification, we shall assume the second epidemic was influenza which was reported as "fatal in a large number of cases" among the Cheyenne and Arapahoe in the late nineteenth century. Fifteen percent of the population died in an epidemic among the Creen Akorores in the Amazon Basin. A 20 percent mortality rate has been reported for Victoria Island, and also for Samoa.[22] Incidence and mortality was high in Huronia, as we have seen. A 15 percent depopulation rate is used here.

Virgin soil smallpox mortality rates are shown in Table 2-2. To keep the estimates conservative, we shall calculate smallpox depopulation in Huronia at 50 percent, but also (considering the rates cited for other horticultural groups) at 60 percent. Table 2-3 shows estimates of total epidemic depopulation based on original population figures of both 20,000 and 30,000.

Calculating total depopulation using the 50 percent rate for smallpox gives a cumulative mortality rate of 61.8 percent. If smallpox mortality was 60 percent, the cumulative rate is 69.4 percent. If the original Huron population had been around twenty thousand, only six or seven thousand would have remained, which is too low in light of the post-epidemic census. If these estimates are conservative, it is possible that Brother Sagard, a French missionary in Huronia in the 1620s, was correct when he reported a Huron population of 30,000 to 40,000.[23]

Table 2-2 Depopulation Rates from Virgin Soil Smallpox Epidemics

Group	Rate of Depopulation
	(percent)
A California Valley group	75
Cherokee	50
Catawbas	Nearly 50
Piegans	50-60
Onahas	50
Nantucket Indians	64
Pueblo	74
Arikara (smallpox and enemy raids)	92
Mandan and Hidatsa (smallpox and enemy raids) (late eighteenth century)	56
Mandan (1837-38)	90

Sources: H.F. Dobyns, "Estimating Aboriginal Population. 1. An appraisal of Techniques with a New Hemisphere Estimate," *Current Anthropology* 7 (1966):411; A.W. Crosby, "Virgin Soil Epidemics as a Factor in the Aboriginal Depopulation in America," *William and Mary Quarterly* 33 (1976):293; J.B. Tyrell, ed., *David Thompson's Narrative of His Explorations in Western America, 1784–1812* (Toronto: The Champlain Society, 1968), 323; S.F. Cook, "The Significance of Disease in the Extinction of New England Indians," *Human Biology*, vol. 45, no. 173 (n.d.):5; E.W. Stearne and A.E. Stearne, *The Effects of Smallpox on the Destiny of the Amerindian* (Boston: Bruce Humphries, Inc.; J.F. Taylor, "Sociocultural Effects of Epidemics on the Northern Plains: 1734–1850," *Western Canadian Journal of Anthropology*, 1977, vol. 7, no. 4 (n.d.):62, 65.

Table 2-3 Estimated Depopulation Rates for the Three Major Epidemics in Huronia, and Size of Remaining Population, Calculated for Estimated Original Huron Populations of 30,000 and 20,000.

		Original Population of 30,000		Original Population of 20,000		
Epidemics	**Mortality Rates**	**Fatalities**	**Population Remaining**	**Fatalities**	**Population Remaining**	**Cumulative Depopulation**
1634–1635 (measles?)	10% (50% incidence, and 20% case mortality)	3,000	27,000	2,000	18,000	10%
1636–1637 (influenza?)	15%	4,050	22,950	2,700	15,300	23.5%
1639–1640 (smallpox?)	50% (60%)	11,475 (13,770)	11,475 (9,180)	7,650 (9,180)	7,650 (6,120)	61.8% (69.4%)

Note: Smallpox figures are calculated for both 50 and 60 percent depopulation

People's reactions to disasters are said to be determined as much by their interpretation of events as by the physical damage sustained. A two-thirds reduction in population would have seemed extremely serious to the Huron. What were their feelings as their family members and countrymen died by the hundreds, year after year? How did they interpret this on-going crisis, and how did they see the future? Reports indicate that their perceptions changed over time.

During the first epidemic, they were quite stoic: "What shall I say of their strange patience in their poverty, famine and sickness? We have seen whole villages prostrated—yet not a word of complaint." By the following spring, however, there was apprehension, dread, and despair. "What wilt thou have?" one is reported to have said, "our minds are disordered." Their distress grew out of the unprecedented severity of the epidemic and the great number of deaths. What made matters worse was that they could not identify the person or spirit causing these misfortunes, and thus they did not know which remedies would be appropriate. Their fears increased. By the end of the second epidemic, at a council where the headmen were listing their dead, they "looked at one another like corpses, or rather like men who already feel the terrors of death." Emotional restraint disappeared, and they alternately threatened and cajoled the Jesuits in their attempts to find the cause or cure for the disease.[24]

Rumours circulated within Huronia and throughout the northeast about what the epidemics meant and who was responsible. Various local spirits were suspected, as were human agents, some of whom were killed. But the main suspects were the Jesuits who were considered to have extraordinary powers. Father Lalemont reported that a Huron had said, "that since we were in the country, and had sown our doctrine there, one saw no longer aught but misfortune and misery, and no more old men were to be seen; that the whole country was going to decay and ruin . . . that if the cause of all these evils were not suppressed, they would soon see their entire nation annihilated."[25]

By 1639, the Jesuits were reporting that "the death of their nearest relatives takes away their reason." Some asked the Jesuits "not to make them linger, but to despatch them promptly" as they had the others.[26] By this time the disaster had lasted five years, and they had no reason to believe it would end, especially if they could not discover the cause and thus the cure. They felt they were being intentionally destroyed as individuals, as families, and as nations.[27]

A disproportionate number of children died during the smallpox epidemic, and these deaths were considered the hardest to bear as children represented the hope of the future. They would protect and repopulate the country. An old Neutral woman said when she saw some Jesuits approaching bringing (as she thought) disease that she "only regretted her grandchildren, who might have been able to repeople the country."[28]

The Huron felt that the Jesuits were destroying them by refusing to share with them their powers over disease, famine, drought, and enemy attacks; by interfering with their own powers in many fields; and by conspiring with their enemies.

Their anxiety over diminished numbers related not only to their personal losses and their image as a strong and prosperous country, but also to their position *vis-à-vis* their traditional enemies. They knew the plight of the disease-weakened Wenro. The Huron continued to raid during the epidemic period. Although there had been no attacks on their villages, there were frequent rumours of imminent attacks, which the Jesuits reported came to nothing. At the council in the summer of 1637, although the epidemic still raged, and although they were distracted by grief and anger, warfare was discussed before the epidemics, which suggests there was much concern about war matters. Their vulnerability was perhaps greater than ever before. By this time they realized that natural reproduction over time would not suffice. An old war captain, who said he had never spoken previously at these councils but that all the headmen of his group had died, said: "I have seen maladies in the country before, but never have I seen anything like this; two or three Moons sufficed for us to see the end of those, and in a few years our families being restored, we almost lost the memory of them. But now we already count a Year since we began to be afflicted, and we see as yet no probability of soon beholding the end of our misery."[29] Three years later, only one-third of the Huron remained. Moreover, they did not know if the epidemics were over, or if the being responsible would not continue to inflict damage until they all had perished.

As we have seen, a major problem was their vulnerability to enemy attacks in their weakened state both during epidemics, and, having lost so many, afterwards. One strategy used by the Huron to restore their strength was a traditional method of increasing population, amalgamation with other groups. The Wenro, and perhaps another group seeking refuge, filled the empty places in their longhouses. Another traditional method used throughout the northeast to replace members killed in warfare was to capture and adopt enemy women and children (all but the males old enough to fight, who were killed). By integrating these captives into their own families or families who had lost members in war, they restored family size and ensured future increases. In the 1620s, Brother Sagard reported "of this experience I have seen many instances."[30] In other parts of the world where blood-feud warfare was practised, this strategy was used to replace people who died in virgin soil epidemics. For example, as a Piegan leader advised his warriors before their first raid after a smallpox epidemic,

> The young women must all be saved, and if any has a babe at the breast it must not be taken from her, nor hurt; all the boys and lads that have no weapons must not be killed, but brought to our camps, and be adopted amongst us, to be our people, and make us more numerous and stronger than we are. This, while it weakens our enemies, makes us strong.

There is evidence that this policy was followed in the northeast.

Post-Epidemic Warfare

Data of post-epidemic warfare is sparse and irregular in nature because of the geographical location of the observers—the Jesuits in Huronia and at the St.

Lawrence region. They mentioned some of the Huron, Algonkin and Montagnais war parties that they knew about. However, the results of these sorties are often not reported, and may not have been known. Sometimes the French were aware that the males were absent, but were not sure whether they were hunting or on war parties. The effects of raids on Iroquois and others are not known, whereas Iroquois attacks on Algonkin and Huron groups, and the outcomes, were known. Despite the uneven data a pattern emerges. Analysis of the epidemic and warfare data for the western Iroquois, eastern Iroquois, St. Lawrence groups, the Neutral, and the Hurons suggest that captures of large numbers of the enemy were attempted following epidemic depopulation.

Despite yearly warfare between the western Iroquois and the Huron during the 1630s, the only Huron reported captured by the western Iroquois were warriors, for example, a large group captured in 1634 and the elders of a war party captured in 1639. However, immediately after their first recorded epidemic (smallpox) of 1640–41, western Iroquois attacks in southeastern Huronia increased. By the summer of 1641, the paths in the southeastern parts of Huronia were considered dangerous because of the presence of the enemy. A Huron war party intercepted and scattered a group of 300 Iroquois warriors near Huronia. In 1642, they were everywhere in Huronia, and "almost throughout the year various parties of the enemy who have crept into the country under the cover of the woods and of the night, have everywhere and at almost all seasons of the year committed massacres. . . . Even women, and children at the breast are not in security within sight of the palisades of their own Villages." They destroyed a Huron village—the first such incident recorded—and killed or captured all but 20 inhabitants. In the summer of 1643, "war continued its usual ravages. . . . The villages were in a state of continual alarm, and captives were taken by the hundreds." In the spring of 1645, "a band of Iroquois—having landed near one of our frontier villages .. . surrounded a company of women who were just going out for work in the fields, and so quickly carried them off in their canoes, that two hundred men in arms, who ran up at their first cries" could not save any of them.[32]

The western Iroquois may have had an epidemic in 1646-47, as the eastern Iroquois did. In 1647, 300 Onondaga and 800 Cayuga and Seneca planned a joint attack on Huronia. It was called off, but the Seneca attacked a Neutral village "where they took away all the captives they could."[33] In the next two years they destroyed four Huron villages and captured many refugee Huron. However, there is no record before the epidemics of their destroying villages or capturing numerous noncombatants.

The only reported epidemics among the eastern Iroquois were in 1634 and 1646. As there were no Jesuit observers in their villages during most of this period, we do not know when or if other infections were introduced. They may have been infected around 1640, as many neighbouring groups were, including the western Iroquois, and they had captured some diseased Huron. The Jesuits reported large captures in 1642 and 1643, and again from 1647 on. Captures of small groups and of Huron traders increased as well, many of the latter being kept alive contrary to traditional practice.

Like the western Iroquois, many more warriors were active in enemy territories—mostly the Ottawa and St. Lawrence River region—and for all seasons of the year after 1641. It is quite clear that they sought captives to adopt. In 1642, they travelled further up the Ottawa River than ever before, over the ice, to a winter camp of Algonkins, where they "killed those whom they first met and took away alive as many as they could to their own country. They killed only the men and the more aged women, sparing about 30 of the younger ones in order that they might dwell in their country and marry as if they had been born there."[34] In 1647, even before the end of their current epidemic, they captured 100 Algonkins from two hunting parties. Shortly after, they attacked 30 Algonkin families far up the Ottawa River and brought many home. The timing of the large captures of women and children suggests that these captures were in response to epidemic deaths.

Although many war parties are reported for the Ottawa and St. Lawrence River groups, no large captures are reported. In 1635, after their first epidemic, Montagnais from Tadoussac attacked the Bersiamites, and in 1636, attacked a fishing party of 300 Iroquois at Lake Champlain, killing twenty-eight and capturing five. They had wanted to capture more, but the speed of retreat made that impossible. In 1637 they went to Mohawk territory with some Algonkin, but were ambushed before they could attack. For these groups, war parties are mentioned for every year, but destinations and outcomes are not always described. However, by 1640, the Jesuits reported that the Algonkin and Montagnais had decreased in numbers to such an extent that the Iroquois had no fear of them. The Algonkin complained that they were now like women—they could "only flee."[35] Possibly being so much nearer the sources of infection, extensive depopulation occurred earlier here than in Huronia. The Jesuits do report individual captives and, living in small groups as they did, small and even individual captures may have been their objective.

In 1645, downriver from Quebec, a war party of headmen passed Miscou "on their way to war . . . . They threw themselves on the first prey that fell into their hands; they came back victorious, and desired by these massacres to allay the grief and sorrow of all the Country, which is afflicted by the death of many persons who have died during the past few years." They "had killed seven Savages and taken thirteen or fourteen prisoners, most of whom were children." The deaths precipitating this raiding could have been war deaths, but there had been epidemics in this region since 1634. In 1645, the Abenakis suffered an epidemic which "destroyed a good part of their nation," and many died in an epidemic in Tadoussac. These captures could have been in response to epidemic deaths.[36]

From 1638 to 1641, the Jesuits reported that the Neutral suffered disease, famine, and war. By 1640, the Neutral were concerned about restoring their population. The number of pre-epidemic captures by the Neutral are unknown, but in 1641 over 170 captives were brought home, and the next year 2,000 Neutral warriors destroyed an enemy village defended by 900 warriors. They captured 800. Of these they burned 70 warriors, blinded and stranded the old men, and brought the rest home. This is the only data we have for the Neutral, as the Jesuits were rarely in their villages.

For the Huron, there is evidence of more captures in the 1630s than in the 1640s, but these were warriors who were tortured and killed. However, Huron parties went out every year during and after the epidemics. The Jesuits mentioned, and then only in passing, only four integrated captives: an Iroquois woman, 25 years old, "whose life the Huron had spared"; an Iroquois man, "a captive among the Hurons, and had become Naturalized with them"; and, as reported in 1647, two "young men of the Nation of Fire . . . both captives of war, who, having been taken when quite young, have been preserved alive."[37] The capture and integration of many enemy women and children reported for other groups after epidemics is not reported for the Huron in any detail. However, in the Jesuit Relations of 1640-1641, the Jesuits reported that during attacks, the Huron either killed women and children immediately, or let them live. (This was the usual practice in the northeast; following an attack, if the warriors thought that some or all of their captives would not survive the trip back to the warriors' villages, or if there were insufficient warriors to help them make the journey, the captives were killed.)

In 1646, the Jesuits reported: "Our Hurons too have had, in their turn, success in warfare, have put to flight the enemy, and have carried off their spoils and some number of captives"—but, they add, "these have served as victims to their flames."[38] This could be true, but it is highly unlikely that all of their captives were warriors, and would therefore be killed. Possibly the Jesuits were more aware of the captives who were tortured and killed than those who had been adopted. Or they may have been uninterested in captives unless they were to be killed, and thus could be baptized. For whatever reason, the results of many war expeditions are not reported. For example, the report of a Christian war party composed of Christian converts that went west in 1642 does not include the outcome of that sortie; although there was a description of the non-Christian party who set out at the same time but who reportedly fled from the enemy. Adopted captives of the Fire Nation are mentioned twice in 1647, and they could have been captured in 1642. The omission of the Christian war party's experience could exemplify a selective reporting which has resulted in so little data on Huron captives.

The Jesuits may, for political reasons, have omitted or deleted references to Huron achievements in war. Their reports, after being edited in Quebec and France, were published in Europe as a means of increasing support for the missions. During the early 1640s they were requesting additional help from Europe, including military aid against the Iroquois whom they considered to be destroying their missions. They thus may have decided that they would gain more sympathy and support by depicting the Huron as victims, fighting in defence or for revenge (understandably, in light of the Jesuit descriptions of Iroquois barbarism). If this was the Jesuit strategy, and the Iroquois were to be depicted as villains who were disrupting not only normal life but also attempts to convert the Huron, it explains their vivid, exaggerated, and, in some cases, untrue portrayal of Iroquois warriors' behaviour and goals. For example, the Huron traders captured in 1644 would, they assured their readers, "serve as prey for the flames, and for their stomachs hungering after the flesh and blood of all these people."[39] Elsewhere they report that many of these particular captives were kept alive and integrated, despite their being adult males. Moreover, in that report, the party capturing them included three former Huron. Likewise the Jesuits, despite their report of the adoption of Algonkins captured far up the Ottawa River, often predicted torture and death for women and children captives. In another report, they state that "the Iroquois followed and massacred them," that those not immediately killed would "become the objects of their sport, and food for the flames and for their stomachs."[40]

Only in the latter part of the 1640s, and in the 1650s, did the Jesuits acknowledge that the Iroquois increased the size of their villages and war parties with captives. After an attack on the Algonkins at Lake Nipissing, the "poor women and children were as usual, dragged away into captivity," and after an attack on the Neutral, they took an "exceedingly large" number of captives, especially "young women, whom they reserve, in order to keep up the population of their own villages."[41] These reports followed the Huron dispersal and the closing of the mission in Huronia.

If the Jesuits failed to detail the capture and integration of enemy captives by the Huron, they did describe the other Huron strategy to increase their population—the taking in of the disease-ridden Wenro women and children. Perhaps the Jesuits felt this good deed would enhance the Huron image in Europe, and thus increase support for their mission. Indeed, they apparently succeeded, for in the early eighteenth century the French historian Charlevoix wrote that the Huron welcomed the Wenro after they had suffered a "fearful massacre at the hands of the Iroquois, and received them with an affection that would have done honour to a Christian people,"[42] not realizing, of course, that by this seemingly altruistic act the Huron were bolstering their own depleted numbers. It is possible that the lack of data after 1640 on captures by the Huron and St. Lawrence groups reflects a bias in Jesuit reporting.

There is other evidence that enemy captives were sought after the epidemics. Attacks increased on places where women and children were, such as villages, camps, and women's working parties. Also, more captives who formerly would have been killed were kept alive. Huron traders captured by the Mohawk eastern Iroquois who, as adult males, would traditionally have been killed, were adopted by families who had lost members, and many were successfully integrated. Although some escaped and returned to their own villages, others accepted the transition, and soon appeared in Iroquois war parties. Another type of captive traditionally killed were the first captives taken in the spring.

These were ceremonially sacrificed to ensure future success in raiding. However, it was reported that for at least one year the Mohawk let these first captives live.

Another indication of the desirability of captives were the larger war parties, so that a good number of captives could be escorted home. In addition, the eastern Iroquois attempted to make peace with the French twice during the 1640s on condition that the French stop protecting the Algonkins.

It seems clear that changes in warfare after the epidemics resulted from a change in motivation. Groups depopulated by epidemics desired enemy captives to increase their numbers. In contrast to the lurid descriptions of Iroquois aims written by Jesuits in Huronia and Quebec in the early 1640s is the report by FatherJogues, who was held captive in a Mohawk village during the same period. He concluded that the Iroquois wanted "to take, if they can, all the Hurons; and, having put to death the most considerable ones and a good part of the others, to make of them both but one people and only one land."[43] In this, of course, they partly succeeded, because when the Huron dispersed, some groups moved to Iroquois villages to join their countrymen already integrated there.

The evidence suggests that this strategy was not an Iroquois ploy to eliminate a trade rival, but an aim shared by many of these groups. Jogues' statement of Iroquois intentions matches exactly the behaviour of the Neutral when they destroyed an enemy village after their epidemics. The fact that others, and not only the Iroquois, were raiding to capture and amalgamate enemy individuals renders Hunt's description of this warfare—"the wars of the Iroquois"—inappropriate. Although it has been thought that only Iroquois raiding changed, it appears to have been a general phenomenon, a shared response to epidemic depopulation.[44]

The results of this post-epidemic warfare—the success of the Iroquois in maintaining their territory and cultural identity while others failed to do so—is probably another reason why the warfare has been thought of as mainly that of the Iroquois. Though it must be stressed that, in the end, there were probably more non-Iroquois in their villages than Iroquois, they achieved what others had failed to do.

Taylor suggests that the "sudden and dramatic changes in demography and territory" which follow virgin soil epidemics result from different rates of depopulation and differences in the timing of epidemics between groups.[45] Those who had lost fewer, or had not contracted certain infections, or at least not yet, may have pressed their advantage over weaker and more vulnerable enemy groups who were currently having an epidemic, or had lost more of their numbers.[46]

Over time, as raiding continued this variation in group strength increased, leading eventually to the dispersal of some groups and the strengthening of others, in the words of a Piegan warrior, "while it weakens our enemies [it] makes us strong."[47]

Thus, the close examination of the epidemic experience and of the conditions, attitudes, and behaviour reported during that time suggests that the changes in warfare and in the consequences of warfare after the virgin soil epidemics resulted more from responses to epidemic effects than from fur-trade aspirations.

Notes

1. See K.D. Patterson and G.W. Hartwig, "The Disease Factor: An Introductory Overview," and G.W. Hartwig, "Social Consequences of Epidemic Diseases; the Nineteenth Century in Eastern Africa," in *Disease in African History*, edited by G.W. Hartwig and K.D. Patterson (Durham, NC: Duke University Press, 1978); J.C. Ewers, "The Influence of Epidemics on the Indian Populations and Cultures of Texas," *Plains Anthropology* 18 (1973): 104–15; A.W. Crosby, "Virgin Soil Epidemics, . . ." in *The American Indian: Past and Present*, edited by R.L.Nichols (New York: 1986), 39–46.
2. A virgin soil epidemic (the Black Death) affected Europe in the 14th century and likewise caused changes—religious, political, economic, social, and demographic—following the loss of 40 to 50 percent of the population. See B.F. Tuchman, *A Distant Mirror* (New York: Alfred A.Knopf, 1979).
3. G.T. Hunt, *The Wars of the Iroquois: A Study in Intertribal Relations* (Madison: University of Wisconsin Press, 1940).
4. The terms "Iroquoian" and "Algonquoian" used here are as defined by Trigger: "In keeping with internationally accepted usage, the term Iroquois refers only to the Confederated Five Nations of Upper New York State: the Mohawk, Oneida, Onondaga, Cayuga, and Seneca. The term Iroquoian is reserved for the broader linguistic grouping to which they, the Huron, and many other tribes belonged. Likewise, Algonkin refers specifically to the tribal grouping that inhabited the Ottawa Valley and adjacent regions early in the seventeenth century, while Algonkian refers to a more widespread linguistic grouping to which the Algonkin belonged." B.G. Trigger, *The Children of Aataentsic: A History of the Huron People to 1660*. (Montreal: McGill-Queens, 1976), xxiii.
5. Hunt, *Wars of the Iroquois*.
6. W.N. Fenton, "The Iroquois in History," in *North American Indians in Historical Perspective*," edited by E.B. Leacock and N.O. Lurie (New York: Random House, Inc., 1971); E. Tooker, "The Iroquois Defeat of the Huron: A Review of Causes," *Pennsylvania Archaeology* 33 (1963): 115–23; A.W. Trealease, *Indian Affairs in Colonial New York: The Seventeenth Century* (Ithaca, NY: Cornell University Press, 1960).
7. Hunt, *Wars of the Iroquois*.
8. Trigger, *Children of Aataentsic*.
9. B.G. Trigger, *The Huron: Farmers of the North* (New York: Holt, Rinehart and Winston, Inc., 1969); C.E. Heidenreich, *Huronia: A History and Geography of the Huron Indians, 1600–1650* (Toronto: McClelland and Stewart, 1971).
10. R.G. Thwaiters, ed., *The Jesuit Relations and Allied Documents: Travels and Explorations of the Jesuit Missionaries of New France 1610–1791*, vol. 8 (New York: Pageant Book Company, 1951), 33, 87, 107.
11. *Ibid.*, vol. 8, 89; vol. 7, 221; vol. 11, 9.
12. *Ibid.*, vol. 14, 83; vol. 15, 57.
13. Trigger, *Children of Aataentsic*.
14. Thwaites, *Jesuit Relations*, vol. 12, 245; vol. 15, 23; vol. 13, 163, 165; vol. 15, 89.
15. *Ibid.*, vol. 18, 23; vol. 19, 87, 217; vol. 20, 27; vol. 17, 223.
16. *Ibid.*, vol. 14, 73; vol. 15, 73, 129; vol. 8, 131; vol. 13, 155; vol. 19, 235, 237; vol. 13, 195; vol. 14, 49; vol. 23, 117; vol. 19, 189.

17. C.W. Dixon, *Smallpox* (London: 1962).
18. As was usual in virgin soil epidemics at contact, where the importance of hygiene and quarantine were unknown, Huron behaviour—both the continuation of normal routines and activities related to the epidemic (for example, mortuary and curing practices, visiting, assemblies for various purposes)—increased incidence and mortality rates and exacerbated the symptoms. For a full description and discussion, see S.M. Johnston, "Epidemic Effects as Causes of Warfare in the Northeast after 1640" (Master's thesis, Carleton University, 1982).
19. Trigger, *Huron*, 13; Heidenreich, *Huronia*, 91–108.
20. J.V. Wright, "A Review: The Children of Aataentsic, A History of the Huron People to 1660," *Canadian Journal of Archaeology* 1 (1977): 183–85.
21. E.W. Stearne and A.E. Stearne, *The Effects of Smallpox on the Destiny of the Amerindian* (Boston: Bruce Humphries, Inc., 1945).
22. Ewers, "Influence of Epidemics," 109; Crosby, "Virgin Soil Epidemics,"; I. Taylor and J. Knowelden, *Principles of Epidemiology* (London: 1964).
23. G.W. Wrong, *The Long Journey to the Country of the Hurons* (Toronto: The Champlain Society, 1939).
24. Thwaites, *Jesuit Relations*, vol. 8, 129–31, vol. 13, 235; vol. 15, 41.
25. *Ibid.*, vol. 17, 115. For a description of the traditional Huron view of disease, their perceptions of and mental and emotional responses to the epidemics, their attempts to discover cause and/or agent, and cure, their perceptions of the French role in the epidemics, and their attempts to discover the secret remedies of the Jesuits, see Johnston, "Epidemic Effects."
26. Thwaites, *Jesuit Relations*, vol. 19, 91; vol. 17, 123.
27. Europeans responded similarly to the horrors and the unprecedented numbers of deaths caused by the plague. They feared they were being exterminated. Because so much had been destroyed, they felt things could never return to normal. " 'Men and women wandered around as if mad' and let their cattle stray 'because no one had any inclination to concern themselves about the future.' " Tuchman, *Distant Mirror*, 99.
28. Thwaites, *Jesuit Relations*, vol. 21, 221.
29. *Ibid.*, vol. 15, 43.
30. Wrong, *Long Journey*, 19.
31. Tyrell, *David Thompson's Narrative*, 339.
32. Thwaites, *Jesuit Relations*, vol. 22, 305; vol. 27, 63-65; vol. 29, 249.
33. *Ibid.*, vol. 33, 81-83.
34. *Ibid.*, vol. 22, 265.
35. *Ibid.*, vol. 25, 157.
36. *Ibid.*, vol. 28, 33–35, 203.
37. *Ibid.*, vol. 33, 109; vol. 29, 251; vol. 30, 91.
38. *Ibid.*, vol. 29, 251.
39. *Ibid.*, vol. 26, 19; vol. 22, 249.
40. *Ibid.*, vol. 22, 249.
41. *Ibid.*, vol. 36, 189, 177.
42. P.F.X. Charlevoix, *History and General Description of New France*, vol. 2 (Chicago: Loyola University Press, 1962), 121.
43. Thwaites, *Jesuit Relations*, vol. 24, 297.
44. The inter-relationships between the disease, famine and war that characterized these areas and people's responses to them affected post-epidemic behaviour in many ways. For example, did food scarcity cause the unusually long periods of male absence from villages which occurred after the epidemics? Did these long sorties provide them with more opportunity for raiding enemy areas, while leaving their own women and children vulnerable to enemy capture? If so, it would help to explain the extension of raiding to more seasons of the year, as well as the destruction of so many

villages and large captures. Did the sense of powerlessness resulting from their ineffectiveness in dealing with the epidemic disaster result in attempts to restore and demonstrate power through success at war, which would help to explain the increase in warfare? For descriptions of responses to virgin soil epidemics generally and an analysis of post-epidemic behaviour in the northeast, see S. Johnston, "Epidemic Effects."

45. Taylor, *Sociocultural Effects*, 76.
46. In the 14th century, when the Scots heard that the English were suffering from the plague, they delightedly assembled to invade. However, before they could proceed, they were themselves infected. Tuchman, *Distant Mirror*.
47. Tyrell, *David Thompson's Narrative*, 339.

Chapter 3
Ktaqamkuk Ilnui Saqimawoutie: Aboriginal Rights and the Myth of the Micmac Mercenaries in Newfoundland

Dennis Bartels

White hostility to the Newfoundland Micmac land claim seems to rest largely upon the widely-held Newfoundland folk-belief that French colonial authorities brought Cape Breton Micmacs to Newfoundland in the sixteenth and seventeenth centuries and paid a bounty for every aboriginal Beothuck that the Micmacs killed. Anthropologists' advocacy of the Micmac claim has involved publicizing historical evidence that this folk-belief is false. Advocacy has also involved situating the Micmac claims in the broader context of the ethical and legal justification of aboriginal rights in Canada.

In 1981, the Ktaqamkuk Ilnui Saqimawoutie[1] (KIS) and the Conne River Indian Band Council, together representing about 1,800 Newfoundland Micmacs, submitted a comprehensive land claim to roughly the southern third of the island of Newfoundland. Several anthropologists and individuals with anthropological training carried out historical or ethnographic research on Micmac use and occupancy of Newfoundland which has incorporated into the Micmac claim. These include Huguette Giard, Jean Morriset, Douglas Jackson, Dennis and Alice Bartels, Dr. Peter Usher, and Jerry Wetzel, Research Director for the KIS who received anthropological training at Memorial University of Newfoundland and elsewhere. Important contributions to the Micmac claim were also made by non-anthropologists. Pat Anderson researched historical records from the British colonial period; Professor Doug Sanders researched the legal basis of the claim; John Fife assisted in editing; Dr. David McNab, a historian, researched records from the British colonial period; and Pam White produced maps for the claim.

The Micmac Mercenary Myth

Many non-Native Newfoundlanders and, possibly, the provincial government, did not take the Micmac land claim seriously at first because it contradicted the widely-held Newfoundland folk-belief that in the sixteenth and seventeenth centuries, French colonial authorities brought Cape Breton Micmacs to Newfoundland, and paid a bounty for every aboriginal Beothuck that the Micmacs killed. This folk-belief has been referred to elsewhere as the Micmac Mercenary Myth.[3] In light of this myth, Newfoundland Micmacs are often seen as one of several relatively recent groups of settlers (like the Irish) who are not aboriginal, and who are historically tainted with the murder of the

Beothucks. Although elements of the myth are present in a 1968 edition of a Newfoundland history text by Leslie Harris (current president of Memorial University of Newfoundland) which is still widely used in Newfoundland elementary schools,[4] there is a great deal of evidence that the myth is false. The historian, Leslie Upton, has argued that the "mercenary myth" was introduced in 1827 by William Epps Cormack in his inaugural address to the Beothuck Institution, and was without supporting evidence. Upton claims that English fishermen and settlers, not the Micmacs, killed most of the approximately 1,000 Beothucks living in Newfoundland in the late eighteenth and nineteenth centuries.[5] Upton concludes that the myth was,

> . . . a very comforting explanation, as it relegated the English to a minor role in finishing off what others [i.e., the Micmacs] had begun.[6]

Evidence adduced by Upton, and others against the myth, was published in *The Newfoundland Quarterly* by an anthropologist belonging to the Support Groups,[7] a magazine which is widely read by Newfoundlanders who are interested in Newfoundland history and culture. Ralph Pastore, a historian-archaeologist at Memorial University, also published evidence that the Micmacs did not kill the Beothucks.[8] It is, perhaps, significant that the most recent "official refutation" of the Micmac land claim by the provincial government (1982) does not mention the "mercenary myth."

The "Magic Date"

Most parties with an interest in the Newfoundland Micmac land claim argue that establishment of the claim requires demonstration of Micmac use of Newfoundland prior to the "magic date." For the provincial government,[9] this date seems to vary between the date when English sovereignty over Newfoundland was established and the date of initial European contact with Newfoundland in the fifteenth and sixteenth centuries. The issue of "the date" is complicated by the provincial government's apparent belief[10] that establishment of the Micmac claim requires demonstration that there were *permanent Micmac settlements* (villages) in Newfoundland prior to the assertion of English sovereignty. The weakness of these arguments was demonstrated in a Support Group document written by Professor Adrian Tanner, an anthropologist who teaches at Memorial University. Tanner points out that: (a) the lack of permanent settlement does not necessarily invalidate a claim to aboriginal rights in light of the "nomadic nature of aboriginal land tenure"; and (b) whenever English sovereignty over Newfoundland was "asserted" (and this is a matter of some controversy), newly-discovered archival sources from the French colonial period indicate that Micmacs were almost certainly there first.[11] In the same Support Group document (1982), Professor Tanner points out that comprehensive land claims fall solely under the jurisdiction of the federal government. The provincial government's attempts to "refute" the Micmac land claim thus constitute unwarranted intrusions into areas outside its jurisdiction.

Newfoundland Micmacs based their land claim on the premise that

Newfoundland has been part of Micmac hunting and fishing territory since "time immemorial,"[12] presumably because Cape Breton Micmacs regularly voyaged to Newfoundland in order to hunt and fish in pre-contact times. Ralph Pastore has argued that Micmacs could not have made the voyage from Cape Breton to Newfoundland without European technology—i.e., shallops.[13] Thus Micmacs could not have regularly hunted and fished in Newfoundland prior to European contact in the fifteenth and sixteenth centuries, a conclusion which the provincial and federal governments may welcome. Other anthropologists have disputed this claim, drawing on historical and ethnographic evidence to demonstrate the possibility that Cape Breton Micmacs could have travelled to Newfoundland in birchbark canoes on a regular basis in pre-contact times.[14]

Archaeological Evidence

The provincial government has claimed that archaeological evidence shows that sites in areas covered by the Micmac claim were actually occupied by Beothucks.[15] Professor Stuart Brown, an archaeologist at Memorial University, has disputed this claim in a long letter to the St. John's *Evening Telegram*, reprinted by the Support Group:

> As a professional archaeologist I strongly object to the misuse of archaeological evidence in the provincial government's rebuttal of the Micmac land claims both in the form of public statements by the Premier and the published assessment of the claim authored by Dr. Albert Jones [Government of Newfoundland and Labrador 1982].
>
> In their statement of claim, the Federation of Newfoundland Indians (FNI) asserts that archaeological research on the south coast of the island has been very limited and thus far has failed to establish evidence of prehistoric occupation by either Micmac or Beothuck Indian groups. While acknowledging the limited research and accepting the lack of evidence for a prehistoric presence, Dr. Jones argues there is indeed evidence for a prehistoric presence, Dr. Jones argues there is indeed evidence for a prehistoric Beothuck occupation "anterior to the sporadic visits of the Micmac." In considering this "evidence," Dr. Jones ignores the fact that no viable archaeological definition of Beothuck material culture exists. Until quite recently, prehistoric artefacts that could not be ascribed to the Maritime Archaic or Dorset Eskimo cultures became Beothuck by default. In recognition that there may be a prehistoric Micmac presence in the southern part of the island and that the immediately prehistoric situation may be more complex than previously suspected, most archaeologists operating in the province prefer to use the neutral term "recent Indian" for such finds. . . .[16]

Other Contributions by Anthropologists

The more general issue of the legal and moral basis for Native land claims, and for this claim in particular, has been dealt with by Professor Tanner in public lectures and newspaper articles.[17] The Support Group, including Professor Tanner and Dorothy C. Anger, has cooperated with leaders of major religious denominations in St. John's in attempts to mobilize public opinion in support of the Micmac claim and other Native land claims in Labrador. Ms. Anger has carried out genealogical research on behalf of Micmacs in western Newfoundland and published on the resurgence of Newfoundland Micmac culture.[18]

Whatever the outcome of the struggle of Newfoundland Micmacs for negotiation of their land claims, anthropologists working on issues surrounding the claim have focussed scholarly and public attention on first evidence against the mercenary myth; and second, unresolved problems of Newfoundland Micmac history and prehistory. Hopefully, this contribution will be recognized by future generations of Newfoundlanders and Newfoundland Micmacs alike.

Epilogue

In late June 1984, the Federal Cabinet agreed to register Conne River Micmacs as status Indians. The Cabinet also ordered a study on the effects of creating a 2.6 square-kilometre reserve at Conne River. The study was to be completed by 30 September 1984.

Newfoundland Micmacs living outside Conne River—for example, at Flat Bay, on Newfoundland's West Coast—will not be included in the Conne River registration.

On 2 October 1986, the Supreme Court of Canada ruled that, although Indian affairs are a federal responsibility, lands involved in the Micmac land claim fall under provincial jurisdiction. Therefore, any legal action regarding the Micmac land claim will have to begin in a provincial court.

Acknowledgements

I wish to thank the following members of the Indian and Inuit Support Group of Newfoundland and Labrador: Professor Adrian Tanner (Anthropology, Memorial University of Newfoundland); Dorothy C. Anger, M.A.; Professor Phyllis Artis (Department of English, Memorial University of Newfoundland). I also wish to thank Professor Charles Davis (Biology, Memorial University of Newfoundland). These people provided information and valuable comments. They are, of course, in no way responsible for my interpretations and conclusions.

Notes

1. Ktaqamkuk Ilnui Saqimawoutie translates as "Newfoundland Indian Government" in the Micmac language.
2. Ktaqamkuk Ilnui Saqimawoutie and the Conne River Indian Band Council (henceforth KIS), *Freedom to Live Our Own Way in Our Own Land* (Conne River, Newfoundland: Ktaqamkuk Ilnui Saqimawoutie and the Conne River Band Council, 1982), iii.
3. Dennis Bartels, "Time Immemorial? A Research Note on Micmacs in

Newfoundland," *Newfoundland Quarterly*, vol. 75, no. 3 (1979).

4. A later edition of Harris' text, which omits the mercenary myth is now used in many Newfoundland and Labrador elementary schools.
5. Ingeborg Marshall argues that tuberculosis " . . . played a significant role in the eventual demise of the Beothuk group." Ingeborg Marshall, "Disease as a Factor in the Demise of the Beothuk Indians," *Culture*, vol. 1, no. 1 (1981): 76.
6. Leslie Upton, "The Extermination of the Beothuks," *Canadian Historical Review*, vol. 57, no. 3 (1977): 147.
7. Bartels, "Time Immemorial?"
8. Government of Newfoundland and Labrador, *Assessment and Analysis of the Micmac Land Claim in Newfoundland* (St. John's, Newfoundland, 1982).
9. *Ibid.*, 115, 93.
10. *Ibid.*, 115.
11. Indian and Inuit Support Group of Newfoundland and Labrador, "The Newfoundland Government's Rejection of the Micmac Land Claim" (St. John's Newfoundland, 1982, unpublished position paper). Also see Tanner's Chapter in Part II.
12. KIS, "Freedom," 1.
13. Ralph Pastore, *Newfoundland's Micmacs: A History of Their Traditional Life*, Newfoundland Historical Society Pamphlet, No. 5 (St. John's, Newfoundland, 1978), 9–10.
14. Bartels, "Time Immemorial?" P.F.X. Charlevoix, *History and General Description of New France*, translated by Dr. J.G. Shea, vol. 1 (London: Francis Edwards, 1902), 264; Frank G. Speck, *Beothuk and Micmac*, Indian Notes and Monographs (New York: Heye Foundation, 1922).
15. Government of Newfoundland and Labrador, *Micmac Land Claim*.
16. Quoted in Support Group, "Rejection of Micmac Land Claim."
17. Adrian Tanner, "Do We Owe Micmacs?," *Humber Log*, January 2, 1983.
18. Dorothy C. Anger, "The Micmacs of Newfoundland: A Resurgent Culture," *Culture*, vol. 1, no. 1 (1981).

Chapter 4
Families of Mixed Descent in the Western Great Lakes Region

Harriet Gorham

The extensive contact between Indians and Whites that the fur trade encouraged in the southern Great Lakes region between 1670 and 1830 fostered the appearance of a population of mixed Indian-White ancestry in the area. These people, whether the offspring of casual sexual unions or relationships regularized by some form of community recognition, had to find their place within the social environment of the region; an environment that for almost a century and a half was profoundly shaped by the fur trade. Many of these "mixed blood" individuals remained with their mother's band and were raised as Indians. Accustomed to the Indian way of life, they were generally identified as "Indians" by most Indians and Whites in the area. However, not all individuals of mixed Indian-White ancestry were adopted by Indian groups in the region; others were more closely involved with the activity of the White fur trade settlements and participated more or less directly in the fur trade and various "Indian departments" that were active in the region. People of mixed-descent lived in or about the fur trading settlements such as Sault Ste. Marie, Michilimackinac, or La Baie, and were employed either as traders, interpreters, or Indian agents, and assisted their husbands in their work. It is these mixed-bloods, who, in a general way, filled a liaison role between the Indian and White societies represented in the Great Lakes region, that are the focus of this essay. While aspects of their trading and business activities are not difficult to trace, the historical record is almost silent about their perception of their own ethnic identity or the attitude toward them that was held by the rest of the fur trade community. Were these people Métis?

The mixed-blood "fur traders" of the Great Lakes region bear some resemblance to the mixed-blood fur traders and buffalo hunters of the Red River area, who were known as the Métis during the nineteenth century. Both groups shared a similar mixed Indian and White ancestry, and earned their living primarily from the fur trade and related activities, subsistence farming, and hunting. Individuals from both regions filled important social roles in their communities as go-betweens and liaisons between adjacent Indian and White groups. Both groups were at least nominally Roman Catholic, and further similarities in use of language, style of dress, construction of housing, arts and crafts could also be enumerated. During the late eighteenth and early nineteenth century the two groups may possibly have influenced each other's development through contact between individuals on the trading frontier to the southwest of Lake Superior and along the Mississippi—Red River water route.[1] Some of the Métis at Pembina may have been descended from mixed-blood traders from the

Michilimackinac area, and a number of Great Lakes families are known to have settled in the Red River area during the 1820s and 1830s.[2]

It is clear, however, that the mixed-blood people of the Great Lakes region never developed a sense of shared ethnic identity comparable to that expressed by the Métis as the New Nation after 1816. A few isolated mixed-blood individuals in the Great Lakes region may have been influenced by the sense of "nation" exhibited by the Red River Métis after the Battle of Seven Oaks, but, if so, they were never able to interest or lead other mixed-bloods in the Great Lakes region to take significant collective action to protect their shared interests. Throughout the period of their dependence upon the fur trade, from approximately 1680 to 1830, individuals of mixed Indian and White ancestry in the Great Lakes region appear to have functioned more as a disparate collection of individuals rather than as a cohesive group. They lived in small widely-scattered settlements such as Sault Ste. Marie, St. Joseph, La Baie, Michilimackinac, and Prairie du Chien, or they maintained their own small trading establishments along the water routes between such centres. Their individual importance within such communities varied from the larger centres, such as Michilimackinac, where the requirements of government administration, Montreal fur trade financiers, and Indian diplomacy shaped local activity, to the smaller centres such as La Baie, where the interests of mixed-bloods such as Charles de Langlade, and later the Grignon and Lawe families, had a significant impact on the daily affairs of the local inhabitants. As individuals, most mixed-bloods demonstrated a greater awareness of the uniqueness of their way of life as fur traders and their attachment to their homeland in the Great Lakes region, than to any clear sense of distinctiveness created by their mixed ancestry.

This study combines elements from both "objective" and "subjective" approaches to the study of ethnicity to analyze the level of ethnic consciousness that may be found among the mixed-bloods of the Great Lakes region during the fur trade period before 1830.[3] Research efforts focussed on locating examples of self-ascription and ascription by outsiders of mixed-blood individuals to a distinctive ethnic group. The other important focus of research was the determination of the major characteristics of the mating and marriage patterns of these people. The main findings from these three lines of inquiry will be discussed further on.

Self-ascription, ascription by outsiders, and mating and marriage patterns can be useful indicators of the definition of group boundaries and criteria for group membership, as well as the extent of group exclusivity, solidarity, and protectiveness. They can also provide valuable information about the nature and quality of the group's relationships with other groups, outsiders' perceptions of the group's function within the larger social structure, and the group's own understanding of its purpose. On a more personal level, examples of self-ascription can reveal much about the individual's perception of his or her own ethnic identity, how the group has transmitted that concept to the individual, and how it has been reinforced by the larger society.[4]

Self-Ascription

Upon initial observation the mixed-blood "fur traders" of the Great Lakes region appear to conform to the theoretical definitions of an ethnic group on the basis of sharing certain objective criteria such as common language, religion, style of dress, housing construction, and some forms of artistic expression.[5] However, an examination of the historical record yields little evidence that mixed-blood individuals in the Great Lakes region identified anything distinctive about their mixed Indian-White ancestry, or acknowledged their relationship to a larger Métis ethnic group. The mixed-bloods of the Great Lakes seemingly lacked one of the more significant characteristics of an ethnic group: self-ascription on the part of the individuals to a larger group. Furthermore, rather than jealously protect the ancestral and cultural integrity of their own group, they seem to have been very open to contact with representatives from other racial or cultural groups, favouring exogamous mating and marriage patterns that re-established contact with both their Indian and White trading partners. Exogamy was beneficial to many mixed-blood trading families and the absences of self-proclaimed "distinctive" ethnic identity enabled interested individuals to mix more freely with both their "client" and "patron" groups. This lack of self-ascription by mixed-bloods during the eighteenth and early nineteenth centuries may have been encouraged by the failure of both Indian and White societies in the region to distinguish individuals of mixed ancestry simply on the basis of their mixed ethnicity. The presence of a small group of people within the mixed blood population, who were able to function as a moving bridge between the two larger societies, unencumbered by rigid ethnic identities, may have been crucial to successful transactions between Indian and White interest groups.

Ascription by Outsiders

In Canadian historical writing "Métis" has been used to describe people of mixed Indian-White ancestry who were both French-speaking and Roman Catholic. More specifically, the term has been used to refer to the Métis of the Red River valley who first expressed their sense of distinctive ethnic identity as the "New Nation" at the Battle of Seven Oaks in 1816, and later went on to fight for their collective rights in the Riel uprising of 1870 and the Northwest rebellion of 1885. In the Great Lakes region during the period under study, the expression "Métis" was virtually never used to refer to mixed-bloods. After 1820, the term "half-breed" came into common use to describe people of mixed Indian and White ancestry. This paper, assuming that the term implies a degree of collective ethnic consciousness, will use the term "Métis" to refer only to the mixed-bloods of the Canadian prairie. In preference to "half-breed", "mixed-blood" will be used to describe the people of mixed Indian-White ancestry in the Great Lakes region. Although both of these terms arose out of the theories of scientific racialism which were popular in North America during the mid-nineteenth century, "mixed-blood" carries fewer derogatory connotations than "half-breed."[6]

The correspondence of the traders, administrators, officers, and missionaries who worked in the Great Lakes region during the latter half of the eighteenth century reveals almost no use of any special terms or expressions that might have been used to distinguish persons of mixed Indian-White ancestry from other residents native to the area.[7] The terms French, French-Canadian, and Canadian were used almost interchangeably to refer to all French-speakers whether originally from Lower Canada or from the Great Lakes region, with only infrequent references to an individual's Indian ancestry. Mixed-bloods in the employ of the government administration were referred to by their proper names with little mention of their racial or ethnic backgrounds.[8] References or generalizations about "half-breeds," "half-Indians," or equivalent terms do not appear in the correspondence.

Throughout the late eighteenth century British officers and administrators often felt somewhat uneasy about the loyalties of their mixed-blood interpreters and Indian agents. In general, however, the British were more apprehensive of the Canadians' lingering attachment to the French government than they were of the likelihood that they would make common cause with the Indians. One significant exception to this, of course, occurred during the Pontiac uprising of 1763, when British officers and traders were very edgy about the sympathies of the French population.[9] During the eighteenth century there existed very little overt prejudice against individuals of mixed Indian-White ancestry in the official correspondence. Even Lieutenant-Governor Patrick Sinclair's notable dislike for the Canadian and mixed-blood traders in his employ at Michilimackinac during the American Revolution apparently stemmed from their continued interest in commerce during the war.[10]

The Catholic missionaries who visited Detroit, Michilimackinac, Sault Ste. Marie, and other remote settlements during the eighteenth century, also did not distinguish individuals of mixed Indian-White ancestry from their other parishioners. The papers of Father Marchand, Bouquet, Potier, Payet, Meurin, Gibault, Burke, Tabeau, and others, contain virtually no such references.[11] For example, in 1796, Father Levadoux described the greeting he received from the people of Michilimackinac in the following terms:

> At the time of my arrival there were two to three thousand persons engaged in trading. . . . I cannot tell you how gladly I was welcomed at that post. Everybody, Englishman, Frenchman, and Indian, all tried to surpass themselves in expressing the joy my coming gave them.[12]

It was not until the 1820s that a few scattered references to half-breeds began to appear in the writings of Father Richard and Crevier, indicating the existence of a separate ethnic category for mixed-bloods.[13] In 1823, Father Gabriel Richard wrote that at St.Joseph and Prairie du Chien:

> . . . as also in Mackinac, there are more than 60 to 80 Canadian Catholic families, or halfbreeds who nearly all speak the language of the Indians with whom they are joined in marriage. In my last mission at Mackinac and Green Bay I married at least ten Canadians or halfbreeds to full-blooded Indian women.[14]

Richard and Crevier appear to have been conforming to outside usage rather then reflecting distinctions being carefully made within the Canadian and Catholic community. None of the missionaries commented on any special self-identification by people of mixed Indian-White ancestry with their own mixed heritage.

Not many letters, diaries, or other documentation that might shed some light upon the attitudes of many mixed-blood individuals toward their own ethnicity appear to have survived from the eighteenth century.[15] Although most mixed-bloods were unable to write, it is unlikely that those who could write would have been inclined to commit such self-reflection to paper on a regular basis. Some information about their sense of ethnicity can, however, be derived from inference.

For some mixed-blood individuals the vagueness of their ethnic identity during the fur trade period before 1820 permitted them to adopt different ethnic identities over time or to selectively communicate elements of their ethnic background as the social situation demanded. In this way they were able to pass back and forth between Indian and White social environments. For example, Billy Caldwell, an English-speaking mixed-blood of Mohawk descent, was known by a series of different ethnic identities as his social status and economic position underwent changes. Caldwell spent his childhood on a Mohawk reserve near the Grand River, but then passed his adolescence among the British élite in Detroit, and as a young man he held a position with the British Indian department. After the War of 1812, he was known as a "mixed-blood" fur trader at Chicago, and finally as a Potawatomi "chief" living with "his people" west of the Mississippi.[16]

Another example of an individual who was able to operate successfully within this sliding, ethnic and social "category," was Charles de Langlade. Born in 1729, de Langlade was the son of a prominent Odawa woman and a French fur trader. He was raised, in part, at his mother's village of L'Arbre Croche, and received both formal instruction from the Jesuit missionaries there and informal guidance from his maternal uncle, LaFourche, then the chief of the L'Arbre Croche Odawa. As an adult, de Langlade achieved recognition as a victorious Indian warrior, able to lead armies of Western Indians into battle and across the continent to fight in the Seven Years War (1753–60) and the Amercian Revolution (1776–83). De Langlade was a half-pay lieutenant and superintendant of Indians at LaBaie under both French and British regimes.[17] Charles de Langlade cultivated the status of an accomplished warrior and leader among his maternal Odawa band and extended his influence outward to other groups of Great Lakes Indians through his reputation for victory, skills as an orator, and gifts and trade goods.[18] His position with the Indian department, in which he frequently was responsible for the distribution of Indian supplies and gifts, certainly did not diminish his popularity. The Menominee reputedly gave him the name "A-ke-wau-ge-ke- tau-so," meaning "he who is fierce for the land."[19] De Langlade's credibility with his Indian associates suggests that he must have communicated effectively his identification with his Indian parentage and cultural heritage when among his Indian kin.[20]

The respect de Langlade was able to command from his Indian supporters contributed directly to his status within White society. His military superiors acknowledged him to be " . . . very brave, to have much influence on the minds of the savages, and to be very zealous when ordered to do anything."[21] In return for his diligence, de Langlade was generally treated with respect. The official correspondence of both the French and British administrations rarely alluded to his Indian origins and generally referred to him simply by his family name or as a Frenchman. De Langlade also married a White woman, Charlotte Bourassa, a most unusual marital match for a mixed-blood man.[22] These facts imply that de Langlade was able to move quite comfortably within White society, and just as he was able to play-up his Indian heritage, he was able to selectively emphasize the White elements of his ethnic background.

Development of Discrimination

In the years following the War of 1812, Great Lakes society became increasingly stratified, and racial prejudices were expressed more openly. Mixed-bloods in the Great Lakes area became subject first to suspicion as British partisans in what had become American territory, and then to the racial discrimination that was becoming more overt in American society during the early nineteenth century. As agriculture, logging, and mining increased in importance in the region, and the fur trade declined, government-Indian relations grew more institutionalized, diminishing the need for mixed-blood individuals to act as liaisons between Indians and Whites. Discriminatory regulations and practices drove the mixed-blood traders into dependency upon the American Fur Company, resulting in the loss of their independence and their control over individual trading decisions.[24] Mixed-blood *voyageurs* were let go by the Company, in favour of more "docile" employees.[25] The mixed-blood population was increasingly viewed as an oddity, and as a convenient labour force of trappers, interpreters, and guides. The role of mixed-blood men and women in creating such towns as Michilimackinac, Green Bay, Chicago, and Milwaukee was quickly forgotten.

The terms "half-breed" and "half-Indian" came into currency and were used most often to describe members of the labouring class who lived on the edge of settlements or Indian reserves. Individuals, who had been accustomed to a degree of respect as leading members of their communities, were now sometimes labelled as "half-breeds."[26] Outsiders distinguished the small clusters of houses belonging to the "half-Indian and mongrel French" from those of the new

American majority in the rapidly expanding towns of the Great Lakes basin.[27] An ethnic category for people of mixed Indian-White ancestry was now more carefully delineated; but they were stigmatized as being indolent and primitive.[28]

The personal letters and recollections left behind by mixed-blood individuals after 1820 reveal a sense of confusion about their ethnic identity and an apprehension about the future. Mixed-bloods, such as William Johnston, Elizabeth Fisher Baird, and Augustin Grignon, demonstrated considerable knowledge of the culture and practices of their Indian relatives, and a definite sympathy and concern for the deterioration of Indian culture.[29] Although they readily acknowledged their Indian background, they seemed anxious to identify themselves as "White". They were associated with the old French bourgeois trading class or with the small group of independent Scots or Irish traders that had to some extent replaced the French within the local fur trade social hierarchy. They referred to other members of the old French trading families simply as French, without specific mention of Indian ancestry. They most certainly did not want to be associated with the "half-breed" labouring class in their communities.[30]

William Johnston, Elizabeth Baird, and Augustin Grignon were able to express their identification with the Great Lakes region as their home, and their membership within fur trade society, far more precisely than they were able to articulate a sense of their mixed ethnic heritage. Augustin Grignon seemed to summarize his experience best when he referred to his family, friends, and neighbours as "borderers," and to the physical and social demands of the "border life."[31] Such statements acknowledged his participation in a social world and a way of life which he recognized as being unique to the Great Lakes region, or to similar fur trade "frontiers," without using ethnic labels to distinguish it. Mixed-blood individuals were caught between the Indian and White societies that surrounded them and certainly were subject to the pressures associated with each of those groups. The treaty-signing process after 1824 forced some mixed-bloods to choose between Indian and White cultural heritages in order to remain near family and friends.[32] After 1820, it became increasingly difficult to maintain a social position that bridged both Indian and White societies.

Mating and Marriage Patterns

Throughout the eighteenth century and into the nineteenth century the Great Lakes mixed-bloods were able to maintain close contact with both Indian and White groups in the area. This was in no small part due to their preference for exogamous mating and marital choices. An examination of available baptismal and marriage records, as well as other sources, reveals that despite the presence of a significant mixed-blood population able to serve as prospective marital partners by the mid-eighteenth century, the Great Lakes mixed-bloods generally preferred exogamy. As successive generations of mixed-blood children reached maturity, they tended to mate and marry outside their own group and renew the cycle of intermarriage.

A discussion of the implications of exogamous mating and marriage for the ethnic development of the mixed-blood people of the Great Lakes region is handicapped by the gaps that exist in the historical material. The available documents consist of a few surviving marital and baptismal registers from the Roman Catholic missions in the regions, that were compiled between 1698 and 1838. Not only are some of these registers damaged and incomplete, they also trace the marital activities of only one segment of the population: those who resorted to the Church to sanction and record their marriages and the births of their children. The habits of the rest of the population, who chose to maintain only temporary alliances, or who sought community approval for their relationships in other ways, remained largely unrecorded save for the casual remarks of soldiers, traders, missionaries, administrators and travellers. The marriages of Native women who were reluctant to compromise their traditional Indian ways and beliefs by conversion to Roman Catholicism, or in later years, those who chose civil or Protestant ceremonies, were not fully recorded in the Roman Catholic records.

The disentangling of personal relationships that took place over two hundred years ago, and the tracing of genealogies, is also complicated by the fact that many of these alliances were conducted in the seclusion of an Indian hut, and the resulting children were raised in the historical obscurity of an Indian village. The details of their life were thus left to oral history rather than to the written record. Taken together, these factors skew the literature in favour of those mixed-blood individuals who were perhaps most closely associated with White society and subscribed, at least intermittently, to the expectations of White ceremonial practices.

The reconstruction of mixed-blood families and marriage practices is also rendered more complex by the presence of White women at Detroit, Michilimackinac, St. Joseph, and the settlements in the Illinois country. At St. Joseph, for example, marriages between White Canadians accounted for 38 percent of the marriages reconstructed between 1720 and 1773, and approximately 23 percent of the baptisms registered were of White (Canadian) children. At Michilimackinac, marriages between Whites accounted for 32 percent of the marriages registered between 1698 and 1765, and 18 percent of those recorded between 1765 and 1838.[33] Unlike the fur trade country in the Canadian West, fur traders' wives cannot be assumed to have been of Native ancestry.

Despite their limitations, the Church registers are still a significant source of information for the examination of mixed-blood mating patterns. The Michilimackinac and St. Joseph registers point to the growth of the mixed-blood population through new Indian-White unions and through mixed-blood exogamy.[34] Between 1698 and 1765, fully 27 percent of the marriages recorded at Michilimackinac were between Canadians and Indians, and 21 percent were between Canadians and mixed-blood individuals (noted as Métis on Tables 4-1 to 4-4). During this period, 39 percent of the baptisms were of mixed-blood children.[35] Between 1765 and 1838, the number of marriages between Whites and Indians diminished to only 14 percent in favour of marriages between Whites and mixed-blood individuals which accounted for 51 percent of the total.[36] Between 1765 and 1797, 71 percent of the children baptized at Michilimackinac were of mixed Indian-White ancestry.[37]

At St. Joseph, White families from the garrison comprised a significant proportion of the households, and marriages between Whites accounted for 39 percent of the marriages, while marriages between Canadians and Indians only accounted for 6 percent. Baptisms of mixed-blood children totalled 40 percent.[38]

The figures drawn from the two registers indicate an almost total absence of endogamy. At Michilimackinac, marriages between mixed-blood individuals accounted for less than 5 percent of those recorded between 1698 and 1838, and

Table 4-1 Marriages by Ethnicity, Michilimackinac, Baptismal and Marriage Registers 1698–1838

Ethnicity	Number	Percent
Between Canadians	20	32
Between Canadians and Indians	17	27
Between Canadians and Mixed-bloods	13	21
Between Mixed-bloods	1	2
Between Mixed-bloods and Indians	3	5
Between Indians	1	2
Uncertain ethnic origin	7	11
	62	100

Source: Peterson, "People in Between," 122.
1765-1838

Ethnicity	Number	Percent
Between Euro-Americans[a]	8	19
Between Euro-Americans and Indians	6	14
Between Euro-Americans and Mixed-bloods	22	51
Between Mixed-bloods	2	5
Between Mixed-bloods and Indians	2	5
Between Indians	0	0
Between blacks	1	2
Uncertain ethnic origin	2	5
	43	101

Source: Peterson, "Prelude to Red River," 50.
a. Canadians and/or Americans.

Table 4-2 Births by Ethnicity, Michilimackinac, Baptismal and Marriage Registers 1698–1797

1698–1765

Ethnicity	Number	Percent
Mixed-bloods	136	39
Euro-Americans	78	22
Indian	115	33
Black	4	1
Uncertain Ethnicity	18	5
	351	100

1765–1797

Ethnicity	Number	Percent
Mixed-bloods	94	72
Euro-Americans	8	6
Indian	13	10
Black	2	2
Uncertain Ethnicity	14	11
	131	101

Source: Peterson, "Prelude to Red River," 51.

Table 4-3 Marriages by Ethnicity, St. Joseph Baptismal Register 1720–1773

Ethnicity	Number	Percent
Between Canadians	12	39
Between Canadians and Indians	2	6
Between Canadians and Mixed-bloods	12	39
Between Indians	3	10
Uncertain Ethnic Origin	2	6
	31	100

Source: Paré and Quaife, "St. Joseph Baptismal Register," 201–39.

Table 4-4 Baptisms by Ethnicity, St. Joseph Baptismal Register 1720–1773

Ethnicity	Number	Percent
Canadians	30	31
Mixed-bloods	39	40
Indian (children)	9	9
Indian (converts)	9	9
Uncertain Ethnic Origin	10	10
	97	99

Source: Paré and Quaife, "St. Joseph Baptismal Register," 201-39.

at St. Joseph, no such marriages appear on the record. Rather than shun intermarriage with other groups, these mixed-blood families apparently found mixed-ethnic marriages to be quite acceptable. Interestingly, the marriages involving mixed-blood individuals recorded in the Church registers are primarily those of mixed-blood women. The marital preferences of mixed-blood men, however, cannot be deduced from the Church registers.

Although patterns of mixed-blood mating and marital practices in unions outside the Church are more difficult to determine, information pieced together from scattered sources again appears to indicate that exogamous partnerships were most common. Mixed-blood men such as Charles de Langlade and his son, Charles de Langlade Jr., Charles Gaultier, Jean Baptiste Cadotte Jr., Michel Cadotte, the Grignon brothers of Green Bay (LaBaie), and others, generally took Indian women as their first wives. Some later marriages were to mixed-blood women, but often these women had close ties to an Indian band.[39] The marital choices of the offspring of *voyageurs* and Indian women may have been more limited. Edward Biddle observed in 1816 that the aging *voyageurs* profited by arranging short-term marriage contracts between their mixed-blood daughters and transitory *voyageurs* and traders.[40] In later years, the mixed-blood component of the Great Lakes Indian bands may have supplied the fur trade with Indian wives.

Comments made by mixed-blood individuals suggest that intermarriage was generally viewed in a positive light by the fur trade and the mixed-blood community. Augustin Grignon wrote that

> The traders and settlers, as a general thing lived on very friendly terms with the natives. No doubt these amicable relations were much promoted by the intermarriage of the early French and Indians.[41]

The union of a mixed-blood man with an Indian woman could renew and reinforce old family ties with established trading partners, or could initiate new ties with a more distant band. Similarly the marriage of a mixed-blood woman to an incoming trader strengthened the ties between new traders and older, more established trading families in the area, reducing the threat of potential competition.

This apparent preference for exogamous matches was largely a result of their specialization in the fur trade and occupations associated with the Indian department. Country marriages removed the institutional barriers to cross-cultural relations and led to a heightened level of contact with, and understanding of, both their parent groups. Intermarriage renewed social and economic ties with the Indian and White trading communities, and could bring individuals greater economic and social stability in a society built around the fur trade. Exogamous mating gave mixed-blood traders important trading contacts and provided them with cultural and social information to add to that which they had obtained already from their parents and families. It also increased their suitability for go-between roles.

Mixed-blood exogamy, however, had its limits. Very few marriages appear to have taken place between White women and mixed-blood men. The marriage of Charles de Langlade to Charlotte Bourassa was an exception. This is in part due to the smaller number of White women, compared to Native women, available for marriage, but it is also likely that their hands in marriage were generally reserved for White traders or soldiers. No more do the records indicate that mixed-blood women raised in the trading settlements commonly lived with Indian men.[42]

Family reconstructions suggest that there may have been a slight trend toward mixed-blood endogamy toward the middle of the nineteenth century. The younger generations of Grignons, Lawes, Vieaus, Laframboises, and Cadottes married other mixed-bloods more frequently than had their parents' and grandparents' generations.[43] It is possible that desirable mates from other groups may no longer have been as available to them in the post-fur-trade era.

Sexual contact and mating patterns between the races in Great Lakes society were subject to certain constraints: status, class, physical necessities, economic realities, and attitude. Among the mixed-bloods of the Great Lakes, inter-ethnic contact, especially in the form of community-approved male-female relationships, appears to have been the expression or the result of economic concerns. This suggests that class, although not overtly recognized as such, may have been a more significant factor motivating apparently common behaviour than was a sense of shared ethnic background. The marriages documented in the St. Joseph and Michilimackinac church registers indicate that it was far easier to cross ethnic barriers in marriage than it was to overcome class and occupational distinctions. Traders tended to marry the daughters of other traders or Indian women of influential families, while *voyageurs* married the daughters of other *voyageurs* or Indian women from less prestigious families. A *voyageur* rarely married a woman from the trading class or from the Indian "nobility." This suggests that occupational and class factors were more significant in the regulation of marital choices than were issues of ethnicity, and that inter-ethnic contact was channelled along class lines.[44] The mixed-blood trading population may very well have formed an occupational class, or even two, rather than an ethnic group.

For all the difficulties inherent with the information available to document the mating preferences of the mixed-blood "trading" population of the Great Lakes region, the degree of exogamy that appears to have been present among them is highly significant. Their apparent willingness to marry outside of their own "mixed" ancestral and cultural group stands in contrast to the mating preferences of Métis groups at Red River or elsewhere in the Canadian Northwest during the nineteenth century.[45] It suggests that close contact with the ethnic groups around them was a high priority, and that the preservation of an established ancestral or cultural group was of secondary importance.

The presence of such extensive exogamy among the mixed-blood population suggests some problems for the transmission of a common ethnic identity among them. The exposure of so many individuals to inter-ethnic contact and marriage may have hindered the group's ability to communicate a cohesive concept of a common ethnic identity from one to another or to transmit their common culture to succeeding generations. Continual intermarriage may have injected new cultural influences into family groups and weakened existing traditions. Some doubt might be raised about the degree of cultural difference that persisted between representatives of various cultural groups in the Great Lakes fur trading settlements by the nineteenth century. Lyle M. Stone and Donald Chaput argue that, by 1760, cultural differences between Indian nations of the Great Lakes region had been greatly reduced by inter-tribal alliances, close residential proximity in the centralized Indian settlements near missions and important trading centres, conversion to Christianity, trade, and intermarriage with Whites and Indians from other nations.[46] A similar blurring of cultural differences may have occurred between long-term residents of trading settlements, most of whom lived with Native wives, and were exposed to similar social, economic, and political experiences, and who, over time, adopted similar fur trade dress, crafts, and housing styles. Endogamy is usually regarded as an important feature of most ethnic groups. How could a mixed-blood group such as this evolve and pass on a common set of traditions which could firmly establish a shared culture and ethnic identity?

The Requirements for the Development of an Ethnic Identity

The case of mixed-bloods of the Great Lakes raises many interesting questions for the study of ethnicity. How is a sense of ethnicity transmitted within "mixed-ethnic" groups? More attention needs to be paid to the transmission of ethnic identity, social roles, and gender roles from generation to generation in families of mixed ethnic parentage or ancestry. In particular, the role of women in this process should be more carefully examined. Often, women may provide the most consistent element in a family unit, and thus may be the most available cultural role models. Since an individual's interpretation of his or her ethnic heritage is seldom an even mix of Indian and White influences, could ethnic orientation or identification be linked with acquired gender roles and social roles as learned through the socialization process?

The examination of ethnicity among an historical group of people, of necessity looks for fairly obvious examples of collective action and of shared attitudes. On the other hand, such an undertaking is really an attempt to analyse thoughts and feelings that are of a very personal nature for most individuals and may not be very well documented by the historical record. An individual's sense of his or her ethnicity should not be viewed as a static element of his or her character. For some people, ethnicity may have been of greater importance in determining their sense of self than in others. One's sense of ethnicity may also shift with time. At one stage of an individual's life, Indian heritage may be very important to the sense of ethnic identity, and at another stage it may not be quite so influential. The pendulum may also swing back and forth more than once.

It should be remembered that the Great Lakes mixed-bloods lived in the midst of a complex social and political environment. The Great Lakes region was the homeland of a number of Indian nations, some of which had originally been significantly culturally different from others. The region also contained territory that, at times, was coveted by three major colonial powers: France, England, Spain, and finally by the United States. The Great Lakes region had been the scene of numerous battles, conflicts, and political intrigues. It had also witnessed many dramatic events of the struggle between the White man and the Indian, such as Pontiac's Uprising in 1763, the Battle of Fallen Timbers in 1794, and the Black Hawk War in 1832. Mixed-blood individuals frequently found themselves in the middle of this hotbed of commercial, political, and military activity. The complexity of the environment should be kept in mind when comparing the Great Lakes mixed-bloods with the Red River Métis, or other mixed-blood groups. When White settlers arrived in the region after 1820, they came by the hundreds of thousands, a veritable flood when compared with the settlement process of the Canadian West. The Indians of the Great Lakes region faced deportation beyond the Mississippi, and armed conflict with the American government. To many of the people of mixed Indian-White ancestry in the Great Lakes region, resistance to the American westward surge may have appeared hopeless.

This essay has attempted to illuminate a few key points about the mixed-bloods who lived in the region to the south of the Great Lakes between 1760 and 1830. It has limited itself to a discussion of those people of mixed ancestry who were more actively involved in the fur trade and Indian department, and whose lives were closely connected with the activity and social milieu of the Great Lakes fur trade settlements, rather than those mixed-bloods who were fully adopted by Indian bands and are therefore assumed to have identified themselves primarily as Indians. The group under study included a significant number of independent traders, clerks, and interpreters who were descendants of the old French bourgeoisie that controlled the fur trade before 1760. This was a more "élite" group than the mixed-blood *voyageurs* of the Great Lakes region, or many of the Métis at Red River. In many respects, we have been tracing the career and marital choices of a very different socio-economic group than the Red River Métis. The Great Lakes mixed-blood population appear to have had virtually no sense of themselves as being part of a distinct ethnic group on the basis of their mixed Indian-White ancestry, nor were they set apart as such by the Indian and White groups in the region. After 1820, when a negative ethnic category for "half-breeds" did develop, no leadership emerged from among these people to fight their worsening social and economic situation, and to stimulate a sense of common ethnicity among them. Any potential leaders may have identified too closely with White interests because of extensive business and family connections. The seeds for the development of a sense of ethnic tradition may also have been scattered by the general preference of these people to marry outside their own "group," and to re-establish contact with the Indian bands and White traders with whom they did business. So prominent were the economic and social concerns in their daily lives, as evidenced by their mating and marriage patterns, that common economic issues were probably of greater relevance to their lives than were concerns couched in the terms of ethnicity. The Great Lakes mixed-bloods might be better described as an economic class, with subdivisions into traders and *voyageurs*, rather than as an ethnic group.

This essay has briefly examined the level of ethnic identification found among the mixed-bloods of the Great Lakes region between 1760 and 1830, a period in which the fur trade was a central force in their lives. The case of the Great Lakes mixed-bloods has been tentatively compared with that of the Red River Métis during the early- and mid-nineteenth century. Further work is necessary to make this a more thorough and illuminating comparison. An extension of this examination of ethnicity to other mixed-blood groups, both historical and current, might be made to more completely understand the circumstances that lead to the creation of such groups, how the transmission of ethnicity is achieved in multi-ethnic families, and perhaps most significantly, what conditions are necessary for such collections of people to form into a viable ethnic group that values shared characteristics and traditions, and expresses common concerns.

Acknowledgements

I would like to thank the Hudson's Bay Company for permission to use its records held on microfilm at the Public Archives of Canada in Ottawa. I would also like to thank the Archives de l'Archevêché de Québec for permission to use their records in Québec and for the helpfulness of their staff.

Notes

1. Reuben Gold Thwaites, ed., "Register of the Baptisms of the Mission of St.Ignace du Michilimackinac, 1695–1821," in *Collections of the State Historical Society of Wisconsin* (*WHC*), vol. 19 (Madison: State Historical Society of Wisconsin, 1910), 48, 81; Jonathan Carver, *Travels Through the Interior Parts of North America in the Years 1766, 1767, and 1768* (Minneapolis: Ross & Hines, 1956), 50; Peter Pond, "The Narrative of Peter Pond," in *Five Fur Traders of the Northwest*, edited by Charles M. Gates and Grace Lee Nute (1933 reprint, St. Paul: Minnesota Historical Society, 1965), 46; John McDonnell, "Some Account of the Red River (about 1797)", "Arrangements of the Proprietors, Clerks, Interpreters, etc. of the North-West Company in the Indian Departments, 1799 (the Old Company)", and "Liste des 'Bourgeois', Commis, Engagés, et 'Voyageurs', de la Compagnie du Nord-Ouest, après la Fusion de 1804," in *Les Bourgeois de la Compagnie du Nord-Ouest*, edited by L.R. Masson, vol. 1 (New York: Antiquarian Press, 1960), 269–270; 62, 64; 409.
2. Donald Chaput, "The 'Misses Nolin' of Red River," *The Beaver*, 306 (1975): 15–17; Public Archives Canada, Ottawa, Hudson's Bay Company Archives, PAC/MG 20/E/5/8-11 Statistical Statement of Red River, 31st May 1827; Public Archives Canada, Ottawa, PAC/MG 9/E/3/2, Manitoba Census vol. 1, Red River 1831–1847: Lower Settlement and Grantown, 1831, 1834, 1838, 1840.

3. Charles F. Keyes, "Towards a New Formation of the Concept of Ethnic Groups," *Ethnicity* 3 (1976):208; Jeffrey Ross, "The Mobilization of Collective Identity: An Analytical Overview," *The Mobilization of Collective Identity: Comparative Perspectives*, edited by Jeffrey Ross and Anne Baker (Lanham, MD: University Press of America, 1980), 6–17.
4. Fredrik Barth, "Introduction," in *Ethnic Groups and Boundaries*, edited by Fredrik Barth (Boston: Little, Brown, & Co., 1969), 10–15; Fredrik Barth, *Models of Social Organization*, Occasional Paper no. 23 (Royal Anthropological Institute of Great Britain and Ireland, 1966), 17–18; Michael Hechter, "Ethnicity and Industrialization: On the Proliferation of the Cultural Division of Labor," *Ethnicity* 3 (1976):214–24; Michael Hechter, "Group Formation and the Cultural Division of Labor," *American Journal of Sociology* 84 (1978):293–318.
5. Jacqueline Peterson, "The People in Between: Indian-White Marriage and the Genesis of a Métis Society and Culture in the Great Lakes Region, 1680–1830" (Ph.D. diss., University of Illinois at Chicago Circle, 1981), 154–85.
6. Reginald Horsman, *Race and Manifest Destiny* (Cambridge, Mass.: Harvard University Press, 1981), 98–157.
7. The journals and papers of travellers, fur traders, military and administrative personnel were surveyed for ethnic references which alluded to the Indian heritage of mixed-blood individuals. The *Michigan Pioneer and Historical Collections* (40 volumes) and the *Wisconsin Historical Collections* (20 volumes) are particularly rich sources of these records, including many transcripts of documents from the French and British colonial periods collected from the Public Archives of Canada and elsewhere.
8. General Haldimand to Major DePeyster, Montreal, 30 August 1778, General Haldimand to Major DePeyster, Quebec, July 3, 1779, Major DePeyster to General Haldimand, Michilimackinac, 24 October, 1778, Major DePeyster to General Haldimand, Michilimackinac, 27 October, 1778, "Haldimand Papers, 1776–1784," Michigan Pioneer and Historical Collections (MPHC), vol. 9 (Lansing: Thorp & Godfrey, State Printers, 1886), 353–54, 361–63, 374–76, 376–77; "Haldimand Papers, 1762–1799," MPHC 10 (1888), 210–672.
9. Major DePeyster to General Haldimand, Michilimackinac, 1 June 1779, Lieutenant Governor Hamilton to General Haldimand, Detroit, n.d. (September, 1778), "Account of the Expedition of Lieutenant Governor Hamilton—1778," "Haldimand Papers, 1776–1784," MPHC 9, 382-83, 464–70, 489–516.
10. Lieutenant Governor Patrick Sinclair to Captain Brehm, Michilimackinac, 7 October 1779, Captain Brehm to Lieutenant Governor Sinclair, Quebec, April 17, 1780, Lieutenant Governor Sinclair to General Haldimand, Michilimackinac, n.d. (February, 1780), General Haldimand to Lieutenant Governor Sinclair, Quebec, 10 August, 1780, Lieutenant Governor Sinclair To Captain Brehm, Michilimackinac, 8 July 1780, "Haldimand Papers, 1776–1784," MPHC 9, 525, 530–3, 533–38, 545–46, 569, 569–70, 578–79.
11. The papers of the Catholic priests who were active in the Great Lakes region between 1760 and 1830 have been scattered between the archives of the Archdiocese of Quebec, Baltimore, and the parish of Detroit. Various letters and diaries have been published in George Paré, *The Catholic Church in Detroit, 1701–1888* (Detroit: Gabriel Richard Press, 1951); Thomas O'Brien Hanley, ed. *The John Caroll Papers,* 3 vols. (Notre Dame: University of Notre Dame Press, 1976); *Annales de l'Association de la Propagation de la Foi* (Paris: La Librarie Ecclesiastique du Rusand 1826-30); and the *Collections of the Illinois State Historical Library.*
12. George Paré, *The Catholic Church in Detroit, 1701–1888* (Detroit: The Gabriel Richard Press, 1951), 269.
13. Paré, *Catholic Church*, 337–38; Joseph Crevier à Mgnr. Panet, Sandwich, 19 Février

1831, Correspondence, Archives de l'Archevêche de Québec, Québec, AAQ 320 CN Haut Canada 1/90.

14. Paré, *Catholic Church*, 592–93.
15. More material of this kind is available for the nineteenth century. Between 1855 and 1915, the editors of the Wisconsin Historical Collections and the Michigan Pioneer Historical Collections interviewed some of the early residents of Wisconsin and Michigan, providing an interesting portrait of Great Lakes Society as it underwent the transition from a fur trade base to an agricultural/lumbering/mining economy, and entered into the early stages of the industrial era. It should be noted that many of the articles dealing with the early years of the century are in the form of recollections transcribed between 1850 and 1870 and so tend to be coloured by the passage of time and changing attitudes.
16. James A. Clifton, "Personal and Ethnic Identity on the Great Lakes Frontier: The Case of Billy Caldwell, Anglo-Canadian," *Ethnohistory* 25 (1978):73–80.
17. Augustin Grignon, "Seventy-Two Years' Recollections of Wisconsin," *WHC*, vol. 3, edited by Lyman C. Draper (Madison: State Historical Society of Wisconsin, 1857), 197–99, 212–14, 217; Reuben G. Thwaites, ed. "The French Regime in Wisconsin, 1743–1760," *WHC*, vol. 18 (Madison: State Historical Society of Wisconsin, 1908), 130–31, editor's note; Extract from the journal of Montcalm, May 11, 1759, Extract from Pouchot *Mémoir* (1759), Thwaites, "The French Regime in Wisconsin, 1743–1760," *WHC*, vol. 18, 209–10, 210–13; Joseph Tassé, "Memoir of Charles de Langlade," *WHC*, vol. 7, edited by Lyman C. Draper, (Madison: State Historical Society of Wisconsin, 1873–76, 152; Major De Peyster to General Haldimand, Michilimackinac, 27 October 1778, Major De Peyster to General Haldimand, Michilimackinac, 29 January 1779, Major De Peyster to General Haldimand, Michilimackinac, 14 June 1779, "Haldimand Papers, 1776–1784," MPHC 9, 376, 377–78, 383–86.
18. Grignon, "Seventy-Two Years," 212; Major De Peyster to General Haldimand, 14 June 1779, "Haldimand Papers, 1776–1784," MPHC 9, 383–86.
19. Grignon, "Seventy-Two Years," 223.
20. Charles Gaultier, "Gaultier's Journal of a Visit to the Mississippi, 1777-1778," *WHC*, vol. 11, edited by R.G. Thwaites (Madison: State Historical Society of Wisconsin, 1888), 105.
21. Governor Duquesne to the French Minister of the Marine, October 25, 1752, Thwaites, "French Regime," 128–31; Captain George Etherington to Monsieur Langlade, fils, 10 June 1763, Reuben G. Thwaites, ed., "British Regime in Wisconsin, 1760–1800," *WHC*, vol. 18 (Madison: State Historical Society of Wisconsin, 1908), 253.
22. Marriage contract between Charles de Langlade and Charlotte Bourassa, August 11, 1754, Thwaites, "French Regime," 135–40.
23. Horsman, *Race and Manifest Destiny*, 98–157; Clifton, "Personal and Ethnic Identity," 82; Jennifer Brown, "Linguistic Solitudes and Changing Social Categories," *Old Trails and New Directions: Papers of the Third North American Fur Trade Conference*, edited by Carol M. Judd and Arthur J. Ray (Toronto: University of Toronto Press, 1980), 147–59.
24. T.L. McKenney to Honourable Henry Southard, 6 January 1818, Lewis Cass to John Bowyer, Indian Agent at Green Bay, Detroit, January 22, 1818, Ramsay Crooks, Robert Stuart to John Jacob Astor, New York, January 24, 1818, Jacob Franks to John Lawe, Montreal, 11 March 1818, Lewis Cass to Agents at Mackinac, Green Bay and Chicago, Detroit, April 23, 1818, Robert Stuart to Governor Cass, Mackinac, 21 November 1819, John Lawe to Mrs. Hamilton, Michilimackinac, 12 September 1824, Robert Stuart to John Lawe, Mackinac, January 21, 1825, Robert Stuart to Messrs. Lawe and Dousman, Mackinac, August 13, 1825, R.G. Thwaites,

ed., "The Fur Trade in Wisconsin, 1812–1825," *WHC*, vol. 20 (Madison: State Historical Society of Wisconsin, 1911), 12–16, 16, 17–31, 34–36, 43, 55–56, 136–37, 351–52, 368–71, 378–79.

25. Peterson, "People in Between," 255.
26. Henry Rowe Schoolcraft, *Personal Memoir of a Residence of Thirty Years with the Indian Tribes on the American Frontier with Brief Notices of Passing Events, Facts, and Opinions, A.D. 1812 to A.D. 1842* (Philadelphia: Lippincott, Grambo & Co., 1851), 478; James Duane Doty, "Official Journey, 1820, Expedition with Cass and Schoolcraft," *WHC*, vol.13, edited by R.G. Thwaites (Madison: State Historical Society of Wisconsin, 1895), 179; Paré, *Catholic Church*, 342; John Shaw, "Personal Narrative," *WHC*, vol. 2, edited by Lyman C. Draper (Madison: State Historical Society of Wisconsin, 1856), 226; James W. Biddle, "Recollections of Green Bay in 1816-1817," *WHC*, vol. 1, edited by Lyman C. Draper (Madison: State Historical Society of Wisconsin, 1855), 58; Alfred Brunson, "A Methodist Circuit Rider's Horseback Tour from Pennsylvania to Wisconsin, 1835," *WHC*, vol. 15, edited by R.G. Thwaites (Madison: State Historical Society of Wisconsin, 1900), 284; William H. Keating, *Narrative of an Expedition to the Source of St. Peter's River, Lake Winnepeek, Lake of the Woods, etc. Performed in the Year 1823* (Reprint, Minneapolis: Ross & Haines, 1959), 75.
27. John H. Fonda, "Early Reminiscences of Wisconsin," *WHC*, vol. 5, edited by Lyman C. Draper (Madison: State Historical Society of Wisconsin, 1868), 225; James Duane Doty, "Northern Wisconsin in 1820," *WHC*, vol. 7, edited by Lyman C. Draper (Madison: State Historical Society of Wisconsin, 1876), 197.
28. Fonda, "Early Reminiscences," 225.
29. William Johnston to Jane Schoolcraft, August 29, 1833, William Johnston, "Letters on the Fur Trade—1833," *Michigan Pioneer and Historical Collections* vol. 37 (Lansing: Wynkoop, Hallenbeck, Crawford Co., 1909–1910), 163–65; Mrs. H.S. Baird, "Indian Customs and Early Recollections," *WHC*, vol. 9, edited by Lyman C. Draper (Madison: State Historical Society of Wisconsin, 1882), 303; Elizabeth Baird, "Reminiscences of Early Days on Mackinac Island," *WHC*, vol. 14, edited by R.G. Thwaites (Madison: State Historical Society of Wisconsin, 1898), 17.
30. William Johnston to Jane Schoolcraft, August 4, 1833, August 29, 1833, September 20, 1833, Johnston, "Letters," 145–48, 163–65, 177–80; Mrs. H.S. Baird, "Indian Customs," 323; Elizabeth Baird, "Reminiscences of Early Days," 17, 19, 34, 40; Elizabeth Baird, "Reminiscences of Life in Territorial Wisconsin," *WHC*, vol. 15, edited by R.G. Thwaites (Madison: State Historical Society of Wisconsin, 1900), 207, 212, 217, 222, 236; Grignon, "Seventy-Two Years," 212, 218, 219, 226.
31. Grignon, "Seventy-Two Years," 212, 235.
32. Felix M. Keesing, *The Menomini Indians of Wisconsin* (Philadelphia: The American Philosophical Society, 1939), 146.
33. Jacqueline Peterson, "Prelude to Red River: A Social Portrait of the Great Lakes Métis," *Ethnohistory* 25 (1978):50; Peterson, "People in Between," 122.
34. Thwaites, ed. "The Mackinac Register: Register of Marriages, 1725–1821," *WHC,* vol. 18 (Madison: State Historical Society of Wisconsin, 1908), 469-513; George Paré and Milo M. Quaife, eds. "The St. Joseph Baptismal Register," *The Mississippi Valley Historical Review* 13 (June 1926):201–39.
35. Peterson, "People in Between," 122, 123.
36. Peterson, "Prelude to Red River," 50.
37. Peterson, "People in Between," 123.
38. Paré and Quaife, "St. Joseph Baptismal Register," 201–39.
39. Grignon, "Seventy-Two Years," 198–99, 237; Peterson, "People in Between," 161–62; A.C. Osborne, ed. "The Migration of Voyageurs from Drummond Island to Penetanguishene in 1828 and List of the Drummond Island Voyageurs," *Ontario*

Historical Society Papers and Records 3 (1901):147–48; B.W. Brisbois, "Traditions and Recollections of Prairie duChien," *WHC*, vol. 9, edited by Lyman C. Draper (Madison: State Historical Society of Wisconsin, 1882), 283; Thwaites, "Mackinac Register," 490–92, 499; William W. Warren, *History of the Ojibway Nation.* (1885; reprint Minneapolis: Ross & Haines, 1957), 9–14; Graham A. MacDonald, "Commerce, Civility and Old Sault Ste. Marie," *The Beaver* 312 (1981):22.

40. Peterson, "People in Between," 211, 215; James W. Biddle, "Recollections," 58–59.
41. Grignon, "Seventy-Two Years," 261.
42. Paré and Quaife, "St. Joseph Baptismal Register," 201-39; Thwaites, "Mackinac Register," 469–513.
43. Peterson, "People in Between," 161–62, 163, 165–66; Warren, *Ojibway Nation*, 9–14.
44. Paré and Quaife, "St. Joseph Baptismal Register," 201–39; Thwaites, "Mackinac Register," 469–513.
45. D.N. Sprague and R.P. Frye, comps. "Table 1: Geneologies of Red River Households, 1818–1870," *The Geneology of the First Métis Nation* (Winnipeg: Pemmican Publications, 1983); Trudy Nicks, Native Responses to the Early Fur Trade at Lesser Slave Lake (Paper presented at the 5th North American Fur Trade Conference, Montreal, Quebec, May 30, 1985).
46. Lyle M. Stone and Donald Chaput, "History of the Upper Great Lakes Area," *Handbook of North American Indians*, vol. 15, Smithsonian Institution, edited by Bruce Trigger (Washington, D.C., 1978) 603, 605, 606.

PART II
The Boreal Forest

This region was once known to ethnologists as the Eastern Woodlands. It thus represented one of the many "culture areas" into which an earlier generation of scholars sorted indigenous societies. No doubt these taxonomies then served their purpose, but here I wish to argue for a different view of the relations between this region and the peoples in it. Let us begin by asking what common factors may have shaped the native cultures of the Boreal forest. I believe that most would accept that one of the most significant factors influencing the Boreal forest peoples stemmed, in recent centuries, from outside the region. Here I refer to the Canadian fur trade, which began in this region. Few would now deny its influence. Yet this influence was not simply a matter of native loss and European replacement. On the contrary, the meeting of European and indigenous cultures during the fur trade produced something new and different from either of the parent cultures. Eleanor Leacock writes in this connection of a "viable synthesis of old and new" (also see John Foster in Chapter 8).

How new? Much ink has been spilled over that question. In fact, a controversy raged for years over the historical standing of the Boreal forest cultures known to classic ethnology. Scholars argued in particular about the status of systems of land tenure known to early ethnographers, who found the Boreal forest Algonkian lands divided into "family hunting territories", wherein hunting rights resided in a male "owner". Would similar relations of production have been found among the Algonkians before Europeans arrived among them? Eleanor Leacock, in her chapter on "The Innu Bands of Labrador" argues that they would not. Doubtless she is correct.

Nevertheless, granting that the present relations of production of the Boreal forest reflect a "viable synthesis of old and new", the question "How old?" is not very interesting. More important questions arise when we consider how these relations of production came to the fore. Leacock is doubtless correct in maintaining that they arose with the fur trade. Nevertheless, this was not simply a matter of the old giving place to the new; the new relations of production served a conservative function as well. In particular, they permitted a foraging mode of production to coexist with the institutions of mercantile capitalism. Some scholars maintain that such coexistence is impossible. Eleanor Leacock, for example, argues that food-sharing, egalitarianism, and communal living end with production for exchange:

> With production for trade, however, the individual's most important ties, economically speaking, were transferred from *within* the band to without, and his objective relation to other band members changed from co-operative to the

> competitive. With storable, transportable, and individually acquired supplies—principally flour and land—as staple foods, the individual family becomes self-sufficient, and larger group living is not only superfluous in the struggle for existence but a positive hindrance to the personal acquisition of furs [original emphasis].[1]

In the passage that follows, Leacock goes on to argue that production for exchange likely led to "a sense of proprietorship" over hunting territories. In this she is doubtless correct. Nevertheless, the implication is left that production for exchange is antithetical to food-sharing, egalitarianism and communal living—in short to the foraging mode of production. Here I must differ.

Let me add as well that Dr. Leacock also presents some evidence that native relations of production need not be completely transformed by the exigencies of fur production. For example, she makes some reference to the custom of "hunting partnerships" (in this volume). These are partnerships among several men who combine forces to exploit particular winter hunting grounds. With their families, they comprise a group not unlike the "multi- family lodge groups" of some 10–20 individuals which Leacock notes were a consistent feature of Boreal forest native social life in the past. Leacock says of these groups that several families depended on each other, thus ensuring "greater security than individual families could achieve."[2] However, what was good in the past often remains so in the present, as Dr. Leacock's own evidence seems to show. Nor did all food-sharing end when Indians began producing furs for exchange. Here is Leacock on food-sharing, past and present, in her contribution to this section:

> The stringency of life in the north woods enforces so immediate an interdependence that sharing is a more total, spontaneous, or unstructured affair than the reglated reciprocity generally obtained in more settled societies. Starvation is a constantly occurring threat, though usually a fairly localized one, and people do not hesitate to turn to others for help. The Jesuits marvelled at the unstinting, unhesitating way Indians who were themselves in trouble shared with others who were in greater straits. In the hinterland *it is still unquestioned that help will always be forthcoming*, even from a bitter personal enemy [author's italics].

Even more telling is this selection:

> I had occasion to question one of my informants, Thomas Gregoire, about a latter day incident where he had given the last of his flour and lard to two men from a neighbouring band. This meant returning to the post sooner than he had planned, thereby reducing his possible catch of furs. I probed to see whether there was some slight annoyance or reluctance involved. . . . He said with deep, if suppressed anger, "Suppose now, not give them flour, lard—just dead inside."

This anecdote shows in sharp relief the contradiction in which native hunters are caught. In some circumstances, they may wish to produce more furs, but cannot go back on their obligation to share food with needy neighbours. Here ideology plays its part, as Tanner and Feit show. What we might call a "hunter's ethic" dictates the sharing of food with those in need. This, in turn, sustains the social relations in terms of which production takes place. (Recall that I urged earlier the role of ideology in reproducing the social relations of production.)

Thus, the foraging mode of production persists among Boreal forest natives, even though they produce furs for the market. Production for exchange does not always put an end to egalitarianism and food-sharing. In *Bringing Home Animals: Religious Ideology and Mode of Production* Adrian Tanner explains how the natives of the Boreal forests balance off the reproduction of the forager's style of relations of production against production for the market. Briefly put, Boreal forest Indians make use of a "single set of social relations" within the "multi-family hunting group" to organize the production of both subsistence and market products. Although they are subordinate to the capitalist merchants within the context of market relations, the production of fur is itself subordinate to the requirements of subsistence. As long as the system can allow the Indians to produce enough fur to satisfy their needs for imported supplies, and to continue to "produce subsistence sufficient for the social formation to reproduce itself, it is able to handle the contradiction inherent in these two aims."[3] Thus, the contradictions are real, but they can be overcome; for the bush Cree at least, the foraging mode of production persists, as it has for generations.

In fact, natives of the Boreal forest have developed the ability to manage such contradictions over generations in which they have mixed production for use with production for exchange. This is no mean feat, but they have had a long time to practice. How long is shown by John Foster's chapter, "The Home Guard Cree and the Hudson's Bay Company: The First Hundred Years." These were bands of Cree of the Hudson's Bay lowlands who supplied the posts with game and handicrafts, acting at times as couriers and guides. As much as modern Boreal forest Indians, they combined subsistence and production with production for exchange (although John Foster does not put it that way). Here we are dealing with a synthesis of cultural elements. Perhaps Foster goes too far in the passage that follows, but his point is taken:

> In time it would be possible to blend elements of Cree and British ways. Expressed in another manner, it would, in time, become difficult to identify specific behaviour as Cree or British.

And, like Tanner's Cree hunters, the Homeguard likely made use of a "single set of social relations" to organize the production of subsistence and market products. They met with some success, Foster adds, since their population seemed to be on the increase during the eighteenth century. Evidently they used the resources from the Hudson's Bay posts to increase their numbers and reproduce their egalitarian social formation. This should be seen as the result of conscious adaptation by the Homeguard, as Foster implies, and as I have argued elsewhere.[4]

Notes

1. Eleanor Leacock, *The Montagnais "Hunting Territory" and the Fur Trade*, Memoir No. 78 of the American Anthropological Association (1954): 7.

2. *Ibid.*
3. Adrian Tanner, *Bringing Home Animals: Religious Ideology and Mode of Production of the Mistassini Cree Hunters* (St. John's: The Institute of Social and Economic Research, 1979), 4–5 *et passim.*
4. Bruce Cox, "Comments on Optimal Foraging Theory in Anthropology," *Current Anthropology* 24 (1983):644.

Chapter 5
The Significance of Hunting Territories Today[1]

Adrian Tanner

This article, in one sense, constitutes an ethnographic report on a specific institution, the hunting territory, as observed in 1971 among the members of a Mistassini band of the northwestern boreal forest region of Quebec. Yet it is of necessity more than just a description, as the context of the lengthy debate in the literature about the origins of northern Algonquian hunting territories cannot simply be ignored. Although not concerned with this historical question, I am in this paper interested in some other matters which have been raised within the debate. I am, moreover, concerned with another, relatively short-term, historical question, that of the way modern hunting territories operate over time, particularly from one generation to the next. I thus make some reference to literature on the Mistassini from earlier in this century to obtain a time perspective on the operation over a few generations. However, this is not another survey of the hunting territory question; specific references will be few, and, with the exception of Knight's work, I will not attempt to summarize or review the arguments of others.

The Mistassini were first studied by Speck, albeit at a distance, through interviews made during a number of summer visits, between about 1915 and about 1930, to the village of Pointe Bleue, 150 miles south of Mistassini territory. A group of Algonquians, distinct from the Pointe Bleue group and identified as Mistassini (presumably on the basis of self-identification and winter residence), were at the time using the Pointe Bleue trading post each summer, possibly due to kinship ties with the Lac St. Jean band, or to better prices there, in preference to Mistassini Post which was much closer to their hunting grounds. Speck obtained from these informants a map of all the Mistassini hunting territories, as well as some data on the inheritance pattern as it was in the 1920s.[2]

While conducting 15 months of field research among the Mistassini Cree on various subjects I obtained, from interviews with almost all the current territory owners, a map of the hunting territories as they are now recognized. My data covered a larger area than Speck's because they included the Nichicun group, who had by then become part of the Mistassini band, at least for administrative purposes. Since 1976 these hunting territories have become incorporated into the administrative structures established under the James Bay and Northern Quebec Agreement, and continue to function.

When my own and Speck's data were analyzed within the context of current Mistassini genealogical material, some continuities in the territories could be seen from Speck's time on to the present, but the territories also showed considerable and problematic changes. These changes were reviewed in a previous article, which included an overlapping map of the territories as recorded by Speck and by myself.[3] Current owners were also questioned about the principles underlying land use, hunting territory ownership and inheritance, and, although there were some contradictions within many informants' accounts of the present system, they gave a similar account of these principles to that published by Speck. Informants also spoke of changes in the land tenure system resulting from the government's introduction of registered traplines and beaver quotas.

Since in this paper I am concerned with how the present day system of hunting territories operates, and not with the institution as it existed fifty or more years ago, discrepancies in the data stemming from changes in the institution since Speck's time might well be set aside. However, similar sorts of discrepancies were noted by Knight,[4] in reference to the data he collected among the adjacent Rupert House band, for which he proposed a solution. I have also encountered the problem of discrepancies between informants' general statements and data on actual territorial usage in recent years. The understanding of hunting territories presents us with problems, quite apart from that of their origins. In this paper, as part of my attempt to adequately describe the institution, I will critically evaluate Knight's solution for the discrepancies in the data.

Criticizing Knight's hypothesized solution on the basis of Mistassini material might be seen as taking something of a liberty with his paper, since it was based on data from a different group, but I feel the procedure can be justified. In the first place, many of the discrepancies Knight notes between his observations and Speck's generalized description of hunting territories are very much the same kind of discrepancies as I found within my own data, and between my own data and Speck's account of the Mistassini territories. Secondly, in his article, Knight extends conclusions from Rupert House to the northeastern Algonquians generally.

By rejecting at least part of Knight's analysis, I am not thereby either challenging or agreeing with his position on the question of the origin of hunting territories. I propose to look at the hunting territory system as including a set of ideas and symbolic associations, as well as an ecological adaptation. My aim is to present a more adequate account of the institution than previous ones, but one which takes account of, rather than rejects out of hand (as it seems to me Knight has done), Speck's initial, and, no doubt, flawed description of it.

* * * * *

Speck's claim that the northeastern Algonquian hunters had a system of land ownership which had (and apparently still has) for anthropology a double significance. For one thing, he saw it as a challenge to the classical evolutionary theory which assigns a key role, and a historically relatively late date, to the emergence of a fully-developed institution of private property, an idea associated with Morgan, Marx, and Engels. This challenge has been countered by many, and the ensuing debate has, over the years, been lively, and has produced a search for new supporting facts, without, however, any conclusive evidence being brought forward by either side.

This intense interest in the origins of hunting territories has, it seems to me, led to a neglect of the other aspect of significance for anthropology to which Speck's "discovery" made reference, what he called the "family hunting band". I am calling this unit the "hunting group", while the term "band" is reserved, in the case of nomadic hunters, for the larger temporary seasonal gatherings. Speck referred to the former group as "the basis of Algonquian social organization," but in a number of attempts he never managed to define it purely in sociological terms, only that it was a group "united by blood or marriage, having the right to hunt, trap or fish in a certain inherited district bounded by some rivers, lakes or other natural landmarks."[5]

Although for some bands Speck gave a precise description of how hunting territories were defined geographically, his description of the social structure of the hunting groups is much more general. It is merely described as an ideal extended family, that is, a couple and their married sons. However, the examination of the composition of actual hunting groups shows this description to be less than adequate. Rogers[6] has assembled evidence to show that, in fact, almost any link by marriage or clanship was used in the formation of hunting groups, while Leacock (in this volume) shows that some groups had no kin links between member nuclear families. Subsequent attempts have not as yet provided us with a satisfactory social structural account of the hunting group, which is the basic residential unit among many nomadic Algonquian hunters, beyond its tendency to be composed of primary kin links and shared residence.

In this regard, the hunting territory might well be seen as the crucial organizational focal point in the social structure, at least for many northern Algonquian peoples.[7] This connection between the hunting territory and the hunting group was echoed, for example, by the title of Rogers' monograph *The Hunting Group—Hunting Territory Complex among the Mistassini Indians*.[8] Perhaps Speck was right to define the hunting group in terms of its rights to a particular hunting territory. And if the hunting group effectively has to be defined as the group that shares the use of a hunting territory, the precise workings of the system of territories needs to be considered in the sociological analysis of hunting groups.

* * * * *

In his critique of Speck,[9] Rolf Knight begins by addressing himself to the discrepancies between his recent data and Speck's earlier account. He ends by questioning whether, even during the fur trade period fixed territories could have existed over the long run. He produced contemporary evidence from the Rupert House Cree to indicate that there is a far greater degree of territorial mobility of hunters from year to year than can be accounted for by using a strictly kin-defined hunting group confined exclusively to one fixed inherited territory.

In my 1972 paper on Mistassini hunting territories, I noted various discrepancies in data as well as the movement of hunters between territories. Discrepancies between my data and Speck's description included cases of: (a) territories which seemed to have "moved" over the 50 year period; (b) inheritance by persons other than the owners' sons; (c) sons obtaining ownership of a territory a long distance from that of their fathers; and (d) owners hunting for one or more winters in areas far distant from their own territories. Internal discrepancies were mainly between different statements about how the hunting territory system worked, and between such statements and actual practice. For example, a hunter would state that, before the introduction of government beaver quota restrictions, anyone could, and did, hunt and trap anywhere he wanted; yet, in many cases, the same person would also carefully trace back over two or three generations his own kin-inherited rights to "his" territory, whose location he described in some detail. Moreover, there was ample evidence, from data obtained from the Hudson's Bay Company manager who visited each camp twice each winter, that many owners actually did hunt the same territories year after year. For other territory owners, however, the data on their actual land use indicated a considerable year to year mobility between territories. It is important, to note that there were no discrepancies between various informants as to who was a territory "owner", and where each such individual's territory was located.

In another article I gave several reasons why hunters move locations from one year to another.[10] Some hunting groups do return year after year to their territories as a matter of course, but in other cases, the hunting territory owners, acting as group leaders, follow a more varied pattern of land use. Toward the end of each summer, these individuals play a particularly important role in assembling a group that may be quite different from the previous year, and in planning where that group will spend the following winter season. Many of these hunting territory owners do not use their own territories year after year. As often as every three or four years, some may hunt on other territories, either leading groups onto another's territories with the owner's permission, or by joining groups led by other men. By following such a pattern, they, in effect, practise the indirect exchange of hunting privileges. Some territories are abandoned entirely, particularly if the population of game animals drops drastically or if the owner dies without heirs.

Comparisons between Speck's map and recent data showed cases where territories appeared to "move" over a period of time. This happened when a group moves its activities over the years onto unused adjacent land. In other cases a group of close relatives, who hold a number of adjacent territories, may effectively pool all their land and use it as a single block for a number of years. Subsequently the land becomes divided as individual owners have their own individual territories again; however, division may not take place according to the earlier boundaries. The result is that if maps of the territories of a single family are compared over time, a major shift may appear to have taken place.

At the same time, the folk model of the hunting territory remains essentially as it was in Speck's time: a specific area of land to which one has kin-based inherited rights.[11] It is a concept that is distinguished from the recently introduced "registered trapline" and fixed quota area system of the provincial government, even though the government scheme was, to some extent, based on the prior existence of hunting territories. For the Cree, there is no contradiction between their system of territory ownership and the long-run need for adjustment.

In his argument for the unworkability of hunting territories over the long run during the fur trade period Knight uses a distorted account of the hunting groups. This is perhaps intentional on his part as a rhetorical device to attack Speck's entire account of the hunting group and the hunting territory. However, as I pointed out earlier, other modern ethnographers, including Rogers and Leacock, have previously shown that hunting groups are far more flexible in composition than in Speck's account. Knight points out that if biological extended families were restricted to a single territory, after a number of generations, the result would be a large variation in the man/land ratio between different territories.[12] The reason given is that the demographic variability between families resulting from differential fertility and mortality would, over several generations, result in the enlargement of some groups and the reduction of others.

The flexibility in hunting group composition which I observed among the Mistassini has been reported by others in the region. According to Leacock (in this volume), in the Labrador area there are no suggestions that the wife is expected to move into the household of her husband, and until quite recently, it was not predominant. (This conclusion refers to the observed pattern, and not to a formal rule.) On the other hand, according to Rogers, the husband is required to live for a time in the area of the wife's home. Over its life, an average household, composed of a nuclear family (with the possible addition of a widowed person and unmarried adopted people) may belong to several different hunting groups.[13] According to Honnigmann, in northern Quebec "the hunting groups in a given territory were fluid, people at will breaking off from one to join another."[14] Rogers on the other hand, calls the Mistassini hunting group "a relatively stable unit,"[15] and one gets the same impression from reading Speck.

My own impression of the current stability of hunting groups among the Mistassini is that there is a great deal of variation. For instance, in the Nichicun sub-group of the Mistassini band most households are long-term members of one or another winter hunting group. While these groups continue to exist in people's minds, they do not always come together as actual hunting groups each winter. I recorded the activities of all of the Nichicun families over a ten-year period, and showed that territory owners, for example, spent from one-quarter to two-thirds of their winters as guests of other hunting groups. During these years, the other families on their own hunting group usually separated and became guests in other hunting groups.

Nichicun does not, however, appear to be entirely typical of the whole Mistassini band in respect to this pattern of frequent mobility from year to year. The region tends to be a frontier zone for the Mistassini band as a whole, with Mistassini Post over three hundred air miles to the south. Most Nichicun families, who spend the summer at Mistassini, now use aircraft to return to their winter hunting areas. Because of its relative isolation, and the resulting high transportation cost of hunting there, a shortage of hunters spread themselves too thin. A winter hunting group must contain at least two households, and many prefer a larger group for reasons of sociability. The pattern of exchange of hunting privileges between Nichicun territory owners permits the formation of adequately sized hunting groups, and, at the same time, enables owners to retain control of their territories by making regular use of them every few years. This kind of fluid pattern of hunting group composition also occurs to a lesser extent among the groups hunting closer to Mistassini Post, even though there is no similar surplus of land. This is because that pattern also conforms to the practice of annually reforming hunting groups. The territory owner is the focus of this process. As Speck pointed out, one particular individual, and not a group of kinsmen, is recognized as having title to a territory. Among the Mistassini, this individual also annually organizes the formation of the hunting group. Each summer those territory owners, who intend to hunt on their own land the following winter, invite other households to join them. As pointed out earlier, it is usually a foregone conclusion which families will accompany him. In the case of more fluid hunting groups, the leader may be approached by someone wishing to join his group, particularly in the final weeks before departure when everyone is outfitting for the winter. Some groups have the same core of two or more households year after year to which other households or single persons may be added for a single winter, or even for only part of the winter.

Of course, the hunting group leader does not decide unassisted who to include in his group. In addition to other members of his family, the Hudson's Bay Company manager and the provincial government administrator of beaver quotas may play influential roles in the process. Even the band chief (who is in charge of welfare) may be called in to give an opinion on whether a man can be given sufficient welfare payments to purchase an outfit, or the nurse may be asked whether a man is sufficiently healthy to join a group with an isolated territory.

Under normal circumstances the chief and the nurse are stabilizing influences, if only through the pressure of bureaucratic inertia. However, the Company manager, by controlling credit, also attempts, in a few cases, to align efficient trappers with rich territories. With the current extensive use of aircraft he can easily prevent a man from joining a group with a distant territory. However, he more often uses persuasion, since his effective monopoly today consists in his greater accessibility than his competitors, which makes it difficult, but not impossible, for a trapper to bypass him. The administrator of beaver quotas, by setting a limit on the total number of beaver each group is allowed to catch, places an upper limit on the number of adult men who may join a particular group. But because hunting groups work a long way from direct supervision, it is possible for individuals to circumvent regulations. For example, an individual may trap beaver using another man's quota, or trap his own quota in an area other than the one stipulated by the administrator. Thus, since the programme of beaver conservation depends on the voluntary co-operation of trappers, the administrator must use persuasion in influencing the formation of hunting groups.[17]

This account of the annual formation of the hunting groups has direct bearing on the issue raised by Knight about Speck's description, in the earlier part of this century, of the hunting group and the hunting territory. Knight's article concludes that without "regular and reliable survival security" a complete system of private hunting territories could not be maintained. A strict reading of Speck's description of hunting groups and hunting territories has already led Knight to the conclusion that in the central and southern regions of the Labrador peninsula this system of land tenure suffers from a number of defects which, in the long run, threaten survival. These defects can be summarized as: (1) fixed territories, (2) hunting group membership determined by a unilocal residence rule,[18] and (3) unilineal inheritance[19] of territories. I take these to be at the root of Knight's objection to Speck's account of the composition of the hunting group.

My data show that hunting territory boundaries are not fixed immutably over the long run, at least not in the Mistassini region of the central and southern part of the Labrador peninsula, except in the ideology of the present owners, and perhaps also in the testimony of the owners who were interviewed by Speck. Shifts in the location of territories do not necessarily break the continuity of the system. Also, membership in hunting groups is static and unilineal only in the ideology of some informants, and not in the data we now have on actual hunting group composition in the area. When questioned about hunting group composition, informants usually stressed father-to-son inheritance and residence after marriage in the area of the husband. Actual factors of group composition are more varied; in the short run, for instance, those influencing the annual process of hunting group formation include the group's need for security, and to adapt to its resources, as well as their preferences of kinship or friendship.

* * * * *

One more implication of Knight's work on hunting territories remains to be examined. If Speck's descriptions of hunting territories were in error, was this due to the bias of his informants, and if so, did this originate with the Indians he interviewed, or the traders? "An increasing amount of evidence leads me to believe that hunting territories were partly a myth propagated by some sections of the Hudson's Bay Company, and initially disseminated by a small number of anthropologists and their students at one or two universities."[20] Nevertheless, according to Knight, the Hudson's Bay Company did not approve of the idea of a beaver preserve until 1932.[21] The Hudson's Bay Company did nothing before that. Unless Knight has other evidence which he has yet to make public, it is not clear how the Hudson's Bay Company's reluctant part in the establishment of a "beaver preserve exclusively restricted to Indian trappers"[22] could explain the propagation of the idea of family hunting territories by academics some twenty years earlier. At the same time, it is quite possible that Speck's earliest descriptions, oversimplified and inflexible as they were, did rely heavily on the summary accounts of the institution which he obtained from Hudson's Bay Company managers, since at that time he was dependent on interviews at the summer trading posts. As I have already pointed out, Speck's earliest descriptions tally quite closely with the account given to me by present-day Mistassini hunting group leaders.

I will leave aside the question of the bias of the Hudson's Bay Company managers, who clearly did and do have an interest in the territories in that they make use of hunting groups in the organization of fur production and trade. There are, however, additional ideas and beliefs of the Quebec Algonquians which can provide us with another source of understanding as to what constitutes their ideological basis for land tenure practices.[23]

Lips has pointed out that many Indians in this area believed that it was the animals, and not men who were the true owners of the territories.[24] While some present-day Mistassini also believe this, at least one was of the opinion that, ultimately, God owns the land. This was stated, by the younger of two brothers who had shared a particular hunting ground since the death of their father.

God in this case refers to the Christian God, and there is little evidence today of a distinct non-Christian supreme being. In matters of hunting success and weather control, direct prayer to the Christian God is not commonly practised, except in a generalized way.[25] More often, such specific concerns are handled through the mediation of a number of spiritual entities, or through rituals directed toward some living or recently killed game. They, in turn, are controlled not by God, but by major spiritual entities such as *wa:pinu*, *chi:we:tinshu:*, or the "animal masters" who control the movements of various game. Although God may be said to ultimately own the land, the territory owner derives his authority from the animals. Furthermore, the relationships which the Mistassini hunters establish and maintain with game and spiritual entities are similar to human relationships.

These relationships with animals were established in mythic times through the curiosity of culture heroes such as *chikapes* who learned about the animals by living with them, and, in some cases, by marrying them. One such animal marriage myth tells of the differing territorial activities of a number of animal species, and the effect of these activities on the men who married them. In the version I collected at Mistassini, the hero first tries living with, in turn, a Canada jay and a caribou, both by nature nomadic animals. In another version of the same myth, collected at North West River, Labrador, the hero tries living with, successively, a fox, a caribou, a porcupine, and a jay. In both versions these animal marriages have two things in common which contrast them with the later marriage with the beaver woman: (1) they are nomadic, and (2) they are temporary. In the case of the beaver marriage, the change from moving camp every day to living in a fixed dwelling is a condition to which the hero agrees in order to continue the relationship. Although the couple is eventually forced to flee when the hero's brother, a shaman, breaks into the lodge (thereby starting the human practice of beaver hunting), the myth emphasizes the sedentary nature of the beaver. This myth is an example, very common among Algonquians, of sexual relations being an image for the relations between a hunter and his prey. (For an analagous situation among the norther Ojibwa, see Dunning.[26]) In the myth, the establishment of sexual relations is explicitly given as the reason by which today's hunting techniques originated. The story indicates a strong contrast between the hero's relationship with a set of animal wives at the beginning of the story, and his later relationship with the beaver woman. Beaver hunting, like the beaver marriage, is continuous (throughout the hunting season) and imposes some degree of a sedentary nature on the hunter. Hunting of the other animals mentioned is, by contrast, discontinuous, and involves to some extent adopting temporarily the nomadic characteristics of the prey. Finally, in the myth, as in present-day hunting and in current Mistassini ideology, the beaver ranks ahead of the other animals mentioned.

Among Mistassini hunters the beaver is, in fact, second in importance only to the bear in terms of religious ideology. All activities involving bears are dominated by religious considerations, even though economically it is not of major importance. Bear hunting, however, is normally confined to the spring and autumn so that the beaver is effectively the primary focus of both economic and ritual activity throughout the winter. The start of the winter hunting season is marked by a feast utilizing the first beaver killed, and beaver fat is given an especially important place in the feast held at the time the hunting group first moves into its main winter camp. As in the myth just referred to, an image of symbiosis is used to express the proper relationship between men and beavers. For instance, if a hunter is hurt by a beaver (he might, for example, be bitten while examining the tunnels in the banks of a beaver pond), the wound is said to hurt only at night, when beavers are active.

Other examples can be found where ritual importance is attached to objects symbolizing human/beaver relations. When a beaver lodge is first found, pieces of stick with teeth marks on them are taken from the top and from the tunnel entrances. These latter are the remnants of beaver food, which may jokingly be referred to as "bones." The ages of the beavers in the lodge are calculated by a hunter placing the sticks in his mouth. Later these sticks are carried back to camp and shown around and discussed with others in the group. Those sticks showing the teeth marks of particularly large beavers are placed at the head of the sleeping place of the hunter, in the same location where objects used to foretell hunting success, and other ritual objects, are placed.

A final example of the Mistassini notion that the behaviour of men, including their territorial behaviour, is parallelled by that of the beavers is the movement of beavers on land which starts in spring. This movement is said to be a sign for hunters to turn their attention to otter, water birds, and muskrat, and usually marks the start of the move to the spring camp.

This material indicates, not so much that Mistassini ecological behaviour is influenced by that of the beaver, but that hunters of this group make use of, and elaborate, a whole range of ideas, beliefs, and practices, all predicated on the relationship between men and beaver. There is, moreover, a complex of commonly expressed ideas and ritual practices which indicate that there are important relationships between hunters and all species of game animals, and that much of the responsibility for maintaining continuity in these relationships in large measure falls upon the hunting group leader. Consequently, there is a need for society to maintain continuity in these relationships at such a person's death.

Symbolic transactions between men and animals are channelled not only through the hunting group leader, but also through other older individuals. Hunting itself is a major means by which such relationships are established. The hunter who has, over many years, killed an extraordinary number of a particular species is felt to have a friendship relationship with that animal. Such an animal may be spoken of as the man's "pet," and this special relationship is usually marked by the hunter collecting, and sometimes decorating, an inedible part of the animal. These "tokens" are of two kinds: the skulls and forelimbs of certain animals, which are displayed by hanging in a tree; and other tokens which can include the chin or the claws of a bear, the head of a water bird, or a ring of fur from the forelimb of a beaver. The second kind are not displayed as trophies, but are usually kept hidden. In either case, the animal "friend" may be given part of the credit for the kill. By this means, old men, who rarely go more than a mile from the hunting camp, can sometimes take credit for the success of active hunters.

The concern of other hunters for the loss of an old person's spiritual power is noticeable when such a person dies. A watch is kept at the grave for the first few nights following the burial, and the non-appearance of a member of the species who had been the old man's "friend" is taken to mean that the animal is sad at his friend's death and will therefore leave the area. In practice, any unusual behaviour of such an animal during this period, not only at the graveside, is taken as a hopeful sign. If it is made clear that the animal will stay, the reason sometimes given is that the friendship relationship with the animal has been taken over by another member of the hunting group, usually the man's son.

The bush grave sites of spiritually powerful men become marked by the tobacco or animal bones sometimes left there for the dead man's spirit. Grave sites of others buried on the hunting territory are also visited when people are in the area. Several were pointed out to me by the Nichicun hunting group I lived with, even though the individuals buried there were rarely spoken of otherwise. Some people believe that the individual's spiritual part which stays near the grave can be acquired by someone close, a category which can include sons and sons-in-law, and in one case at least, a wife. In the case of animal friendship, the transference takes place within a short time of death. Other spiritual connections remain associated longer with the grave site before they either vanish or are taken over.

Other techniques used in maintaining relations with animals, in addition to animal friendship, favour the knowledge and experience of the aged. For instance, stories illustrating the effectiveness of dreaming, dream interpretation, sorcery, wish power and the power of songs almost invariably involve an old man.

Given that the Mistassini are concerned with the inheritance of the spiritual power of old men, can such ideas be seen as a model for the way in which the inheritance of rights to animal resources is conducted? In cases of spiritual power the inheritor appears always to be a co-resident, and is on warm terms with the deceased. Often he is a son, a brother, a son-in-law, or some unrelated friend or companion. However, inheritance of a territory by such a man is not the explicit ideal, which is the son. However, because of the frequent adoptions, particularly in families with many children, the kinship category of "son" is to some extent defined by residence. The cases of territorial inheritance at Mistassini for which there is detailed information suggest that inheritance is usually by a person within the same hunting group, although there are exceptions.

In practice, inheritance to the hunting rights, and the spiritual relationships, of a hunter are gradual processes. As the territory owner gets old he has fewer direct encounters with animals, which are left to younger members. After the death, relations with animals are passed on, not necessarily to a kinsman, but to *uwi:chiwa:kan* ("his friend" and, by connotation, "a co-resident"), the same term used to refer to the man/animal relationship. Even prior to death, some of his spiritual power can be acquired by a close companion, including the companion's wife, who can then use wish power to influence the hunting success of her husband.

The government's introduction of permanent residences for band members at Mistassini Post, and the availablity of welfare, has recently changed the issue. Old people, in the majority of cases, now spend their last winters at Mistassini Post, and are buried there. Some kind of transference of hunting privileges must therefore take place before death. The process of becoming a territory owner begins, for some hunters, as early as their late teens. A young man may speak about a certain part of his group leader's territory as "his," although this subdivision of the territory may later be forgotten if group membership changes. However, in most of the actual cases in which two brothers own adjacent territories, I was told that the land had originally been a single territory which had been divided between the brothers before the father died. In some cases, it appears that the divided areas effectively continued to be managed as a single unit, even after the death of the father, with a single group alternating from one year to the next between the two halves. Although the wishes of the dead are respected, it is becoming more common for a territory effectively to be inherited before the death of the former owner.

Mistassini Cree ideology (as well as their practical concerns) places emphasis on animals rather than on land, and thus suppresses the question of the clear definition of boundaries. A hunting territory is a unit which is most often defined by naming the lakes, rivers or mountains within it, rather than with boundary markers. In practical terms, the definition of a territory boundary is not as often used in keeping outsiders off one's land, as it is in making sure, in advance, that the hunting and trapping activities of one group do not overlap with those of another. A hunting territory is a unit of management. Each winter a group makes plans to conduct particular kinds of activities in particular areas at particular times. These plans can be seriously interfered with if another group makes use of one of these areas prior to, and without the knowledge of, the first group. The same applies to the activities of individual hunters within the hunting group.

The following case provides an illustration. I spent part of one winter with a section of a hunting group that had temporarily split in two. An expedition was made by my section to a particular region to hunt for beaver and moose. In one area, we found several beaver houses which had been trapped earlier that winter without our knowledge by the other section of the group, on its way to its predetermined area. However, it had been understood by a previous arrangement that they would not trap en route. This misunderstanding had only minor consequences in wasted time for our group, but it caused considerable comment.

Such a case points out the need for prior knowledge of where neighbouring groups will operate. This problem is not confined to the trapping of fur-bearing animals. Any animal which confines itself to known localities in particular seasons, such as moose with their "yarding" behaviour, or bear, can be managed, in the sense that a group can plan with a fair degree of certainty to utilize it during a certain period. I observed these kinds of strategies in a small unselected sample of Mistassini hunting groups in 1969–70, and they have also been reported among the neighbouring Waswanipi by Feit (in this volume).

To prevent any overlapping of hunting activities between members of adjacent groups, boundaries are discussed during the summer. In addition, markers are used to indicate the fact that traps have been set such as when a hunter traps in an area peripheral to that of his neighbour. This happened in the group I was with when we became aware that others were in the vicinity. These markers were placed in case a hunter should pass by to warn him that others have already trapped the area.

To summarize the Mistassini ideology as it relates to hunting territories, the ideals of fixed tracts of land and father-to-son inheritance, which Speck emphasized, are today explicitly held. But so are other ideological principles which emphasize the management and inheritance of rights to animals and power over animals (rather than rights to land) by persons, of whatever kinship status, who have, by long-term residence and hunting success, established membership in the hunting group led by the territory owner.

While Knight seems to think that hunting territories have broken down at Rupert House, apparently due to game shortages, my own conclusion is that the system is not threatened by demographic variations between families or changes in the ecological productivity of land. The institution is able to survive the adjustments needed to adapt to these conditions. The description of the hunting territory system by Speck turns out to have been inadequate in a number of respects. He presented part of his informant's ideals about land tenure as if it were the system itself. He ignored the role of the hunting territory as an administrative unit for the production of fur. But his work remains the *one* description of the system which comes closest to indicating the sociological basis for Algonquian land tenure.

* * * * *

To conclude I will make two points arising out of Knight's comments on my earlier version of this article. Both are related to his general contention that in that article I give general support for Speck's notion of hunting territories as essentially correct, in contradistinction to his own. I believe that *both* Speck and Knight give sadly inadequate accounts of the institution; Speck, because he presented only the folk ideology of the social aspect of the institution as if it were the entire institution itself, and Knight, because he presents the institution of hunting territories as being essentially irrelevant, a recent invention of outsiders.

My first point concerns Knight's defence of his hypothesis that hunting territories could not, on ecological grounds alone, have survived in the long run, even under fur trade conditions. If Knight's only point is that hunting territories would be unworkable if they were as rigidly structured as Speck's early descriptions suggest they were (and setting aside the fact that Speck did admit that some flexibility does occur), he is, of course, quite probably correct. However, as I have shown earlier, our knowledge of hunting territories and hunting groups has advanced since 1915, and before Knight's article in 1965. Field studies have shown that in practice, territories are more flexible than Speck's description, which was based on interviews alone, would suggest. Knight's elaborate and entirely hypothetical ecological arguments challenge what is today an imaginary problem. My own hope would be that ecological research could be put to better use analyzing something in the real world.[27]

My second point involves Knight's comments[28] on my reference to Mistassini religious beliefs as these relate to land tenure. He says that, on the basis of the religious material, I conclude that Speck's account of hunting territories and hunting groups was essentially correct because this account approximates Cree concepts of how the system would work best. I am then accused of verging on the sin of "theological ecology," whatever that may be. I did not write anything remotely similar to the ideas he attributes to me—my own views on the relationship between religious beliefs and ecological adaptation, expressed elsewhere,[29] are actually quite opposed to the ideas of which I am accused. I leave the reader to refer to that source, and will only restate here my view on the value of Speck's work on hunting territories. Speck's account of hunting territories is important in my view, in that he came closest (and certainly closer than Knight) to giving an indication that hunting territories have an important sociological basis. This importance comes from the central significance hunting territories have in the operation of hunting groups, since common residence and shared rights to land-based resources are the groups' structural focus. Thus, despite his inadequate field-work, Speck was clearly aware of this significant point, one that, in the hands of some modern scholars like Knight, is in danger of being overlooked.

My statement has nothing to do with any supposed parallel between Speck's account and the Cree's own religious concepts. These concepts have been referred to in this paper since I believe that no account of a land tenure system can be complete without including the system of ideas which is used to validate the distribution of resources, and especially in this case to validate any changes in the system that are necessitated to maintain it over the long run.

Notes

1. An earlier version of this paper was published in *Cultural Ecology*, a precursor of this volume. While the aim of the paper remains essentially the same, I have taken the opportunity to go over the text, eliminating a few passages that were irrelevant, and expanding and adding references to a work of mine published since the first version. I have also added a new passage at the end which answers some of the points made in Knight's review of the earlier version (Knight, 1974).
2. Frank G. Speck, "Mistassini Hunting Territories in the Labrador Peninsula," *American Anthropologist* 25 (1923):452–71.
3. Adrian Tanner, "Existe-t-il des territoires de chasses?" *Récherches amerindiennes au Québec* 1 (1972):5–6.
4. Rolf Knight, "A Re-examination of Hunting, Trapping and Territoriality among the Northeastern Algonkian Indians," in *Man, Culture and Animals*, edited by A.P. Vayda and A. Leeds, American Association for the Advancement of Science, Publication 78 (Washington, D.C., 1965).
5. Frank G. Speck, "The Family Hunting Band as the Basis of Algonquian Social Organization," *American Anthropologist* 17 (1915):290.
6. Edward S. Rogers, *The Hunting Group—Hunting Territory Complex among the Mistassini Indians* (Ottawa: National Museum of Canada, 1963).
7. This is not to overlook the fact that other groups, such as the so-called Naskapi, manage perfectly well without hunting territories. It is note-worthy that these people do not have structured stable winter-long hunting groups, and have a much more flexible leadership system, both of which relate to the lack of a system of territories.
8. Rogers, *Hunting Group*.
9. Knight, "Re-examination".
10. Tanner, "territoires des chasses."
11. One explanation for the disparity between statement and actual practice may well be that the Cree tell a consciously over-simplified description to naïve outsiders, because the real situation is felt to be too difficult for them to understand.
12. Knight, "Re-examination," 33.
13. Rogers, *Hunting Group*, 55–56.

14. John J. Honnigmann, "The Indians of Nouveau-Quebec," in *Le Nouveau-Québec. Contribution à l'etude de l'occupation humaine*, edited by Jean Malaurie and Jacques Rousseau (Paris: Mouton, 1964), 332.
15. Rogers, *Hunting Group*, 67–68.
16. Adrian Tanner, *Bringing Home Animals: Mode of Production and Religious Ideology among the Mistassini Cree Hunters* (St. John's: The Institute of Social and Economic Research, 1979), chapter 9.
17. Tanner, *Bringing Home Animals.*
18. The unilocal residence rule states what *particular* class of relatives a couple will live with after marriage. That is, it does not offer a choice of several classes of relatives.
19. Unilineal inheritance is the passing of property through only *one* descent line for all members of society; that is, always through the male line or always through the female line. No choice is allowed.
20. Rolf Knight, *Ecological Factors in Changing Economy and Social Organization among the Rupert House Cree*, National Museum of Canada, Anthropological Papers No. 15 (Ottawa, 1968), 26.
21. *Ibid.*, 29–30.
22. *Ibid.*, 30.
23. Tanner, *Bringing Home Animals.*
24. Julius Lips, "Naskapi Law," *Transactions of the American Philosophical Society* 37 (1947):379–492.
25. This statement probably does not apply to recent converts to the Pentacostal Church. At the time of my research the Mistassini band was almost entirely Anglican. Since then about half have joined the Pentacostal Church, which actively discourages non-Christian religious practices.
26. Robert W. Dunning, *Social and Economic Change among the Northern Ojibwa* (Toronto: University of Toronto Press, 1959).
27. Even if Knight only *intended* his article to dispute Speck's original description of hunting territories, Marvin Harris has claimed that Knight actually concludes something quite different. Harris writes, "[Knight] doubts that family territories even with the fur trade could have been a viable adaption for more than a small part of the population for any prolonged period;" Marvin Harris, *The Rise of Anthropological Theory: A History of Theories of Culture* (New York: Thomas Crowell, 1986), 359. But if hunting groups are flexible in the way I have stated, then they could well have had long-run viability. Ironically, Harris and Knight need the inaccuracy of Speck's description of the hunting territory, or their whole argument about the unviability of the institution collapses.
28. Rolf Knight, "Grey Owl's Return: Cultural Ecology and Canadian Indigenous Peoples," *Reviews in Anthropology* 1 (1974):349–59.
29. Tanner, *Bringing Home Animals.*

Chapter 6
Waswanipi Cree Management of Land and Wildlife: Cree Ethno-Ecology Revisited

Harvey A. Feit

Introduction[1]

It is a common assumption that game animal hunters exercise little control over the resources on which they depend or the environments in which they live. Peoples who have domesticated animals manage the environmental side of the man/nature relationship for they control, to varying degrees, the distribution and reproduction of some animals which they utilize. This control can be expressed by saying that they manage their resources. The lack of such management is often assumed to be virtually the *sine qua non* of hunting as opposed to other subsistence types. What powers hunters have are usually analyzed in terms of how they exercise control over themselves, and how they are affected by the unintended ecological consequences of their own actions. Hunters regulate the man/nature relationship primarily by regulating man, by controlling the human population size, the human population density, and the distribution of goods and services, and human desire itself. The scarcity, mobility, unpredictability, and difficulty of the capture of animals leaves the game hunter with little to hope for, except that he kills the animals he needs and adjusts himself to the results. It has been repeated again and again that there can be little planning and little foresight because so much of the outcome of the hunt is chance.

Yet studies in contemporary wildlife management indicate that human hunting itself has significant effects on the standing crop, production, yield, age structure, sex balance, and often size and health of the harvested animal populations, and studies of fishing give similar results.[2] It is possible to anticipate the consequences of hunting or harvesting patterns, and it is therefore possible for hunters to control some of the critical parameters of the harvested population through their choice of resource utilization strategies. Hunters can then, at least theoretically, exercise some control over the distribution and reproduction of the animal populations which they harvest, and may, in some sense, manage their resources as well as themselves. This paper explores how one group of subarctic hunters, the Waswanipi Cree, utilize the resources available to them in order to demonstrate the hypothesis that they are managing their resources. The ecological system of knowledge of Waswanipi hunters, their ethno-ecosystem, implies a process of management.

Some Features of Waswanipi Ethno-Ecosystem

Waswanipi hunters say that they only catch an animal when the animal is given to them. They say that, in winter, the north wind, *chuetenshu*, God, and the animals themselves give the hunters what they need to live. In the culturally constructed world of the Waswanipi, the animals, the winds, and many other phenomena, are thought of as being "like persons" in that they act intelligently and have self-will and idiosyncrasies, and understand and are understood by men. Causality, therefore, is personal, not mechanical or biological, and it is, in our experience, always appropriate to ask "Who did it?" and "Why?" rather than "How does it work?" The bodies of the animals received by the hunter nourish him, but the soul is reborn, so that when men and animals are in balance, the animals are killed but not diminished, and both men and animals survive. The balance is reciprocal, and in return for the gifts, the hunter has obligations to the animals and *chuetenshu* to act responsibly. He is expected to completely use what he is given, and to act respectfully toward the bodies and souls of the animals by observing the highly structured procedures for retrieving the animal, butchering it, consuming its flesh, and disposing of its remains. It is expected that men will kill animals swiftly, and avoid causing them undue suffering. It is also understood that men have the skill and technology to kill many animals, too many, and it is part of the responsibilities of the hunter not to kill more than he is given, and not to "play" with animals by killing them for fun or self-aggrandizement.

This last stricture is critical in the Waswanipi ethno-ecology, because it means that, in their view, the hunter has a considerable influence over his hunting. Men should only catch what is given to them, but in practice, what is given to them is a function of what they have done before. Thus, much of the time, when hunters are asked about why their hunt was good or bad, they reply in terms of how they hunted the year before. Failure to catch animals when expected is a critical concern of the Waswanipi. In their view, uncertainty is always attached to their activities, but a lack of success is distinguished from this uncertainty, in certain cases, by the duration of the period without harvests. For example, beaver traps set at a lodge may not have any animals in them when they are checked after three or four days. This is usually because "the beaver don't want to be caught yet," and the traps are left for an additional three to four days. If, however, there are no, or few catches, within a longer period of time, most informants suggest about two weeks, then a hunter is not just confronting the whims of the animals, he is having "bad luck." Bad luck is the result of a decision on the part of *chuetenshu* or the animals that a man should not get what he wants—usually because he has failed to fulfill one or more of his responsibilities. One of the most important responsibilities is not to kill too many animals. Thus the hunter is often confronting the consequences of his own activity when he goes hunting, and this confrontation occurs through the will of *chuetenshu* and the animals.

The relationships that are posited in the Waswanipi ethno-ecosystem make it possible for hunters to choose a number of different ways of hunting. Since it can be known more or less well in advance that animals will be "mad" at transgressions of the hunters' responsibilities and will bring "bad luck," a hunter can to some degree plan for this contingency.

The striking feature of this account is that while the explanation, the causality that animates the Waswanipi ethno-ecosystem model, is very different from a scientific account, the structural relationships described are partially isomorphic with those of a scientific account of the relationships of hunter to animal population. Despite the difference in world views, the Waswanipi are recognizably concerned about what we would call ecological relationships, and their views incorporate recognizable ecological principles. Prominent among these are the equivalents of concepts that man/animal relationships are systemic, and that a sustained yield use of the animal populations is possible through a process of management. But, is choice, in fact, possible in the subarctic region known for its relatively large unpredictability?

Waswanipi Hunting Recipes

Waswanipi hunters utilize a variety of animal resources, the most important being beaver and moose, followed by various species of fish (particularly pickerel, whitefish, pike, sturgeon, and burbot), hare, and various species of grouse (spruce grouse, ruffed grouse, and willow ptarmigan). Beaver, moose, and fish are the most important subsistence resources providing an average of 39, 29, and 5 percent of the total calories available for human consumption during the winter hunting season, the remainder being primarily purchased foods, with some hare, small fur-bearing animals, and fowl.[3] Beaver and fish are relatively stable resources. The sedentariness, predictability, and success of the trapping techniques available for beaver are, as has been recognized for some time, well suited to management.[4] Moose, however, have generally been considered mobile, erratic, and sparsely distributed, and moose hunting itself considered a very unreliable activity.[5] It is therefore appropriate to analyze the Waswanipi recipes for moose hunting.

Waswanipi hunters say that it is *chuetenshu*, the north wind, who controls winter precipitation and who is especially important for the moose hunts. During the early winter, as the snow accumulates, the moose begin to have trouble walking as their legs penetrate deeply into the snow, and their bodies start to drag. Moose, therefore, move to locations that have relatively lower snow accumulations due to their vegetational cover and topographic conditions. Waswanipi say that the moose move to the hardwood covered hills which are exposed to the wind. By early January, such conditions have normally occurred, the moose are concentrated in these suitable areas, and they generally confine themselves within them to the established paths of snow packed by repeated use. Once this has happened, hunters say it is easy to hunt moose. To locate moose they search the hills for tracks or signs which can be followed, and when tracks or signs are found many hunters report that they are happy because they "will be eating moose."

If the approaching hunter is heard or scented, the moose will flee, but the depth of the snow will quickly tire the animal, and it will frequently stop to rest, thus giving the hunter a chance to catch up. At most, the people say, after one and a half, or two hours, of steady walking on snowshoes a man will have completely exhausted a moose running in high snow, and the animal will stand its ground and be killed. However, many hunters say that, given the snow conditions, they can often predict where the moose will run. Furthermore, Waswanipi prefer to hunt on "moose days" when there is a slight wind that covers low noises made by the hunter and when the temperature is cold so that wet snow does not stick to their snowshoes and make walking difficult. If it is too cold the snowshoes make excessive noise on the hardened snow and the branches of trees and shrubs are brittle and easily cracked. Under these conditions, it is possible to often avoid pursuit of the moose entirely, or to terminate the chase quickly.

That moose give themselves to men is also indicated to the hunters, by the behaviour patterns of the animal. When moose are alerted by a noise they respond not by immediately taking flight, but stand and look in the direction of the sound, trying to see or scent its source.[6] The moose will then flee. This is the moment the moose offers himself to the hunter, and this is the moment for the kill. If it is not then shot, it will run some distance, how far depends on snow conditions, and then stop and look back in the direction from which it has come.

There are also, according to the Waswanipi, even better conditions for hunting moose, although these only occur briefly toward the end of winter. In late March and early April, the sun melts the topmost layer of snow, and during the nights and on colder days, an icy crust is formed. Moose break through this crust as they walk and cut their legs against the edges of the holes. Moose find it difficult to run under these conditions and often simply will not—even in full view of the hunters. Under these conditions the Waswanipi say moose hunting is easy, and they are then often assisted by dogs which are trained to bring a moose to bay, or to run a semi-circle around it so that the moose, caught between man and dog, "freezes."

Waswanipi hunters, then, have a detailed knowlege of moose behaviour, and so can hunt moose specifically when the animals are concentrated in a few locations which can be easily searched, when the moose are immobile, or less mobile than the hunter, and at times when moose behaviour is relatively predictable. Most of the relationships of the Waswanipi recipes have been reported by scientists, although many have only been scientifically described in the last decades.

Waswanipi have a very substantial knowledge of the environment in which they live and this knowledge makes plausible their claims for the reliability, efficiency, and affluence of their subsistence system. Their expertise also suggests that it is possible to choose when to use resources. For each animal species the Waswanipi harvest, they attempt, as for the moose, to utilize it at times when the chance of success is high and the efficiency of capture is optimized. The Waswanipi account of their annual cycle is a model for integrating the various harvesting activities so that each resource is used at periods of high vulnerability and efficiency, and ideally, so that at least two resources are available at each period throughout the hunting season. But, given the low productivity of subarctic ecological systems, can decisions on the time and place of resource utilization actually manage the resource system, and can hunters control some critical parameters of the resources on which they depend?

Waswanipi Resource Management

During the 1968-69 hunting season, an analysis of moose and beaver caught by all Waswanipi hunting groups indicated that no group went short of food, and that most groups caught moose and beaver in surplus of their subsistence requirements. Some groups caught more than double their subsistence requirements. A majority of bush hunting groups provided significant quantities of meat for other Waswanipi residents near towns, and many groups cached meat caught in winter to add variety to their summer diet. However, despite this affluence, there is considerable variation in the dependence on the resources available to different Waswanipi hunting groups. In a detailed sample of all the foods available for human consumption in four hunting groups during the 1968–69 hunting season, beaver accounted for approximately 25 to 45 percent of the total calories available for human consumption, moose for 15 to 40 percent, and fish for 1 to 15 percent. These variations suggest that a number of different harvesting strategies are in use among different hunting groups, and that a multi-dimensional management process may exist.

On the basis of existing biological data it is possible to make rough estimates of the production of the primary resources available to Waswanipi hunters, as well as to estimate the efficiency of their harvesting techniques, and their human subsistence requirements. The production of the major animal resources used by Waswanipi hunters, measured as calories for human consumption produced per square mile per annum on a sustainable basis, indicates that fish are substantially more productive than beaver, and that beaver are 50 percent more productive than moose. The production of hare obviously varies over a wide range because of the great amplitude of its population cycles. On the other hand, the efficiency of harvesting activities, assuming the present range of harvesting time and intensity, also varies. Moose hunting is by far the most efficient harvesting technique ranging from 65,000 calories for human consumption per person-day to nearly 110,000 calories per person-day; beaver efficiency varies with season, but the seasonal averages are 9,000 to 27,000 calories per person-day, while winter fishing produces 10,000 calories per person-day, and small game capture up to 3,000 calories per person-day. For comparison, averages of maximum human subsistence requirements at Waswanipi for the winter bush population are estimated to be 4,200 calories per person per day, of which a minimum of approximately 1,200 calories is provided by purchased foods.

Given these parameters, it is clear that, to meet human subsistence requirements, there are a number of alternative sources of subsistence that could be chosen in a large number of combinations. However, since the biological production of moose and beaver are relatively low, the critical feature for the hunters is managing their harvest so that the populations of these species are not depleted. This is necessary because it is clear from experience elsewhere that beaver are easily over-hunted, and it seems likely from our study of Waswanipi moose hunting that this species could also be over-hunted. The Waswanipi themselves say that limiting the kill is a part of their responsibility.

One important way that Waswanipi regulate the harvests of the animals, and the production and distribution of animals, is by rotational hunting. By not occupying a given hunting territory every year, the hunters allow the populations and harvests of animals to grow. Some men regularly rotate their use of land, others let their grounds rest occasionally, and some practise rotation by dividing the territory into sub-sections so that each section can be used in turn. Of the twenty-two territories in use during 1968–69 and 1969–70 there were only six cases where men actually hunted on the same territory or sub-section both years. From year to year, hunters constantly evaluate the state of the animal populations on the land they hunt, and any drop in the success of the hunt, the number of animals sighted, or the number of animal signs, is taken as an indication of over-hunting or of other transgressions by the hunter. The state of the animal populations on a given territory is constantly monitored and Waswanipi can discuss the population trends on their territories, and compare them to what they were last year, ten years ago, or when they had first started hunting.

Territorial rotation is a critical mechanism for managing the size of the animal populations. The size of the harvests are directly related to the frequency of hunting on a territory. During our study, hunters who were on territories that *were used the year previous* to the recorded year (1968–69 or 1969–70) caught fewer moose and beaver per square mile than men hunting on territories *not used one year previous* to the recorded year, and these men had a lower catch density than men who hunted on grounds *not used for two or more years* previous to the recorded year. In short, the catch densities increased with the expected increases in the animal population densities. These increases in harvest densities are a result of both increased game densities, and Waswanipi harvesting decisions which responded to these changes.

The value of a short-term rotation system is that it allows hunting activity to be concentrated within a more limited geographical area than if an area was used continuously, thereby increasing harvesting efficiency; and, it may also serve to keep the animal population at the high rate of productivity characteristic of expanding populations, by periodically reducing the population significantly and then allowing it to expand for two or three years before re-harvesting.

On rotated territories, the average harvests of moose and beaver were well below estimated sustainable yields for intermittently harvested moose and beaver populations. Furthermore, all groups that were on territories that had been rotated caught high levels of moose and beaver relative to their subsistence requirements. In the four hunting groups for which we have detailed samples it is clear that when moose and beaver catches are high, relative to subsistence requirements, over 4,000 calories per adult per day in two cases, the fish and small game do not amount to over 300 calories per adult per day available for human consumption.

But not all men can rotate their territories, or sections thereof, because of the size of their families or because of a lack of access to other territories. These men must hunt the same land each year. It is interesting to note that it was only among groups using a territory hunted the year previous to the recorded year that some groups did not have sufficient moose and beaver to meet basic subsistence demands. From our four-group sample it can be suggested that when the catches of moose and beaver drop to about the 3,000 calories per adult per day range or below, dependence on fish increases to over 600 calories per adult per day, and although purchases of foods do not rise, they become more important as a percentage of available foods, accounting for approximately 40 percent of the total, moose and beaver providing an average of only 50 percent of the total. The Waswanipi use the most efficiently harvestable resources, namely moose and beaver, first, and then they shift to other less efficiently harvestable but more productive resources, particularly fish.

For the region as a whole, harvests of moose and beaver were within the estimated sustainable yields of the populations. The average density of animals killed as a percentage of the average density of the surveyed population is the same or within the range of the estimated production for moose. The moose harvests on Waswanipi hunting territories, including White sportsmen's harvests which account for approximately 25 percent of the total harvest, amounted to between 18 and 21 percent of the estimated moose populations. This falls within the ranges of net moose productivity determined by biological research in other subarctic regions, where net productivity has varied from 17 to 25 percent. The beaver harvests on Waswanipi hunting territories amounted to an average of 0.77 and 0.71 beaver per colony, based on the estimated number of active colonies in the region. The minimum permissible harvest level would normally be 1.0 beaver per colony, and this level would normally permit some increase in beaver populations. Often 1.25 beaver per colony would be a sustainable yield in a relatively stable population. Based on Waswanipi reports to the governments, beaver lodge counts have remained relatively steady over the fifteen years prior to this research. The harvests of moose and beaver in the Waswanipi region are therefore apparently limited to the net production of the populations.[7]

Conclusions

The data we collected supports the interpretation that Waswanipi hunters do manage their harvests of moose and beaver and the distribution and reproduction of the harvested populations, either by rotational use of the territories, or by an increased use of alternate resources to supplement moose and beaver in the subsistence diet.

Waswanipi hunters use the animal resources available to them on a sustained yield basis while increasing the efficiency and enhancing the security of their subsistence activities insofar as this is compatible with sustainable yields.

Afterword, 1973

The priority that Waswanipi men give to ecological factors can serve as a model for the non-Natives who plan to utilize other resources in the subarctic region. All use should be based on a multiple-use management plan. Such a plan would necessitate that governments recognize that rational management of the animal resources of the region is already practised, and if these resources are affected it is essential that the Indian people themselves be represented on the planning body. The Indian people of the region must be allowed to articulate their own needs and to help evaluate the impact of other uses on the resources of the region. Their agreement should be obtained before the resources which they are now managing and utilizing are affected by plans to develop the non-wildlife resources of the region.

Postscript, 1986

Two questions have been asked on a number of occasions about the analyses presented in this article. Is the finding that Waswanipi hunters' practices lead to conservation of the major wildlife populations they harvest a result of the conscious decisions of the Cree, or could it be that either the hunters cannot catch any more than they do, or alternatively that it would not be efficient for them to catch any more than they do? Second, do these management practices continue, given the rapid change presently occurring in the region? I will address each of these issues in turn by summarizing the results of recent re-studies and re-analyses of the original data on Waswanipi hunting culture and practices.

Eric Alden Smith suggests that, rather than following a strategy of long-term management, a more likely hypothesis is that Waswanipi hunting practices are "primarily devices to increase foraging efficiency and optimize time allocations, only incidentally having the effect of 'managing' prey populations."[8] In support of this hypothesis, Smith asserts that "it is difficult to see how a strategy of long-term resource management could repay the costs to individual foragers of foregoing immediate returns for uncertain future returns," given the "drastic and unpredictable fluctuation that has been documented for populations of most prey species in the subarctic."[9] I will re-examine this hypothesis, as well as the evidence on which its reasonableness is asserted to rest, in the context of reformulating and re-evaluating the major assertions of this article.

To formalize the main strategies which are explicitly and implicitly organized in the original analysis, I would propose three dynamic goals which are pursued situationally by Waswanipi hunters: (1) to harvest intensively utilized resources within sustainable yields so as to avoid depletion of these wildlife resources in the long run; (2) to reduce hunting labour costs by harvesting more efficiently harvestable wildlife resources in preference to less efficiently harvestable resources, insofar as this is compatible with the sustained yield strategy; and (3) to choose a harvesting pattern, for example, rotational harvesting, which not only reduces labour cost but also reduces the variability of harvests in the long-term.

That Cree practices keep harvests of wildlife within the sustainable yields of the species populations is documented above. Additional evidence comes from repeated aerial surveys of the game populations of the region by the Quebec and Canadian wildlife services, some of which only became available after the original article was published.

A series of four surveys of moose populations gives an indication of trends in the regional moose populations over a nine year period, 1968 to 1976. The first survey was completed at the beginning of the calendar year in which the field research on which this article was based began. The second survey was completed one year after the field-work, and the other two were conducted three and four years later. The estimated moose densities were similar before and after the field-work period, being marginally higher by about 20 percent in 1971–72 than in 1968. Numerical comparisons are not possible with the data in the reports from the later surveys, but the author of the 1976 report concluded that the findings were generally comparable to those of 1971–72.[10]

For beaver populations, results of aerial surveys made six years and two years before initial field-work, and seven years after the first field study was completed, were compared with each other and with Waswanipi hunters' maps of beaver lodges collected during field-work. Again the surveys indicate relatively stable populations, with similar population densities at the beginning and end of the series, and a small rise of less than 20 percent followed by a decline during the middle of the period.[11]

The relatively limited variability of both the moose and beaver populations during this period is the clearest evidence that the Waswanipi were harvesting the most efficiently utilizable wildlife populations within sustainable yields.

While these data also indicate that moose and beaver populations varied in density over a relatively moderate range during a period of a decade or more, the Cree hunters report longer periods of relative stability or slowly changing trends. This is not to deny the substantial fluctuations which are common on many small game and fur-bearer populations in the subarctic regions, nor the longer term sequence of stages through which the boreal forest passes;[12] but the relative stability of the moose and beaver populations in the Waswanipi region is all the more striking and important because of these other fluctuations.

Indeed, given the pervasiveness of substantial fluctuations, and the relatively modest fluctuations of moose and beaver, it would seem *prima facie* that the most likely hypothesis is that this relatively modest variation is partially the result of Waswanipi hunting practices, as well as of moose and beaver population dynamics and environmental variables. This conclusion supports the third strategy hypothesized above, although more extensive data will be required to fully test this strategy.

Turning to Smith's assumption that the drastic and unpredictable fluctuations documented for most prey species in the subarctic can be readily generalized to all herbivorous species, and made the basis of generating hypotheses concerning hunting strategies, it is clear that the Waswanipi data do not substantiate his assertion.

The second strategy of giving priority to the harvesting of more efficiently harvestable wildlife resources is reflected in the intensity of the use of the various game populations of the region. The definition of intensity used is the percentage of the sustainable yield of each wildlife population which was harvested by Waswanipi hunters. Over the two-year initial study period, the estimated range of the percentage of sustainable yields for moose which were actually harvested was between 80 and 100 percent. Beaver harvests varied between approximately 55 and 75 percent of sustainable yields, and fish were estimated at 35 percent of potential yields. Data were not available to estimate sustainable yields for other species populations. This confirms that in practice the Waswanipi were harvesting the more efficiently harvestable wildlife species more intensively than less efficiently harvestable species.

Is there any evidence that these outcomes are the result of conscious choices on the part of Waswanipi hunters? Ethnographically, I have noted in the original article that the Waswanipi hunters speak of their harvests as being given to them by God, the spirits, and the animals themselves, and they say that they should only kill animals that are given. This conceptualization makes clear that hunters perceive that they must decide which animals to kill, and that hunting is not just a function of running across animals or signs of animals, but of evaluating in cultural terms whether each potential encounter with an animal involves the "gift" of an animal or not.

Actually, the choice does not only occur in the encounters, but begins before setting out to look for animals, because the Waswanipi say they dream or are otherwise told of the animals they will be given. The most publicly accessible demonstrations of this thought process are the plans which hunters often have and express. For example, a hunter will say that "maybe I will get *X*-number of moose this winter." Or the sighting across a lake of a moose with two young during the summer may provoke a response that the hunter will get two or three moose the coming season. Or a hunting territory "steward" may tell someone he invites to use the territory that he can take *X* moose, if he can get them. These plans are always subject to additional information on and from the game, and are often revised, but they do guide hunting activity and effort. These statements demonstrate that, from a Waswanipi point of view, the hunter must choose what to harvest in accordance with his knowledge of the will of the spirits and the animals.[13]

Waswanipi harvesting is organized around the system of hunting territories. Each territory is under the stewardship of a hunter, usually an active elder. The territory system has been recognized by governments in recent decades for purposes of organizing beaver trapping, but the system predates official recognition, and it serves the Waswanipi for a much wider range of harvesting activities than just trapping fur-bearers. There are approximately 225 adult Waswanipi men, of whom approximately 50 are stewards. Stewards generally have the right and obligation, socially and spiritually sanctioned, to decide whether a hunting territory should be harvested for big game and fur-bearers during any season, and they allocate long-term rights and seasonal privileges to use the territories to hunters who do not have their own. They can thus decide, roughly or precisely, how many hunters will use a territory, and they can indicate to those who do use it how many of each major kind of game they can harvest. They can direct where, when, and how game should be taken although this direction is normally kept to a minimum, and it takes the discreet form of suggestions and providing information, thus observing the relative autonomy of each hunter. Their supervision is widely respected. The decisions, therefore, are made by socially located individuals bound in a complex system of rights and responsibilities.[14]

Behavioural indicators that harvests are a result of decisions are also available. If decisions were taken only on the basis of short-term efficiency considerations, and not on the basis of long-term plans and year-to-year monitoring of game populations, then it is hard to explain why moose in particular are not hunted out. Moose are three times more efficient to harvest than are beaver, the next most efficient resource. It is unlikely, given that annual per hunter harvests of moose average between two and three animals, that the efficiency of moose hunting drops off so quickly after that number that it is no longer more efficient to harvest another moose rather than to harvest beaver or alternative species. That is, we would not expect that the return rates do not drop off until the moose populations are more or less depleted. This is supported by evidence in the literature that moose can be, and have been depleted on occasion by hunters.

Indeed, the actual practices of the Waswanipi indicate that it would be efficient, although only in the short-run, to harvest moose at non-sustainable levels. The critical case is what happens in conditions where the strategy of maintaining harvests at sustainable levels is modified. This occurs, for example, when a group of hunters uses a hunting territory which they know will not be hunted again for one or more years. This was the case in 1968–1970 for a limited number of territories that were distant from settlements and roads. Hunters could not afford the cash outlay required to return to these territories every year, and the territories were therefore used periodically, hunted for one or more years, then left for several years. In these circumstances, hunters would say they "cleaned out" an area, by which they meant they took more than they would if they were returning the following year, but not so much that the wildlife populations would not recover after one or more years of not being harvested.

While there are a limited number of such cases, the harvests of moose and beaver taken in these circumstances are higher per unit area hunted than in other hunting territories, and they exceed the estimated annual sustained yields of the areas being hunted. This indicates that under exceptional circumstances, when hunters are ready to temporarily exceed sustainable yields, they find it efficient to take more moose and beaver than they would in normal circumstances. It also indicates by implication that the relative efficiency of harvesting of these species has not declined significantly at these more elevated levels of harvesting. The limiting of moose harvests is therefore not a function of short-term declines in efficiency, but of long-term planning within a culturally structured system.

Further evidence of conscious choice is found in the allocation of hunters' time. Based on hunters' diary records and reports of the main hunting activities they engaged in during each day of the winter hunting seasons, I allocated each day or half-day to the primary activities. During the 1968–69 winter hunting period, the percentage of hunting person-days spent in various activities were on average: 8 percent moose hunting, 59 percent beaver hunting, 5 percent fishing, 2 percent waterfowling at the end of the winter period, 20 percent harvesting small game, and 6 percent fine-fur trapping (Table 6-1). It is difficult to explain the limited allocation of hunting effort put into hunting moose, except by conscious choice. Declining efficiency is not the cause. The risk involved is not sufficient explanation because moose hunting was successful on approximately 25 percent of hunting days, and the size of each harvested animal offsets the risk, as the high efficiency of moose hunting indicates. Neither were environmental conditions limited in any apparent way. Snow depth was sufficient over the entire mid-winter period, and approximately 65 percent of winter days had the right precipitation conditions, and 75 percent had the right wind conditions for moose hunting.

The fact that such a limited percentage of hunting effort is spent moose hunting is a strong indication that what limits the harvest is how much time the Waswanipi decide to spend trying to hunt moose, and this I have argued responds to their monitoring of the conditions of the game populations and their desire to generally harvest at what they perceive to be sustainable levels.[15]

That moose and beaver populations appear to go through limited variability, and appear to be relatively or partially predictable, results both from their relationships to the boreal forests and other components of the environments of the region, and also from the activities of the Waswanipi hunters themselves. The Waswanipi not only adapt to the natural environment/material world, they make that world conform in some of its aspects to the cultural images the Cree themselves hold of how it should be. This point would be trivial were we talking about agriculturalists, horticulturalists, or pastoralists, but it has still not been widely appreciated that it may also apply to some hunters.

One consequence is that it is very likely that both the activities and strategies of hunters will be misconstrued unless the systems of knowledge, values and

Table 6-1 Percentage of Hunting Person-Days Allocated to Different Hunting Activities, Diary Records, Winter Hunting Season, 1968–69

Hunters Reporting in Diaries[a]	Hunting Periods Covered by Diary[b]	Percentage of Hunting Person-Days Spent:						
		Moose Hunting	Beaver Hunting	Fishing	Waterfowl Hunting	Grouse Hunting	Hare Hunting	Fine Fur Hunting
52 and 61	1/5 to 5/25	12	70	1	7	1	1	7
53 and 59	1/9 to 5/1	13	29[c]	N.A.[d]	0	10	37	10
68	1/16 to 5/5	0	78	9	0	4	7	2
All		8	59	5	2	5	15	6

Notes:

a. The diaries which had sufficient data for tabulation included: one diary covering the activities of two fully active, intensive hunters, who often hunted as partners (hunters 52 and 61); one diary covering a single young intensive hunter, who did no moose hunting during the period covered (hunter 68); and one diary covering an active, intensive but aged hunter who worked with a part-time hunter (hunters 53 and 59). The adventitious sample of four intensive and one part-time hunters, is from a population of 88 hunters, of whom 53 are intensive hunters. It may be useful to note that from the perspective of bush food produced per adult food consumer in their co-residential hunting group, hunters 52 and 61 produced the third highest level of food per unit of nutritional demand, and hunters 53 and 59 produced the second lowest, of the total of seventeen groups. The two cases therefore bracket the range of hunters' successes.

b. The period covered by the diaries is from early January to May 1969, and it includes both the mid-winter and late-winter moose hunts. It does not include the fall moose hunt, but the available data suggests that the inclusion of this period would not have substantially changed the results, because the intensive early fall rutting hunt is followed by a period of very limited moose hunting, until snow accumulations reach winter levels, and furthermore, summer moose hunts are not numerous.

c. Beaver data for hunter 59 are incomplete, and the tabulated time allocation may therefore be lower than if full data were available; however, the diary indicates that hunter 53 hunted at only five beaver colonies, an exceptionally low number, suggesting that time allocations for beaver hunting were indeed low.

d. Not available.

decision making are also made part of the frame of analysis. This is the case even though it is also true that behaviour does not necessarily conform in any simple fashion to cultural models. But cultural structure and action cannot even be adequately examined unless both sides of the analysis are completed. For example, I would argue that one would not recognize the significance of the fact that the Waswanipi take higher harvests on hunting territories which will be left fallow for one or more years, unless the patterns of knowledge and decision making had been sought from informants.

To return to the original point, and Smith's hypothesis, it is not surprising that the Waswanipi seek to conserve resources, it would be surprising, and require explanation, if they did not do so.[16] To recast Smith's argument, given that there is conscious decision making, it is difficult to see how a strategy of foregoing uncertain but necessary future returns for certain immediate depletion of resources could make any sense. Yet this is precisely what the hunters would have to do if their hunting practices were solely devices to increase foraging efficiency and to optimize time allocations.

Furthermore, the Waswanipi do not simply consider costs to individual foragers, the system of hunting territories involves them in consideration of individual, kin-group and community needs and costs, because the complex social organization of stewardship involves reciprocal duties and responsibilities to the living, and by way of inheritance to those deceased and yet to be born. Waswanipi hunters have occasionally asked, in deep puzzlement, as to why the non-Natives, who exploit the forests and the land of their region, can act with such clear disregard for the longer-term consequences of their own actions.

Thus, a further consequence of the need to pursue the analysis of cultural knowledge is that it helps to open up questions about inconsistencies, conflicts, and problems with the wider world. While it is beyond the scope of the present paper to explore these issues, a brief review of current developments may serve to raise them.[17]

The question of how the Waswanipi pattern of hunting has been reproduced in the period since the early 1970s can only be addressed briefly. Nevertheless, some indication of developments and responses can be summarized. During the 1970s and 1980s, massive development schemes have taken place in the James Bay region, and the Waswanipi area has been opened to more intensive industrial development. The same period has seen a land claims agreement implemented which recognizes Indian rights to hunt, to govern their own communities, and to participate in the co-management of the region, as well as government rights to develop the natural resources of the region.

The major changes in the socio-economic conditions of hunting during the decade under consideration have been:

- an increase by about 45 percent of the number of people who make hunting their main productive acitivity, due primarily to the guaranteed annual income support programme (ISP) established under the James Bay and Northern Quebec Agreement (JBNQA) for families who hunt;

- a 35 percent increase in the amount of time hunters and their families spend away from the settlements, responding in part to the structure of benefits under ISP;
- a substantial increase in the availability of cash incomes, and a consequent increase in the use of snowmobiles and other industrial commodities, with some indication that this has increased hunting efficiencies;
- a substantial increase in the domestic unit production of traditional or specialized housing, equipment, clothing and other bush services;
- an increase in the rate of use of more distant hunting territories;
- an enhancement of traditional social forms and hunting practices, along with some innovation and development of community-wide hunter decision-making structures;
- an increase in the rate at which forestry companies are clear-cutting Waswanipi hunting lands;
- an increase in the accessibility of the region to outsiders, due in large part to the improved transportation and communication necessitated by large scale regional development schemes.

Each of these changes, with the possible exception of the increase in cash incomes *per se*, would have been expected to lead to pressures toward increased harvests, or to declining game populations, and to problems conserving game by self-imposed limitation of the harvests, especially for intensively harvested species.

Intensive research on Waswanipi game harvests was conducted as a result of the land claims agreement process between 1972 and 1979. The author conducted follow-up research in 1981–82, and successive years. The long-term harvest data from the mid 1970s shows a relatively stable harvest of beaver during the period, with some decline in the early 1980s. The moose harvests on the other hand, increased following the agreement, but have declined back to earlier levels during the mid-1980s following a decision by community elders and stewards that the higher levels of harvesting could not be sustained. Changes in the distribution and abundance of moose are now occurring due to extensive clear-cutting of forests on Waswanipi hunting territories. Thus, the interpretation of trends in moose populations and harvests is now complicated by this factor.

At the community level, there were no downward trends in the total available weights of food from harvesting, and the system of hunting management has generally continued to work to regulate harvests and manage wildlife on those lands not disrupted by industrial developments.

At the level of hunting territories, the logging has been extremely disruptive, as lands and wildlife in which a lifetime of knowledge and care have been vested have been clear-cut, and disrupted for at least a period of one or more decades, until appropriate regeneration is established. This forces people into marginal hunting, breaks the continuity of knowledge of the land and wildlife, and makes it impossible for the affected hunters to pass on their skills and understanding of a particular area to the next generation. The Cree are currently seeking to modify through administrative and political action the conditions under which forestry companies are permitted to operate in the region.

An account of hunting practices and society which does not consider the Cree system of management decision making will continue to seriously underestimate the consequences of regional development on Waswanipi hunters and their efforts to protect wildlife and enhance the possibilities for continuation of their own ways of life.

Notes

1. Source: Harvey A. Feit, "L'Ethno-écologie des Cris Waswanipis; ou comment les chasseurs peuvent aménager leurs resources," *Recherches amérindiennes au Québec*, vol 1, no. 4–5 (1971). Reprinted by permission of the author and publisher. The author has revised this article, updated the calculations and added a postscript for this volume. The re-study and re-analysis of the material in this article, and in the 1986 postscript, were funded by a research grant from the Social Sciences and Humanities Research Council of Canada (410-81-0241). The original version of this paper was an early resumé of portions of a larger study, the research for which was supported by grants from the National Museum of Man, 1969–72, the Northern Research Committee of McGill University, 1968–71, and the Steinberg Summer Research Fellowships, 1968–69. Results of the initial research appear in Harvey A. Feit, *Waswanipi Realities and Adaptations: Resource Management and Cognitive Structure* (Ph.D. diss., McGill University, 1978). This study has benefited from the comments and advice of Richard F. Salisbury, many of which were incorporated in the present paper.
2. R.F. Dasmann, *Wildlife Biology* (New York: John Wiley & Sons, Inc., 1964); K.E.F. Watt, *Ecology and Resources Management* (NewYork: McGraw-Hill, 1968).
3. Harvey A. Feit, Waswanipi Realities and Adaptations: Resource Management and Cognitive Structure (Ph.D. diss., McGill University, 1978).
4. F.G. Speck and L.C. Eiseley, "Montagnais-Naskapi Bands and Family Hunting Districts of the Central and South-eastern Labrador Peninsula," *American Philosophical Society Proceedings* vol. 85, no. 2 (1942).
5. R. Knight, "A Re-examination of Hunting, Trapping and Territoriality Among the Northeastern Algonkian Indians" in *Man, Culture and Animals*, edited by A. Leeds and A.P. Vayda (Washington, D.C.: American Association for the Advancement of Science, 1965).
6. R.H. Denniston, II, "Ecology, Behaviour and Population Dynamics of Wyoming or Rocky Mountain Moose, *Alces alces shirasi*," *Zoologica*, vol. 41, no. 2 (1956):14.
7. It will be realized by ecologists familiar with the subarctic that this evaluation is based on the principles presently used by various game management personnel as operational rules of thumb, rather than on scientifically acceptable evaluations of the actual production and hunting yields of the animal populations.
8. Eric Alden Smith, "Anthropological Applications of Optimal Foraging Theory: A Critical Review," *Current Anthropology*, vol. 24, no. 5 (1983):625–51.
9. Smith, "Anthropological Applications."
10. J.-M. Brassard, and R. Bouchard "Inventaire aérien des ongulés sauvages, section située dans le nord de l'Abitibi (Janvier 1968)," Québec Ministère du Tourisme, de la Chasse et de la Pêche, [Quebec, 1968]. J.-M. Brassard "Inventaire aérien du gros gibier," Québec Ministère du Tourisme, de la Chasse et de la Pêche, [Quebec, 1972]. M. Morasse, "Rapport d'inventaire aérien de l'original dans la partie sud de la

municipalité de la Baie James," Québec Ministère du Tourisme, de la Chasse et de la Pêche, [Quebec, 1975]. R. Audet, "Distribution de l'Orignal dans la région de la Baie James, de la rivière Eastmain à l'Harricana," Québec Ministère du Tourisme, de la Chasse et de la Pêche, [Quebec, 1976]. Feit, *Waswanipi Realities*; and "North American Native Hunting and Management of Moose Populations," *Viltrevy, Swedish Wildlife Research*, in press.

11. Charles A. Drolet, *Contribution à l'étude du castor (Castor canadensis Kuhl) a la Baie James* (M.S. diss., Université Laval, 1965); G.A. Emond, "Initial Aerial Survey of Beaver Preserves: Nottaway, Rupert House, Nemiscau, Mistassini, Roberval, Abitibi, Waswanipi," study prepared for Department of Indian Affairs and Northern Development (Ottawa, 1967); Daniel Banville, "Inventaire aérien des colonies de castor au sud de la rivière Eastmain—octobre 1977," Québec Ministère du Tourisme, de la Chasse et de la Pêche, [Quebec, 1978]. Feit, *Waswanipi Realities*.
12. For a review see Harvey A. Feit, *Mistassini Hunters of the Boreal Forest: Ecosystem Dynamics and Multiple Subsistence Patterns* (M.A. diss. McGill University, 1969).
13. A more comprehensive account of these concepts will be found in Feit, *Waswanipi Realities*. Also, see Adrian Tanner, *Bringing Home Animals*. (London: C. Hurst, 1979).
14. A more comprehensive account will be found in Feit, *Waswanipi Realities*, and "Legitimation and Autonomy in James Bay Cree Responses to Hydro-Electric Development " in *Indigenous Peoples and the Nation State*, edited by Noel Dyck (St. Johns: Memorial University, Institute for Social and Economic Research, 1985), 27–65.
15. Feit, *Waswanipi Realities*; and "North American Native Hunting."
16. Related issues are discussed in Colin Scott, *The Semiotics of Material Life Among Wemindji Hunters* (Ph.D. diss., McGill University, 1983); Fikret Berkes, "Fishery Resource Use in Subarctic Indian Community," *Human Ecology* vol. 5, no. 4 (1977):289–307; "Waterfowl Management and Northern Native Peoples With Reference to Cree Hunters of James Bay," *Musk-Ox* vol. 30 (1982):23–35; and Harvey A. Feit, "James Bay Cree Indian Management and Moral Considerations of Fur-bearers" in *Native People and Renewable Resource Management* (Edmonton: Alberta Society of Professional Biologists, 1986):49–65.
17. See Harvey A. Feit, "The Future of Hunters Within Nation States" in *Politics and History in Band Societies*, edited by Eleanor Leacock and Richard Lee (Cambridge: Cambridge University Press, 1982):373–417; "Conflict Arenas in the Management of Renewable Resources in the Canadian North" in *National and Regional Interests in the North* (Ottawa: Canadian Arctic Resources Committee, 1984):435–58; and, "Hunting and the Quest for Power: the James Bay Cree and Whitemen in the Twentieth Century" in *Native Peoples: The Canadian Experience*, edited by R. Bruce Morrison and C. Roderick Wilson (Toronto: McClelland and Stewart, 1986):171–207.

Chapter 7
The Innu Bands of Labrador[1]

Eleanor Leacock

I should like to preface my discussion of the Innu band with some general remarks on history, acculturation, and evolution, as they are presently viewed. First, it is now recognized that aboriginal peoples, especially in the New World, were influenced by European commercialism earlier than was previously assumed. Much of what was formerly considered to be aboriginal represents instead an early phase of acculturation, a relatively viable synthesis of old and new that preceded the severe shaking up or outright destruction of Indian societies. So far as I know, it was William Duncan Strong who first clearly formulated this point. From his Columbia University seminar on "Time Perspective and the Plains" came studies of early Indian-white contacts and influences in the Plains and other areas that laid the basis for much of the ethnohistorical research that followed.

Today it is surprising to remember that Speck and Cooper took 1670 (the date when the first Hudson's Bay Post was established at James Bay) to represent the significant starting point for European influence in Labrador. It is well known that fur trading became a lively enterprise soon after Columbus' first voyage to the New World, and may even, in some slight degree, have preceded it. The Micmacs, who sighted Cartier's ships in 1534, waved furs on sticks to entice the men ashore, and throughout the sixteenth century there was constant competition among French companies for control of the St. Lawrence trade. Approximately forty years before the establishment of the James Bay Post, Charles L'Allemant wrote:

> Before the time of the association of those Gentlemen to whom the King gave this trade for a certain time . . . the Savages were visited by many people, to such an extent that an Old Man told me he had seen as many as twenty ships in the port of Tadoussac. But now since this business has been granted to the association . . . we see here not more than two ships which belong to it, and that only once a year about the beginning of the month of June. These two ships bring all the merchandise which these Gentlemen use in trading with the Savages; that is to say the cloaks, blankets, nightcaps, hats, shirts, sheets, hatchets, iron arrowheads, bodkins, swords, picks to break the ice in Winter, knives, kettles, prunes, raisins, Indian corn, peas, crackers or sea biscuits, and tobacco. . . . In exchange for these they carry back hides of the moose, lynx, fox, otter, black ones being encountered occasionally, martens, badgers, and muskrats: but they deal principally in Beavers, in which they find their greatest profit. I was told that during one year they carried back as many as 22,000. The usual number for one year is 15,000 or 12,000, at one pistole each, which is not doing badly.[2]

Many such passages found in the *Jesuit Relations* and other accounts indicate how important early European influence was in this area. I do not think it is necessary to review the argument that one result of this influence was the development of the so-called "family hunting territory," which represented the "successful" acculturation phase of Indian history.

Currently the historical perspective of the New World takes better account of very early European-aboriginal contacts, and, as the archaeological record has unfolded, a fuller sense of pre-contact complexities has developed. Previously there was a vague notion that the aboriginal societies which we painfully attempt to reconstruct had existed for untold generations as more or less stable entities. Scholars now take a second look at the possible pre-European influences of more complex cultures on simpler ones, and there is greater sensitivity to the ebb and flow of culture histories as changing ecological conditions affected subsistence patterns, population density, and movement.

As for evolution, today there is no longer great interest in arguing "evolution" versus "history", though there are, of course, many different phrasings of the relationship between the two and a consensus does not exist. I do not know how many of us here today would see "evolution" as referring to basic and general historical processes, which, when expressed in theoretical terms, enable us more easily to interpret sequences of individual and unique events. In any case, central to evolutionary theory, as is generally understood, is a statement of the relationship between economic arrangements and other aspects of society. Up to a point, such a relationship is widely accepted as important; that is, there is fair agreement that the economy sets obvious limits on possible social developments. For example, under unusually favourable circumstances, hunting-gathering-fishing societies can reach a greater degree of complexity than simple agricultural societies, but I doubt if one would argue that they could equal the potential opened up by agriculture, and achieve urbanization. Or, as another instance, some may still want to call status differences in pre-urban societies "classes," but I believe no one now disputes that such "classes" are different from classes in urban society.

The argument begins when the economy is understood not just to limit, but also to determine various aspects of social organization. I do not want to introduce a spurious argument about a partly semantic matter, because of course, limitation is necessarily determination of a sort, and determination can only be determining limits. However, the issue is one of degree, and of how actively and specifically the economy influences other parts of culture. The concept of determination implies a strong active influence, but it definitely need not imply a mechanically narrow influence, and it certainly should not imply a one-way influence. Deterministic theories based purely on productivity fail to give proper consideration to the relationship established among the members of a society by the form of productive work. On the other hand, non-evolutionary ecological arguments, although they seem to take these relationships into account, can also neglect them. Speck argues that the "family hunting territory" resulted from the nature of game available in the forested area below the Height of the Land in Labrador compared to that found to the north. This is an ecological argument in the narrow sense.

The relationship between the economy and the rest of the society is often discussed in terms of "stages," or significantly different types of production techniques, economic arrangements, and related social and political forms. In using the concept, it is important to avoid too static an implication; that is, an over-emphasis on the relative equilibrium achieved at each "level of integration," at the expense of a dialectical orientation toward conflicting tendencies that lead to a major or revolutionary reintegration. An evolutionary approach generally implies the qualitative leap of Marxian-Hegelian dialectics, thought this is not often explicitly stated. From an evolutionary point of view, social development does not simply involve a series of cumulative changes. Instead, there is the point at which a real transformation is effected, and something qualitatively different has developed.

The theoretical problem, which we are discussing in this chapter, is to define the nature of band organization. One aspect is the question of what is intrinsic to the hunting-gathering "stage." Service's statement concerning the limits ordinarily set by a hunting-gathering technology expresses, I think, virtual consensus about what can readily be observed, although there would doubtless be arguments about one or another specific aspect of his formulation:

> . . . there are no special economic groups or special productive units such as guilds or factories, no specialized occupational groups, no economic institutions such as markets, no special consuming groups or classes. The economy, in short, is not separately institutionalized, but remains merely an aspect of kinship organization; in the usual modern sense of the word, there is no formal economy at all.
>
> The same is true of other cultural functions. There is no separate political life and no government or legal system about the modest informal authority of family heads and ephemeral leaders. Likewise, there is no religious organization standing apart from family and band; and the congregation is the camp itself.
>
> The fact that the family and band are simultaneously the sole economic, political and religious organization greatly influences the character of these activities. The economy, polity, and ideology of the culture of bands is unprofessionalized and unformalized; in short, it is familistic only.[3]

Thus, it is clear what band organization is not. It does not include specialization of labour beyond that based on sex, nor include class divisions, a formal priesthood, or hierarchical political organization. In addition, basic sources of livelihood are not privately owned. More problematic is the question of what band organization *is*. A well worked out statement is needed to describe how relationships function in the hunting collective in their own right as well as how they contrast with institutions of urban society. Hickerson[4] makes such a statement when he points out that distribution of food is a right, not an obligation (our concept), among simple peoples, and is valued as such.

Service stresses that the custom by which a man is expected to marry outside his own band and the wife is expected to reside in the domicile of her husband (exogamous patrilocality), is basic to band organization. He writes, "The most significant rules among patrilocal bands are *reciprocal band exogamy* and the associated *virilocal* [*patrilocal*] *marital residence* mode, for it is these that create the patrilocal structure of the band."[5] Later he elaborates,

> Both the internal structure of each band and the external associations among certain bands are created by rules of exogamy and virilocal residence. A "natural" biological group is amorphous except for the dominance hierarchy, sexual pairs, if any, and mother-child dyads. However, once reciprocal virilocal marriage exchanges between two such groups have become modal for more than one generation then the relations between the two groups have a character invested with new, cultural, determinants. The simplest is the common moiety arrangement of two, or often several groups arranged as two sides which intermarry. . . .[6]

Service re-evaluates material on those bands Steward considered to be either "composite"—the Algonkians, Athabascans, Andamanese, and Yahgan—or at the "family level of integration"—the Basin Shoshone and Eskimo. He argues that all were originally structured around patrilocal exogamous units. Service writes that in a hunting-gathering society "a woman is a more 'liquid asset' in a band than is a male" and "the fraternity of males is the unit of most solidarity."[7] "Virilocality is expectable," he feels, "because of the importance of the solidarity of the males in hunting, sharing game, and particularly offense-defense. This necessity could be expected to continue from early to late times, until the epoch of modern acculturation."[8] Thus, "all the people are each a part of their *father's* group, not the mother's; she remains in some sense an outsider, particularly in the early years of the marriage."[9]

In the Labrador area, however, in no case, early or late, is there evidence for this relatively permanent core of related males who are joined by outside females. There are no suggestions that the wife is required to join the band of her husband, and, until quite recently, this was not even predominant. Nonetheless, this is an area where hunting was of overwhelming importance, and an area where pressure from the Iroquois to the south, and against the Inuit on the east Labrador coast and the north shore of the lower St. Lawrence River, was important from the early post-contact period. Groupings related through men have been strengthened, as I have documented elsewhere,[10] while early records, especially the *Jesuit Relations*, supply rich evidence for the prior importance of ties through the mother. One finds reference to the husband going to live with the wife's group (matrilocality) as the ideal pattern for the Innu,[11] and reference also to inheritance by the sister's son,[12] as well as many instances where a man either lives with or close to his wife's father.[13] The closeness of bonds with a son-in-law is revealed in LeJeune's account of a dying man who is being cared for by the Jesuits. The man's wife, "his children, his son-in-law, his friends, and his fellow-savages, his Manitousiouets, sorcerers, or jugglers" all try to make him come away with them. When he persistently refuses, it is a son-in-law who stays with him until his death.[14] References to the role of women show them to be extremely important in decision making,[15] and they sometimes join a hunt.[16]

Long after the fur trade and other external pressures toward the patrilineal "family hunting territory" were introduced, matrilocality remained important in the area. Speck refers a number of times to the prevalence of father-in-law ties and shows at least half of Mistassini trapping partnerships to be of this type.[17] In Southeastern Labrador, where the "hunting territory" system had not yet been established by 1950, one could document a marked shift from prevalent matrilocal band exogamy toward band endogamy and a greater proportion of patrilineally structured hunting partnerships. For instance, there was only one family at Natashquan whose male members had been born there, and although this was seen as a natural course of affairs, it was one that was changing since the younger generation no longer moved away to marry.

Any suggestion that patrilocality (in which the wife goes to live with the husband's group) increases individual efficiency in hunting economy, because a man works in an area he has known from childhood, is contradicted by evidence from Labrador. This had been another argument for patrilocality. Much travelling about and moving from one band to another has been noted, first by the Jesuits and, in fact, by all recorders of Indian life. There is every indication that this movement is old, and is well established. Changes in trading post locations, the intrusion of white trappers and settlers, and the depletion of game have caused shifts in the general distribution of the population, and, in post-contact times, in the yearly cycle. However, the attitudes expressed by my informants about individual movements do not indicate that this is disrupting what were formerly stable groups. Instead, there is a feeling of constantly increasing restrictions, the most recent being against band exogamy which is directly discouraged by trading post officials and missionaries, and indirectly influenced by other factors.

Mathieu Medikabo, a man of 60, spoke of the time when the whole south-eastern area was "one hunt," with St. Augustine, Musquaro, and Natashquan people crossing over the Height of Land to descend to Northwest River in mid-winter. Now there are too many white people. Mathieu's father had crossed over to hunt in Newfoundland one year; he had found good hunting, but the area had then become subject to "a different government" and it was no longer possible to go there. Mathieu himself had hunted at Musquaro until his first wife died and had lived at Natashquan about twenty years when I worked with him in 1950. His prodigious knowledge of the area is shown by one of the sketch maps he drew for me. (The only map I had at the time left the Labrador interior one large blank!) The territory it covered is roughly 40,000 square miles, yet this map did not exhaust Mathieu's knowledge, for at different times he would select different smaller stream and pond systems to draw in further detail, according to the topic of our discussion.

Although Mathieu Medikabo's familiarity with his environs encompassed in great detail the territory hunted by about forty men in two bands, it seemed to represent fairly standard knowledge for the older generation with whom I worked. A moment's reflection will make clear how important such knowledge was for survival in the north country. Familiarity with only one area is far too limiting, whereas intimate knowledge about animal habits in relation to types of terrain applies widely and affords a large number of alternative choices for hunting, and greater flexibility of response to changes in the animal population, and to various intra- and inter-group relations. As one informant put it, "everyone Indian, no like'em this one, going to hunt the other one."[18]

In summary, there is no evidence for patrilocality as an organizing principle in Labrador. Instead, the evidence favours matrilocality. However, as early as 1632, patrilocal as well as matrilocal tent groups were described by the Jesuits. Was this the result of male-oriented trading ties and the disruption resulting from the Iroquois invasions, or did the exigencies of life in the north woods, with its extremely low population density, always call for the "expediency" (mentioned by Service as a later consideration) that did not allow a rigid system to be maintained? There is little question about exogamy being the former practice. It persisted until recent times in southeastern Labrador[19] and characterized the even more remote Barren Ground and Davis Inlet Bands as they were when Strong worked with them in 1927–28.[20] Information regarding the exogamous unit is, however, lacking for the earlier period. This brings us back to the original question: what was the structure of the Innu band?

There is no doubt that the large and loosely organized "composite" band, comprised of relatively independent nuclear families first described in detail by Speck, is a recent phenomenon that followed the dependence of the Innu on the fur trade.[21] Earlier groupings in southwestern Labrador, described by the Jesuits in the 17th century, represented seasonal fluctuations in the number of people who could gather at different times of the year. They were of four types, or orders of magnitude:

(1) the multi-family group inhabiting one lodge or "cabin";
(2) several such groups forming a co-operating unit most of the year;
(3) the named group usually referred to as the "band", which consists of two or more of the previous groupings inhabiting the same roughly defined territory and uniting, or trying to, for short periods, during the summer at the St. Lawrence coast or some large interior lake; and
(4) the gathering of people from several such "bands".

It is the relationship between the second and third types of groups, with respect to exogamous units and post-contact changes, that is both the most pertinent and the least clear. For over 350 years the size, composition, and location of the third and fourth categories have increasingly been determined by the location of missions and trading posts, while the first two have been undercut by the individualizing effects of fur trapping and trading. The relation between the second and third categories is further obscured by the fact that some of the named groups considered to be in category three were perhaps originally in category four. Examples of seventeenth century references to the four groupings follow.

The multi-family lodge group (10 to 20 Innu). One point is clear: the basic socio-economic unit was not the nuclear family but the multi-family group inhabiting a lodge, although the breaking away of individual families apparently began early in cases where Indians attached themselves to missions or trading posts. The Jesuits referred to "large cabins" that contained "a number of men, women and children." In a few instances the number of people in such lodges was given. LeJeune reported ten, sixteen, and nineteen in the "cabins" in which he wintered in 1632-33. In each there were several mature hunters.[23] There is a later reference (1673) to thirty-four persons occupying two cabins.[24] Elsewhere there is reference to the small size of the average Indian family, with two or three, rarely more than four children, in contrast to the French who may have had eight, ten or twelve children.[25] In isolated areas, the multi-family lodge persisted until late. In 1905, Wallace met a group of Indians on the George River, including 11 adult males, who lived in two "wigwams," with three fires in the larger one. These Indians, he said, "had not accustomed themselves to the use of flour, sugar, and other of the simplest luxuries of civilization and their food was almost wholly flesh, fish, and berries."[26]

The aggregate of several lodge groups, or the winter band (35 to 75 Innu). In the fall, several lodge groups left the shore together to go inland. Usually by late December they were forced to separate to hunt over a wider area, remaining close enough to lend mutual aid. LeJeune's group of thirty-five split into two on December 24, and when Druilletes went inland in 1647 with a party of fifty, they divided around Christmas time.[27] In February 1670, Albenal, travelling with a group of fifteen to twenty met with a "cabin of Savages," and wrote of "two large cabins about six leagues from us."[28] Contact was also maintained among the larger groups. LeJeune referred to another camp of forty-five, a day's travel away,[29] and several times during the winter other Indians came to them for help. In the case of Druilletes, four cabins came from another quarter, where they had been starving.[30]

The account of Crespieul's winter in 1763 in the Lake St. John area illustrates the network of expanding and contracting Indian encampments spread through the north woods. Setting out in late September, Crespieul first stayed with "five cabins" of Papinachois. He then met a large encampment awaiting him at Chicoutimi. He ascended to the interior with "six canoes," or about twenty-five to thirty Indians who were joined by "four families" of Outabitibees. "All together we entered the woods, to seek our livelihood and to meet a great number of Savages who were to come down in the spring." He spent November with "two cabins" of thirty-four persons, and, before setting off for Hudson Bay, he visited Albenal, who was staying with "four cabins" of Indians. Upon his return, he stopped with "two cabins" of Outabitibees about four miles from his original group. Crespieul returned to prepare for a journey to the Mistassini and Papinchois and revisited Albenal before leaving. In the spring there were warnings of Iroquois raiding in the area, and the Indians he was accompanying gathered and fortified themselves. Later, after making contact with a large camp, he set out for the Coast, encountering "four large cabins" on the way. He arrived back at Chicoutimi at the end of May, where many Indians awaited him.[31] In the fall of 1676, Crespieul left for Lake St. John, and spoke of "five cabins" of Indians from the area who awaited him, as well as "four families" of Algonkians from Three Rivers, and several individuals who came from the woods upon hearing of his arrival. He left on November 30 with "eight families" to "enter the forest."[32] Assuming that "family" refers to a nuclear family, the camps mentioned vary from the minimal unit of about fifteen people to groups of about seventy-five in addition to the larger numbers that temporarily gathered in warmer seasons.

There are several specific references to the size of the multi-lodge groups, which the Jesuits often referred to as "bands," using the term "tribe" or "nation" to refer to the larger aggregates. In 1646, it is reported that Indians arrived at Tadoussac "in small bands, one after another". In one case, two hundred came from a "single nation," but "these poor people, withdrawing into their forests, usually separate themselves into three bands."[33] This would indicate groups of sixty to seventy persons each. In 1642, Vimont reported that thirteen canoes, carrying about sixty Atticamegs, arrived in Sillery from their St. Maurice area.[34] Nouvel visited the Papinachois, to the east of Tadoussac, some years later. In the fall of 1662, he contacted a group of sixty-eight, who had fortified their camp because of reports that Iroquois were in the area.[35] The following spring he met a party of sixty-four at Lake Manicouagan.[36] At Sept-Iles, a mission record served a "tribe" of 150 people, the Oumamiois, who "go about in two small bands" in the winter.[37]

The named group commonly called the band (150 to upward of 300 Innu). Reference has already been made to the Oumamiois group of 150, and a "nation" of 200, the former divided into two "winter bands," the latter into three. On Druilletes's 1647 trip, he left Tadoussac with a group in eight *chaloupes*, or French open boats, and several canoes. This assemblage divided after crossing to the south shore of the St. Lawrence, and Druilletes's party of fifty left two *chaloupes* at the Coast. This would indicate a total aggregate of about two hundred. Druilletes's group returned to the shore on March 3, and by April 14 all had gathered to proceed to Tadoussac and farther up the St. Lawrence River.[38]

In 1648, the Atticamegs were reported to have arrived in "three bands," the last consisting of forty canoes, making the total considerably larger than the previously mentioned groups.[39] In 1669, toward the end of May, Albenal arrived at the place where 150 Papinachois were assembled.[40] This may or may not have comprised all Indians called Papinachois, since the following spring contact was made with a group of about the same number.[41] The next summer, he went to baptize a band on Hudson Bay, and on his return to Lake St. John he met and baptized a party of 150 Mistassini. He later met an assemblage of two hundred Indians, whose identity he did not give, and exacted a promise from them to come to Lake St. John the following year. Still later in the summer, the Mistassini band he had previously contacted arrived at Lake St. John.[42] The 1681 record refers to the very short periods during which the scattered "tribes" assembled in greater numbers. The Mistassini are mentioned gathering, but only for three weeks, at Lake Kenogami, which is located further down the Saguenay than Lake St. John "after which they separate into small bands, for fear that, by keeping together in too great numbers, they may suffer from hunger."[43]

Buteaux's trip, in the spring of 1652, illustrated that numbers came together to the extent they could. Although in this case the situation was somewhat influenced by the presence of a priest, it was doubtless similar to the older patterns. In March, Buteaux visited about forty Atticamegs, who split into two parties to make canoes. When finished, his group set out for a place where "all" were gathered arriving May 18. Several days later, the entire encampment embarked in thirty-five canoes (about 150 to 160 people), and arrived at "another assembly, about twenty-five leagues hence." Here they feasted on moose, beaver, and bear's fat, and departed for another gathering, three days away, with sixty canoes (or approximately 260 to 280 people). However, "hunger compelled this gathering to disperse."[44]

Gatherings of people from several bands (up to 1,500 Innu). Groups this large gathered at trading posts in the spring and summer. The Atticamegs, who arrived in 1648 in numbers of over three hundred, met four hundred Indians at Trois-Riviéres,[45] where a trading post had been established for some thirty years. A post had functioned at Tadoussac, farther down the St. Lawrence River, since 1599. In 1645, there were 350 hunters with their families at Tadoussac, or from 1,200 to 1,500 individuals. (This is not our estimate, but one given in the record and is in agreement with the average family size.[46]) However, this number was reduced by disease, and, in the summer of 1650, there is a reference to only eight hundred Indians having assembled.[47] It is stated in 1669 there were ordinarily 1,000 to 1,200 Indians at the post, but because of a smallpox epidemic, there were scarcely one hundred left.[48] These gatherings included people other than Innu. At Chicoutimi, up the Saguenay from Tadoussac where a post was established in 1650, Crespieul in the late 1670s, speaks of Abenaki, Inuit, and Algonkian families awaiting him, as well as people from a number of neighbouring Innu groups.[49] Though the magnitude of these encampments indicates that they were post-contact, they doubtless had some roots in old patterns of Indian trade and visiting. There is reference, for example, to reciprocal hunting visits between the Innu and Abenaki.[50]

In later times, as White settlement increasingly limited the freedom of the Indians to move about their territory, the large summer assemblages in most places became restricted in size, while in the upper St. Lawrence River area they became impossible. By the middle of the nineteenth century, the two largest gatherings reported by Hind occurred at the Mingan and Sept-Iles posts, with 500 and 350 Indians respectively. The western-most post on the St. Lawrence River, at Tadoussac, served only one hundred Indians, and settlements at other posts throughout the Labrador peninsula ranged from 75 to 250 Indians.[51]

To return to earlier groupings and their relevance to the question of aboriginal band structure: which was the exogamous unit, the smaller fall and spring band or the larger summer band? To what extent was the larger band already affected by the fur trade? Was the 150 to 200 figure, with two or three sub-bands, the earlier norm for one band, and had the Atticamegs, close to an old trading post, already increased in numbers? Buteaux's interior group grew briefly to over three hundred, but could not maintain this size for more than several days, even in the summer. Did this grouping comprise people from two bands, who habitually came together for socializing, trading, and out-marrying? Formerly these people had traded with the Hurons according to Buteaux;[52] doubtless some trade in this area was of long standing. When some Atticamegs invited one of the Jesuits to come to their country, they pointed out that tribes from farther north would be gathering at the same place.[53] Certainly peoples commingled on one another's band "territory" with great ease. There is a suggestive reference to the mission at Lake St. John where missionaries attended gatherings of the "Porcupine nations," given in the plural.[54] (Their name apparently follows from the prevalence of porcupines in the area. Such animal names, *Atticameg* or White-fish, were rapidly replaced by locality names associated with trading posts.)

The occurrence of out-marrying groups at the third level, numbering around 150, agrees well with the recently disappearing band exogamy of Eastern Labrador. In that area there were also winter hunting parties akin to the tent-groups, and traces of two band subdivisions at St. Augustine and Northwest River. There was a feeling of closeness among those contiguous bands that most commonly interchanged their members. The pattern was for people from the Natashquan, Musquaio, and St. Augustine bands to cross over the Height of Land and go down to the Northwest River for the summer, and vice versa. Similarly, the northern wing of the Northwest River band apparently formed another intermarrying and interchanging network with the Barren Ground, Davis Inlet, and other northern peoples. The Barren Ground and Davis Inlet people summered together at Indian House Lake. Apparently population was sparser in the northern barrens than in the woodlands to the south, although the extremely small size of the Barren Ground and Davis Inlet peoples, which, at the time Strong worked with them numbered 56 and 36 respectively, was the result of severe smallpox, measles, and Spanish Flu epidemics in 1918.[55]

In the absence of direct evidence, it is impossible to say whether exogamy was a binding or a preferred custom, or whether the minimal exogamous unit was a band subdivision rather than the band. Nevertheless, exogamy did obtain. In addition to its persistence in eastern and northern Labrador there was the occurrence in the northern-most bands of an institution tied in with closely linked exogamous groups; that is cross-cousin marriage, as well as the kin terms appropriate to the practice.[56] The exogamy was not patrilocal, but matrilocal in emphasis, though how absolute this was remains a further question. In any case, to leave the matter at this, and simply substitute matrilocal exogamy for patrilocal exogamy as the organizing principles of Labrador band life, is not sufficient. There is the need, mentioned above, for a fuller description of means whereby effective co-operative units are maintained among such peoples. Material on life in the north woods suggests two mechanisms that provide a beginning: complete, rather than reciprocal sharing, and a great latitude for individual choice. The first makes possible the second, and both seem essential for survival.

The stringency of life in the north woods enforces so immediate an interdependence that sharing is a more total "spontaneous" or "unstructured" affair than the regulated reciprocity generally obtained in more settled societies. Starvation is a constantly recurring threat, though usually a fairly localized one, and people do not hesitate to turn to others for help. The Jesuits marvelled at the unstinting and unhesitating way Indians who were themselves in trouble shared with others who were in greater straits. In the hinterland it long remained unquestioned that help would always be forthcoming, even from a bitter personal enemy.[57]

It may be necessary to qualify that in speaking of "complete" sharing by hunters, it would be absurd to imply that everything, including small catches of fish or rabbits, is always shared. In making a differentiation between the sharing of game with everyone present, and sharing whatever there is available in times of trouble, on the one hand, and the reciprocal exchange of simple agriculturalists, on the other, I would not deny a long-run generalized principle of reciprocity among hunters. But the reciprocity is generalized, and the point seems to lie in the difference between sharing as enabling the dependence of anyone on anyone else, and regularized sharing as a means of equalizing the distribution of goods.

I had occasion to question one of my informants, Thomas Gregoire, about a latter day incident where he had given the last of his flour and lard to two men from a neighbouring band. This meant returning to the post sooner than he had planned, thereby reducing his possible catch of furs. I probed to see whether there was some slight annoyance or reluctance involved, or at least some expectation of a return at some later date. This was one of the very rare times Thomas lost patience with me, and he said with deep, if suppressed anger, "Suppose now, not give them flour, lard—just dead inside." The finality of his tone and the inference of my utter inhumanity in raising questions about his action were more revealing than the incident itself.

With regard to latitude for individual choice, flexibility in the movements of individuals and groups seems indicated from earliest times, with a constant shuffling and reshuffling of personnel to serve several purposes, namely: (1) the sensible distribution of the population through the hunting area; (2) the balanced age and sex composition of any group; (3) another aspect of the second point, the re-forming of groups in cases of starvation; and (4) the allowance of sufficient choice so that the tent groups, thrown so closely together for such long periods, could be as congenial as possible. (The Jesuits commented on how remarkably well groups lived and worked together, but LeJeune also commented on the deep grudges that occasionally were held.)

The question is whether this movement of families is a "breaking down" of formerly more stable groups, or simply an "expedient" response to new conditions, different in its specific content, but not in form, from the "expediency" always required. In eastern Labrador, moving about is considered desirable, whether to find a spouse, to be with a loved relative or friend, or simply to get to know a new territory. Moves are phrased as matters of individual choice, and friendship is important in determining hunting partners.

Patterns of marriage show the formation and re-formation of congenial groups, with weddings of brother and sister pairs, or parent-child pairs (such as a widowed mother and a son marrying into another band at the same time) as common occurrences. As an example of family moving practices, Mathieu Medikabo, the map-maker, came to Natashquan at the same time as his step-sister. She "married Natashquan," a patrilocal move when considered by itself, yet with her came not only her mother, brother, and step-brother, all widowed and with marriage in mind, but also her sister and sister's husband and children!

Whether such flexibility was or was not pre-Columbian has important implications for our problem of determining what is intrinsic to the social organization of foraging peoples. More is known about the upper limits of hunting and gathering economies where the predictability, accessibility, and sufficiency of food resources are roughly equivalent to that provided by early agriculture, than is known about the lower limits. While it is agreed that the principle of exogamy is essential, limiting as it does competitiveness within closely co-operating groups, the question is how loosely this practice can operate in relation to post-marital residence and the permanence of band affiliation. I have suggested that there are good reasons for tolerating far more ambiguities in the uncertain north woods than is possible for people with larger more permanent residence groups who rely on clear unilineally defined and mutually exclusive divisions of the population for handling socio-economic relations, and who marry out of the kin group, but not necessarily out of the local group.

However, the exogamy, cross-cousin marriage, and related terminology of eastern and northern Labrador raise the question: are these remnants of formerly existing clans? A similar question is raised by the uneven distribution of matrilineality (descent through the female line), cross-cousin marriage, and exogamy among Athabascans in British Columbia and the Yukon. Are they the result of Northwest Coast influence, as is generally felt, or evidence of a previously more formal level of organization throughout Canada? Or, to return to Labrador, do cross-cousin marriage and exogamy represent "incipient" clan organization, socially desirably alternatives which provide the basis for clans? In this discussion of cross-cousin marriage among Algonkians generally, Eggan points out that its essence is to "create multiple bonds between a limited group of relatives and maintain these from generation to generation, rather than tying nonrelatives together in an expanding system."[58] He goes on to say this form of residence tends to intensify local relationships at the expense of cross-group ties. However, when combined with local group exogamy, it strengthens both internal and external ties, just as the fully developed clan does. Should further ethnohistorical, archaeological, and linguistic research happily combine to clarify the nature of pre-Columbian social organization among native Canadian hunters, the question would still remain: where do they stand in their historical relation to hunting-gathering societies in other parts of the world? The Athabascan and Algonkian hunters, who inhabit the vast interior of North America, far from the centres of higher culture, provide excellent candidates for "pure" marginal cultures. There is, at best, limited influence from settled peoples on their peripheries; there seems to be nothing indicating an earlier horizon of denser population like that in the Inuit area; nor were they pushed into marginal regions by advancing higher cultures in the same sense, say, as the once widespread Bushmen. Furthermore, the extreme marginality of the north woods economy, with starvation periods as a recurring danger, contrasts even with that of the Kalahari Desert. The Bushmen may have to tighten their belts in the dry season and forgo having as much meat as they would like, but they can rely on the vegetable foods which form the greater part of their diet. Certainly the uniquely elaborated definition of marriageable partners among the Australians was made possible by the relative dependability, predictability, and stability of the major part of their food supply, in contrast to the uncertainty of weather conditions and animal movements and distribution in the north.

At first, the marginality of the native Canadian hunters might seem to make them good models for more "primitive" or "earlier" forms of social organization. Yet a moment's thought makes it clear that this is not the case. Their extreme dependence on meat, albeit supplemented by fish, and, in the short summer, some vegetable food, represents a late and specialized adaptation in the evolution of man, so far as we can tell from our present knowledge. Thus, from the long historic view, we cannot say that the ancient forbears of today's Canadian hunters did not have more formal organizational patterns adapted to a more sedentary foraging-hunting economy, patterns which were lost in adjusting to northern conditions, either in the Old or the New World.

Although we may conclude with more questions than answers about Innu band organization, some things can be said with certainty. I have spoken of the wide latitude afforded the individual for choice of movement and group affiliation, and have suggested it is not a recent breaking down of a structure but an old adaptive pattern that takes place within a structure, one that, in fact, enables the structure to exist. (Indeed, it is not so different in kind, although perhaps in degree, from the flexibility found among hunting-gathering peoples generally, a good example of which is given by Hart and Pilling's discussion of the Australian Tiwi.[60]) In any case, it is far from a simple matter. Albeit maddening to the field worker in its lack of formal definition, it involves a highly sophisticated process of evaluating population composition and territorial resources, and making one's choices both in relation to them and to personal preferences of oneself and others. This much, at least, is very clear: the "individualism" this both necessitates and enables is far from the "atomism" said to characterize the north-eastern Algonkians. Seventeenth century material reveals that minimal units consisted of not one, but several nuclear families, that several such units co-operated closely much of the year, and that these larger groupings joined with others in a constantly fluctuating cycle of seasonal movement, aggregation and separation. Recent field studies indicate that in-group cohesion and out-group ties are strengthened by exogamy and a tendency to cross-cousin marriage, and both early and late data indicate a strong matrilocal emphasis. This is the structure within which individual decisions are made. If their range is wide, it is necessitated by the conditions of north woods life and is only made possible by complete interdependence or the "total" sharing of available resources.

Notes

Source: "The Montagnais-Naskapi Band," in *Contributions to Anthropology Band Societies*, edited by David Damas (Anthropological Series, No. 84, National Museums of Canada), 1969, 1–17. Reprinted by permission of the author and publisher.

1. The Algonkians of Labrador call themselves Innu, just as their congeners in Northern Quebec are Cree.
2. R.G. Thwaites, ed., *The Jesuit Relations and Allied Documents,* vol. IV (Cleveland: Burrows Bros., 1906), 207.
3. F.R. Service, *Primitive Social Organization, an Evolutionary Perspective* (New York: Random House, 1962), 108–109.
4. H. Hickerson, "Some Implications of the Theory of the Particularity, or Atomism, of Northern Algonkians," *Current Anthropology*, vol. 8, no. 2 (1967), 313–43.
5. Service, *Primitive Social Organization*, 66–67.
6. *Ibid.*, 69.
7. *Ibid.*, 49–50.
8. *Ibid.*, 67.
9. *Ibid.*, 69.
10. E. Leacock, "Matrilocality in a Simple Hunting Economy (Montagnais-Naskapi)," *Southwestern Journal of Anthropology* (1955), 31–47.
11. Thwaites, *Jesuit Relations*, vol. XXX, 169.
12. *Ibid.*, vol. VI, 255.
13. *Ibid.*, vol. V, 163, 33; vol. XIV, 143–45; vol. XVI. 49; vol. XXXI, 149; vol. LVI. 151.
14. *Ibid.*, vol. VI, 125.
15. *Ibid.*, vol. VII, 61; vol. XIV, 183.
16. *Ibid.*, vol. II, 77.
17. F.G. Speck, "Social Structure of the Northern Algonkian," *Publications of the American Sociological Society* (1917):91, 97–98; F.G. Speck, "Mistassini Hunting Territories in the Labrador Peninsula," *American Anthropologist* 25 (1923):462; F.G. Speck, "Family Hunting Territories of the Lake St. John Montagnais and Neighboring Bands," *Anthropos* 22 (1927):392.
18. From the author's field notes.
19. Leacock, "Matrilocality," 35–36.
20. W.D. Strong, "Labrador Winter," unpublished manuscript.
21. E. Leacock, *The Montagnais "Hunting Territory" and the Fur Trade*, Memoir No. 78 of the American Anthropological Association (1954), 19–23.
22. Thwaites, *Jesuit Relations*, vol. V, 105.
23. *Ibid.*, vol. VII, 121.
24. *Ibid.*, vol. LIX, 31.
25. *Ibid.*, vol. LII, 49.
26. D. Wallace, *The Long Labrador Trail* (New York: Outing Publishing Co., 1907), 135–36.
27. Thwaites, *Jesuit Relations*, vol. XXXII, 269.
28. *Ibid.*, vol. LIII, 73.
29. *Ibid.*, vol. VII, 121.

30. *Ibid.*, vol. XXXII, 271.
31. *Ibid.*, vol. LIX, 27–47.
32. *Ibid.*, vol. LX, 247.
33. *Ibid.*, vol. XXIX, 139–41.
34. *Ibid.*, vol. XXIV, 67.
35. *Ibid.*, vol. XLVIII, 279.
36. *Ibid.*, vol. XLIX, 49.
37. *Ibid.*, vol. LIX, 57–59.
38. *Ibid.*, vol. XXXII, 259–73.
39. *Ibid.*, 283.
40. *Ibid.*, vol. LII, 85.
41. *Ibid.*, vol. LIII, 85.
42. *Ibid.*, vol. LVI, 207–11.
43. *Ibid.*, vol. LXII, 221–23.
44. *Ibid.*, vol. XXXVII, 19–63.
45. *Ibid.*, vol. XXII, 283.
46. *Ibid.*, vol. XXIX, 123.
47. *Ibid.*, vol. XXXVI, 223.
48. *Ibid.*, vol. LII, 85.
49. *Ibid.*, vol. LX, 245; vol. LXI, 85–87.
50. *Ibid.*, vol. XII, 187.
51. H.Y. Hing, *Explorations in the Interior of the Labrador Peninsula* (London: Longman, Green and Co., 1863), 117.
52. Thwaites, *Jesuit Relations*, vol. XXXVI, 65.
53. *Ibid.*, vol. XXXVII, 139.
54. *Ibid.*, vol. XXXVII, 211.
55. Strong, "Labrador Winter."
56. W.D. Strong, "Cross-Cousin Marriage and the Culture of the Northeastern Algonkian," *American Anthropologist* 31 (1929).
57. J. Lips, "Public Opinion and Mutual Assistance Among the Montagnais-Naskapi," *American Anthropologist*, 39 (1937):222–27.
58. F.Eggan, ed., *Social Anthropology of North American Tribes* (Chicago: University of Chicago Press, 1955), 532.
59. C.W.M. Hart and A.R. Pilling, *The Tiwi of North Australia* (New York: Holt, Rinehart and Winston, 1962).

Chapter 8
The Home Guard Cree and the Hudson's Bay Company: The First Hundred Years

J.E. Foster

Prior to James Walker's timely and devastating criticism of Canadian historians' treatment of the Indian in his article, "The Indian in Canadian Historical Writing," the Indian rarely elicited much attention from historians.[1] On the infrequent occasions when historians showed some scholarly interest, the focus of their attention centered on the nature of the relationship between the European and the Indian. (Their methodology, if not their interests, ensured such an orientation.) In what was Rupert's Land in the eighteenth century, historians emphasized the peaceful nature of the relationship between the Hudson's Bay Company and the Indians.[2] The remarkable feature of this *entente*, of course, was its enduring nature. With but occasional lapses into awkward incidents, the relationship that began with the voyage of the *Nonsuch* extended to the surrender of the Company's territories to the Canadian Government. To explain its enduring and peaceful attributes, historians have emphasized both economic and socio-political factors.

In most traditional historical works, British manufactured goods, particularly metal products, had a revolutionary impact upon the stone-age technology of the primitive Indian. Although the Indian enjoyed an improved standard of living with these products, he paid a significant price in the loss of his traditional skills. In time, he became dependent upon the fur trader,[3] which was a factor in explaining the Indians' enduring peaceful relationship with him. The other important factors contributing to the nature of the relationship were the policies of the Hudson's Bay Company's Governor and Committee in London. Occasionally ignorant of local conditions, but always honourable and well-meaning, the Governor and Committee emphasized policies that saw the Indian treated "by fayre and gentle means."[4] Similarly the officers in the field, with but few exceptions, took effective action to realize the "fayre and gentle means" as they were elaborated in directives from London.[5] Perhaps historians of a generation ago were essentially correct in identifying the economic dependence of the Indian and the "fayre and gentle" policies of the Company as the cardinal factors explaining the relationship between trader and Indian. However, more recent works in history, and the relevant social sciences, question the assumptions that underlay earlier historical works, and suggest a re-examination.[6] In this paper, the re-examination will center on the relations between the Home Guard Indians and the Hudson's Bay Company in the century prior to the Company's penetration of the interior in strength.

Until relatively recently, historians failed to distinguish between Indians in the fur trade except on the basis of tribal designations somewhat vaguely related to cultural areas. Thus in such standard works as A.S. Morton's *A History of the Canadian West to 1870–71* and H.A. Innis' *The Fur Trade in Canada*, the Home Guard Indians were not distinguished from other Indians.[7] In a more recent work of impressive scholarship, E.E. Rich's monumental study *The History of the Hudson's Bay Company, 1670–1870* in two volumes, five references were made to the Home Guards in volume one with double that number in volume two.[8] Scholars in the social sciences have also not been particularly interested in the Home Guards. Their track record, however, is superior to that of historians.[9] Thus before the Home Guards can be examined in detail, it is necessary to remove some of the obscurity that surrounds them in the historical record.

To understand the Home Guard Cree it is necessary to study Rupert's Land in the last quarter of the seventeenth century and the first three-quarters of the eighteenth century from the perspective of the fur trade. The trappers who supplied the bulk of the furs that passed through the Company's coastal factories were at a distance from Hudson Bay, extending far into the interior. Between the trapping Indians and the British trader were the "Upland" or "Foreign" Indians. These were the middlemen who controlled and, through their annual voyage to the coast, facilitated the exchange of furs for British products. On the coast, living near the Company's posts, were small bands of coastal Cree who specialized in supplying the trading posts with goods and services derived from the new world environment. These were the Home Guards. Their small furs, provisions, goods such as toboggans and snowshoes, and services as guides and couriers were significant factors contributing to the profitability of the fur trade.

The role of the Home Guard in the fur trade defined their way of life. After noting the linguistic connection between the Cree on the Saskatchewan and those on the coast of Hudson Bay, Andrew Graham wrote:

> At the Forts there are natives which we style home-guards or home-Indians, and by the trading natives Winepeg or Muchiskewarck Athinuwick, which last word signifies Indians, who are employed as hunters to supply the Forts with provisions, which is not inconsiderable, and are paid for such according to their dexterity and shooting. They also carry packets, and haul trading goods from forts to forts. They are trusted goods to the value of twenty or thirty beaver in October, when the fall goose season is over, when they go a little distance inland and traps martens, etc. Towards May they pitch in again to the forts to kill geese etc.; in the interim they pay their debts, and what furs may remain they trade for brandy, and gets merry. The number of them at one of the capital forts are from 150 to 200 men, women and children. . . .[10]

Graham continued:

> There are commonly two families of home-guards entertained at each fort (besides widows, orphans and helpless people) all the winter to hunt, go with packets, make snow-shoes etc.; and are allowed oatmeal, pease and salt meat, besides the offal and game they can kill over and above the complement charged them. . . .[11]

From Graham's description of their annual cycle of activities, it is apparent that the coastal Cree were enmeshed in the fur trade. To a significant degree their well-being was linked to that of the fur trade itself.

The historical significance of the economic dependence of the Home Guard upon the coastal factory lies as much in the views and attitudes of the participants as in the economic circumstances themselves. The question is whether the Home Guards and the British-born personnel of the post regarded the economic relationship between them in a negative or positive light. Needless to say it is virtually impossible to determine a precise Home Guard view; yet much evidence would suggest that it is possible to indicate probable responses.

From the documents it is apparent that, similar to other Indian peoples, the Home Guards selected European goods that enriched aspects of their way of life. As with all Indians, it would appear that they appreciated the portability and durability of manufactured British products. Alcohol and tobacco met an appreciative reception as well. But the coastal Cree, by virtue of their proximity to the trading post and their role in the fur trade, were in a position to profit more. Their economic relations with the trading post improved their margin of safety in terms of their survival in a harsh environment. With large supplies of both European and Country provisions, goods and services, the trading post was an inexhaustible storehouse that the Cree could draw upon when they were in need. Even the most skilled hunter could suffer a temporary setback. If word of need could be carried to a coastal factory survival was assured.

> The hungry are fed, the naked clothed, and the sick furnished with medicines, and attended by the factory surgeon; all this gratis. And if unable to purchase guns, etc. when they go from the Forts, such are delivered to them upon a promise of future payment, at the same rate as if traded with furs already produced.[12]

The Home Guards may well have played down their own economic dependence upon the British but emphasized the economic dependence of the British upon themselves. The officers and servants of the post may well have agreed with such an assessment.[13] In particular, Home Guard supplies of provisions were crucial to the operation of the coastal factories. The historian Richard Glover would possibly challenge such a statement. In his most recent works he has questioned the extent of British dependence by challenging the myth of inexpertise in new world skills of the Company's personnel in this era.[14] Glover has noted a number of British officers and servants skilled in trapping, hunting, and fishing, as well as in the use of the canoe and snowshoes. However, using these individuals in such tasks was unprofitable at critical times of the year. During the leisurely months of winter, officers and servants skilled in the ways of the new world could supply important amounts of furs and provisions to the factory's storehouse and larder.[15] But at other times participation in such activities was not only unprofitable, but impossible. The brief summer season, opening with the arrival of the Upland Indians and closing with the departure of the annual supply ship, strained the personnel resources of the coastal factories, often to the point of collapse.[16] If the necessary quantity of country provisions were to be obtained, the Home Guard Cree had to conduct the spring and autumn goose and caribou hunts. In addition, their offerings of small furs were of significant interest to the officers in charge of the coastal factories.[17] On balance, it is probable that the personnel of the Company's posts were not dependent upon the Home Guard for physical survival. But they would know that, in a major way, the pleasantness of their stay in Rupert's Land was dependent upon the Guard fulfilling their role in the fur trade. Such an understanding would also not be lost on the Home Guard.

No evidence to date clearly indicates that the Home Guard negatively assessed their economic relationship with the trading post. Some documents suggest that the consumption of liquor probably should have been a concern to the coastal Cree.[18] Glover, however, would suggest that Home Guard practices with liquor were not significantly different from practices in Great Britain at the time.[19] While this is a useful perspective to keep in mind, it is necessary to note that a contemporary British observer was moved to comment critically:

> The English brandy [kills] . . . many of them before the young ones grow to maturity. Indeed they are so degenerated as scarcely to be able to endure their native labours and climate.[20]

Perhaps more critical questions to be asked than the amount of alcohol consumed would be the question of the amount of time devoted to the pursuit of goods and furs to trade for liquor, and the amount of resources, both fur and provisions, directed toward the purchase of liquor. While some British observers viewed the situation negatively, there is no evidence that would suggest that the Home Guards would have agreed.

There seems little doubt that the Home Guard would evaluate the trading post in positive terms, particularly in respect to its role as a storehouse of provisions and goods. But unknown to them at the time, they may have been paying a sizeable price for the benefits derived from the fur trade. The price, of course, was the reduction of their fur and provision resources to the point where they would no longer support the population. Such an experience awaited the woodland tribes of the interior in the early decades of the nineteenth century: intense trapping, stimulated by the fur trade competition, joined with natural calamities to deplete resources.[21] Such an experience, however, had not occurred among the Home Guard before 1770. Momentary times of crisis occurred when the spring and autumn goose hunt failed;[22] but survival through a hard year, with extensive support and encouragement from the Company, was often followed by a good year.[23] If the coastal Cree were making significant inroads into their resources, neither they nor the Company were aware of it in the years before the Company's penetration of the interior.

Population figures further suggest a probability that the Home Guards viewed their circumstances in a postive rather than a negative light. Although population figures are tenuous at best, learned "guestimates" indicate a slow but steady increase in population over the years following initial contact.[24] Such figures imply not only adequate resources, but also effective exploitation of those resources. In addition, on at least one occasion, there was a significant migration from the forest interior to the coastal region of the Hudson Bay.[25] At a time when the general movement of Indian peoples was toward the West, a migration in the opposite direction is of much interest. It would indicate that, in the minds of some Indians, the circumstances of the Home Guards were superior to their own.

In essence, the economic relationship between the Home Guards and the personnel of the trading post emphasized, in the minds of the participants, not the economic dependence of either party but, the economic interdependence of both. It seems most plausible that the participants' recognition of this fact contributed substantially to their relatively peaceful relations extending over the years. In relations involving Coastal Cree and the Company, however, social relationships existed which were not primarily economic in nature. It would be stretching the limits of credibility to see economic motives predominating in a game of checkers between a British-born servant and a Home Guard hunter.[26] A similar situation exists in terms of relations between British males and Indian women. No doubt economic factors were operative, perhaps even predominant, in many relationships, particularly in their early phases. But it becomes obvious that, in time, factors of a social and perhaps political nature became determinants in some of these relationships.[27] Put simply, many of the relations involving the two peoples suggest factors other than those of an economic nature regulating behaviour.

It would appear that to understand the nature of the relationship between the Company and the Home Guard it is necessary to postulate a social system embracing the various factors regulating Indian-White relations. It would seem probable that such a system would encompass the economic relationship as well. Further the participants in such a social system would have to be able to understand its operative features. Such a situation would be impossible, at least in the early period of contact. The British-born officers and servants would view the Home Guard Cree from the perspective of British ways. If cultural differences were to lose the quality of strangeness, and the hint of threat that this entailed, adjustments had to be made. No doubt the numbers of the British-born relative to the Home Guard, and their interest in acquiring furs, were factors encouraging a "broad-minded attitude" toward the different ways of their Home Guard neighbours. In addition, it seems distinctly possible that the Home Guard took purposeful actions to reduce what they thought the other party might view as strange. Nevertheless, while much flexibility and good will may have been intended, the British view of the system regulating their relations with the Home Guard would be rooted in British ways.

What would be true of the British-born officers and servants would be equally true of the Home Guard Cree. Again, relative numbers and economic interests, and the acquisition of British products, would encourage a positive and flexible response. The Home Guard would want to remove the quality of being a stranger from the newcomer. The newcomer would have to cease being "they" and become "we" for purposes of social interaction.

In effect, two social systems would regulate social relationships on the coast of Hudson Bay. Such a situation was impossible for any period of time unless there was a compatible intertwining of the systems in key areas. In time it would be possible to blend elements of Cree and British ways. Expressed in another manner, it would, in time, become difficult to identify specific behaviour as Cree or British. If such changes reflected corresponding changes in the values and attitudes of the participants, might one not postulate a distinct socio-cultural entity on the shores of Hudson Bay?

To formulate a British view of the system that regulated social relations in the coastal factory, an understanding of the English social system in the two centuries prior to the emergence of the Industrial Revolution is helpful. Peter Laslett in his book *The World We Have Lost* postulates the patriarchal household of parents and children, master and servant, as the fundamental social system in England at this time.[28] In such a system, domestic and economic organization and function were the same.[29] The patriarch of the family was as father and employer to the other members, and they were as children and servants to him.[30] Sexual activity was restricted to the patriarch and his spouse, and denied to others.[31] Institutions of society, the law, and the church worked with varying earnestness to have practice comply with theory.[32] It would be this social system of the patriarchal households that British-born officers and servants would carry to the shores of Hudson Bay.

At first glance, the complement of a coastal factory did not fit the image of a patriarchal household. The number of men involved, and the absence of women and children, emphasized a difference. Yet the complement of the trading post was remarkably similar to that of a ship which, in turn, was but a variant of the patriarchal household.[33] The special social circumstances of the ship would appear to have led to greater precision in defining privileges and responsibilities among the different grades in the social hierarchy. Perhaps for such reasons, the image of the social world of the ship was in the minds of those who established and monitored the social world of the trading post.[34] A minor but useful example of this borrowing from the world of ships can be seen in the treatment of venereal disease. In the navy medical treatment was free except for cases of venereal complaints. In such cases, the patient was required to pay a month's wages to the surgeon.[35] Perhaps the best example of the patriarchal household, refracted through the social world of the ship, to emerge in the trading post is the means by which the society of the trading post structured and regulated its relations with Indian women.

The official policy of the Governor and Committee in London with respect to the Indians in general and the Indian women in particular, was non-fraternization.[36] Only on occasions of business should social contact occur, and only the officer-in-charge would be involved in any meaningful relationship. The ban against social contact with the Indians in general emphasized the concern of the Governor and Committee with the conducting of private trade; the ban against fraternization with Indian women emphasized the concern that the women would debauch the officers and servants, that they would consume too many provisions and trade goods, and that they would provoke unpleasant incidents between the officers and servants and the adult males of their band.[37] In a remarkably short period of time, it would appear that the personnel of the coastal factories determined that, one, Indian women would not debauch them, two, Indian women need not consume too many provisions and trade goods, and three, they need not provoke untoward incidents with their fathers and husbands. As a result, the officers evaded the letter of the official policy and instituted an unofficial policy which, nevertheless, preserved the patriarchal household. In this unofficial policy, the Governor or the officer-in-charge of the coastal factory had an Indian woman as "bedfellow."[38] She, and possibly her family, were permanent residents of the post. Other officers were permitted to entertain a lady in their apartments, but never overnight.[39] It would appear servants were expected not to undertake liaisons.[40] The recurrence of venereal complaints among them would indicate that they developed an unofficial policy of their own which the officers accepted tacitly.

A significant facet of the social relationships involving British officers and Indian women was the tendency of these relationships to move in the direction of a familial context. The careers of the mixed-blood officers Moses Norton and Charles Price Isham emphasized the paternal interest that their fathers had taken in their upbringing.[41] For many officers, it became necessary to change the context in which they placed a number of their Home Guard customers. They were no longer simply Home Guards; they were grandparents, aunts and uncles, and cousins to their mixed-blood children.[42] In such circumstances the feeding of starving Indians was no longer an act of enlightened economic self-interest; by the early years of the eighteenth century, it had become a family responsibility. This view is confirmed in the observation of Andrew Graham who noted the familial context encompassing the Home Guards:

> The Englishmen's children by Indian women are far more sprightly and active than the true born natives; their complexion fairer, light hair and most of them fine blue eyes. These esteem themselves superior to the others, and are always looked upon at the Factories as descendants of our countrymen.[43]

Graham's next sentence is most illuminating:

> The Indian parent and step-father are remarkably fond of them; and by this means receive much benefit by taking care of them when young, for they continue in the same family until they marry.[44]

The socio-cultural context from which the Home Guard Cree would view social relations with the British newcomers does not emerge with detailed clarity in the documents. Nevertheless, some materials describing the ways of the Home Guard Cree in this period permit plausible inferences. The hierarchical and authoritarian social system of the trading post would most certainly appear alien, if not ridiculous, to the coastal Cree. The lowly status of the youthful labourer must have drawn comment, particularly in the years of initial contact.[45] The power and authority of the officer-in-charge would draw comment as well.

Perhaps most important was his control of the warehouse and storehouse.[46] His ability to command men may have indicated "much medicine." Such an individual would be a valuable ally to any hunter and his immediate family. Benefits would possibly accrue to the band as well. Should such an individual express an interest in forming what could be viewed as a marriage relationship with a woman of the band, the overture would probably be welcomed.[47] An overture of this nature from a servant of much less status may well have been refused.

While the Home Guard Cree had more flexible attitudes toward what the British would term fornication and adultery, it is equally apparent that liaisons between Indian women and British officers and servants were viewed as marriages.[48] Indian males apparently expected the British to treat them in a manner appropriate to their kinship with the female. The failure to observe these social niceties, as the Europeans of the French Fort Bourbon and the first Henley House could attest, could bring swift and bloody reprisal.[49] It is apparent that, in their relations with Indian women, the British-born of the trading posts had to act in a manner consistent with the familial criteria of the Home Guard social system.

In the century following the establishment of the fur trade, the image of the social world of the coastal factories of the Hudson's Bay Company emphasizes the intertwining of two social systems. Further, it would appear that it was the familial aspects of both systems that minimized abrasive incidents and facilitated peaceful interaction. The patriarch household of England experienced significant problems in adjusting to the coastal factories. But the problems, expressed in terms of strains in the master-servant relationship, involved the Indians only minimally. In terms of relations with the Home Guards, the ways and means of the patriarchal household concept seemed to be most functional. Similarly, the perspectives of the Home Guards, which perceived relations in a kind of familial context, facilitated an enduring peaceful relationship. The familial contexts in which the participants could place their relationship ensured a vehicle for facilitating cross cultural relations. While much study remains to be accomplished, one cannot help but notice the similarity in the relationship between the Home Guard Cree and the Company in the eighteenth century, and the relationship between the Bush Indians of the West and the Company in the nineteenth century. Among other things, such relationships may offer insights into an Indian perspective in terms of the treaties signed during the 1870s.

Notes

Source: *Approaches to Native History in Canada.* Edited by D.A. Muise. National Museum of Man, History Division, Paper No. 25. Reprinted by permission of author and publisher.

1. James W. St. G. Walker, "The Indian in Canadian Historical Writing," *Historical Papers* (Canadian Historical Association, 1971). Also see "The Indian in Canadian

Historical Writing, 1972–82" in *As Long as the Sun Shines and Water Flows*, edited by I.A.L. Getty and A.S. Lussier (Vancouver: 1983).

2. Arthur S. Morton, *A History of the Canadian West to 1870*, edited by Lewis G. Thomas (Toronto: University of Toronto Press, 1973, 146, 194, 321. Morton's interpretation is cautious and scholarly. Later historians of repute have not challenged Morton's conclusion.
3. *Ibid.*, 13. The economic dependence is underlined but the relationship is placed in a positive context. E. Palmer Patterson, *The Canadian Indian: A History Since 1500* (Don Mills: 1972), 39; the negative context is emphasized.
4. E.E. Rich, *The History of the Hudson's Bay Company, 1670–1870*, vol. I (London: 1958), 145.
5. *Ibid.* All standard historical subjects are replete with examples. In addition note Glydwr Williams, ed., *Andrew Graham's Observations on Hudson's Bay, 1767–91* (London: 1969), 322.
6. For historians a particularly notable work is A.J. Ray, *The Indian in the Fur Trade, 1660–1870* (Toronto: 1974).
7. See Morton, *Canadian West*, 933, for traditional historical sources on the Indians.
8. Rich was one of the first historians to perceive an Indian perspective on a sophisticated level. See E.E. Rich, "Trade Habits and Economic Motivation among the Indians of North America," *Canadian Journal of Economics and Political Science* XXVI (1960). Reprinted with brief introductory remarks as "The Indian Traders," *The Beaver* (Winter 1970).
9. See Ray, *Indians in the Fur Trade.*
10. Williams, *Graham's Observations*, 192.
11. *Ibid.*
12. *Ibid.*, 327.
13. *Ibid.*, 281.
14. K.G. Davies, ed., *Letters from Hudson's Bay, 1703–40* (London: 1965), Introduction by Richard Glover, xvii.
15. *Ibid.*, xviii–xxi.
16. *Ibid.*, 28, 40, indicate the problems the post's complement experienced at shipping time.
17. *Ibid.*, 80.
18. Williams, *Graham's Observations*, 152, 155, 156.
19. *Ibid.*, xxxix.
20. *Ibid.*, 192.
21. Ray, "Chapter Six", *Indians in the Fur Trade.*
22. Davies, *Letters*, 80.
23. *Ibid.*, 87. The year following the failure of the goose hunt at Albany Fort, Richard Staunton mentioned no difficulties in his annual letter to Governor and Committee.
24. Compare population figures in Williams, *Graham's Observations*, 192, 330, with Charles A. Bishop, "Ojibwa, Cree, and the Hudson's Bay Company in Northern Ontario: Culture and Conflict in the Eighteenth Century," in *Western Canada Past and Present*, edited by A.W. Rasporich (Calgary: 1975).
25. Williams, *Graham's Obersvations*, 281.
26. *Ibid.*, 168.
27. Davies, *Letters*, 292, suggests a situation which would be defined as prostitution in a British context. Williams, *Graham's Observations*, 145, however, indicates behaviour which could be construed as affection.
28. Peter Laslett, *The World We Have Lost* (London: 1971), 2.
29. *Ibid.*
30. *Ibid.*
31. *Ibid.*, 3.

32. *Ibid.*
33. *Ibid.*, 11.
34. Davies, *Letters*, xxiii.
35. *Ibid.*, 247.
36. Williams, *Graham's Observations*, 248.
37. Rich, *Hudson's Bay Company* 102; and Morton, *Canadian West*, 129.
38. Williams, *Graham's Observations*, 248.
39. *Ibid.*
40. The numerous efforts to restrict liaisons between servants and Indian women may well reflect a fear of a "family" emerging. A servant as a "patriarch of a household" was difficult to incorporate into the trading post social structure.
41. Williams, *Graham's Observations*, 145.
42. *Ibid.*
43. *Ibid.*
44. *Ibid.*
45. *Ibid.*, 262.
46. *Ibid.*, 263.
47. Needless to say Philip Turnor's famous explanation or rationalization is of interest here. See J.B. Tyrrell, ed., *Journal of Samuel Hearne and Philip Turnor* (Toronto: 1934), 593.
48. Williams, *Graham's Observations*, 157, 175, 176.
49. Morton, *Canadian West*, 129, 253.

PART III
The Prairies

Scholars have argued that a single society may operate with more than one mode of production. Thus, we may see elements of feudal, capitalist, even foraging modes of production in combination within a single social formation. If there ever were a people to whom this applies, it is surely the Métis of the Red River Settlement before Confederation. It is difficult to think of the settlement during those times without also picturing the battalion of voyageurs, drovers, fur company servants, and small farmers, who embarked each summer with their Red River carts on the annual buffalo hunt. This picture, however evocative, is nevertheless incomplete. Remember also the classic archival picture of Louis Riel with his provisional government: a dozen men wearing neckties, stiff collars, and what we would now call three-piece suits. These were the mill owners, free fur traders, and organizers of the cart trade to St. Paul, Minnesota. As for the buffalo hunters, their slogan was, "Divide while anything remains, and beg while all is done" (cited in Sprenger's chapter, "The Métis Nation"). The entrepreneurs were four-square against the Hudson's Bay Company's monopoly while it lasted, but perhaps not united on much else. (This is a touchy point, and not yet resolved, as Jennifer Brown shows in her contribution, "The Métis: Genesis and Rebirth.") It is a nice point whether the Settlement could be regarded as a single social formation. Indeed, it is not clear that all settlers regarded themselves as part of a unitary "New Nation," although that label finally stuck. In Part I, we examined the case of families of mixed Indian-White ancestry in the Michigan Territory at the southern end of the cart trail from the Red River Settlement. It appears that these families never came to think of themselves as a "new nation," although outsiders may have regarded them in those terms.

In this section, Jennifer Brown's contribution stresses the influence of European scholarly opinion concerning "mixed-bloods" on outsiders' perceptions of the settlement. Among the racist scholars and popular writers of the period, personality traits and even cultural institutions stemmed from racial inheritance. These might be positive, as in Henry Schoolcraft's view;[1] he had found confirmation of "the most sanguine expectations of the philanthropist, in regard to a mixed species." They might be less than positive. In either case, these prevalent views of the nineteenth century probably led others to see the Red River Settlement as a single social entity, when it was likely not so.

Furthermore, outsiders did more than spill ink over the "racial" traits of the settlers. One who could put his views into practice was George Simpson, Governor of the Hudson's Bay Company's Northern Department after 1821. Governor Simpson saw those of mixed descent as a unitary group, inheritors of unfortunate character traits, and belonging at the bottom of the social scale:

> The half-breed population is by far the most extended about the [Red River] Settlement and appear to require great good management otherwise they will become in my opinion dangerous to its peace. . . . They will not enter the [Company's] service and moreover they are not the class of people that would be desirable on any terms as they are indolent and unsteady merely fit for voyaging, under those circumstances it is necessary to watch and manage them with great care. . . .[2]

"Watch them and manage them" he did, with the result that opportunities in the Company's service became few for those of mixed descent. Soon those who might earlier have aspired to careers as officers or "gentlemen" were recruited to the Company's service only at the lowest level; and there they remained. By the 1850s about half the servants employed by the Northern Department were of mixed descent; as were very few of the Department's "gentlemen." Did this sense of narrowing horizons contribute to a growing feeling, at mid-century, of solidarity and national identity among settlers of mixed descent? Perhaps it did, but there were pulls as well as pushes toward that solidarity.

One such "pull" came from the annual buffalo hunt, described in Herman Sprenger's contribution to this section. Sprenger shows the hunts enjoyed wide participation, with over 1,200 Red River carts setting out during the hunt of 1840. Alexander Ross, a long time resident of Red River, believed that the buffalo hunt drew "into its illusive train, not only the hunters, but almost every class of our population."[4] Marcel Giraud concurs; during years of crop failure, all settlers might join in the hunts, even the winter hunts. Here is Herman Sprenger's translation of Giraud:

> In the bad years, when food was scarce in Red River, the Métis proceed in great number, if not completely to the Prairie where they often found an abundance of food. . . . In those winter camps, one not only found the most humble and poorest Métis—those who obstinately refused to make the least concession to the sedentary life. . . . The more prosperous Métis—those who had distinguished themselves by the diligence of their enterprises or who had participated in the political life of the colony—were also well represented there, all yielding to the attraction of the bison hunt as well as to actual need.[5]

Following Ross and Giraud, we begin to see what a remarkable place the Red River Colony truly was. The forager's life was quite often shared, annually perhaps, by the families of entrepreneurs. This life should have contributed to social solidarity among all those who shared it. According to Sprenger, nearly 1,700 settlers embarked on the great buffalo hunt of 1840; this would have been nearly one-third of the settlement's population, using George Stanley's figures for 1840.[6] Recall also, from Part II, that food-sharing is the touchstone of the foraging mode of production. Likely something of this mode persisted, despite some settlers working for wages, or acting as entrepreneurs. In any case, there was food-sharing, though perhaps it was misunderstood by some observers. Here Herman Sprenger cites W.L. Morton's *Manitoba: A History*:

> If the Sioux had been troublesome, or the buffalo distant and the hunt short, then before spring there was hunger in the cabins and *sometimes the charity* of the

> *wealthier and more prudent people* of Red River had to come to the *relief of the brave métis in his distress.*[7] [Author's italics]

Was this "relief," "charity," or simply food-sharing? We cannot know for a certainty, of course. We might speculate, however, that food-sharing would not look like "charity" to men who hunted together on the buffalo plains, however it might have looked to outsiders.

This was a predicament which the Métis of Red River shared with their cousins to the west, the Plains Cree; that is, much of their lives were lived out before an unsympathetic audience of outsiders who also set many of the material conditions of existence. Game laws, reserves, band lists, Indian agents: for over a century now, Canadian Indians have lived their lives hedged about with every sort of regulation and constraint, all meant to protect and "civilize" them. The provisions of various acts have served to keep Indians divided, disorganized, and apathetic, as John Tobias shows in his contribution, "Indian Reserves in Western Canada." In this we stray from adaptation in any narrow sense. Nevertheless, adaptation always means more than getting a subsistence; it also means success in social reproduction, as Tobias indicates, no mean feat.

Notes

1. Henry Rowe Schoolcraft, *Narrative Journal of Travels . . . to the Sources of the Mississippi River in the Year 1820* (1921; reprint, University Microfilms, 1966), 338.
2. Carol M. Judd, "Native Labour and Social Stratification in the Hudson's Bay Company's Northern Department, 1770–1870," *Canadian Review of Sociology and Anthropology*, vol. 17, no. 4 (1980):310.
3. *Ibid.*, 311.
4. Alexander Ross, *The Red River Settlement* (1856; reprint in facsimile, Minneapolis: Ross and Haines, 1957), 243.
5. Herman Sprenger, "The Métis Nation: Buffalo Hunting versus Agriculture in the Red River Settlement 1810–1870," in this volume, citing Marcel Giraud, *Le Métis Canadien* (Paris: Institut d'Ethnologie, 1945), 819–20.
6. George F.G. Stanley, *The Birth of Western Canada* (Toronto: University of Toronto Press, 1960), 13.
7. Sprenger, *Métis Nation*, citing William L. Morton, *Manitoba: A History* (Toronto: University of Toronto Press, 1967).

Chapter 9
The Métis Nation: Buffalo Hunting versus Agriculture in the Red River Settlement, 1810–1870

George Herman Sprenger

The Métis played an important part in the history and development of Western Canada. They are frequently mentioned in much of the literature dealing with the Old Northwest and the fur trade. Yet, in spite of their early prominence, the number of books and articles specifically concerned with the Métis people is very small. Of the works that do exist, almost all are historically oriented and provide the reader with a series of personalities, events, and dates, but little in the way of interpretation or analysis.

During the period under consideration, the early and mid-nineteenth century, the Métis lived in various parts of what is today Western Canda. Most of them, however, were concentrated in southern Manitoba and along the Manitoba-North Dakota border. Many of the Métis made their homes in the Red River Settlement in the parishes of St. Boniface, St. Vital, and St. Norbert. Others lived in St. Francois Xavier (also known as The White Horse Plain and Grantown) on the Assiniboine River some fifteen miles west of the Settlement, and in Pembina (North Dakota), just below the International Boundary line.

The Red River Settlement was located at the forks of the Red and Assiniboine Rivers (the site of the modern-day city of Winnipeg). In addition to the Métis, there were also a number of other ethnic groups who made their home in the Settlement. These were the Métis Anglaise (English-speaking half-breeds), the Kildonan Scots, and a small contingent of French Canadian settlers from Lower Canada (Quebec). The Hudson's Bay Company maintained two posts in the Settlement—Upper and Lower Fort Garry—which were the major inland administrative and supply centres for the far-flung operations of the Company in the Northwest. The Company's officials, servants, and their families lived in or near these forts. At mid-century, the total population of the Settlement was approximately 5,000. Of these, 2,500 were Métis, 1,800 were Métis Anglaise, and about 300 were Kildonan Scots. Of the two other Métis communities, St. Francois Xavier had a population of about 800, and Pembina's population is estimated to have been between 600 and 1,000.[1]

Although the Métis sustained themselves in a variety of ways, such as fishing, trapping for furs, practising small-scale agriculture, and working as wage labourers for the Hudson's Bay Company, they were first and foremost buffalo hunters. The buffalo herds were their major source of subsistence and trade goods. Every summer, and again in the fall, hundreds of Métis families with their Red River carts, horses, oxen and dogs, set out for the "buffalo plains" of North

Dakota. These buffalo hunting expeditions were carefully organized. A leader of the hunt was selected, scouts were chosen, and rules were arranged before the expedition ever set forth.

The great size of these hunting expeditions has drawn comment. Alexander Ross, a resident of the Red River Settlement writing in 1856, felt that the camp of the 1840 hunt covered an area equal to that of a "modern city." This particular expedition contained 620 men, 650 women, 360 children, and 1,210 Red River carts.[2] The artist, Paul Kane, saw a Métis hunt in the summer of 1846 and also commented on its size: "I have often witnessed an Indian buffalo hunt since, but never one on so large a scale."[3] The hunt witnessed by Kane was by no means the largest Red River hunt ever assembled.

The skill of the Métis buffalo hunters has been documented by Lewis Henry Morgan, the anthropologist who visited the Red River Settlement in the summer of 1861, who states:

> The most expert and successful buffalo hunters in America are the half breeds of Pembina, and of Selkirk Settlement around Fort Garry.[4]

Father Antoine Belcourt, a Catholic missionary who accompanied a hunt in the fall of 1845, described the hunters' expertise:

> The rapidity with which the half-breeds charge their guns is astonishing, it not being an uncommon occurrence for one of them to shoot down three buffalos in the space of an acre (arpent).[5]

Also, John McLean, an employee of the Hudson's Bay Company wrote that,

> There are no better horsemen in the world than the Red River "brûlés"; and so long as the horse keeps on his legs, the rider sticks to him.[6]

In this paper I shall attempt to demonstrate that the Métis buffalo hunters played an indispensable role in the history of the Red River Settlement and the fur trade. The importance of buffalo hunting and the fact that it was an adaptive strategy on the part of the Métis, has not been fully appreciated in the past. Most works dealing with the history of Western Canada and the fur trade depict the behaviour of the Métis as irrational, incomprehensible, and non-adaptive. George F. Stanley, for example, states that,

> the French half-breeds were indolent, thoughtless and improvident, unrestrained in their desires, restless, clannish and vain. Life held no thought of the morrow. To become the envied possessor of a new suit, rifle, or horse, they would readily deprive themselves and their families of the necessities of life.[7]

Over the years, the stereotype of the lazy, thoughtless, and improvident Métis has become so ingrained that glaring contradictions have found their way into the literature.

> *There, with pemmican packed away and with fresh meat from the last hunt*, these people enjoyed a round of social activities and waited for another season in the out-of-doors. They were an improvident people for the most part, but like their Indian kinsmen, they were devoted to their way of life.[8] [Author's italics]

Particularly incomprehensible to many writers was the fact that the Métis continued to hunt buffalo in a land that was considered by some to be an agricultural paradise. For example, John McDougall wrote in 1896:

> These were the men who owned the rich portions of Manitoba, the Portage plains, and the banks of the Assiniboine and Red Rivers; but what cared they for rich homesteads so long as buffalo could be found within five or six hundred miles? These owners of the best wheat fields in the world very often started out to the plains and were willing to take their chance of a very risky mode of life, forsooth, because they came of a hunting breed, and "blood is thicker than water". . . .[9]

And George F. Stanley:

> With few exceptions the French half-breeds were neither extensive nor successful farmers. Brought up in the open prairies they preferred the excitement of the chase to the monotony of cultivating the soil.[10]

And Finally, E.E. Rich:

> Descendants of French voyageurs and Indian women, they [the Métis] disliked steady agricultural labour even after they had ceased to roam and had settled in the colony. "Divide while anything remains, and beg when all is done" was said to the be their way of life, and their efforts at husbandry had always been feckless and destructive of the soil. . . .[11]

More specifically, the Métis, because they were hunting buffalo at seeding and harvest time, denied the labour which was necessary for agriculture to prosper.

> After the expedition starts, there is not a man-servant or maid-servant to be found in the colony. At any season but seed time and harvest time, the settlement is literally swarming with idlers; but at these urgent periods, money cannot procure them. This alone is most injurious to the agricultural class. . . .[12]

In short, according to the views of Anglo-Saxon explorers, missionaries, residents of the Old Northwest, and eminent historians of western Canada, the Métis were indolent, thoughtless, improvident, unrestrained in their desires, restless, clannish, vain, and irresponsible. They despised agriculture and their efforts at farming were always destructive of the soil. Their love of open spaces and the freedom of the hunt prevented them from becoming sensible and steady farmers. In addition, their irrational preference for the chase was in part responsible for the slow development of agriculture in the Red River Settlement.

Before one can adequately comment on the validity, or accuracy, of this assessment, the nature of agriculture and animal husbandry in the Red River Settlement, as well as the yearly food requirements of the fur trade economy, must be taken into consideration.

The Nature of Agriculture and Animal Husbandry in the Red River Settlement

Background

Before 1800, the two major fur-trading concerns, the Hudson's Bay Company and the North West Company, exploited separate areas of the fur country. The former conducted its operations primarily along the shores of Hudson's Bay, and maintained comparatively few inland posts, while the latter did almost all of its trading in the interior. During the first decade of the nineteenth century, however, the rivalry for furs became acute and the Hudson's Bay Company suffered as a result. Consequently, its Governor and Committee came to the realization that, if they were to remain competitive with the North West Company, they had to make a concentrated effort to expand their area of operation inland. If this goal was to be achieved, however, an economically feasible method of provisioning the personnel of the new posts had to be devised. The solution to this problem, it was hoped, would be found by establishing an agricultural colony in the heart of the Old Northwest.[13] A Company letter, dated 1815, explained the plan:

> The servants of the Hudson's Bay Company employed in the fur trade, have hitherto been fed with provisions exported from England. Of late years this expense has been so enormous, that it has become very desirable to try the practicality of raising provisions within the territory itself; notwithstanding the unfavourable soil and climate of the settlements immediately adjacent to Hudson's Bay, there is a great deal of fertile lands in the interior of the country, where the climate is very good and well fitted for the cultivation of grain.
>
> It would not appear probable that agriculture would be carried on with sufficient care and attention by servants in the immediate employment of the company, but by establishing independent settlers, and giving them freehold tenures of land, the company expected to obtain a certain supply of provisions at a moderate price. The company also entertained expectations of considerable eventual benefit, from the improvement of their landed property by means of agricultural settlements.
>
> With these views the company were induced, in the year 1811, to dispose of a large tract of their lands to the Earl of Selkirk, in whose hands they trusted that the experiment would be prosecuted with due attention, as the grant was made subject to adequate conditions of settlement.[14]

Quite clearly, then, the founding of the Red River Settlement was basic to the expansionist plans of the Hudson's Bay Company. From the above letter, it is obvious that the demands placed on the colonists were considerable. They had to produce provisions not only for themselves, but also for the personnel of the Hudson's Bay Company. In their efforts to meet these demands the colonists often fell short of their goal. The harsh environment coupled wih a relatively simple technological inventory placed severe limitations on agricultural productivity.

Environmental Factors

Throughout the history of the Red River Settlement, agricultural productivity was consistently hampered by a variety of natural hazards, such as droughts, locusts, frosts, floods, blackbirds, wild pigeons, mice, and mites. Serious and prolonged droughts occurred in the late 1830s, throughout the 1840s, and again in the 1860s. Locusts caused extensive damage during the years

1818 to 1822, and 1864 to 1867. Their depredations were less severe on other occasions, as in 1848 and 1857. Total or partial crop failure due to frosts is recorded at least once in every decade between 1810 and 1870 (see Table 9-1). Serious floods occurred in 1826, 1852, and 1861. Every year, a portion of the crop was lost to large numbers of blackbirds, wild pigeons and mice. The damage caused by mice was exceptionally great in 1825.[15]

In any given year, there was a strong possibility that one or several of these elements or pests would strike. They might affect the entire settlement, or only certain parts of it, in a completely unpredictable manner. To compound matters, the interplay between some of the elements worked to the detriment of the agriculturalists. A flood in the spring delayed seeding time, thereby increasing the possibility that the harvest would be damaged by frost in the fall. Similarly, drought or excessive dampness lengthened the maturation process, again subjecting the crops to the danger of a fall frost. Locusts presented a double threat: after devastating the fields in the late summer or autumn, they laid their eggs in the ground and the following spring their larvae ate the freshly sown crops.

Table 9-1 A List of Partial and Complete Crop Failures in the Red River Settlement

Year	Frost	Locusts	Drought	Other or Unspecified	Source
1813			X	X	W.L. Morton 1949: 306, fn6
1817	X			X	Selkirk Papers in A.S. Morton 1938: 20
1818		X			Stanley 1980:11
1819		X			Nute 1942:246
1820		X			West 1966:22-23; Rich 1967:250
1821				X	Nute 1942:326; West 1966:62-70
1822				X	Rich 1959:507
1823				X	Rich 1959:507
1825				X	MacEwan 1952:20; Giraud 1945:445
1826	X				Giraud 1945:640, fn6; Nute 1942:445
1832				X	Hargrave 1938:102
1836	X				Ross 1957:187-88

Table 9-1 (cont'd)

Year	Frost	Locusts	Drought	Other or Unspecified	Source
1837	X		X		Giraud 1945:778; Glueck 1965:20
1840			X		Bayley 1969:72
1844				X	Giraud 1945:836
1846				X	W.L. Morton 1967: 513, fn73; Bayley 1969:79
1847	X				W.L. Morton 1956: xxviii; Giraud 1945:836
1848		X	X		Giraud 1945:779; W.L.Morton 1956: xxviii
1850				X	Giraud 1945:837
1855	X				Giraud 1945:779
1856	X				Giraud 1945:779
1857	X	X			Giraud 1945:777-79
1861				X	A.S. Morton 1938: 37-38
1862				X	A.S. Morton 1938: 38
1863			X		A.S. Morton 1938: 38
1864		X	X		A.S. Morton 1938: 38
1865		X			A.S. Morton 1938: 38
1866	X	X		X	A.S. Morton 1938: 38
1867		X			A.S. Morton 1983: 38
1868		X			A.S. Morton 1938: 38

Technological Factors

In addition to the setbacks brought about by unfavourable environmental conditions, the productive capacity of the colonists was also handicapped by their unsophisticated, or simple, agricultural technology. Operations such as seeding, reaping, and threshing, were carried out by archaic and time-consuming methods. Seed was broadcast by hand; sickles and cradle scythes were used for reaping; threshing was done by hand flails and the trampling of animals. Before 1824, there were no ploughs in the Settlement, and only spades and hoes were used to prepare the fields. After this date, wooden ploughs with iron points and wooden mould boards, and some with iron mould boards, were introduced. These, however, were not very efficient in the thick and heavy soils of Red River.[16]

Throughout most of the history of the Red River Settlement (1812–70), the benefits of mechanized agricultural machinery, which was to revolutionize farming in the West, were not available to the colonists. Mechanical reapers and threshers reached Red River in the 1850s, but these were few in number (two reapers and eight threshers). Steel ploughs with polished steel mould boards were not introduced until 1867, and mechanical seeders arrived later still. In 1856, there was only one steam-powered flour mill. There were eighteen wind mills and nine water mills, These, however, were subject to the vagaries of nature; for example, the latter had to be shut down during the prolonged drought in the 1860s.[17]

Productivity was further offset by the lack of adequate facilities for preparation and storage. This contributed to significant losses, and affected meat and dairy products as well as cereal crops. The fungous disease smut caused problems for the colony:

> Smut in the cereal grains was a problem then as it is today. But with no smut-mills in the colony and no means of chemical control, this plant disease spread alarmingly and flour was contaminated. Threshed on ice-floors, grain was often damp and badly stored; coupled with smut, this produced flour which, on the whole, increased the popularity of pemmican.[18]

The Company attempted to provide a market for the colony, but its produce was less than satisfactory:

> . . . the Company began to buy their surplus flour, barley, butter and pease as well as the Indian corn which had earlier been sought. The quality of such produce was uneven, and the fur trade suffered (from rancid butter and dirty flour) that the colony might benefit. Simpson, anxious to buy the Company's requirements from the colony, tried to establish an alternative to the dirty "ice-barn" farmers (who threshed their wheat and kept their meat alike on the unsanitary ice-floor of their unsavoury barns) by buying the wheat in the ear and getting it milled according to the Company's specification. The remedy was not completely satisfactory, and the amount of farm produce could never be predicted from year to year.[19]

Several varieties of soft wheat, such as White Russian and Club, were grown in the Settlement. Unfortunately, none of these grains was particularly well-suited to the climate of Red River. The colonists were continually importing new strains,[20] and the flour produced from these wheats was of dubious quality. Lewis Henry Morgan was only one of many travellers who complained about Red River bread:

> The wheat may be good, and they say it is, but we saw no good bread. The flour is dark and the bread heavy. They use a good deal of unleavened bread, but it is very hard.[21]

When Red Fife, a hard spring wheat, was introduced to the Settlement, it quickly replaced the older varieties.

> It yielded well, usually matured before the fall frosts struck in the Manitoba lowlands, and gave a white smooth flour of exceptional baking strength.[22]

Red Fife, however, only reached the Settlement in 1876.[23]

Livestock

Besides horses, the colonists also raised some cattle, sheep, pigs, and chickens. Although the problems encountered here were different than those of raising crops, the end result was similarly not entirely successful. The difficulty of importing significant numbers of large hooved animals, such as cattle, sheep, and pigs, from England via Hudson Bay, or from other parts of Canada via Rainy Lake, need only be mentioned to be appreciated. Consequently, only a few animals reached the Settlement by these routes. Animals were also brought in overland from the United States to the southeast, but the length of the journey and the harshness of the terrain and climate made high casuality rates unavoidable.

In the early 1820s the first attempt to import large numbers of cattle met with failure. Two herds destined for Red River starved en route. Subsequent efforts, however, did succeed, and by 1825, there were several hundred head of cattle in the colony.[24] In 1833, a party from the Settlement purchased 1,475 sheep in Kentucky. The long and difficult journey back proved to be disastrous, for only 251 sheep actually reached Red River. The rest perished on the way.[25]

Once in the Settlement, the animals faced further hardships. Sheep and cattle could not be wintered on the range. Wolves, wild dogs, and long and cold winters severely depleted their numbers. As a result, the animals had to be sheltered and fed over the winter months. This, surprisingly enough, led to further difficulties: wild hay, which was the staple fodder for the winter, was often in short supply, especially during the years of drought or when prairie fires had swept across the nearby plains.[26]

By 1849, although the absolute numbers of sheep and cattle stood at 3,096 and 6,014 respectively, they did not constitute a secure economic base, since the population of the Settlement itself was by that time over 5,000. Indeed, cattle were still being imported in an effort to improve quality as well as quantity, and the numbers of sheep actually declined in subsequent years.[27]

Consequences

The "carrying capacity" of any food-producing economy is seriously limited to the extent that natural disasters are a frequent occurrence. Concurrently, the inability to adequately prepare and store produce for future use exacerbates this situation and further limits the "carrying capacity."[28] Inasmuch as both of these sectors were present for the agriculturalists in Red River, it is not surprising that there are frequent references to food shortages and near-famine conditions. In a letter to William Bayley, a friend in England, John Bunn, a resident of the Red River Settlement, wrote on August 10, 1857 that the community was "often on the verge of starvation."[29] W. Mactavish, Governor of Assiniboia, wrote in 1861: "From 1857 till last year food was positively scarce here and there was difficulty in scraping enough for soldiers."[30] The farmers were expected to produce food, not only for themselves, but also for the Hudson's Bay Company. Sir George Simpson, Governor of the Company, reported in 1857:

> There is at present no sufficient quantity of grains for the use of the settlers. Whether from climate, soil, indolence of the people, we cannot rely on the settlers for our supplies.[31]

And also:

> The banks of the river are alluvial and produce very fair crops of wheat; but these crops are frequently destroyed by early frosts; there is no certainty of the crops. We have been under the necessity of importing grain within these *last ten years* from the United States and Canada, for the support of the establishment.[32] [Author's italics]

Between 1812 and 1870, there were at least 30 reports of partial or complete crop failures (see Table 9-1). These crop failures, and the food shortages which inevitably followed, were largely the result of the combined effects of an inhospitable environment and an unsophisticated agricultural technology. Over the long run, the agriculturalists in the Settlement were incapable of providing the colonists and the personnel of the Hudson's Bay Company with an adequate and reliable source of food.

The Contributions of the Red River Métis

Plains Provisions

Throughout the period under consideration, the farmers' harvests were regularly supplemented by "plains provisions" in the form of pemmican, dried meat, frozen meat, buffalo tongues, and fat. Substantial amounts of these goods were produced by the Métis hunters on their annual summer expeditions. In 1823, for example, the returns of the summer hunt came to 45 tons.[33] Over the years, as the size of the hunt increased, so did the volume of buffalo products. In 1840, the total was 500 tons,[34] and by 1860 it had reached 640 tons.[35] In addition, the returns of the fall hunt generally came to about one-third of the volume produced during the summer.

From the very beginning, the Red River Settlement was, to a considerable extent, dependent upon "plains provisions" for its existence. During the early difficult years, crop failures forced the colonists to spend several winters at Pembina which was closer to the buffalo herds. Here they enlisted the help of the Métis to hunt for meat.[36]

> When the colony was first established upon the Red River, these Free Canadians, as well as the Brûlés, or half-breeds, were on good terms with the settlers. . . the

> latter were occasionally employed by the colonists in hunting for them, and collecting provisions.[37]

After 1827, when the settlement had managed to gain a foothold and began to prosper somewhat, the colonists remained at the Forks throughout the year. However, this did not mean that they no longer depended on buffalo products for a part of their subsistence; these goods were now brought into the Settlement by the hunters. Even during years of successful harvests, "plains provisions" are regularly mentioned as being an important component of a "carefree" winter: "The crops are good, and plain provisions overwhelming. Plenty and gaiety are the order of the day. . . ."[38]

During years when the crops did fail, either wholly or in part (see Table 9-1), and famine threatened the Settlement, it was the pemmican, dried meat, frozen meat, and so on, which saved the colony from starvation.

> The hunters have been coming in during the past few days, from their third and last trip of this season. This is what commonly is known as the "green meat party"—those who go for fresh, in contradistinction from dried meat and pemmican. They have only been three weeks away, and have come in heavily laden with cows meat. *We are happy to hear of such abundance. Our grain crop is rather scimp this year and it is well that meat provisions are plentiful this year.*[39] [Author's italics]

And three years later, in 1864:

> The Dry Meat hunters are dropping in daily and we are happy to be able to state that in general they are well loaded. *It is fortunate in a year such as this when there is a scarcity of Provisions in the settlment, that the hunters should have proved so successful.* The buffalo were near and in great numbers, being driven in this direction it is said by the Sioux; and the "green meat" hunters who are now starting out, expect to kill abundance for their wants. Without having to go any considerable distance.[40] [Author's italics]

Population Pressure

Particularly during the years of famine, the Red River Métis enhanced the Settlement's chances for survival in yet another way, by reducing the "population pressure" around the area of the Forks. "Population pressure" is defined as consisting

> . . . of the demand on subsistence resources resulting from both the density of population and its level of technology in relation to a specific environment. Thus, population pressure exists when subsistence resources are scarce, i.e., when the demand for subsistence resources exceeds the supply.[41]

Every year, the summer hunt drew several hundred (and in later years well over a thousand) men, women, and children, along with large numbers of horses, oxen, and dogs, out onto the plains for a period of about two to two-and-a-half months. Smaller numbers were involved for shorter periods on the fall hunts. While they were out on the plains, the hunters, their families, and livestock lived off the land and thereby reduced the demand on the food resources of the Settlement. This meant that more food was available for the use of the full-time agriculturalists who remained in the Settlement, thus increasing their chances of survival.

Similarly, when severe food shortage occurred in the winter months, those Métis families who usually passed this season in the Settlement, adopted a similar strategy, that is, they simply left the Forks in large numbers and wintered out on the plains or prairie. In his history of Manitoba, W.L. Morton has suggested that at these critical times, the Métis buffalo hunters were helpless and would have starved had it not been for the kindness of certain people in the colony:

> But if the Sioux had been troublesome, or the buffalo distant and the hunt short, then before spring there was hunger in the cabins and sometimes the charity of the wealthier and the more prudent people of Red River had to come to the relief of the brave métis in his distress.[42]

Morton's statement is somewhat misleading since it implies that this was the condition of all the Métis who normally wintered in the Settlement. This is doubtful. At best, it applies only to a few families who for some reason or other (perhaps due to illness or a death in the family) were unable to leave the colony with the others. For the great majority of the Métis people, however, there was no need for charity since they were resourceful enough to provide for themselves. In November of 1836, Thomas Simpson, an employee of the Hudson's Bay Company, wrote:

> The Catholic population of the main river have lost much of their hay by fire; and several families—with a number of horses—have in consequence gone to winter at the "Turtle Mountain."[43]

The crop of 1836 had been a complete failure and it is very likely that as the winter progressed still more Métis families left for Turtle Mountain. Marcel Giraud wrote:

> In the bad years, when food was scarce in Red River, the Métis proceeded in great number, if not completely, to the Prairie where they often found an abundance of food. Thus in 1853, as a consequence of the destruction caused by the flood of the previous year, the Métis of the Red River had used up their provisions of fresh meat. Therefore, they sought provisions in the area of Turtle Mountain where an autumn prairie fire had driven considerable herds of buffalo.
>
> In these winter camps, one not only found the most humble and poorest Métis—those who obstinately refused to make the least concession to the sedentary life. The representatives of the more prosperous Métis—those who had participated in the political life of the colony—were also well represented there, all yielding to the attraction of the bison hunt as well as to the actual need.[44] [Author's translation]

Again, because the Métis families left the colony in large numbers, there was a reduction in the "population pressure." As a result, more food was available for those who remained and their chances of making it through the hard winter were considerably improved.

The Fur Trade Economy

In addition to contributing to the needs of the agriculturalists in the Settlement, the Red River Métis also supplied the Hudson's Bay Company with buffalo products, especially pemmican. The Company, in turn, used these goods for the provisioning of its northern posts and York boat brigades. Although pemmican was not the only type of food used by the voyageurs who manned the brigades, it was, nonetheless, the major item in their diet.

When compared with foods such as domestic meats (beef, pork, mutton) and agricultural produce, the use of pemmican afforded certain advantages. First, since it was produced locally, the Company avoided the high cost of importing large quantities of foodstuffs from England and the Red River Settlement. The latter was not a reliable source. Moreover, pemmican, in relation to its bulk, was more nutritious than the other foods available. This meant that the more profitable cargoes of the canoes and York boats, such as furs and trade goods, could be increased without sacrificing the nutritional quality and quantity of the provisions. The major advantage of using pemmican, however, was that it would keep for years without going bad. Because of its amazing imperishability, large amounts of this food were stored at various points along the river routes and at the northern posts to be used as the need arose. Finally, pemmican was a type of instant food: it did not require any preparation or cooking and was consequently ideal for the voyageurs.[45]

Since it was vital to the operation of the fur trade, the Company annually purchased pemmican from the Métis.[46] After the return of the summer hunt,

> . . . the Hudson's Bay Company, *according to usual custom*, issued a notice that it would take a certain specified quantity of provisions, not from each fellow that had been at the plains, but from each old and recognized hunter.[47] [Author's italics]

For the years 1839, 1840 and 1841, the Company spent 5,000 for the purchase of buffalo products. In 1850, Eden Colvile, an officer of the Hudson's Bay Company, reported that the Company had purchased 400 bags of pemmican (90lbs. each) and 200 bales of dried meat (90lbs. each)—27 tons in all—at Fort Garry, and that in all probability additional amounts had been obtained at the Company's post at Pembina.[48]

Conclusions

The commonly accepted viewpoint that the Métis were a lazy improvident people who preferred buffalo hunting to agriculture because the former activity was exciting while the latter was dull, is not borne out by the available evidence . The theory that their buffalo hunting was detrimental to the development of agriculture in the Red River Settlement is equally inaccurate.

The Métis produced pemmican, dried meat, and other buffalo products on a large scale. This involved a great deal of careful preparation and hard work. The following passage from the letter of Father Antoine Belcourt describes some of the work which went into the making of pemmican. His account begins after the chase, as the men are skinning and cutting up the buffalo:

> Cutting-up is a labor which brings the sweat from the hunter, but our people display a surprising rapidity and adroitness in performing it. Sometimes, in ten hours's time, as many buffalo have been killed and dissected by one man and his family. The profuse perspiration affects them very much, causing inordinate thirst, so that they take the precaution to supply themselves with keg of water, which is transported on the cart that *goes to the meat*. . . .
>
> The meat, when taken to the camp, is cut by the women into long strips about a quarter of an inch thick, which are hung upon the lattice-work, prepared for that purpose, to dry. This lattice-work is formed of small pieces of wood placed horizontally, transversely, and equi-distant from each other, not unlike an immense gridiron, and is supported by wooden uprights (trepieds). In a few days the meat is thoroughly dessicated, when it is bent into proper lengths, and tied in bundles of sixty or seventy pounds weight. This is called dried meat (viande seche). Other portions which are destined to be made into *pimikehigan*, or pemican, are exposed to an ardent heat, and thus become brittle, and easily reducible to small particles by the use of a flail; the buffalo-hide answering the purpose of a threshing-floor. The fat, or tallow, being cut up and melted in large kettles of sheet-iron, is poured upon this pounded meat, and the whole mass is worked together with shovels, until it is well amalgamated, when it is pressed, while still warm, into bags made of the buffalo-skin, which are strongly sewed up, and the mixture gradually cools and becomes almost as hard as a rock.[49]

In view of the frequent occurrences of partial or complete crop failures, it is obvious that the Red River Settlement was anything but the agricultural paradise that some have made it out to be. The primary causes for the slow development of agriculture were the unfavourable environmental conditions and the rudimentary technology of the farmers. These two factors severely limited agricultural productivity and made it impossible for the farmers to meet the nutritional needs of the people of the Settlement and the Hudson's Bay Company. However, the Métis hunters, exploiting the vast herds of buffalo, satisfied these needs with pemmican, dried meat, frozen meat, buffalo tongues, and fat. And over the years, the continuing difficulties of the farmers served as a positive stimulus for the increase and persistence of the buffalo hunt.

It may well be that buffalo hunting was more exciting than farming. More importantly though, it was essential for the survival of the people of the Red River Settlement and the success of the fur trade economy.

Notes

Source: *The Western Canadian Journal of Anthropology* vol. 3, no. 1 (1972). This paper is a slightly revised version of a chapter in my M.A. thesis, University of Manitoba, 1972. I would like to thank Louise E. Sweet, Ray Wiest, Joan Townsend, and John Foster for comments and suggestions on earlier drafts of this paper.

1. William L. Morton, "Agriculture in the Red River Colony," *Canadian Historical Review* 30 (1949):xiv-xxi; Stanley Norman Murray, *The Valley Comes of Age: A*

History of Agriculture in the Valley of the Red River of the North, 1812–1920 (Fargo: North Dakota Institute for Regional Studies, 1967), 40; Elwyn B. Robinson, *History of North Dakota* (Lincoln: University of Nebraska Press, 1966).

2. Alexander Ross, *The Red River Settlement: Its Rise, Progress, and Present State. With Some Account of the Native Races and its General History to the Present Day* (1856; reprint, Minneapolis: Ross and Haines, 1957), 244, 246.
3. Paul Kane, *Wanderings of an Artist among the Indians of North America, from Canada to Vancouver's Island and Oregon through the Hudson's Bay Company's Territory and Back Again* (1859; reprint Edmonton: Hurtig, 1968), 60.
4. Lewis Henry Morgan, *The Indian Journals, 1859-62*, edited with an Introduction by Leslie A. White (Ann Arbor: University of Michigan Press, 1959), 120.
5. Antoine Belcourt, letter of 1851 in *Information Respecting the History, Condition and Prospects of the Indian Tribes of the United States*, edited by H.R. Schoolcraft (Philadelphia: Lippincott, Grambo and Co., 1854), 105.
6. John McLean, *John McLean's Notes of a Twenty-Five Years' Service in the Hudson's Bay Territory* (Toronto: Champlain Society, 1932), 376.
7. George Francis Gilman Stanley, *The Birth of Western Canada: A History of the Riel Rebellions* (Toronto: University of Toronto Press, 1960), 8; see also Alvin C. Glueck, *Minnesota and the Manifest Destiny of the Canadian Northwest; a Study in Canadian-American Relations* (Toronto: University of Toronto Press, 1965), 15; Ross, *Red River Settlement*, 253–54, 261; William L. Morton, *Manitoba: A History*, 2nd ed. (Toronto: University of Toronto Press, 1967), 66; William L. Morton, "A Century of Plain and Parkland," *Alberta Historical Review*, vol. 17, no. 2 (1969):2.
8. Murray, *Valley Comes of Age*, 23.
9. John McDougall, *Saddle, Sled and Snowshoe: Pioneering on the Saskatchewan in the Sixties* (Toronto: Wm. Briggs, 1896), 141–42.
10. Stanley, *Birth of Western Canada*, 8.
11. E.E. Rich, *The History of the Hudson's Bay Company, 1670–1870*, vol. 2 (London: Hudson's Bay Company Society, 1959), 515; see also John Walter Grant MacEwan, *Between the Red and the Rockies* (Toronto: University of Toronto Press, 1952), 46–47.
12. Ross, *Red River Settlement*, 243–44; see also Frank Gilbert Roe, *The North American Buffalo: A Critical Study of the Species in its Wild State* (Toronto: University of Toronto Press, 1951), 399; Morton, "Agriculture in the Colony," 320.
13. Arthur Silver Morton, "The Place of the Red River Settlement in the Plans of the Hudson's Bay Company, 1812–1825," *Report of the Annual Meeting of the Canadian Historical Association* (1930):103–106.
14. *Ibid.*, 105–106.
15. Ross, *Red River Settlement*, 24; MacEwan, *Between Red and the Rockies*, 20.
16. Murray, *Valley Comes of Age*, 38–40; W.L. Morton, *Agriculture in the Colony*, 319; MacEwan, *Between Red and the Rockies*, 204–206.
17. *Ibid.*
18. MacEwan, *Between Red and the Rockies*, 22.
19. Rich, *Hudson's Bay Company*, vol. 2, 408; see also Arthur Silver Morton, *Canadian Frontiers of Settlement*, vol. 2 of *History of the Prairie Settlement* (Toronto: Macmillan, 1938), 26; Marcel Giraud, *Le Métis Canadien; Son Role dans l'Histoire des Provinces de l'Ouest* (Paris: Institut d'Ethnologie, 1945), 759 fn. See also a new translation by George Woodcock, entitled, *Métis in the Canadian West* (Edmonton: University of Alberta, 1986.
20. John Walter Grant MacEwan, *Harvest of Bread* (Saskatoon: Western Producer, 1969), 33; W.L. Morton, *Agriculture in the Colony*, 311–12.
21. Morgan, *Indian Journals*, 127.
22. L. Morton, *Manitoba: A History*, 182.

23. MacEwan, *Harvest of Bread*, 32–33.
24. A.S. Morton, *Prairie Settlement*, 22.
25. Reich, *Hudson's Bay Company*, vol. 2, 511.
26. William L. Morton, "Introduction," in *London Correspondence Inward from Eden Colvile, 1849–1852* (London: Hudson's Bay Record Society, 1956), xxxi-xxxii; W.L. Morton, *Manitoba: A History*, 86; Rich, *Hudson's Bay Company*, vol. 2, 512.
27. Rich, *Hudson's Bay Company*, vol. 2, 512; Youle A. Hinde, "Red River Settlement and the Half-breed Buffalo Hunters," *Canadian Merchants Magazine and Commercial Review* 3 (1858):12.
28. Marshall David Sahlins, *Social Stratification in Polynesia* (Seattle: University of Washington Press, 1958), 124.
29. Denis Bayley, *A Londoner in Rupert's Land; Thomas Bunn of the Hudson's Bay Company* (Sussex, England: Moore and Tillyer, 1969), 96.
30. Giraud, *Le Métis Canadien*, 787, fn 3.
31. *Ibid.*
32. Sir George Simpson in a report of 1857, cited in A.S. Morton, *Prairie Settlement*, 28.
33. R.O. Merriman, "The Bison and the Fur Trade," *Queen's Quarterly* 34 (1926):92.
34. Ross, *Red River Settlement*, 272.
35. "The White Horse Plain Hunters," *The Nor'Wester*, 28 August 1860.
36. Arthur Silver Morton, *A History of the Canadian West to 1870–71; Being a History of Rupert's Land (The Hudson's Bay Company's Territory), and of the North-West Territory (Including the Pacific Slope)* (London: Thomas Nelson and Sons, 1939), 546–56.
37. *Statement Respecting the Earl of Selkirk's Settlement upon the Red River in North America; its Destruction in 1815 and 1816, and the Massacre of Governor Semple and his Party* (1817; Coles Facsimile Edition, 1970), 354; see also Grace Lee Nute, ed., *Documents Relating to Northwest Missions, 1815–1827* (St. Paul, Minnesota: The Minnesota Historical Society, 1942), 354.
38. Thomas Simpson to Hargrave, December 9, 1835 in James Hargrave, *The Hargrave Correspondence, 1821–1843*, edited with an Introduction by G.P.de T. Glazebrook (Toronto: Champlain Society, 1938), 207; see also Simpson to Hargrave, December 1, 1834 in Hargrave, *Hargrave Correspondence*, 160; John Charles to Hargrave, December 2, 1843 in Hargrave, *Hargrave Correspondence*, 454.
39. "Buffalo Hunt," *The Nor'Wester*, 1 November 1861.
40. "The Dry Meat Hunt," *The Nor'Wester* 9 November 1864.
41. Michael J. Harner, "Population Pressure and the Social Evolution of Agriculturalists," *Southwestern Journal of Anthropology*, vol. 26, no. 1, (1970):68.
42. W.L. Morton, *Manitoba: A History*; see also W.L. Morton, *Correspondence from Eden Colvile*, xxxiv.
43. Simpson to Hargrave, November 28, 1836 in Hargrave, *Hargrave Correspondence*, 250.
44. Dans les mauvaises années, lorsque les vivres manquaient à la Rivière Rouge, les métis se portaient en plus grand nombre, sinon en totalité, vers la Prairie qui leur reservait souvent une profusion de nourriture. C'est ainsi qu'en 1853, à la suite des ravages causés par l'inondation de l'année précédente, les métis de la Rivère Rouge, après avoir épuisé leurs provisions de viande fraîche, allèrent chercher leur subsistance dans le secteur de la Montagne à la Tortue où l'incendie qui avait, à l'automne, détruit les pâturages de la Prairie avail refoulé d'importants troupeaux de bisons. Dans ces hivernements, on ne trouvait pas seulement les métis les plus humbles et les plus pauvres, ceux qui refusaient obstinément de faire la moindre concession à la vie sédentaire. Les représentants de la bourgeoisie métisse, ceux qui se distinguaient par l'activité de leurs entre prises ou qui participaient à la vie politique de la colonie y figuraient aussi bien obéissant à l'attrait de la chasse au bison plus qu'à de réeles nécessités. Giraud, *Le Métis Canadien*, 819–20.

45. Merriman, "Bison and the Fur Trade," 82.
46. Harold A. Innis, *The Fur Trade in Canada; An Introduction to Canadian Economic History*, revised ed. (Toronto: University of Toronto Press, 1962), 301; Rich, *Hudson's Bay Company*, vol. 2, 516.
47. Ross, *Red River Settlement*, 273.
48. E.E. Rich, ed., *London Correspondence from Eden Colvile, 1849-1852* (London: Hudson's Bay Record Society, 1956), 33.
49. Belcourt, *Information Respecting Tribes of the United States*, 106–107.

Chapter 10
The Métis: Genesis and Rebirth[1]

Jennifer S.H. Brown

Métis, derived from an old French word meaning "mixed," is one of several terms (michif, *bois-brûlé*, *chicot*, half-breed, country-born, mixed-blood) that have been used to designate people of mixed Amerindian-European descent. Since the 1970s, the use of this French term, formerly used mainly for people of French-Indian background in Western Canada, has increased exponentially among anglophone writers.[2] However, since many such writers (along with politicians and others) either have not been explicit about, or have not achieved consensus on exactly which historical and present-day groups and categories of people of mixed ancestry may properly be defined as "Métis", it is necessary to explain how the term is used in this essay.

Written with a small "m" and italicized, *métis* is used here in the general French sense for all people of dual Amerindian-White ancestry. Capitalized, "Métis" is therefore not a generic term for all persons of biracial descent; it refers to those people who are agreed to possess a distinctive socio-cultural heritage and a sense of ethnic self-identification. Alternatively, the capitalized English form may signify a political and legal category, more or less narrowly defined, as in, for example, Alberta's Métis Betterment Act of 1938, or else left undefined, as in Canada's new Constitution Act, 1982 which recognized the Métis along with (status) Indians and Inuit as distinct native peoples.

Biologically speaking, racial mixing (French, *métissage*) has gone on since the earliest European-Indian contacts along the Atlantic coast. *Métissage* by itself, however, does not determine a person's social, ethnic, or political identity. Many North American whites have some Indian ancestry, and rates of European genetic admixture among status Indian groups in eastern and central Canada and New England range in some instances from 20 to over 40 percent.[3] Over time, and in different areas, people of mixed ancestry have grown up and lived out their lives in a vast variety of circumstances, leading them and their descendants to be categorized and to classify themselves by many different criteria.[4]

Acadia and New France

On Canada's Atlantic seaboard, *métis* families and communities were identifiable in the 1600s, although not classified according to race. Early and often casual unions between European fishermen and native women from Acadia to Labrador produced progeny who matured as Indians among their maternal relatives. Those among the Maliseet were sometimes described as

"Malouidit" because so many of their fathers came from St. Malo on the Brittany coast of France. In Acadia, many French took Indian wives, and some communities became largely biracial. The *capitaines des sauvages*, who served the French governors as interpreters, intermediaries and distributors of annual presents to the Indians, were commonly of mixed parentage. A writer at Louisbourg in 1756 praised these *métis* as "generally hardy, inured to the fatigues of the chase and war, and . . . serviceable subjects in their way."[5]

Some biracial offspring were born of formal church marriages, as Acadian families such as the Denys and d'Entremonts forged both kinship and trading ties with the Micmac.[6] During the seventeenth century French officials supported such marriages in hopes of furthering their policy of frenchification, converting the Indians, and building up the population of New France. "Our young men will marry your daughters and we shall be one people," Samuel de Champlain reportedly told his Indian allies; and some subsequent administrators such as LaMothe Cadillac at Detroit in 1701 continued to encourage those mixed unions which were church-sanctified.[7]

Problems arose, however. Some officials such as Governor Vaudreuil had strong doubts about *métissage* as producing inferior offspring.[8] Further, there was concern that both the Indians and the French traders who sojourned among them had a distressing tolerance for unions unblessed by Christian rite, and that many Frenchmen took up "savage" ways themselves. As New France began its second century, crown policy shifted against intermarriage—reflecting, too, the increased availability of White wives within the colony, both *filles du roi* (French women deliberately imported to marry bachelor settlers) and native-born. The ideal of "one people" (French, incorporating Indian and *métis*) faded. Countless families, both French and Indian, had become genetically mixed, but Indian communities, as such, were not assimilated. Nor did biological *métissage* in New France yield a biracial population that persisted as socio-culturally or politically distinct. Indeed, despite their numbers, people of mixed descent are difficult to identify in early records of New France; they either remained among their mothers' kin as Indians, or were baptized with French names and in almost all instances went on record solely as French.[9]

Métis Communities in the Great Lakes Region

The official discouraging of mixed unions in eighteenth century New France was probably one among many factors that fostered the growth of the first distinguishably *métis* communities around and beyond the Great Lakes. From the 1690s on, these settlements were increasingly remarked upon by clergymen, travellers, and others. Many men who evidently preferred the freedom and opportunities of life in the Indian country to the regulation of church and state in the home colony found livelihoods and new homes around the trading and military posts that were carrying French influence into the interior of the continent. Their native families, whom they might or might not legitimize in the missionaries' terms, had formed nuclei of settlement at several dozen localities by the time the British conquered Canada in 1763. Numerous American and Canadian towns and cities, for example Detroit and Michilimackinac in Michigan; Sault Ste. Marie at the juncture of Lakes Superior and Huron; Chicago and Peoria in Illinois; Milwaukee, Green Bay, and Prairie du Chien in Wisconsin, had their origins in these informal biracial communities. The sizes of these populations are sporadically reported, but some soon became substantial. As of 1700, the Jesuit missionary Étienne de Carheil was deploring the lewdness and apostasy of the hundred or more voyageurs and *coureurs de bois* residing with native women around Michilimackinac.[10]

Carheil and other outsider-critics to the contrary, these communities achieved a moral and social order of their own. French Catholicism remained a part of their heritage, even if attenuated by isolation. Indian constraints also set moral limits. Unions with Indian women involved commitments to and reciprocities with Indian kin and neighbours and earned their own descriptive term, marriage *à la façon du pays*, "according to the custom of the country." Fathers often lived out their lives with these families, whether formally employed at the forts, or subsisting as *gens libres*, freemen who provisioned the posts and served intermittently as guides, interpreters, or voyageurs. Game, fish, wild rice, and maple sugar furnished sustenance, supplemented by the small-scale slash-and-burn or "burnt-stump" agriculture that may have caused Great Lakes *métis* to be labelled *bois-brûlés* or *chicots*.[11]

"Natives of Hudson's Bay"

While these communities were growing during the 1700s, a biracial population of a rather different character was becoming noticeable to the north of the Great Lakes watershed. In 1670, the enormous region draining into Hudson Bay was granted by Charles II of England to his cousin Prince Rupert and other speculators for the exclusive trade of the new Hudson's Bay Company (HBC). After the Treaty of Utrecht in 1713 granted Hudson Bay to the British, numerous HBC posts in Rupert's Land, as the area became known, grew into enclaves among the predominantly Cree Indians, who, as "Home Guard" traders and provisioners, were basic to the company's survival and success.[12] As around the Great Lakes, White women were absent; and Indians eager to consolidate trade and friendship offered wives to the Europeans in "the custom of the country." HBC employees, however, violated strict company rules if they accepted. The HBC directors in London, strongly aware of the costs and problems of maintaining posts so remote from their home base in so northern an environment, sought rigid controls on the numbers of post dependants. Needs to maintain security at the forts, and to minimize expenses and sources of friction with the Indians, reinforced company concerns to maintain servants' celibacy and chastity; and servants in turn attempted to keep their transgressions off the record. By the 1740s, however, when officer James Isham reported that traders' native offspring around the posts had become "pretty Numerious", the HBC London Committee had to acknowledge the limits of its control. By 1810, the Company had given some attention to both the responsibilities and the rewards of educating and training these progeny into "a colony of very useful hands."[13]

These early "natives of Hudson's Bay" did not become classed as a separate ethnic/racial entity in those years. Even if the company could not suppress its servants' marriages, it could and did suppress the growth of dependent post communities and free traders by removing from the Bay all British servants who retired or were dismissed, and by encouraging Indians to disperse to their hunting grounds each winter. A very few HBC officers' native sons gained permission to travel to Britain; but most offspring were assimilated among the Home Guard Cree, and a few became Company servants, by 1800, sometimes classed as "Natives of Hudson's Bay", or even as "English" as for example, was Charles, the half-Cree son of James Isham.

The HBC data from the period before 1810 show that biological mixing in itself was insufficient to occasion "ethnogenesis", as Jacqueline Peterson has termed the Great Lakes and Red River *métis'* rise to recognition and self-consciousness. The HBC offspring lacked the distinct community and economic base upon which to build a separate identity. Through much of the eighteenth century, Company rules gave their trader-fathers good reason to be circumspect about their existence, while at the same time, Cree maternal relatives seem to have readily incorporated the offspring among themselves. HBC word usage also muted their distinctiveness. It was in New France, and in British Canada after 1763, that *métis*, *bois-brûlé*, and later, "half-breed," came into use; HBC men lacked such terms until they picked them up from the Montreal-based traders in the early 1800s. If language is any guide to thought, perhaps HBC writers also lacked (although they later acquired) the increasingly judgemental racial consciousness evident among some of their fur trade counterparts (and among numerous European thinkers) during the early nineteenth century.[14]

Events of the late 1700s brought accelerating changes for both British and Montreal-based fur traders. Around the Great Lakes, the British conquest of New France in 1763 may have heightened a *métis* sense of separateness. As the North West Company gained strength in the 1780s, the British (mainly Highland Scots) took over the leadership of the Montreal fur trade. Most francophones, although their experience and skills continued to be fundamental to the fur trade, were relegated to lower ranks. In 1794, Jay's Treaty fixed the US-Canadian border around the Great Lakes. In the following decades, American settlers and governments displaced and disorganized numerous *métis* communities around the lower lakes, leading many to migrate northwest towards Minnesota and Manitoba.[15]

Ethnogenesis in Red River

It was in Manitoba that the Métis became conspicuous as a socio-political entity in Canadian history. By 1810 they had established roles as buffalo hunters and provisioners to the North West Company (NWC). As supply lines lengthened to Athabasca and beyond, the NWC fur traders became more and more dependent on the pemmican (processed buffalo meat and fat) supplied by the Red River heartland. When in 1811, Thomas Douglas, Fifth Earl of Selkirk, reached an agreement with the HBC to found the colony of Assiniboia with a band of Scottish settlers, the Nor'Westers and their native-born employees and associates saw it as a direct threat to their trade, livelihood and territorial interests.

Events of the next decade are well known: the Pemmican War (1814–15), the killing of Governor Robert Semple and several colonists at Seven Oaks in 1816, the often violent conflicts between the HBC and NWC, and the final merger of the two companies in 1821. Less recognized is the fact that each company's Red River Colony involvement was intensified by the existence of its own native-born constituency. The growing numbers of "Hudson's Bay natives" were a factor in the HBC decision to support the colony. Servants with native wives and families lobbied for the establishment of a community where they could retire and have lands, livelihoods, schools, churches, and other amenities. The HBC itself hoped to reduce costs by relocating dependent populations in a place where, under company governance, they could become self-supporting.

The Nor'Westers and their Métis associates had a more complex relationship. The NWC claimed less control over its Métis and freemen, many of whose biracial connections stretched to both the Great Lakes and the Prairies, and long predated its arrival in the northwest. In the conflict around Red River, this fact served the NWC well, for no matter what support it actually gave to Cuthbert Grant, Jr. (North West Company clerk, local leader, and native-born son of an old NWC partner) and his cohorts, it could and did argue that these men were defending an identity and interest of their own. Leading Nor'Wester William McGillivray admitted in a letter of March 14, 1818 that Grant and the others were linked to the NWC by occupation and kinship. "Yet," he emphasized, "they one and all look upon themselves as members of an independent tribe of natives, entitled to a property in the soil, to a flag of their own, and to protection from the British government." Further, it was well proved "that the half-breeds under the denomination of *bois brûlés* and métifs [alternative form of *métis*] have formed a separate and distinct tribe of Indians for a considerable time back."[16]

McGillivray's statement (although he was an interested party) helps to document the maturation of a network of communities amounting, probably, to several hundred people who resided in the Red River and Assiniboine River drainages, from the Pembina and Brandon areas to Lake Winnipeg. By 1818, when these communities were gaining attention from McGillivray and others as a distinct native people, the concept of a Métis Nation was already taking root.

Red River to the 1870s

From 1821 (when the North West and Hudson's Bay companies merged) to 1870, Red River's overwhelmingly mixed-descent population continued to reflect its dual origins: Montreal, the Great Lakes and Prairies, and the NWC; and Great Britain, the Orkney Islands (a major HBC recruiting ground), and Rupert's Land. The extent to which these subgroups were allied is debated. Some argue for their solidarity on the basis of their numerous intermarriages, business ties, and shared involvements in the buffalo hunt, the HBC transport brigades, and Louis Riel's provisional government of 1869-70.[17] A contrary view emphasizes the split between the Roman Catholic francophones and the Protestant anglophone "country-born"[18] as they were sometimes known. The debate reflects in part the complexity of the evidence and in part the fact that many individuals, such as members of the Alexander Ross family, suffered personal ambivalence about their Indian heritage and about Métis political activism.[19]

Whatever their internal ties and tensions, the rapidly growing population of "half-breeds" in the northwest was, by the 1830s, increasingly seen as an aggregate, as racial interpretations of human behaviour gained ground in nineteenth century European thought and writing.[20] As such, they were often stereotyped and disparaged. For example, in his characterizations of the Company's "half-breed" clerks and postmasters, HBC Governor George Simpson, from the mid-1820s to 1832, showed biases that were common among other Europeans (clergy, colonists) arriving in the Red River region, and among numerous scientific and popular writers of the period. Attributes of race or "blood" were linked with cultural and behavioural traits to produce judgements that science later proved untenable. Such views, applied to biracial groups, covered a wide range; hybrids were everything from "faulty stock" or a "spurious breed"[21] to "the natural link between civilization and barbarism," as Alexis de Tocqueville put it in the 1830s.[22] Daniel Wilson, writing of the Red River half-breeds in 1876, offered a contrast to racial determinism, noting that racial traits did not set limits to adaptiveness or potential. Besides demonstrating "a remarkable aptitude for self-government" in their organization of the buffalo hunt, the Red River Métis showed "capacity for all the higher duties of a settled, industrious community."[23]

Events of the decade in which Wilson wrote offered few outlets for the qualities that he perceived. The 1840s had seen a rising entrepreneurial spirit in Red River.[24] New challenges to the HBC trade and administrative monopoly in Red River were expressed in the trial and freeing of trader Pierre-Guillaume Sayer in 1849, and, in the 1840s and 1850s the anti-HBC lobbying efforts in London by Alexander Kennedy Isbister, the part-Cree grandson of HBC Chief Factor Alexander Kennedy. Other events, however, soon overshadowed the free traders' gains and the issue of HBC power. Eastern Canadian interest in developing the West was heightened by Henry Y. Hind's glowing report of its agricultural potential. The subsequent planned transfer of Rupert's Land from the Hudson's Bay Company to the new Canadian government in 1869 led surveyors to begin to map Red River without regard for local residents' holdings. This touched off Louis Riel's establishment, in 1867–70, of a provisional government in Red River. The Canadian government's bargaining with Riel led in 1870 to the passage of the Manitoba Act, which secured the admittance of a small portion of Manitoba to Canada and provincial status and, most important for the Métis, stated that 1,400,000 acres of land would be allotted for their children.

This promised land was lost in the next decade, however. The settlers and troops who arrived in the new province from 1870 on were hostile to the prior inhabitants, many of whom were "beaten and outraged by a small but noisy section"[25] of the newcomers, according to a report by the new governor, Adams Archibald. Métis landholders were harassed, while new laws and amendments to the Manitoba Act undermined their power to fend off speculators and new settlers.[26] Of the approximately ten thousand people of mixed descent in Manitoba in 1870, two-thirds or more are estimated to have departed in the next several years. While some went north and some went south to the United States (where they already had ties through the Red River cart trade to St. Paul, Minnesota, and the buffalo hunts to Montana), most headed west to the Catholic mission settlements around Fort Edmonton (Lac Ste. Anne, St. Albert, Lac La Biche), and to the South Saskatchewan River where they founded or joined such settlements as St. Laurent (now St. Laurent-Grandin), Batoche, and Duck Lake.[27]

As they grew, the Saskatchewan River communities sought to secure clear titles to their river lots from the Canadian government, in the face of governmental efforts to survey the whole region into squared sections. Lieutenant Governor Alexander Morris thought in 1880 that the claimants' land case was clear: "They will, of course, be recognized as possessors of the soil and confirmed by the Government in their holdings." He urged that the Métis who still depended on the buffalo hunt have lands assigned to them since that resource had increasingly failed.[28] The government, however, ignored or responded very slowly to Métis concerns, while at the same time negotiating the major western Indian treaties and pre-empting land for the railways. The relative blame for subsequent events has been variously assigned by researchers to government incompetence or connivance, to agents fostering Canadian Pacific Railways, and other interests, and to poor guidance of the Métis' interests by their own priests and leaders.[29] Whatever the precise importance of these various factors, they probably all contributed toward building the crisis in which the Saskatchewan Métis, in deep frustration, took up arms under Louis Riel and Gabriel Dumont in the Northwest Rebellion of 1885.

After 1885

The Métis defeat at Batoche, and the execution of Riel in the same year set off a second dispersal, particularly to Alberta, and a renewed weakening of Métis political influence and cohesiveness. Sir John A. Macdonald in 1885 viewed them as without distinct standing: "If they are Indians, they go with the tribe; if they are half-breeds they are Whites,"[30] in contrast to his 1870 acceptance of their distinctness.[31] Where Métis individuals did receive land allowances, or money equivalents, these were usually granted in scrip or transferable certificates which unscrupulous speculators often pressured them to sell cheaply on the spot. The "scrip hunters" who followed the Treaty 8 Half-Breed Commission as it made its awards to Métis in the Dene (Northern Athabascan) settlements, for example, bought up many $240 scrip certificates for cash amounts of $70 to $130.[32]

From 1885 into the mid-1900s, poverty, demoralization, and the opprobrium commonly attached to being "half-breed" led many people of Indian descent if they could, to deny or suppress that part of their heritage.[33] In 1896, Father Albert Lacombe, concerned for Métis interests, founded St. Paul des Métis, northeast of Edmonton, on land furnished by the government. For financial and other reasons, by 1908, the colony had failed as a formal entity, and settlers from Quebec began to dominate the area.[34] Here, as elsewhere, the Métis who remained found themselves on the lower socio-economic levels.

Some other developments after 1900, however, were more positive. In 1909, the Union Nationale St-Joseph de Manitoba, founded by former associates of Riel and others, began to retrieve from documents and memories their own history of the events of 1869-70 and 1885, resulting in A.-H. de Tremaudan's *History of the Métis Nation in Western Canada*.[35] The 1920s and 1930s saw the rise of new leaders—notably James Patrick (Jim) Brady and Malcolm Norris—who, as prairie socialist activists, built a new political and organizational base to defend their people's interests. Many Métis and ex-treaty Indians had been squatters on Crown lands in north-central Alberta. Threatened by a federal plan to place these lands under provincial jurisdiction, Joseph Dion and others organized petitions and delegations to the Alberta government to seek land title for the squatters. After Brady and Norris joined the movement in 1932, the first of several provincially based organizations was founded—the Métis Association of Alberta, open to all persons of Indian ancestry.[36] Its efforts led, in 1934-35, to the province's appointment of the Ewing Commission to "make enquiry into the condition of the Half-breed population of Alberta." Despite reverses, the association eventually secured land for Métis settlements and passage of the Métis Betterment Act in 1938. In the same year, the Saskatchewan Métis Society (later the Association of Métis and Non-Status Indians of Saskatchewan) was founded.

From the mid-1960s on, Métis political activity intensified with the founding of numerous other organizations such as the Manitoba Métis Federation, the Ontario Métis and Non-Status Indian Association, and the Louis Riel Métis Association of British Columbia. Confronting such issues as the federal government's White Paper of 1969 and the Constitution of 1982, Métis representatives repeatedly faced questions about whether to pursue their concerns jointly with status and/or non-status Indians, or on their own. From 1970 to 1983, the Native Council of Canada (NCC) alone represented Métis interests on the national level. For the 1983 First Ministers' Conference, however, the two NCC seats were both allocated to non-status Indian delegates; and the Métis National Council was formed to secure distinct Métis representation there and elsewhere.

Reflecting the historical diversity of their communities across Canada, people who identify themselves and are accepted as Métis (or in some localities, half-breeds) have not necessarily shared a consensus about what organization may best represent them in Ottawa. Western Métis who view themselves as "a distinct indigenous nation with a history, culture and and homeland in western Canada"[37] are generally affiliated with the Métis National Council. Those who define their claims as based more on aboriginal than national rights, and whose *métis* roots may reach to Quebec, Ontario, the Maritimes, or elsewhere, rather than to the prairie heartland of Louis Riel and Gabriel Dumont, appear more inclined to affiliate (as Métis or Non-Status Indians) with the Native Council of Canada.[38] The open-ended recognition, and non-definition, of Métis in the Constitution Act, 1982, present new issues, challenges, and opportunities which will be explored and tested for many years to come.[39]

Métis Renaissance: The 1980s

Whatever courses the Métis may follow in their evolving political history, the late twentieth century has been a time for their revival and renewal in both Canda and the northern United States. In Canada's 1981 federal census, nearly 100,000 people identified themselves as Métis, and many thousands more may legitimately be able to rediscover past histories and affiliations, suppressed or forgotten, through which they may link themselves to Métis communities. In 1985, the Manitoba Métis Federation (which has claimed a population base of between 80,000 and 100,000 people in Manitoba alone) launched proceedings to pursue land claims dating from the Manitoba Act, 1870.

In the United States, where governments have given no recognition to ethnic categories between those of Indian and White, people of mixed descent have been obliged to establish either Indian or White identities.[40] Yet there, too, Métisism (to use a recently coined Alberta Métis term) has gained ground among the many thousands of people with Canadian Métis roots and connections who live in Michigan, Minnesota, North Dakota, Montana, and Washington,[41] generating a cultural resurgence with political overtones.

Expressions of Métisism range far beyond the political. In literature, both Métis and non-Métis authors have brought the past and present lives of Métis people to centre stage with varying success. Maria Campbell's *Halfbreed*[42] (1973) and Beatrice Culleton's novel, *In Search of April Raintree*[43] (1983) stand out.[44] Winnipeg is home to a publisher that is Métis in both focus and management—Pemmican Publications. Métis language and linguistics are growing fields of study.[45] Arts and artisanry that are now recognized to be distinctively Métis rather than tribal or simply "Indian" have received long-delayed recognition in Alberta's Glenbow Museum exhibition, "Métis," which toured Canada in 1985–86.[46] Film and television attention to Métis themes has increased; 1986–87 saw the launching of a new four-part National Film Board dramatic series, "Daughters of the Country," and media commemorations of the 1885 centenary were widespread. Métis historical sites have become foci of intensive research, restoration, and reconstruction.[47]

For the 1980s, it seems fair to speak of a Métis renaissance giving new vitality to communities who have experienced long periods of relative invisibility, economic hardship, and prejudice. Social currents of the 1970s and 1980s have legitimized ethnicity and ethnic pride on a broad scale all across North America, and many Métis people, as the centenary of Batoche approached, were drawn to rediscover and reconstruct their past.

Shifting intellectual currents have also helped; new modes of social history and ethnohistorical analysis have placed ordinary people of all kinds in the mainstream of recent historical writing. As an example, the perspectives of women's history have reinforced the attention paid to Métis history and origins: as long as western Canadian history was European-oriented, patricentric, and patrilineally directed in the reconstruction of its genealogies, native origins and components of those families were readily screened out because the native women from whom they were derived were overlooked. Younger generations, however, are retracing these origins and connections with enthusiasm.

Probably these development have occurred partly because the Indians and "half-breeds" of a century ago have become safely exotic, and many of their descendants have been able to put aside the vulnerability and insecurity long associated with their plight. But there is more to it than this. In a very positive sense, a sea of change may finally be occurring in Canadians' views of their nation's Indian past and native heritage. The Métis, along with Canada's other native peoples, are earning attention as integral parts of our past and present, rather than residing, as formerly, on the shadowy margins of colonial and frontier history. Neither scholars, nor the media, nor the Métis themselves, are likely to allow this trend to be reversed in the foreseeable future.

Notes

1. This essay is a revised and expanded version of the article, "Métis," which appeared in *The Canadian Encyclopedia*. Edmonton: Hurtig, 1985, 1124–27, by permission.
2. Two recent guides to sources on Métis history are: John W. Friesen and Terry Lusty, *The Métis of Canada: An Annotated Bibliography* (Toronto: OISE Press, 1980) and D.F.K. Madill, *Selected Annotated Bibliography on Métis History and Claims* (Ottawa: Indian and Northern Affairs Canada, 1983). The *Canadian Journal of Native Studies*, vol. 3, no. 1 (1983), appeared as a special issue on the Métis since 1870, and contains useful articles on Métis history, claims, language, and other topics. Similarly, *Canadian Ethnic Studies*, vol. 17, no. 2 (1985) was a special issue, entitled "The Métis: Past and Present."
3. Emok J.E. Szathmary and Franklin Auger, "Biological Distances and Genetic Relationships with Algonkians," in *Boreal Forest Adaptations: The Northern*

Algonkians, edited by A. Theodore Steegmann Jr. (New York: Plenum Press, 1983), 298–99.

4. Jacqueline Peterson and Jennifer S.H. Brown, eds., *The New Peoples: Being and Becoming Métis in North America* (Winnipeg: University of Manitoba Press, 1985).
5. Cornelius Jaenen, *The French Relationship with the Native Peoples of New France and Acadia* (Ottawa: Indian and Northern Affairs, 1984), 72.
6. Olive Patricia Dickason, "From 'One Nation' in the Northeast to 'New Nation' in the Northwest: A Look at the Emergence of the Métis," in *New Peoples*, edited by Peterson and Brown, 26.
7. Jaenen, *French Relationship*, 74.
8. *Ibid.*, 74–75.
9. Dickason, "One Nation," 20–23.
10. Jacqueline Peterson, "Many Roads to Red River: Métis Genesis in the Great Lakes Region, 1680–1815," in *New Peoples*, edited by Peterson and Brown, 38–43.
11. Jacqueline Peterson, "Prelude to Red River: A Social Portrait of the Great Lakes Métis," *Ethnohistory*, vol. 25, no. 1 (1978).
12. Daniel Francis and Toby Morantz, *Partners in Furs: A History of the Fur Trade in Eastern James Bay 1600–1870* (Kingston and Montreal: McGill-Queen's University Press, 1983).
13. Jennifer S.H. Brown, *Strangers in Blood: Fur Trade Company Families in Indian Country* (Vancouver: University of British Columbia Press, 1980).
14. Jennifer S.H. Brown, "Linguistic Solitudes and Changing Social Categories," in *Old Trails and New Directions: Papers of the Third North American Fur Trade Conference*, edited by C.M. Judd and A.J. Ray (Toronto: University of Toronto Press, 1980).
15. Peterson, "Prelude to Red River."
16. Jennifer S.H. Brown, "Woman as Centre and Symbol in the Emergence of Métis Communities," *Canadian Journal of Native Studies*, vol. 3, no. 1 (1983):43–44.
17. Irene M. Spry, "The Métis and Mixed-bloods of Rupert's Land before 1870," in *New Peoples*, edited by Peterson and Brown.
18. Frits Pannekoek, "The Rev. Griffiths Owen Corbett and the Red River Civil War of 1869–70," *Canadian Historical Review*, vol. 57, no. 2 (1976):133–49.
19. Sylvia Van Kirk, "'What if Mama is an Indian?': The Cultural Ambivalence of the Alexander Ross Family," in *New Peoples*, edited by Peterson and Brown.
20. Robert E. Bieder, "Scientific Attitudes toward Indian Mixed-bloods in Early Nineteenth Century America," *Journal of Ethnic Studies*, vol. 8, no. 7 (1980).
21. Lewis O. Saum, *The Fur Trader and the Indian* (Seattle: University of Washington Press, 1965), 206.
22. Bieder, *Scientific Attitudes*, 20.
23. Daniel Wilson, *Prehistoric Man: Researches into the Origin of Civilisation in the Old and the New World,* vol. 2 (London, 1876), 264, 265.
24. Irene M. Spry, "The 'Private Adventurers' of Rupert's Land," in *The Developing West*, edited by John E. Foster (Edmonton: University of Alberta Press, 1983).
25. Arthur S. Morton, *A History of the Canadian West to 1870–71*, 2nd ed. (Toronto: University of Toronto Press, 1973), 920.
26. Douglas N. Sprague, "Government Lawlessness in the Administration of Manitoba Land Claims 1970–1887," *Manitoba Law Journal* 10 (1980).
27. Murray Dobbin, *The One-and-a-half-Men: The Story of Jim Brady and Malcolm Morris* (Vancouver: New Star Books, 1981), 23.
28. Alexander Morris, *The Treaties of Canada with the Indians* (Toronto, 1880), 294–95.
29. Compare, for example, Bob Beal and Rod MacLeod, *Prairie Fire: The 1885 North-West Rebellion* (Edmonton: Hurtig Press, 1984); Martin Shulman and Don McLean, "Lawrence Clarke: Architect of Revolt," *Canadian Journal of Native*

Studies, vol. 3, no. 1 (1983); Thomas Flanagan, *Riel and the Rebellion: 1885 Reconsidered* (Saskatoon: Western Producer Prairie Books, 1983).
30. Quoted in Joe Sawchuk, *The Métis of Manitoba: Reformulation of an Ethnic Identity* (Toronto: Peter Martin Associates, 1978), 33.
31. Flanagan, *Riel and the Rebellion*, 62.
32. René Fumoleau, *As Long as this Land Shall Last: A History of Treaty 8 and Treaty 11, 1870–1939* (Toronto: McClelland and Stewart, 1974), 76.
33. Jean H. Lagassé, director, *The People of Indian Ancestry in Manitoba*, 3 vols. (Winnipeg: Department of Agriculture and Immigration, 1959).
34. James G. MacGregor, *Father Lacombe* (Edmonton: Hurtig, 1975), 306–308; Dobbin, *One-and-a-half-Men*, 42–43.
35. A.-H. de Tremaudan, *Hold High Your Heads*, translated by Elizabeth Maguet (originally published as *History of the Métis Nation in Western Canada,* 1936; Winnipeg: Pemmican Publication, 1982).
36. Dobbin, *One-and-a-half-Men*, 61.
37. Peterson and Brown, eds., *New Peoples*, 6.
38. *Ibid.*
39. For a good discussion of these issues and controversies, see Joe Sawchuk, "The Métis, Non-Status Indians and the New Aboriginality: Government Influence on Native Political Alliances and Identity," *Canadian Ethnic Studies*, vol. 17, no. 2 (1985).
40. Verne Dusenberry, "Waiting for a Day that Never Comes: The Dispossessed Métis of Montana," in *New Peoples*, edited by Peterson and Brown.
41. Peterson and Brown, eds., *New Peoples*, 7.
42. Maria Campbell, *Halfbreed* (Toronto: McClelland and Stewart, 1973).
43. Beatrice Culleton, *In Search of April Raintree* (Winnipeg: Pemmican Publications, 1983).
44. For a recent overview of such literature, see Emma LaRocque, "The Métis in English Literature," *Canadian Journal of Native Studies*, vol. 3, no. 1 (1983).
45. John C. Crawford, "What is Michif? Language in the Métis Tradition," in *New Peoples*, edited by Peterson and Brown; Patline Laverdure and Ida Rose Allard, *The Michif Dictionary: Turtle Mountain Chippewa Cree*, edited by John Crawford (Winnipeg: Pemmican Publications, 1983); Patrick C. Douaud, *Ethnolinguistic Profile of the Canadian Métis*, National Museum of Man, Mercury Series, Canadian Ethnology Service Paper, no. 99 (Ottawa, 1985).
46. Ted J. Brasser, "In Search of Métis Art," in *New Peoples*, edited by Peterson and Brown.
47. Diane Payment, *Batoche (1870–1910)* (Winnipeg: Les Éditions du Blé, 1983).

Chapter 11
Indian Reserves in Western Canada: Indian Homelands or Devices for Assimilation?

J.L. Tobias

The reserve system has been a major feature of Canada's Indian policy since Confederation. Originally developed long before Confederation, when lands were set aside for the use and benefit of Indian bands as a means to protect the Indian from exploitation by peoples of European origin, the reserve system in the last decade and a half before Confederation came to be regarded as a training ground in "civilization" where the Indian could be taught to live like a European with European values, and thus made capable of being assimilated. Legislation outlining the goals of the reserve system and establishing the procedure for assimilation was passed in the Legislature for Upper Canada in 1857 in "an Act to encourage the gradual civilization of the Indians in this province. . . ." In 1869 essentially the same bill with a slight change in emphasis was passed by the Parliament of Canada and entitled "An Act for the gradual enfranchisement of Indians. . . ."[1] Both laws were based on the assumption that the reserve was the place where the Indian could be "civilized," meaning Christianized, educated, and be made a farmer. When he had learned these things, the Indian would be tested on his reading and oral knowledge of English (or French in the 1869 Act), and after demonstrating that he was free of debt, of good moral character, and able to look after a farm of at least fifty acres, he was enfranchised—meaning he lost his status as an Indian and was admitted to the same rights as the White man.[2]

The reserve system was designed for use in the settled regions of the dominion, meaning the provinces which had entered Confederation. No thought had been given to applying it in the more remote areas of those provinces, or in the Northwest Territories or Manitoba. In fact, the governments of Canada in the 1870s had given little thought to how they would deal with the Indians in those areas, preferring instead to ignore them if possible, and allow them to follow their traditional way of life until such time as settlement reached their area. Indian concern for their future source of livelihood, and fears that their lands would be taken from them, led these Indians to threaten violence and to prevent government survey teams from entering the region. Indians also stated that they would not allow settlement of the west beyond the Red River settlement until Indian ownership of the land had been recognized and duly surrendered. In this manner, the Indians of Manitoba and the Northwest Territories forced the governments of Canada to devise a policy for dealing with the matters that were of grave concern to them.[3]

The policy determined upon was the traditional one of taking surrender of Indian title to the land by documents called treaties. In addition, the governments agreed to extend the reserve system to these peoples whenever they were ready to accept it. As explained to the plains Indians, the reserve system was to provide them with a homeland, where they could learn, if they so chose, a new way of making a living. Nothing was said about this being compulsory; in fact, the Indians were often told they could practise their traditional way of life—hunting—as well as farming. They were assured that the government would not interfere with their religion or try to alter their culture.[4] Realizing that their game resources were almost depleted, most Indians of the prairies welcomed what was being promised them, and accepted the treaties and the idea of reserve as homeland. In essence, this was what they sought by their earlier agitation—a guarantee of a place for them to live and to receive assistance in developing a new economic base for their society.[5]

Having dealt with the Indian title to the land, the government assumed that it had allayed Indian fears. It did virtually nothing to implement the promise of reserves. This was not due, as some commentators say, to the fact that the Indians refused to settle or choose reserve sites, for many of the treaties stipulated the sites where the reserves were to be located and the formula for determining their size, while in the treaty areas where no reserve sites were defined in the treaties themselves, the Indians had within a year not only selected the sites for these homelands but many had also settled on them.[6] Having done this, the Indians expected that the reserve lands would be surveyed and the farm equipment and tools that were promised as part of the reserve provisions in the treaty would be immediately sent. This did not happen, as the government assumed that the Indian would continue to hunt, and the treaty provisions on reserves would not have to be implemented until the Indian's traditional source of livelihood was no longer available. In taking this attitude, the government ignored the reports from the field that the buffalo were an endangered species and would disappear as an economic base for the plains Indians in less than a decade.[7]

Desire for economy of administration costs for Indian affairs was largely responsible for the government doing little more than pay annuities, and provide ammunition and twine for the plains Indians until 1880. Implementation of the reserve system would require expansion of staff within this department, and entail heavy expenditure on agricultural equipment and animals. It was considered to be cheaper to allow Indians to fend for themselves while there was still game and no settlements in the area which would be disrupted by the Indians continuing to hunt in their traditional manner.[8] This belief was a common feature of Canada's Indian administrators, for it persisted until well into the 1960s. Reserves and the reserve system would only be implemented when the Indians' old way of life was not possible, either through depletion of the game resource, or when hunting areas were required for settlement or economic development purposes for non-Indian communities. Not until 1879 did the government begin to take any steps to implement the reserve and farming provisions of the treaty in more than a token scale, even then not all the farm animals and equipment were sent, but by then the Indians faced starvation and, as a result, their early attempts at farming had little impact on the grave hunger crisis that struck. For the most part, the people who were sent to help them learn to farm, had to spend much of their time issuing rations to starving people.[9]

Indian reaction to the government's slowness in establishing reserves and teaching them to farm was one of grave disillusionment and discontent with the treaties. Most Indian leaders knew by 1870 that their buffalo would not be able to provide them with all their needs for much longer, and accepted that they would have to get their sustenance from other means.[10] The Plains Cree, in particular, had accepted the treaties because they believed that through them they would be assured not only a homeland, but also would learn to farm. Agriculture was only one means, for they sought to have the government provide them with the skills, tools, and training that would make their reserves virtually self-sufficient homelands, by having blacksmith shops, carpenters, mills, and instruction in farming techniques.[11] The Treaty Commissioners refused to commit themselves or the government to these demands. Nevertheless, the Indians, including Big Bear (the principal Plains Cree leader), found the government's more limited offer in the area of economics acceptable. What kept some of the bands from initially accepting the treaty was the refusal of the Treaty Commissioners to guarantee that the Indians would not be compelled to accept an alien legal and cultural system.[12]

Failure to provide all the materials to help the Cree develop a new economic base and slowness in setting aside the lands they wanted resulted in much dissatisfaction with the treaties and discontent with the government. By 1881, many of the Cree leaders protested to Governor General Lorne about the inadequacy of the treaties and of the government's promises to help them meet the crises that faced them.[13] By 1884, meetings among the leaders of the Cree people were taking place with the view to having the treaties revised to provide for more assistance in farming and the creation of an Indian territory.[14] That year, several confrontations between Indians and police occurred when the North-West Mounted Police attempted to prevent or break up the meetings. That no blood was shed was due to the desire of both sides to avoid violence.[15] The Indian movement for a large homeland and revised treaties came to an end when troops were sent into the North to put down the Métis Rebellion of 1885, and subsequently against the more prominent leaders and bands of the Indian movement.

Having asserted its power in the northwest, the government then proceeded to introduce a reserve system and an Indian policy that was hoped would, within a generation or two, not only "civilize" the Indians, but make them assimilatable. Commissioner of Indian Affairs for Manitoba and the Northwest Territories, Hayter Reed, called it the "tribal system": all chiefs who through their actions and words during the crisis of 1885 had not given unwavering loyalty to the government were to be deposed, and their bands left without leaders or spokesmen. All other chiefs and headmen were allowed to hold office until they resigned or died, after which the bands would not be allowed to replace them. Not until the bands were considered advanced enough in civilization would they be allowed to select their own leaders according to the election provision of the Indian Act.[16]

The Indians were to look to the employees of the Department of Indian Affairs for help. To facilitate this, the number of employees of the Department working in the northwest was greatly increased. Thus, after 1885, the number of Indian agencies was increased from two to ten in the region we now know as Saskatchewan. Most agencies were also provided with farm instructors for each reserve. These persons were not to deal with bands, but individuals. Thus, even where chiefs and councils were retained, they were not to be treated as spokesmen for the band. Nor were the agents to show them any deference as leaders of the band, unless the holders of these offices were strong supporters of the policy the Department was implementing. All chiefs and councillors opposing such policies and encouraging their people not to accept the new system were to be treated as "incompetent" to hold office, and deposed. In fact, to facilitate this policy, the Indian Act was amended to legitimize the deposition of life chiefs and councillors.[17]

Indian society was to be atomized. Thus, the government would deal with individuals, and not with bands. To prevent the Indians taking concerted resistance to any policy, individuals were not to be allowed off the reserve without a pass signed by the Indian agent, stating the reason for the person being off the reserve, and how long he might remain off it. To facilitate the enforcement of this measure, the Indian Act was amended to give the Indian Agent the power of a Justice of the Peace to enforce the sections of the criminal code dealing with vagrancy and loitering.[18] The government's desire for atomization extended to breaking up the villages in reserves, and to putting an end to communal farming and ranching. What the Indian had to be taught was to be an individual farmer or cattle raiser on his own piece of land. Thus, reserves were subdivided into forty acre plots, and individuals were given their own parcel of land to farm.[19]

Education was necessary for assimilation, and was used to undermine the tribal system. At first, schools on the reserves were thought to be the answer, but poor student attendance and performance resulted in their closure and the promotion of residential schools. Day schools were abandoned because the government thought that the homelife of the Indian child counteracted whatever was learned in school. The prevailing belief was that the adult Indian could not be changed or made to accept new values, but that a child removed from the Indian environment and placed in a carefully controlled "civilized" environment, could be. To provide the government with the authority to remove the children from their home environment, the Indian Act was amended to permit the Governor in Council to commit children to residential schools and make whatever regulations he considered necessary for running them.[20]

Complementary to the education policy was the attempt by the Government to discourage the traditional religious and ceremonial practices of the adult Indians. Again, legal authority was first obtained by additions to the Indian Act banning all ceremonials where torture and mutilation were involved. Later, amendments also forbade the holding of all give-away dances, or any type of native dances, without the written permission of a senior official of the Department of Indian Affairs.[21] By the mid-1890s, the government took the final step in destroying the Indians' ability to live in their traditional manner by making them subject to the game laws of the Territories.[22] By these measures to deprive the plains Indians of their leadership, social organization, religion, their children, and their old source of livelihood, the government sought to prevent the reserve from becoming an Indian homeland and to use them instead as devices of assimilation.

To drive home the point that the reserve was not to be regarded as a homeland, or that the Indian owned the reserve, Indians were forbidden to dispose of any resource from their reserve without first securing a permit to do so. This policy extended even to the disposal of the crops and animals the Indian raised on the plot of land assigned to him. To prevent circumvention of this law, anyone who purchased goods from an Indian who did not have such a permit was made liable to a fine.[23] Not only were the Indians regulated in how they disposed of their produce, they had to follow certain rules in their farming activities. Thus, we find that for a time, they were forbidden to use farm machinery and labour saving devices, even if the Indians had personally funded the purchase of such instruments.[24]

Indians resented what was being done to them, and tried to resist as best they could the efforts to change their way of life. Many refused to tolerate the restrictions placed on their economic activity, and abandoned farming when they were not allowed to farm in the manner their White neighbours did or in the manner they wished. Thus, the breakup of the communal farms led on many reserves to a drastic reduction in crop production, while on others the ban on machinery caused many Indians to give up farming; government policy, rather than promoting agriculture, had just the opposite effect. The only advantage produced by restrictive regulation, and the Indian abandonment of agriculture that resulted, was that the government no longer had to try to placate angry farmers complaining that Indian agricultural produce was depriving them of a market.[25]

The Indians tried to circumvent the bans on their religious practices, both by holding secret dances on remote sections of reserves, and by hiring lawyers to defend those convicted of holding dances.[26] Particular exception was taken to the interference of the farm instructors and agents in the politics of the reserve. On several reserves where traditional chiefs were deposed and no new men allowed to assume the post of chief, the Indians refused to farm or send their children to school until the chiefs were reinstated. Often this tactic was successful and the deposed chiefs were reinstated.[27] Subdivision of the reserve was also resisted and, rather than farm as the government wanted them to, most Indians simply gave up farming.[28] As for the effort to impose the hunting laws on Indians, protests of treaty violation were made, and many continued to hunt where game was available, despite the laws.[29]

The Indians also tried to prevent their children being sent to residential schools, not only because the children were taught to be ashamed of their parents' way of life, but largely because such a high percentage of their children died from diseases contracted at the schools.[30] Also, among the older men who were present when the treaties were made, a movement of protest against the assimilationist policy developed. The policy was attacked as being a violation of the promises made by the Treaty Commissioners that the reserve would be the Indian homeland, and the chiefs and councillors officers of the Queen. However, the government did not change its policy, and tried to break up the movement before it got too strong.[31]

By 1920, the government became convinced that the reserve policy had failed in both east and west. In the east, where numerous Indians were qualified for enfranchisement, most refused to take this step, preferring to live on the reserve and defend what they regarded as their rights. In the west, passive resistance to the policy had developed when the Indians refused to engage in farming if it had to be done on the government's terms. Realization of what was happening caused the government to plan to do away with the reserve system.[32] In this, the government was merely responding to the feeling of the electorate which regarded the reserves as anachronisms, holding back the "progress" of the areas where they existed. Public opinion wanted Indians removed from valuable lands so that further development of the region could occur. Demands for making Indian land available to non-Indians was quite strong on the part of communities next to reserves. The government tried to accommodate such requests by taking surrenders of reserve lands whenever possible in the west, and passing laws establishing a procedure by which reserves within or next to towns could be abolished. In these surrenders, the Indian Act was amended to make inducements to give a surrender more attractive.[33] Nevertheless, some bands proved reluctant to give up their lands, and on several occasions the requirements for legal surrender, as set in the Indian Act, were not met.

An examination of just how well the reserve system worked to promote assimilation showed that only 250 persons had chosen to enfranchise between 1857 and 1920.[34] This made it clear that the Indian still regarded the reserve as a homeland and that they would not give it up. Believing that more people would enfranchise if they were not required to have land, the Indian Act was amended to permit enfranchisement on such a basis. Five hundred people decided to enfranchise under this provision within a five year period, but all of them had been living off the reserve for several years before the amendment was passed. When this step had little impact on encouraging the Indians living on the reserve to enfranchise, the Indian Act was amended to allow the government to appoint boards to examine the qualifications of people living on reserves for possible enfranchisement. Those judged capable of being assimilated would then be enfranchised, even if they did not want to be.[35] Protests of such a procedure led to repeal of this provision but it was reintroduced a few years later and remained part of the Indian Act until 1951.[36]

The Government of Canada did not limit its efforts to further assimilation by the measures designed to have more people enfranchised. It also tried to put an end to the reserve as homeland by giving the government power to lease out the reserve lands without first taking a surrender, and making provincial laws on general police matters applicable on the reserve.[37] In addition, after 1947, following recommendations made by the Joint Committee of both the Senate and the House of Commons, policies were introduced that for the first time made the Indians citizens of Canada without being enfranchised. Also, agreements were made with the provinces to have Indian children educated in provincial schools with White children in return for the Federal government paying part of the capital costs for school buildings, as well as tuition fees for Indian students. Increasingly, the Indians were integrated into the services, such as welfare and health care insurances provided by the province, in return for the Federal government paying some of the costs for provision of these services. By the mid-1960s, Indians were given the vote and allowed intoxicants. All these things, it was hoped, would promote assimilation.

An examination of the success of these measures in promoting enfranchisement or assimilation demonstrated this was not the case. Therefore, in 1969, the Government of Canada in a policy statement on Indian Affairs announced that it intended to do away with special status and legislation for the Indians. It would, within a five year period, turn over reserve lands to Indians, as well as have the provinces provide all services to Indians.[38] In essence, the Indian was to be assimilated by government fiat. Announcement of this policy brought a storm of protest from the Indians and increased political acitivity, all designed to preserve the special status for Indians and to retain the reserves. Indians announced in no uncertain terms their opposition to assimilation; they were, and are, still trying to promote the idea of the reserves as Indian homeland, although in a somewhat different form. Partial success has crowned Indian efforts, for the 1969 policy has been withdrawn. At the moment, we have a government still promoting the goal of assimilation facing an Indian community opposed to this goal, and trying to develop a policy that will reconcile the two contradictory ideas.

Notes

Source: D.A. Muise, ed. *Approaches to Indian History in Canada*, National Museum of Man, History Division. (Ottawa: paper no. 25. Reprinted by permission of author and publisher.)

1. *Statutes of the Province of Canada*, 20 Victoria, Chapter 26, 1857; *Statutes of Canada*, 32–33 Victoria, Chapter 6, 1869.
2. *Ibid.*

4. *Public Archives of Canada*, Ottawa, Record Group 10, Indian Affairs files (hereafter cited as *PAC*, RG–10), volume 3576, file 378; volume 3586, file 1137; volume 3604, file 2543; volume 3609, file 3229; volume 3625, file 5366; volume 3636, file 6694-1; volume 3616, file 4490. *Public Archives of Manitoba*, Winnipeg, Adams G. Archibald Papers (hereafter cited as *PAM*, Collection title), Archibald to Secretary of State for the Provinces, January 5, 1872; Archibald to Kusisheway, January 4, 1872; Archibald to Pascal Breland, February 22, 1872; Joseph Howe to Archibald, June 30, 1872; *PAM*, Lt. Governor's Collection, Alexander Morris to Minister of the Interior, July 7, 1873. William Francis Butler, *The Great Lone Land* (Vermont: Rutledge, 1970), 358–62, 369. John MacDougall, *Opening of the Great West-Experience of a Missionary in 1875–1876* (Calgary: Glenbow Alberta Institute, 1970), 20–21.
4. Alexander Morris, *The Treaties of Canada with the Indians of Manitoba and the North-West Territories* (Toronto: Belfords Clarke & Co., 1880), 28–29, 96–97, 120–21, 204–209, 211, 268–69.
5. *Ibid.*, 31, 118–23, 215–21, 270–74; "The Reminiscences of Peter Erasmus," as told to Henry T. Thompson, *Glenbow Alberta Institute*, Calgary, Alberta, 250–62.
6. Treaties 1, 2, and 7 stipulate the site of the reserves; see Morris, *Treaties of Canada*, 313–20, 338–42, 368–75. Most of the bands living in the Treaty 4 and 6 area had made known within a year of taking treaty where they wanted their reserves—some were even living on those sites. *PAC*, RG–10, volume 3625, file 5489, Indian Commissioner W.J. Christie to Minister of the Interior David Laird, October 7, 1875; volume 3, file 6694-1, W.J. Christie to Alexander Morris, October 12, 1876.
7. *PAC*, RG–10, volume 3609, file 3229; volume 3625, file 5489; volume 3636, file 6694-1; volume 3672, file 10, 853; volume 3665, file 10,094 entire files; *Opening Up the West: Being the Official Reports of the North-West Mounted Police from 1874-1881*, 1877 Report (Toronto: MacLean, Roger & Co., 1973), 22–23.
8. *PAC*, RG–10, volume 3625, file 5489; volume 3636, file 6694-1, volume 3716, file 22,367; volume 33635, file 6567; volume 3665, file 10,094.
9. *PAC*, RG–10, volume 3672, file 10,853; volume 3619, file 425; volume 3700, file 17,027; volume 3665, file 10,094; volume 3686, file 13,364, volume 3704, file 17,858; volume 3648, file 8162-2; volume 3699, file 16,580.
10. Morris, *Treaties of Canada*, 169–71; "The Reminiscences of Peter Erasmus", 251–58; Butler, *Great Lone Land*, 270–71, 358–60; J. Hines, *The Red Indians of the Plains: Thirty Years Missionary Experience in Saskatchewan* (Toronto: MacLean, Roger & Co., 1916), 78–79, 188–89.
11. *PAC*, RG–10, volume 3636, file 6694-2; volume 3625, file 5489, W.J. Christie to Minister of the Interior D. Laird, October 7, 1875. Morris, *Treaties of Canada*, 115–23, 210–23.
12. *Ibid.*; see also Morris, *Treaties of Canada*, 236–41.
13. *PAC*; RG–10, volume 3768, file 33,642, "Notes of the Governor General's Conversations with the Indian Leaders of the North-West (1881)."
14. *PAC*; RG–10, volume 3682, file 12, 667, Indian Commissioner Dewdney to Supt. General of Indian Affairs, April 28, 1884; volume 3686, file 13,168, Agent MacDonald to Indian Commissioner, May 15, 1884; volume 3745, file 29,506-4, volumes 1 and 2; volume 3576, files 309A and B; volume 3697, file 15,423; volume 3701, file 17,109.
15. Confrontations took place in Sakemay and Poundmaker Reserves and next to Pasquah Reserve where the Mounted Police, hoping to arrest Piapot in the middle of the night found themselves totally surrounded—in all of these incidents the police blundered into impossible situations and avoided complete annihilation only because the Indians did not wish to use violence. *PAC*, RG–10, volume 3576, file 30,913; volume 3666, file 10,181; volume 3745, file 29,506-4. *Settlers and Rebels*

Being the Official Reports to Parliament of the Activities of the North-West Mounted Police from 1882 to 1885 by the Commissioner of the NWMP (Toronto: MacLean, Roger & Co., 1973). The report for 1884 gives an edited and somewhat favourable, toward the police, account of these incidents.

16. PAC, RG–10, volume 3584, file 1130, Asst. Commissioner of Indian Affairs, Hayter Reed to Indian Commissioner, re: Future Management of Indian Affairs, n.d. (ca. July 1885); file 1130-1B, Deputy Supt. General of Indian Affairs L. Vankoughnet to Dewdney, October 28, 1885.
17. *PAC*, RG–10, volume 3671, file 10,836; volume 3720, file 22,897; volume 6809, file 470-2-3, volume 11, part 4; volume 3939 to 3941 all contain files numbered 121, 598 which go into detail in the government's policy regarding chiefs and councils in the period 1888–1890 and the Indians' reaction to this policy. Government of Canada, Ottawa, *Sessional Papers* (hereafter cited as *CSP*), 30 Victoria, 1887, no. 6, p. 109; *CSP*, 52 Victoria, 1887, no. 16, p. 128.
18. PAC, RG–10, volume 3584, file 1130 and 1130-1B, Reed to Commissioner, Future Management of Indian Affairs, n.d.: Vankoughnet to Commissioner, October 28, 1885; volume 3832, file 64,009; volume 2446, file 93,503; volume 2497, file 102,950; volume 3378, file 77,020; volume 6809, file 470-2-3, volume 11, part 4. *Statutes of Canada*, 33 Victoria, Chapter 29, 1890; 58–59 Victoria, Chapter 35, 1895.
19. *CSP*, 50 Victoria, 1887, no. 6, pp. 108–09; 52 Victoria, 1889, no. 16, p. 128; 53 Victoria, 1890, no. 12, pp. 165–66; *PAC*, RG–10, volume 3964, file 138,285.
20. *PAC*, RG–10, volume 3947, file 123,764-2; volume 6808, file 470-2-3; volume 11; *Statutes of Canada*, 57–58 Victoria, Chapter 32, 1894.
21. *PAC*, RG–10, volume 3825, file 60,511, volumes 1 and 2; volume 6809, file 472-3, volume 11, part 4; *Statutes of Canada*, 53 Victoria, Chapter 27, 1884; 58–59 Victoria, Chapter 35, 1894; 4-5 George V, Chapter 35, 1914.
22. *PAC*, RG–10, volume 2378, file 77,020; volume 2832, file 69,009; volume 2446, file 93,503; volume 2497, file 102, 950; *Statutes of Canada*, 53 Victoria, Chapter 29, 1890.
23. *PAC*, RG–10, volume 6809, file 470-2-4, volume 11, parts 4 to 6; volume 6810, file 470-2-3, volume 12, parts 7 and 8. *Statutes of Canada*, 47 Victoria, Chapter 27, 1884; 58–59 Victoria, Chapter 35, 1895; 4–5 George V, Chapter 35, 1914; 10–11 George V, Chapter 50, 1920; 20–21 George V, Chapter 25, 1930.
24. *PAC*, RG–10, volume 3847, file 82,250-4; volume 3806, file 52,332; volume 3864, file 148,285; *CSP*, 45 Victoria, 1882, No. 6, p. 40; 51 Victoria, 1888, No. 15, p. 190; 50 Victoria 1887, No. 6, pp. 108–109; 53 Victoria, 1890, No. 12, p. 112.
25. *PAC*, RG–10, volume 3857, file 32,250-4; volume 3806, file 52,332; volume 3864, file 148,285.
26. The law was interpreted for many years as banning White man's dances, and Indian tea dances or round dances; *PAC*, RG–10, volume 3825, file 60,511, volumes 1 and 2, entire files.
27. *PAC*, RG–10, volumes 3934 to 3941, files that begin with 121,689.
28. *PAC*, RG–10, volume 3845, files 73,406-8 and 9; volume 7769, file 28,114-2; volume 3806, file 52,332; volume 3851, file 82,250-4; volume 3864, file 148,285.
29. *PAC*, RG–10, volume 6732, file 420-2 *passim*.
30. *PAC*, RG–10, volume 3880, file 92,449; volume 3940, file 121,698-13; plus many others; P.H. Bryce, *Report on the Indian Schools of Manitoba and North-West Territories* (Ottawa: Department of the Interior, 1907).
31. *PAC*, RG–10, volume 4053, files 379,203-162; volume 3939, file 121,698-8.
32. *PAC*, RG–10, volume 6810, file 470-2-3, volume 12, part 7.
33. *Ibid.*, and part 10, also RG–10, volume 6809, file 470-2-3, volume11, part 4; volume 6809, file 470-2-3, volume 11, parts 5 and 6. *Revised Statutes of Canda* 1906, Chapter 81; Statutes of Canada, 61 Victoria, Chapter 34, 1896; 6 Edward VII, Chapter 20, July 13, 1907; 9-10 Edward VII, Chapter 28, 1910; 1-2 George V, Chapter 14, 1911; 9-

10 George V, Chapter 56, 1919; 2 George VI, Chapter 31, 1938; 8-9 George V, "An Act to Amend the Indian Act," May 24, 1918.

34. *PAC*, RG–10, volume 6810, file 470-2-3, volume 12, part 7, "Memo on Enfranchisement."
35. *Ibid.*; volume 6809, file 470-2-3, volume 11, part 6; *Statutes of Canada*, 8–9 George V, May 24, 1918.
36. *PAC*, RG–10, volume 6810, file 470-2-3, volume 12, parts 7–9. *Statutes of Canada*, 10–11 George V, Chapter 50, 1920; 12–13 George V, Chapter 26, 1922; 23–24 George V, Chapter 42, 1933.
37. Statutes listed under fr. 34, and 12–13 George V, Chapter 26, 1922; 20–21 George V, Chapter 25, 1930; I Edward VIII, Chapter 20, 1936; *PAC*, RG–10, volume 6810, file 470-2-3, volume 12, parts 7–9.
38. *Statement of the Government of Canada on Indian Policy 1969*, presented to the First Session of the 28th Parliament by the Honourable Jean Chrétien, Minister of Indian Affairs and Northern Development (Ottawa, 1969).

PART IV
The Pacific Region

In the Introduction to this volume, we considered the position of the Indians of the North Pacific Coast. There I noted doubts in the literature as to whether these Indians shared in the foraging mode of production. Richard Lee,[1] for example, maintains that these societies did not take part in the foraging mode of production, even though they subsisted on the products of field, forest, and tide. Thus, among the Tsimshian, Kwakiutl, Nootka, and their neighbours, production was not organized in an egalitarian manner. Just how much this was so is shown by Leland Donald's chapter on "Slave Raiding in the North Pacific Coast." Furthermore, Professor Donald argues that, contrary to current opinion among anthropologists, slave labour played an important part in the region's production. Professor Donald speculates that the anomalous position of the societies of the Northwest Coast derived from the presence of slaves:

> Nowhere else in North America do we find slavery important either numerically or productively. I suspect that many of the other distinctive features of the culture area are associated with the fact that many of the Northwest Coast societies were, like the Nuu-chah-nulth-aht, based on slave labour.[2]

Donald posed that question in the context of an implicit comparison with Athens in the fourth century B.C. or the southern United States during the eighteenth century. This may strike some of the wrong resonances because, although Northwest Coast society was hierarchical, slavish even, it was not patriarchal. In fact, early observers often reported that women were the dominant sex in many coastal societies. Thus, Robert Haswell, commanding the trading sloop *Adventure* in 1792,[3] referred to Cunneah's wife as "Chief of the Haida" because of her dominant role in trading. Evidently Captain Vancouver formed a similar opinion of the Tlingit women he encountered. Furthermore, for some women, things got even better as time went on, as the contributions by Jo-Anne Fiske and Lorraine Littlefield show. Up and down the coast, women forged an important (often dominant) role in the marine fur trade. This was possible, Littlefield argues, because men feared to damage reputations of generosity by haggling over the price of furs and crafts. Women evidently did not labour under any such stricture, allowing them often to control such transactions. Jo-Anne Fiske shows that among the Carrier of central British Columbia, the salmon fishery became "the business of women." This came to pass when the *Barricade Treaty* of 1911 prohibited what had been male means of fishing.[4] Men could no longer co-operate in the construction and operation of salmon weirs, nor would they net salmon. Thus, Carrier women took over the fishery. There is also an ideological side to this control of production, as we might expect from earlier discussions:

> Salmon fishing remains the strongest affirmation of women's rights, responsibilities and ties to the land. It is the right of women to follow their foremothers as owners and managers of fishing sites. It is also their responsibility to nourish their people. This entails more than the mere feeding and care of dependents and the impoverished. It calls for political actions which seek to preserve Carrier culture, protect the environment and retain it for the future generations. . . ."[5]

In the chapters by Littlefield and Fiske, commodity production and (for the Carrier) the ironies of state intervention gave native women a wider economic scope. Nevertheless, native women did not always benefit from state intervention. Quite the contrary, as Fiske's discussion of the role of the state in Carrier trapping shows:

> Land and resources were wrenched from the Carrier at the discretion of state agents. Lines deemed unused or underexploited were transferred to White trappers . . . [Nevertheless] women continued to trap.[6]

The state's intervention in native subsistence production is also the theme of the final contribution to this section. Recall that in Part III, we saw that Canadian Indians, for more than a century now, have been hedged about with every sort of regulation and constraint, all intended to protect and "civilize" them. This has led, as we have seen, to keeping Indians divided, disorganized, and apathetic. James McDonald puts this somewhat differently: he writes of the provincial Fisheries Act of 1901 as "marginalizing the Tsimshian in their own environment."[7] In another telling phrase, McDonald also writes of the "redefinition" of native resources by the federal and provincial governments. Thus in the 1880s, the Tsimshian learned that anyone who held a timber lease on Crown lands could prevent their cutting trees for house timbers or storage boxes; in the 1920s, they were prevented from taking bark from hemlock or cedar trees on Crown lands. No more could they collect the eggs of grouse, robins, blackbirds, thrush, wild ducks, geese, swans, shorebirds, or cranes. And so on. "Rich as the natural resources were," McDonald concludes, those "available to the Indians became impoverished."[8]

Such changes, and the demands of commodity production, wrought large transformations in the Tsimshian yearly round of subsistence activities. Furthermore, these changes

> . . . were not simply adaptations to their given environment, but accommodations to the socially defined environment being created under the new political economy that was emerging in the region. As capitalist production became dominant, the Tsimshian political economy was assigned to a marginal position.[9]

The next act in that drama has yet to be written. Can the Tsimshian move their political economy from its present position marginal to the Canadian and world economies? Perhaps so, but a remedy must depend on the Tsimshian regaining the right to harvest fully the resources of their territory.

Notes

1. Richard Lee, "Is There a Foraging Mode of Production?" *Canadian Journal of Anthropology*, vol. 2, no. 1 (1981).
2. Leland Donald, "Was Nuu-chah-nulth-aht (Nootka) Society Based on Slave Labour?" in *The Development of Political Organization in Native North America*, edited by E. Tooker. Proceedings of the American Ethnology Society, (1979).
3. R. Haswell, "Log of the First Voyage of the Columbia," in *Voyages of the Columbia*, edited by F.W. Howay (Boston, MA: Historical Society, 1940).
4. Chapter 14 of this volume.
5. Chapter 14 of this volume.
6. Chapter 14 of this volume.
7. Chapter 15 of this volume.
8. Chapter 15 of this volume.
9. Chapter 15 of this volume.

Chapter 12
Slave Raiding on the North Pacific Coast

Leland Donald

This paper is a brief discussion of the conjunction of two important but relatively neglected aspects of Northwest Coast ethnography: slavery and warfare. Its primary purpose is to describe and discuss inter-group attacks which had as one of their outcomes the capture of prisoners who subsequently became slaves. As background to this discussion, the paper begins with short overviews of slavery and warfare as practised by the aboriginal inhabitants of what is commonly called the Northwest Coast culture area.

Slavery was practised and warfare was important throughout the North Pacific Coast region of North America. This paper concentrates on the Northwest Coast culture area which is defined here as the coastal belt of societies stretching from Yakutat Bay in the north to the mouth of the Columbia River in the south. It should be remembered, however, that slave raids occurred in the wider region as well.[1]

The time period considered here is that best covered in the ethnographic and historic sources, roughly 1780 until 1880, with the emphasis on the first half of that period. During this time the aboriginal inhabitants of the region were transformed from people living in autonomous societies to survivors of those societies who had forcibly been incorporated into the larger Canadian and American nations. Obviously it was a period of great social change for the aboriginal inhabitants of the region.

Northwest Coast Societies were not politically unified above the local community level. Therefore, in matters of raiding and warfare the most useful unit of analysis is the local community—usually the winter village. The material on which this paper is based was assembled during an extensive study of Northwest Coast slavery and other inter-group relations. Altogether nearly eight hundred published and unpublished, historic and ethnographic, sources were combed for data.[2] One goal of the research was to locate all data as precisely as possible in space and time. In order to insure a balanced coverage of the regions while maintaining a focus on specific communities, files were constructed for each village community in the culture area with reasonably full material on slavery. This produced sixteen files based on a single winter village community or on a set of neighbouring and very similar winter village communities. Because of some significant gaps in regional coverage within the culture area, four broader files were added. These twenty files are the basis of most of the generalizations presented in this paper. The twenty files from North to South are (broad files italicized): Yakutat, Chilkat, Sitka, Stikine, *Lower Skeena Tsimshian*, *Haida*, *Bella Coola*, Fort Rupert, Kwakiutl, Moachat,

Clayoquot, Makah, Saanich, Klallam, Lummi, Skagit, Puyallup-Nisqually, Twana, Quileute, Quinalut, and *Lower Chinook*.

Slavery

Slaves were present in all Northwest Coast societies. These very low status persons were labeled by a special term in all the culture area's languages. In many communities, slaves could be distinguished from their fellows by special haircuts, or other external markers. We can confidently call such individuals slaves because their status conforms to that of the usual definition of slave whether that definition emphasizes slaves as "property" or as "socially alienated."[4]

The status of slave was hereditary: the children of slaves were slaves. Slaves had no rights or privileges. Masters could and did exercise physical control over their slaves, even killing them if they chose. Owners did, at times, kill their slaves. Although the occasion of the killing was usually ritual, the particular slaves chosen for the sacrifice might very well have caused problems in a purely secular context. Shakes, the most prominent Stikine leader, for example, had a slave whom he allowed to own slaves, even his own canoe. But, after the slave bragged that Shakes would never do anything to him, Shakes killed him during a ceremony.[5]

Slaves were owned by individuals in their own right or, probably the more usual situation, by the descent groups of which the nominal owner was the head. Some owners held numerous slaves; for example, it was claimed that the famous Moachat leader Maquina, owned about fifty.[6] Others held only one or two slaves. The proportion of slaves in a community also varied greatly from group to group. Sometimes neighbouring villages contained quite different percentages of slaves, although it is a trend for the proportion of slaves to increase as one goes north. (The Lower Chinook were an exception; they had a "northern" rate of slave holding during the early contact period.) The problem of numbers cannot be treated in detail here. A winter village's proportion of slaves would sometimes reach 30 percent and frequently the proportion ranged from 15 to 25 percent. Thus, for some winter villages a major segment of the population was slave.[7]

The economic significance of slaves is a matter of some controversy among students of the Northwest Coast. The orthodox view is well represented by Drucker's statement that, "[a] slave's economic utility was negligible."[8] Recent re-examination of the ethnographic and historic sources, however, shows that slaves were of considerable importance to the economy of many Northwest Coast communities.[9] This economic importance was of two kinds: the labour power of slaves was significant in a range of subsistence and other mundane tasks, and slaves were an important item in inter-group transactions, especially trade.

The available evidence, although not as detailed as is desirable, strongly suggests that, in many local groups, slaves contributed significantly to their master's well-being by their labour at subsistence tasks. It was probably the case that rarely were the members of an owner's household freed from all subsistence work by slave labour. Slaves were also important as literally "hewers of wood and drawers of water." In addition, slaves carried out the duties common to servants in many other areas: the preparation and serving of food, caring of children, running errands, carrying messages, and so on. Indeed, it can be argued that the contributions of slave labour were crucial to freeing members of the Northwest Coast elites to pursue prestige, and otherwise engage in the elaborate activities that have made the region famous: potlatches, elaborate ritual performances, and complex and elaborate art.[10]

The trade in slaves was intense throughout the historic period, especially in the northern part of the culture area. The slave trade was probably less intense but still important in pre-contact times. Throughout the fur trade period, especially the land-based fur trade period (post-1820), the slave trade and the fur trade were significantly linked. There were native middle-men who dealt in slaves in order to deal in furs and the comments of Hudson's Bay employees make the link between the two trades clear. Many prominent native figures of the first half of the nineteenth century owed their positions in large part to their skill in dealing in both slaves and furs.[11]

Slaves were ultimately the product of violence—they were either captives or the children of captives. If a community was attacked, anyone living in the community was a potential slave, although the expressed preference was for women and children. Some of those taken would already be slaves, and like other property taken, merely undergo a change in ownership. Others were free and became slave. And, with occasional exceptions, ex-title-holders were treated like other slaves, being put to the same drudgery and running the same risks as their fellow slaves of commoner origin.

Sometimes a victimized group attempted to ransom or redeem recent captives. A member of an important title-holder family was probaby more likely to be ransomed than a commoner, but many former title-holders spent their lives in slavery. In the historic period, Europeans were readily enslaved under suitable circumstances. When slaves were redeemed, all did not necessarily go well for the former slave. Rituals were performed to remove the stain of slavery, but it seems that the status of slave was so degrading that some of the stain remained. Former slaves seemed to have been at risk of re-enslavement. The slave status of an ancestor could affect a person's life even into recent times. Consider, for example, Colson's account of a Makah man who withdrew from reservation political life after it was rumoured that he was descended from a slave.[12]

The Production of Slaves

Although slaves are human beings, they are also objects and as such must be produced. Slave raids are an important aspect of Northwest Coast slavery because of the way slaves were produced in the region. A person could become a slave on the Northwest coast in one of two major ways: by birth into slavery, or by capture in war. In a few groups people could gamble themselves into slavery, debtors became slaves, orphans were enslaved, or a murderer or his relative could become a slave as a part of restitution to the victim's family. But these methods are rarely reported. Clearly most slaves were war captives, with most of the rest being the children of war captives. There is no way to be sure of the ratio, but the impression given by reading the available material is that a very high proportion of slaves were first generation captives. Since there was an active trade in slaves, many of a group's slaves may not have been captured by group members but were captives who had been obtained in trade. Most of the slaves present in any Northwest community were the direct products of capture either by members of the owner's community or had been acquired in trade from the captors. Where individuals had been born into slavery, their status was ultimately the result of the capture of either their parents, or perhaps their grandparents. Thus virtually all Northwest Coast slaves were the product of violence which directly (or indirectly for those born slave) alienated them from their natural circumstances. This does not make slaves in the region unique, of course, for violent alienation, seizure by force is the ultimate basis of slave status everywhere.

War

Although it has not often been discussed at length or in detail, inter-village fighting was very frequent on the Northwest Coast. Ethnographers have not stressed this, but a careful reading of the texts they collected and of the historic record supports this view.[13] The term "war" will be used here in the sense that it was probably used throughout the culture area, although the only clear description of the use of such a term that I am aware of comes from the Southern Kwakiutl: " *wī'na* indicates not only fights between tribes or clans but also deeds of individuals who set out to kill a member or members of another group."[14] Violent conflicts between members of different winter villages were incidents of "war," and even conflicts between members of different descent groups within the same village may have been viewed the same way. Boas goes on to remind us that relations between groups were complex and we can see why Mauss used the peoples of the Northwest Coast as one of his typical cases of societies possessing a system of "total prestations": "The same term is also used for the procedure customary in the marriage of a young man to a woman of another tribe or clan. The bride is 'obtained in war.' In tales, it is often said that she is given in order to avoid a warlike attack by visitors."[15]

Reading the literature on the entire coast leaves the impression that any time members of more than one group came together there was the possibility of violence. Although they should have been free of such events, even ceremonial feasts (potlatches) might become scenes of inter-group violence.[16]

But, although fighting could break out in many contexts, the organized war expedition was a feature of most, if not all, Northwest Coast Societies. Most accounts in the literature are retrospective descriptions by participants or other informants, while some are accounts by contemporary observers of at least part of an expedition's progress. Although there is variation according to differing circumstances and groups, the general outline of such ventures seems to have been similar throughout the culture area.

McIlwraith offers a generalized picture of Bella Coola warfare based on informants' memories, but his description is consistent with accounts of actual wars. Basic to their warfare was the raid, a planned organized attack on a non-Bella Coola-speaking community. The usual motivation was retaliation for raids by the intended victims. If the inhabitants of a town agreed that retaliation was desirable, a raid would be organized by a prominent man, usually one who held the status of "warrior." Such a leader did not have strong control over his followers. He could compel the services of only his slaves; others followed him only if they wished to do so. Men from other Bella Coola villages might also join the expedition, especially if they desired revenge for the death of a relative. Plans for an attack were usually discussed during the winter months, and raids usually took place in late spring and early summer.

Raiders usually travelled by canoe. As they neared enemy country they began travelling at night, hiding their canoes during the day. During this journey a definite order of procedure was supposed to be followed. There was a fixed order of seating in each canoe (the captain sat in the stern), and a strict ritual for eating and drinking (involving the number four—four bites of salmon chewed four times, four swallows of water). At night the men slept around an unlit fire. Those remaining behind were also required to follow certain rules: the wives were expected to live quietly, as a woman's careless play would lead to the injury of her husband, and her faithlessness would lead to his death.

When the expedition neared the target village, a scouting canoe was sent out. The scouts usually went off at dusk to spy out the enemy position and to try to determine the best plan of attack. If the scout's report was promising, the attackers moved into position near the village. The goal was complete surprise, and if this seemed to be impossible the attack was usually called off. The attack came at dawn: with a fierce shout the warriors would rush to attack the house which they had been assigned. They endeavoured to kill the village men, and take the women and children captive. The successful warriors would then cut off the heads of their victims, seize what loot they could, set fire to the houses, and set out for home before help could come from a neighbouring village.

The victors hurried home, hoping to avoid being cut off by reinforcements from the victims' relatives and friends. On the journey home, each man who had taken a head cut off its scalp. As the canoes neared home, the scalps were displayed and victory songs performed. The prisoners of war usually became slaves, although a few were occasionally ransomed.[17]

Texts describing war, and informants' accounts from many Northwest Coast groups, are similar to the Bella Coola material in many aspects: the surprise attack at dawn, the mixture of practical and ritual preparations and precautions, the primary objects of the raid being killing and looting, the raid ending with a quick retreat, and the possibility of pursuit by the victims and/or their kin.

The motives for these attacks were varied. Among the most prominent and frequently mentioned are revenge, territorial expansion, plunder, and the acquisition of slaves. Often more than one motive was involved. The consequences of such raids—deaths in the community attacked, booty, slaves, houses and other material burned or otherwise destroyed, casualties among the raiders, and possible provocation of a retaliatory attack—should be distinguished from motivation.

There is one point about Northwest Coast warfare which has aroused some interest and controversy: the *causes* of Northwest Coast warfare. The two most influential analyses of war in the region are Codere's[18] discussion of the Southern Kwakiutl and Swadesh's[19] paper on the Nuu-chah-nulth (Nootka). Codere not only denies the importance of Kwakiutl warfare (being unwilling to call it "true warfare"), but strongly argues that what inter-group fighting there was, was not "economically" motivated. Rather she sees revenge and the seeking of prestige as the motivations for Kwakiutl warfare. Swadesh showed that the principal motivation to be found in Nuu-chah-nulth warfare texts was territorial expansion. Clearly economic motivations were significant. Although little systematic work on Northwest Coast warfare has been done, Codere's claims about the motives (or causes, Codere does not clearly distinguish them) of Kwakiutl warfare have been accepted and taken as applying to the culture area as a whole; the Nuu-chah-nulth are treated as an exception in the region. Territorial expansion was certainly an important consequence of inter-group fighting in many parts of the culture area: we have clear evidence of territorial expansion, not only by various Nuu-chah-nulth local groups, but also by the Lequiltok Kwakiutl against several Salish groups, the Kaigani Haida against several Southern Tlingit groups, various Tlingit groups against other Tlingit, and so on.[20]

On the other hand, virtually every account of inter-group fighting on the Northwest Coast contains the motif of revenge. The desire for revenge was often generalized rather than focussed on a specific individual or even a specific local group. If someone from another group killed a community member, revenge might well be sought against the offender's group; but often the would-be revengers would kill the first person they encountered who was not a member of their community, be satisfied, and return home. Revenge was especially likely after the death of a title-holder, even if the death was from apparently natural causes. It often seems that the goal was death, any death, so as to balance the community's loss.

Aside from territorial gain and revenge, the other major motivation for attacks was plunder which might be corporeal or incorporeal. Boxes, blankets, foodstuffs, and ritual paraphernalia were all forms of plunder. If the owners of particular songs, crests, or rituals were killed, not only was the appropriate ritual gear acquired but also their ownership. Such bloody acquisitions were one way that rituals and ceremonies diffused in the culture area.

Captives, most of whom became slaves, were also an important form of plunder. Prisoners could be the by-product of any attack, whatever the motive; but the taking of slaves could also be the primary motive for expeditions. Ten of the sample groups contain explicit statements that the motive for some attacks was the taking of slaves and the same primary motive is implied in several other groups.[21]

Thus attacks could have a variety of motivations. Indeed, most probably had several. With this brief sketch of Northwest Coast warfare as background we can now turn to the kind of expedition which saw the conjunction of slavery and warfare on the Northwest Coast: the slave raid.

Slave Raids

Although the motives for the organizing and carrying out of an attack on another local group were varied, the taking of prisoners who became slaves was a common outcome of successful attacks whether or not one of the initial motives of an expedition was the acquisition of slaves. For ease of discussion, it will be helpful to first consider the consequences of raids in general.

As a part of the widespread pattern of inter-group fighting on the Northwest Coast, neighbouring communities, as well as more distant communities, were attacked. Indeed, in some parts of the region, even those residing within the same village did not have complete immunity from armed attack by community members of different descent groups, acting in co-operation with non-community members. Any of these attacks might result in slaves being taken. In two of the sample groups forcible enslavement by members of one's own local group is reported (Puyallup-Nisquallyl, Yakutat), while in only three groups is such within-group slaving explicitly denied (Lower Chinook, Twana, Bella Coola). For thirteen sampled groups there are reports of enslavement by force of members of the same language unit. For example, slaves are recorded as having been taken from the Ninstints, Kaigani, Skidigate, and Massett—all Haida local groups—by other Haida. There are also records of at least seven Tlingit winter village communities being raided for slaves by other Tlingit, and of at least twelve Nuu-chah-nulth communities having residents enslaved by other Nuu-chah-nulth. Nor was the raiding of groups with the same language confined to the north or central coast for the records show that several Salish-speaking groups were raided for slaves by other Salish who belonged to their own dialect set. It is quite probable that there were many more such raids for most of the records we have do not specify the raided or raiding groups, and, obviously, there were a great many raids of which we have no records at all.

This brings us to the question: what was the pattern of raiding for slaves? Sometimes neighbour raided neighbour, but what sticks in the mind after a reading of the literature are the long-distance slave raids. The accounts, for example, of Haida bringing home Coast Salish slaves after a trip to the southern part of Vancouver Island conjure up images of regular trips during which Haida and other northern people fought and slaved their way back from Victoria to their home villages. The distance from the Queen Charlottes to Victoria and back is considerable and from such accounts we could easily assume that these spectacular journeys were typical of slave raids in general. But such raids need to be placed in a historical context. Fort Victoria was not built until 1843, so the pull on northern Indians to the southern Gulf of Georgia did not become strong until well into the land-based fur trade period.

There is evidence which suggests that slave raids were undertaken at much shorter distances in the early historic period, and that the spectacular long distance raids like those of the Haida were a late development made possible and encouraged by the land-based fur trade, especially by the building of such key posts as Fort Victoria. The ethnographic record is rarely time-specific and is thus of little help with this problem. If we divide the dateable historic record into pre-1845 and post-1845 periods we find that, in the earlier period, almost all groups raided within their own geographic region (86 percent), whereas after 1845 the proportion of raiders and raided who fell within the same region was much lower (41 percent).[22] In pre-contact and early contact times, we can be fairly certain that raids were primarily made on groups that were not far away, and which often spoke the same language.

Predatory Warfare

Slaves were a common by-product of inter-group fighting, even when the conflict was between neighbours and the motives were revenge, territory, or other kinds of plunder. It may even be that this incidental or casual production of slaves was the major source of slaves in pre-contact times. By the time the land-based fur trade was well established (the 1820s), raids whose primary goal was the capture of slaves had become important. Slave raiding became so important that one mid-nineteenth century observer described Northwest Coast fighting as a "cruel system of predatory warfare."[23]

The journal of the Hudson's Bay Company post at Fort Simpson refers to "predatory warfare," and illustrates several other changes that were affecting slavery and other aspects of Northwest Coast life:

> Quatkie [a Stikine Tlingit leader] has a certificate from the Governor at Sitka with his seal of office attached and an English translation highly recommending Quatkie for listening to his counsel instead of killing his slaves on the death of any principal man or his relatives, as is customary among the Stikeen and some other tribes, he spared their lives and gave them their freedom. This is certainly a considerable point gained, but owing to the scarcity of furs the Indians are becoming poorer every year and they are so fond of property of which slaves constitute the principal part of what they possess, I should not think much persuasion necessary to deter them from killing them. I have never known an instance of such taking place among the Chimsyans since I have been here. Could the natives be dissuaded from trafficking in slaves altogether it would be the means of doing away with a good deal of predatory warfare among themselves.[24] (21 June, 1838)

It was a widespread Northwest Coast practice to kill one or more slaves upon the death of important members of the elite. Although among some groups slaves were killed on other ritual occasions, the killing of slaves at elite funerals was practised over most of the coast—from Yakutat in the north down to the Lower Chinook in the south. As the nineteenth century passed, more leaders freed rather than killed their slaves.[25] As the Hudson's Bay Company man writing at Fort Simpson shrewdly implies, the sparing of slaves was more probably due to their growing role as a trade item than to their owners' "enlightenment." His quotation clearly associates slaving and warfare, and mentions a "scarcity" of furs.

By the 1830s the trade in slaves and furs were clearly linked. No evidence suggests that Europeans were significantly engaged in the slave trade in a direct manner in the 1800s, but many Indian middle-men faced with local declines in furs found that slaves were the most important trade goods if they were to obtain furs from their more distant native trading partners. The profits possible when slaves were converted to furs often led them to bypass European trade goods and trading posts in favour of slave trading, which in turn encouraged slave raids.

James Douglas writing from Tlingit country in 1840 clearly connects the fur trade, the slave trade, and predatory warfare:

> . . . the species of property most highly prized among the natives of Tako [Taku] is that of slaves, which in fact constitutes their measure of wealth. . . . Slaves being through this national perversion of sentiment, the most saleable commodity here, the native pedlars, come from as far south as Kygarnie [Kaigani Haida] with their human assortments and readily obtain from 18 to 20 skins a head for them. The greater number of these slaves are captives made in war, and many predatory excursions are undertaken not to avenge international aggressions, but simply with a sordid view to the profits that may arise from the sale of the captives taken.
>
> This detestable traffic, and the evils it gives rise to, are subjects of deep regret to us, but we know of no remedy within our power, as we would use it were it only for the sake of our own interest, which is thereby seriously affected,as the Take [Taku Tlingit] skins are traded before our very eyes and carried off from our very door, by means of a description of property that we cannot compete in.
>
> A few days ago a canoe from Kygarnie brought in four slaves, and a second from Stekine [Stikine Tlingit] brought one which were immediately purchased at the prices stated above.[26]

It seems clear that the fur trade intensified the slave trade on the Northwest Coast, and thus contributed to the growth of predatory warfare. But the predatory warfare complex was not simply an outcome of European contact and the subsequent development of the fur trade. Rather, the predatory slave raid grew out of a traditional Northwest Coast cultural theme: the struggle for prestige. Underlying much political and economic activity in the culture area were the preparations by members of the elite for a "potlatch," those ceremonial feasts where property was given away and prestige acquired. An important potlatch might be years in the planning. The historic record suggests that by the 1830s some powerful members of the elite had found ways to both shorten the preparation time and greatly increase the economic scale of their feasting activity: they conducted raids for captives, most of whom became slaves. The slaves, as objects of wealth, were then either given away or traded for other goods—furs or European goods—which were then potlatched. The skillful leader could profit both from his raid and his subsequent trading activities, gaining both economically through trade, and politically or ceremonially through the potlatch. Donald Mitchell[27] has carefully reconstructed one such raid and its consequences, carried out by Tsibasa, leader of the Kitkatla Tsimshian, and shown that there is evidence that throughoput the culture area, especially in its northern region, such sequences of events became common in the first half of the nineteenth century. Thus it is probable that traditional cultural elements, such as the enslaving of war captives and the striving to increase social status, formed the foundation, when linked up with the new demand created by the fur trade, of the system of predatory warfare within which slave raiding flourished.

Conclusion

In this paper I have argued several major points. Hereditary slavery was an important feature in the societies and economies of the village communities of the Northwest Coast culture area, and they were important economically both for the contribution of their labour power and as items of high trade value. Virtually all slaves were ultimately produced by forcible seizure as either the object or by-product of attacks on other communities.

The motives for inter-village fighting were varied. They could include revenge (usually for the death of a community member), territorial gain, and plunder, which would include slaves.

Fighting often involved nearby neighbours, although villages at greater distances were also attacked. Frequently those attacked spoke the same language as their attackers. Slaves were taken from both groups. In the historic period, the distance involved in raids for slaves grew longer over time.

During the land-based fur trade period, the capture of slaves became a major motive for many attacks, especially in the northern part of the culture area. Slave raiding became so important that a system of predatory warfare developed.

Striving for prestige was a significant elite activity on the Northwest Coast. Slaves were important to the elite both for their exploitable labour and as high-value trade items. During the fur trade, slaves became even more important to the striving for prestige and power because of the high profits that came when the slave and fur trades were linked. Such high potential profits led many leaders to become involved in predatory warfare.

Notes

My colleague Donald Mitchell and I have been working on this project since the mid-1970s. We are grateful for the support of the Social Sciences and Humanities

Research Council of Canada, the University of Victoria Faculty Research Committee, and the Province of British Columbia's Youth Employment Programme.

1. For the Aleut, see Joan Townsend, "Pre-contact Political Organization and Slavery in Aleut Society," in *The Development of Political Organization in Native North America*, edited by E. Tooker (1979 Proceedings of the American Ethnological Society, 1983), 120–32; for a wider perspective on the area north of the Northwest Coast, see Jean Malaurie, "Raids et esclavage dans les sociétés autochtones du détroit Behring," *Inter-Nord* 13/14 (1974):129–55.
2. For other results of this project, see Leland Donald, "Was Nuu-chah-nulth-aht (Nootka) Society Based on Slave Labor?" in Tooker, *Political Organization in Native North America*; Leland Donald, "The Slave Trade on the Northwest Coast of North America," *Research in Economic Anthropology* 6 (1984):121–58; Leland Donald, "Captive or Slave? A Comparison of Northeastern and Northwestern North America by Means of Captivity Narratives," *Culture* V (1985):17–23; Donald Mitchell, "Predatory Warfare, Social Status, and the North Pacific Slave Trade," *Ethnology* 23 (1984):39–48; Donald Mitchell, "A Demographic Profile of Northwest Coast Slavery," in *Status, Structure, and Stratification*, edited by M. Thompson, M. Garcia, and F. Kense (Proceedings of the Sixteenth Annual Conference, Archaeological Association of the University of Calgary, 1985), 227–36; Donald Mitchell and Leland Donald, "Some Economic Aspects of Tlingit, Haida, and Tsimshian Slavery," *Research in Economic Anthropology* 7 (1985):19–36.
3. H.J. Niebor, *Slavery as an Industrial System* (The Hague: Martinus Nijhoff, 1910), 6.
4. Orlando Patterson, *Slavery and Social Death: A Comparative Study* (Cambridge, MA: Harvard University Press, 1982), 13.
5. R.L. Olson, *Social Structure and Social Life of the Tlingit in Alaska*, University of California Anthropological Records, 26 (Berkeley, 1967), 48B–57A.
6. John R. Jewitt, *Narrative of the Adventures and Sufferings of John R. Jewitt While Held as a Captive of the Nootka Indians of Vancouver Island, 1803–1805*, edited by Robert F. Heizer, Ballena Press Publications in Archaeology, Ethnology and History, no. 5 (1975).
7. For an analysis of the census data available on Northwest Coast slavery, see Mitchell, *Demographic Profile.*
8. Philip Drucker, *Cultures of the North Pacific Coast* (Scranton, Pennsylvania: Chandler Publishing Company, 1965), 52.
9. See Mitchell and Donald, *Economic Aspects*; and Donald, *Slave Trade on the Northwest Coast.*
10. See Kalervo Oberg, *The Social Economy of the Tlingit Indians* (Seattle: University of Washington Press, 1973), for the distinciton between "ceremonial" labour and "common" labour in which the importance of slave labour is implicit; and Donald, *Nuu-chah-nulth-aht Society*, where it is argued that slave labour is "fundamental" to Nuu-chah-nulth (Nootka) society as ethnographically known.
11. For a detailed analysis of the slave trade, see Donald, *Slave Trade on the Northwest Coast*; for the link between political prominence and slaving see Mitchell, *Predatory Warfare.*
12. Elizabeth Colson, *The Makah Indians* (Manchester: Manchester University Press, 1953), 220.
13. For another assessment that agrees with this point of view, see R. Brian Ferguson, "A Reexamination of the Causes of Northwest Coast Warfare," in *Warfare, Culture and Environment*, edited by R.B. Ferguson (New York: Academic Press, 1984).
14. Franz Boas, *Kwakiutl Ethnography*, edited by Helen Codere (Chicago: University of Chicago Press, 1966), 108.
15. *Ibid.*

16. See Franz Boas, *Tsimshian Mythology*, Annual Report of the Bureau of American Ethnology, 1909–1910 (Washington: Government Printing Office, 1916), 355 *et seq* for an account of the killing of some Bella Bella potlatch messengers by the Southern Kwakiutl—potlatch messengers were supposed to be under safe conduct.
17. T.F. McIlwraith, *The Bella Coola Indians*, vol. II (Toronto: University of Toronto Press, 1948), 340–44.
18. Helen Codere, *Fighting with Property, A Study of Kwakiutl Potlatching and Warfare 1792–1930*, Monograph of the American Ethnological Society 18 (Seattle and London: University of Washington Press, 1950).
19. Morris Swadesh, "Motivations in Nootka Warfare," *Southwestern Journal of Anthropology* 4 (1948):75–93.
20. Note that all these examples come from the Northern or Central parts of the culture area. The evidence for territorial expansion in the Southern part of the region is much thinner.
21. Attacks, at least one of whose motives was the taking of slaves, occurred among the Yakutat, Chilkat, Sitka, Stikine, Lower Skeena Tsimshian, Haida, Fort Rupert Kwakiutl, Puyallap-Nisqually, Quileute, and Lower Chinook. Slave raiding is a possible motive among the Moachat, Clayoquot, and Saanich.
22. These proportions are significantly different by chi-square test ($P \leq .01$).
23. Richard Charles Mayne, *Four Years in British Columbia and Vancouver Island* (London: John Murray, 1862), 74.
24. Fort Simpson Journal 1838–1840, manuscript, B201/a/4, Hudson's Bay Company Archives, Provincial Archives of Manitoba, Winnipeg.
25. Or they broke coppers instead. For the substitution of coppers for slaves in rituals of destruction, see Martine de Widersprach-Thor, "The Equation of Copper," *Papers from the Sixth Annual Congress, 1979, Canadian Ethnology Society*, National Museum of Man Mercury Series, Canadian Ethnology Service, 78 (1981); Donald, "Slave Trade on the Northwest Coast," 141–42.
26. James Douglas, "Diary of a Trip to the Northwest Coast, Ap. 22 - Oct. 2, 1840," manuscript, British Columbia Provincial Archives. For a detailed discussion of the slave trade-fur trade nexus, see Donald, *Slave Trade on the Northwest Coast*, 147–51.

Chapter 13
Women Traders in the Maritime Fur Trade

Loraine Littlefield

The active economic role of Northwest coast women in the appropriation and distribution of trade goods during the maritime fur trade has been neglected in the literature[1] despite the many historical accounts that document the presence of women in trade transactions, their shrewdness and skill in bargaining, and their role as chief negotiators. The role of women in trade was not a new behaviour arising out of the fur trade and its introduction of new trade goods but a continuation of women's traditional role that had included their active participation in the exchange of trade goods.

Maritime Fur Trade

From 1785 to 1825, a profitable maritime fur trade flourished on the Northwest coast. The fur resources of this trade were the sea otters that inhabited the ecological niche between the Columbia River to the south and Cook's Inlet to the north. The incentive for this trade was the easy harvest of the sea otter herds and the high demand for their pelts on the Chinese market. The first trading vessel dispatched solely for the purpose of the fur trade was the British *Sea Otter* commanded by James Hanna in 1785. In his brief visit to the coast he obtained 560 pelts which fetched a profit of $20,000 in Canton. The promise of such profits encouraged other traders, and during this period it is estimated that over 450 vessels visited the Northwest Coast.[3]

Initially, the main items demanded were iron and copper, with little popularity for trinkets and other trade items. Many vessels stripped themselves clean of everything metal on board in order to appease these demands. However, the coast became saturated with metals within a decade and muskets, blankets, and cloth became the more popular trade items. During the later years, more exotic tastes in trade were expressed in the demand for tobacco, molasses, biscuits, and rum.

Many maritime accounts reveal the desirability and eagerness on the part of the native population to trade. The earliest accounts of exploration[4] noted this eagerness from the start. Later maritime traders,[5] while pleased with this response, were at times astonished at the native shrewdness and mercenary attitude in trade. Indicative of this trading ability is the increased price of sea otter pelts as the maritime trade progressed.[6]

In the beginning of the trade, traders were able to acquire large quantities of sea otter pelts in a fairly short time, however with the increasing competition and the gradual depletion of the sea otter herds this number decreased considerably.

By 1825, the sea otter herds had been so decimated that the maritime fur trade came to a close, and other fur bearing animals and the establishment of permanent fur trading posts now held the most promise for fur trade returns.

Women Traders

While early explorers[7] had noted the presence of women during trade transactions, the first trader to specifically identify women's active participation in trade was an Englishman who recorded his visit and trading experience at Nootka Sound. James Strange,[8] a senior merchant for the East India Company, wrote in his journal in 1786 that in many of his trade transactions with the Nootka Indians, women were not only present, but were principally in control of the trade. He noted also that women traders would increase the price of furs up to three times the price he could have acquired them for if dealing only with their men. This trading activity by Nootka women was confirmed two years later, in 1788, by John Meares,[9] who visited another Nootka community to the south of Nootka Sound at Clayoquot Sound. He too noticed the presence of women during trade transactions, and remarked on their bargaining ability. Like Strange, he complained that women would consistently interfere in his trade transactions and retard the sale until they had procured an additional gift from the transaction.

Other journals described the women on the northern coat of this region as equally shrewd and active in trade transactions. Dixon,[10] one of the first traders to discover the rich fur resources of the Queen Charlotte Islands in 1786, acknowledged that in trade with the Haida the women were equally active and encouraged to come aboard his vessel. Later other traders[11] noted that the Haida men dared not trade their furs without the concurrence of their wives for if they disapproved of a deal it would ultimately fail. Ingraham[12] and Roquefeuil[13] were surprised by instances where men, who parted with their furs without the consent of their women were abused in the most cruel manner.

Still other accounts recorded that such active role in trade was also present among the Tlingit and Tsimshian women. Douglas[14] accompanying Meares in the *Iphigenia* sailing between Queen Charlotte Islands and Cook Inlet, commented that women with large lip plugs (labrets) commanded the canoes trading alongside his vessel. Later Marchand[15] wrote that Tlingit women at Sitka Sound and Yukatat Bay were consistently present during trade transactions, and the men seldom concluded a deal without consulting them. Similarly, Vancouver[16] when surveying this northern coastline in 1792 observed that Tlingit and Tsimshian women took the principal role in all commercial transactions involving the purchase of salmon and furs.

South of Nootka Sound, women participated in and controlled trade transactions. Quimper,[17] during his exploration of the Strait of Juan de Fuca, wrote that women were present at Cape Flattery and Waddah Island, and participated equally in the trade of goods. Bishop,[18] a few years later, recorded that women eagerly traded goods while he anchored at the mouth of the Columbia River. When Sturgis arrived in 1804, he observed that he dealt solely with women in all his trade transactions with the Chinook and Clatsop. Similarly, Lewis and Clark, in their daily entries, wrote repeatedly of the active role of women in trade in this region. Lewis[19] described incidents where women either arrived at the post individually or accompanied by their male relatives in order to trade a variety of goods.

While these maritime accounts document the active participation of women in trade throughout the length of the coast, the fur traders differed in their opinions concerning the nature of this participation. Meares' statement concerning women "interfering" or "retarding" a sale seems to imply that Nootka women were only peripheral participants in trade transactions. However, this statement may reveal more of the fur traders' bias in recording women's roles in trade than it does any sexual variation in roles throughout the coast. For example, the presence of native men in the bargaining process may have been purely a male bias on the part of the European fur traders who were accustomed to directing their trade transactions to men. The lack of terms such as "interfere" and "retard" to describe women's role in trade transactions in later accounts supports this assumption.

Other trade accounts noted that trade transactions needed women's approval in order to succeed. To account for this behaviour, some fur traders felt that women's participation stemmed from a man's respect for her decision-making and not from any other form of formal rights in trade transactions. For example, Alexander Walker,[20] accompanying Strange at Nootka Sound, recorded that Chief Maquinna was principally directed by his young wife Hestoquotto. In Walker's estimation, this control stemmed from her husband's desire to please her and not from any formal authority. Marchand[21] formed a similar opinion in his observation of women's control over trade among the Tlingit. He felt that womens' opinions before concluding a bargain were sought only out of polite respect.

However, this view that women's participation in trade was only a product of men's respect for women's decision-making does not explain those cases where men were actually abused for not consulting women before accepting a trade negotiation. Douglas[22] gives a fairly vivid account of a Tlingit woman at Cross Sound, who, when interrupted in her trade transactions, began to strike a man upon his head with a paddle for close to half an hour, and then ended the abuse by slashing his thigh with a knife. Douglas noted that during this violent exchange no one interfered as this seemed to be this woman's right. Such acts of violence and abuse during trade transactions were also witnessed by other traders.[23]

Such observations led some traders to conclude that in many locations of the coast, women were the superior sex and this accounted for their principal role in trade transactions. For example, during his trade with the Haida of the Queen Charlotte Islands, Haswell[24] referred to the wife of Cunneah as the chief of the tribe because of her dominating role in trade transactions. Vancouver[25] and Douglas[26] formed a similar opinion about some of the Tlingit women they met. While later ethnographies written on the Northwest coast have acknowledged that some women did acquire considerable political power within their society, traditionally this power was vested in men.

Nevertheless, these statements of sex superiority may reflect the fur traders' ignorance of the existence of classes within Northwest coast societies. While recent ethnologists have documented the presence of a ranking system that included nobles, commoners, and slaves as an integral feature of Northwest coast societies, not many early maritime traders were perceptive to the existence of classes. For example, both Vancouver[27] and Malaspina[28] believed that Northwest coast societies were fairly egalitarian, and that the concepts of property and class had not yet arisen. This lack of awareness of class may have misled some traders when observing women's behaviour in trade, for women of high class would have had a superior status over any of the men in their tribe. This superiority would have been apparent during trade transactions.

However, while there were many accounts describing trade transactions with chief's wives, or women of great authority, there are many more accounts that record the active trading role of women who did not have such power. While class may have influenced the type of goods women traded, it does not seem to have restricted a woman's ability (with the exclusion of slaves) to trade. One account in the historical material which acknowledges that women of all classes traded was written by Ingraham[29] after he arrived at Cloak Bay, off the tip of the Queen Charlotte Islands. He was disappointed to find that this particular village had traded all of its furs to previous maritime traders. He complained that the canoes that came alongside his vessel contained women of the lowest class for they had only fish, and not furs, to sell.

Lewis,[30] who with Clark spent the winter on the Columbia River, speculated that the economic role of women stemmed from the usefulness of their labour in subsistence production. In the interior of the continent, where women's status was lower, he noted that hunting, the main subsistence activity, excluded women, while on the Columbia River the Chinook and Clatsop women were active drying fish, and gathering wapittoo roots and berries. This production made a major contribution to the traditional economy and, he believed, gave women a voice in their distribution. Later, fur traders to this region, agreed with Lewis's conclusions. Cox[31] believed that women's role in collecting the wappitto root allowed them an air of independence that he had not seen evident among the interior tribes.

This speculation that women's role in the distribution of trade goods stemmed from their participation in production has some support for many trade goods were produced wholly or partially by women. Even at the start of the fur trade, Portlock[32] acknowledged that many of the trade goods brought out to his vessel were made by women. However, cross-cultural studies[33] into women's economic roles have revealed that women's participation in the production of trade goods does not necessarily ensure that women obtain the rights to distribute them. To understand how women on the Northwest coast acquired these rights, the economic role of women within the traditional fishing economy, and how this role gave them access to trade goods, must each be examined in turn.

Women's Traditional Economic Roles

The traditional economy of the Northwest coast was based largely on marine resources such as salmon, halibut, cod, candle fish, and herring. These fish which were caught off the coast, or in the rivers and streams appeared seasonally, and often in great quantities. While some were eaten fresh, the majority were dried and smoked to furnish food all year round. At certain seasons, seals, sea lions, sea otters, whales, and other larger marine animals were hunted. Also, according to the season, shellfish and vegetable foods, such as shoots, roots, and berries, were gathered and sometimes dried. Land animals were hunted but were of minor importance in the diet.

Men were the fishermen and hunters. In groups, or individually, they furnished the majority of food. Men were also skilled in woodworking, and made a variety of items such as dishes, bowls, spoons, boxes, and other small items. As well as wood, men carved bone and shell to make arrowheads, fishing hooks, and awls. Among men there was some specialization in production, and, either through skill or heredity some individuals carved poles and manufactured large canoes and ritual masks.

Women's role in the traditional economy is confirmed in many of the maritime fur trade accounts.[34] They document that women's primary subsistence activities involved the preparation and curing of fish, as well as digging clams, gathering mussels, sea urchins, and other edible shellfish. Also according to the season, women picked berries and shoots which they often dried in the sun and shaped into cakes. Besides helping in food production, women also wove a variety of items such as baskets, hats, trays, fish-nets, aprons, and blankets. These items were made out of plant materials that women gathered, dried, and coiled. Women also made robes out of furs which were first cured and then sewn together. And finally, but not least, women were responsible for the care and nurture of their children.

Maritime accounts record that there was some margin of flexibility in the sexual division of labour that allowed women to fish and hunt, and men to assist in gathering shellfish and plant foods. This flexibility was noted by Von Langsdorff,[35] a visitor to the Russian post at Sitka. He observed that among the Tlingit women were quite accustomed to firearms and were included in the many hunting expeditions. Also, Vancouver,[36] while surveying the Strait of Juan de Fuca, observed the participation of Klallam men in the gathering of roots and plant materials.

However, there are no historical accounts that document such flexibility in the production of crafts. It seems that, traditionally, women did not carve wood, bone, or shell, and men did not weave baskets or blankets.[37] Whether or not this flexibility in food production was a product of the fur trade, it is hard to judge, but it seems to have been evident in traditional times. Even then the intensive labour needed for the seasonal, and often unpredictable, food resources of the Northwest coast may have necessitated a flexibility in the gender-related division of labour.

While the division of subsistence labour was determined by sex, all such labour was directed by the needs of the household which was the fundamental social and economic unit of the Northwest coast. Each household was autonomous and consisted of a chief or elder, his related family, and slaves. The chief's role was to direct the general subsistence activities of the household. He supervised the men's work, while his senior wives supervised the women and their slaves. During the summer months, individual nuclear families within the household dispersed to the many fishing camps. In the fall, they rejoined their original household group or made alliances to form new ones.

Apart from the active subsistence practices of drying fish and other foods, women were responsible for food management and rationing within the household. Each woman had the product of her family's spring and summer labour stored in boxes or bundles suspended from the ceiling. While this food was shared by the household, individual women were responsible for ensuring that these foods were kept dry and free from insects or mould. Their care in monitoring and rationing this food was crucial: during the later winter months when food supplies were scarce the survival of the household depended upon its stores.

The role of managing the larder may explain the participation of women in trade. Women were responsible not only for scarcity of food stores, but also for any surplus that might have been available for trade outside of the household. However, this role alone would not guarantee women rights to appropriate and distribute trade goods outside of the household. On the contrary, many societies have property relations that allow husbands and elders to systematically appropriate the surplus production of the household. To understand the women's rights to trade goods, the relations of production that enmeshed all Northwest coast household resources must be examined.

Property Ownership

The concept of property ownership was well developed on the coast and was all encompassing. Maritime traders were to discover this fact in their many transactions with these people.[38] There were two recognizable types of property: communal and private. Communal property included food producing areas such as beaches, fishing streams, halibut and codfish banks, hunting territories, berry grounds, as well as smoke houses, and dwelling areas. It also included intangible property such as songs, dances, rituals, and supernatural powers. This property was not owned by one individual, but was managed and administered by a chief or elder of the household. The chief had power to administer and distribute this property based on lineage rights that placed him as the highest ranking member within the household. Other members of his household, while they did not have rights to distribute communal property, did have user rights based on their hereditary affiliations.

Private property, on the other hand, was owned and distributed by individuals. This property included items such as clothing, tools, ornaments, and other personal effects. Individual men owned their fishing gear and woodworking tools, while women owned household utensils such as knives, baskets, mats, and bowls. The majority of items were made by their owners; however, there was an exchange of tasks within the household whereby men carved bowls and other wooden utensils for women to use, and women made nets, clothing, and mats for men to use. As well as gender, the type and amount of property owned by any one individual depended upon that individual's industry and class. Men and women of high class and wealth owned furs, coppers, dentalium shells, slaves, and other prestige items.

Early maritime accounts record the trade of goods that are recognizably women's private property. Women actively participated in the trading of baskets, hats, and their other gender-related crafts. The demand for such trade goods would have ensured women's participation in trade transactions; however, the interest in these goods was often more one of curiosity than one of marketability. While on some voyages, there was a conscientious effort to collect material culture for anthropological and ethnographical research, the majority of these trade goods were acquired by individual crew members who were interested in them for their own personal use. While later accounts during the land fur trade indicate an increase in demand for such crafts, in the maritime period, women's participation in trade would have been negligible if the only goods traded were her personal effects and gender-related crafts.

However, there are many reports in the fur trade accounts that document women trading furs, dried fish, and other goods that are recognizably communal property. In some Northwest coast societies, women could have acquired access to communal property by their hereditary status. For example, in the north, where matrilineal descent groups were predominant, women, who by their age were the highest members of their lineage might have had an ability to control their own lineage property. However, in other regions of the coast where different descent systems existed, women did not necessarily have the same access. To understand how women throughout the coast acquired rights to trade communal goods during the fur trade, let us consider that women had a specific role in traditional trade that was maintained and continued during the fur trade. The following section reveals this role in trade and examines some of the pivotal factors that might have contributed to this role.

Women's Role in Trade

While each household was self-sufficient and autonomous in the production of its own goods, each household traded for goods that were not locally produced. Trade networks linking neighbouring coastal villages and tribal groups gave individual households access to a great variety of trade goods, as well as diversity of cultural interaction. Traditionally, trade took place during the spring and early summer months before intensive food gathering activities began. At this time, each household established its own trading partnerships with other households in neighbouring villages. These trade partnerships and alliances were maintained through either marriage affiliations or trade monopolies of specific food resources. Food was the primary trade good; crafts and other goods were of secondary importance.

Traditional trade included social and political obligations that were expressed in rituals, feasting, and the giving of gifts. This was an integral part of trade and continued throughout the maritime fur trade period.[39] The participants in this aspect of trade were the elders or the chiefs of the households involved. The goods that they traded or exchanged were viewed as gifts to confirm and maintain the status of the household group and their lineage. They included not only tangible communal property, such as furs and other prestige items, but also intangible property such as the rights to rituals, songs, and medicines. Inadvertently the giving of such gifts also enhanced the prestige of the chief who gave them, for prestige on the Northwest coast did not come from the acquisition of wealth but its generous distribution. The more a chief gave, the more status he gained for himself and his household group.

Women did participate and contribute to this social and political aspect of trade. Besides their involvement in the welcoming rituals and food preparation for feasting, women also participated in the giving of gifts. The senior women of the household, depending on their status gave furs and other prestige gifts to the visiting guests. Many of these women were related through kinship or marriage, and consequently these exchanges further enforced the trading alliances. These gifts also confirmed the status of the household group, and in the giving, enhanced the prestige of the women involved.

Once the gift-giving ceremonies were complete, individual families traded with other families on a more informal level. At this level, all individuals (with the exception of slaves) had an opportunity to participate in trade. At this point in the trade transactions, the motives were purely economic and each family tried to maximize their trade returns. The women had a decisive role in this goal. They checked the goods to be traded and kept track of the prices for each item. Sometimes the prices were set by custom, or by the skilful bargaining of the chief; however, at other times women could, through their own shrewdness and experience, manipulate the prices to ensure a better trade exchange.

This role of women in trade, while assured at the times of trade for their own gender-related crafts, might have also been assured for household goods if she had the ability to increase the returns from trade transactions. In a society where status was determined not only by heredity, but also by wealth, this skill had great potential for increasing a woman's status as well as her household's wealth. Women's participation in this regard would have been further enforced because they need not compromise a chief's reputation for generosity in the prestigious distribution of wealth. A chief's status rested on the distribution of wealth, and not on its accumulation. Thus chieftainship had been given a cultural role definition that excluded some men from maximizing (buying cheap and selling dear) during trade transactions. Women evidently did not labour under such strictures, thus allowing them to control goods distributed outside of the household.

The maritime fur trade differed in many respects from traditional trade in that it did not have the same social and political ramifications as inter-tribal trade. In fact, many maritime traders[40] were quite aggravated by the time-consuming welcoming rituals and feasting that first accompanied trade. Their prime concern was to acquire furs as quickly as possible, and move on. Also, the prestige associated with gift-giving had no place in these exchanges. While many maritime traders were forced into gift-giving exchanges, they recorded their dislike for such practices, and declined as much as possible. Such dislike was further increased when many maritime fur traders[41] discovered that gift-giving exchanges actually increased the price of trade goods. In such trade situations, where maximizing was the sole criterion for exchange, women's participation in trade would have been ensured.

Another element that might have ensured women's participation in trade during the maritime period was the increased competition between tribal groups that the infusion of new wealth encouraged. The maritime fur trade, due to its nature of interaction, brought new disparities of wealth between the tribal groups. With this new uneven distribution of wealth came the increasing need for chiefs and their households to validate their status. To do so, there was an increasing need for each household to accumulate more wealth than the other. Some traders noted this competition among different households in trade transactions. For example, Dixon[42] observed in his trade with the Haida that the furs in each canoe were distinct household property and the trade returns kept secret from each other. In the competitive trade transactions that had only maximizing motives a woman's role in bargaining and monitoring prices would have been maintained and continued, particularly if she could increase the returns. Many fur trade accounts seem to confirm that women did have this skill from the beginning of the maritime trade.

However, women's economic control over household goods in trade transactions may have continued during the maritime fur trade with the increasing demand upon food stores. While the main motive of the maritime fur traders was to acquire furs, another important trade item was food: when vessels reached the northwest coast, they were in desperate need of replenishing their provisions. In order to do so, maritime traders became dependent upon the natives of the region to resupply them. In this regard the natives were quite accommodating, and many accounts[43] record instances of women rowing out to the boats to trade food with the crews. Women brought a variety of items such as fresh and dried fish, ducks, shellfish, berries, and shoots.

Many of these foods were produced by women on the spur of the moment while the vessels were anchored in their harbour. During the summer, when food was in abundance and food gathering activities were at their peak, such trading activity probably had no consequence upon the household stores. However, later in the maritime trade period when vessels remained for the winter on the coast, the trade of food provisions had the potential to jeopardize the winter stores of the household group. This increasing demand upon household stores would have increased women's economic power in managing and rationing this food outside of the household for trade transactions.

However, women's active participation in trade during the maritime fur trade may have also increased due to changes in property relations. Drucker,[44] for example, theorizes that the fur trade encouraged the breakdown of communal relations, and fostered private ownership of resources. While it has been argued[45] that women's economic role and participation in the distribution of social production decreases with the formation of private property, there are many cross-cultural instances where private property gave women an increasing role in trade. For example, Afonja[46] and Etienne,[47] in tracing the role of women in trade, noted that within the Yoruba and Baule subsistence economy there was a private but gender-related ownership of property that encompassed all property relations. This gender-related property ownership allowed women rights to trade their own goods.[48]

Gender-related property ownership already existed to some extent on the Northwest coast. If women's control over household goods increased, is it possible that property relations may have been increasingly transformed into private gender-related ownership? Such ownership would have assured women a role in trade with their own gender-related trade goods. There is some evidence in the later ethnographies[49] which indicates that this gender-related property ownership was well entrenched between a woman and her husband at the end of the fur trade. However, such evidence does not reveal whether gender-related ownership increased during this period from that in traditional times.

Conclusion

This paper has examined the role of Northwest coast women in the fur trade, and proposed that this role was not a new behaviour arising from the fur trade, but a continuation of a traditional role that included women in trade transactions. Also, it proposed that some of the key factors that enabled women access to trade goods in traditional trade were the specific relations of production of the Northwest coast, women's role in the management and production of household goods, and a cultural role definition that excluded some men from maximizing in trade transactions.

This paper has also examined how these factors may have increased women's participation in trade during the maritime fur trade. The fur trade, by increasing the frequency and importance of maximizing exchanges, may have increased women's participation in a role that traditionally excluded some men. Also, the increasing demand upon household stores by the maritime crews may have increased women's stewardship of such goods into their use for trade.

Finally, the transformation of communal property to private property may have increased the emphasis upon gender-related ownership of goods giving women increased participation in trade transactions.

Notes

1. Recent fur trade research by Jennifer S.H. Brown, *Strangers in Blood: Fur Trade Company Families in Indian Country* (Vancouver: University of British Columbia Press, 1980); and Sylvia Van Kirk, *Many Tender Ties: Women in Fur Trade Society* (Watson and Dwyer, 1980), has revealed the role of women in marriage alliances and their productive role as a labour force. However, this research only portrays women as supporting men's roles and neglects the economic role of women in the appropriation and distribution of trade goods.
2. W. Beresford, *A Voyage Round the Word: But More Particularly to the Northwest Coast of America; Performed in 1785–88*, edited by Capt. Dixon and Capt. Portlock (London, 1789), 315.
3. F.W. Howay, "A List of Trading Vessels in the Maritime Fur Trade, 1785–94," *Transactions of the Royal Society of Canada*, 3rd ser. 24, section 2 (1930):111–34.
4. J. Crespi, *Missionary Explorer on the Pacific Coast 1769–74*, edited by H.E. Bolton (Berkeley: University of California Press, 1927), 329; F. Mourelle, "Voyage of the 'Sonora' in the Second Bucareli Expedition. . . . The Journal kept in 1775 on the 'Sonora' by Don Francisco Antonio Mourelle," in *Miscellanies* by Daines Barrington (London, 1781), 503; J. Cook, *A Voyage to the Pacific Ocean Performed Under the Direction of Captains Cook, Clerke and Gore, in His Majesty's Ships the Resolution and the Discovery in the Years* 1776, 1777, 1778, 1779, and 1780, vol. 3 (London, 1784), 43.
5. C. Fleurie, *A Voyage Round the World Performed During the Years 1790–92 by Etienne Marchand*, vol. 1 (London, 1801), 92; J. LaPerouse, *A Voyage Round the World in the Years 1785, 6, 7, 8*, edited by M. Milet-Mareau, vol. I (London, 1798), 369; J. Meares, *Voyages made in the Years 1788–89 from China to the Northwest Coast of America* (New York: Da Capo Press, 1967), 141.
6. G. Vancouver, *A Voyage of Discovery to the North Pacific Ocean and Around the World*, vol. I (London, 1798), 348; E. Bell, *A New Vancouver Journal on the Discovery of Puget Sound by a Member of the Chatham's Crew*, edited by E. Meany (Seattle, 1915), 40; J. Espinoza, *A Spanish Voyage to Vancouver and the Northwest Coast in the Year 1792 by the Schooners 'Sutil' and 'Mexicane' to explore the Strait of Fuca*, translated by C. Jane (London: Argonaut Press, 1930), 90.
7. Crespi, *Missionary Explorer*, 329; Fray Tomas de la Pena, *Diary of Fray Tomas de la Pena kept during the voyage of the Santiago—dated 28 August 1774*, edited by G.B. Griffin, the Sutro Collection, Historical Society of Southern California (Los Angeles: Franklin Press, 1891), 122; B. La Sierra, *Diaries of Benito de La Sierra and Padre Miguel de la Campa made on board the Frigate Santiago 1775* (Mexico: D.F., 1919), 19.
8. J. Strange, *Journal and Narrative of the Commercial Expedition from Bombay to the Northwest Coast of America* (Madras, 1928), 25.
9. Meares, *Voyages made in the Years 1788–89*, 141.
10. Beresford, *Voyage Round the World*, 208, 225.
11. R. Haswell, "Log of the First Voyage of the Columbia," in *Voyages of the Columbia*,

edited by F.W. Howay (Boston, Mass.: Historical Society, 1940), 96; Haswell, "Log of the Second Voyage of the Columbia," in *Voyages of the Columbia*, 325; J. Hoskins, "Narrative of the Second Voyage of the Columbia," in *Voyages of the Columbia*, 372; J. Ingraham, *Journal of the Brigantine Hope on a Voyage to the Northwest Coast of North America 1790–92*, edited by M.D. Kaplanoff (Massachusetts: Imprint Society, 1971), 132; J. Caamano, "Extracto Del Diario, 1792," *British Columbia Historical Quarterly* 2 (1938):205; C. Bishop, *The Journal and Letters of Capt. Charles Bishop on the Northwest Coast of America, in the Pacifiç and in New South Wales 1794–1799*, edited by M. Rowe (Cambridge: Hakluyt Society, 1967), 63.
12. Ingraham, *Journal of the Brigantine Hope*, 132.
13. C. Roquefeuil, *A Voyage Round the World Between the Years 1816–19* (London, 1823), 104.
14. Meares, *Voyages made in the Years 1788–89*, 323.
15. Fleurie, *Voyage Round the World Performed During the Years 1790–92*, 242.
16. Vancouver, *Voyage of Discovery*, vol. II, 343, 409.
17. M. Quimper, "Diaro, 1790," in *Spanish Explorations in the Strait of Juan de Fuca*, edited by H. Wagner (Santa Anna, CA, 1933), 123.
18. Bishop, *Journal and Letters of Capt. Charles Bishop*, 125.
19. M. Lewis, *The Lewis and Clark Expedition*, vol. II (Philadelphia and New York: Lipincott Co., 1961), 483, 484, 500, 501, 521.
20. A. Walker, *An Account of a Voyage to the Northwest Coast of America in 1785 and 1786*, edited by R. Fisher and J.M. Bumsted (Seattle: University of Washington Press, 1982), 62.
21. Fleurie, *Voyage Round the World Performed During the Years 1790–92*, 242.
22. Mears, *Voyages made in the Years 1788–89*, 324.
23. Hoskins, "Narrative of the Second Voyage of the Columbia," 208; Vancouver, *Voyage of Discovery*, vol. II, 324; Beresford, *Voyage Round the World*, 290; Roquefeuil, *Voyage Round the World Between the Years 1816–19*, 104; Ingraham, *Journal of the Brigantine Hope*, 132.
24. Haswell, "Log of the Second Voyage of the Columbia," 325, 326.
25. Vancouver, *Voyage of Discovery*, vol. II, 409.
26. Meares, *Voyage made in the Years 1788–89*, 323.
27. Vancouver, *Voyage of Discovery*, vol. II, 253.
28. A. Malaspina, *Politico-Scientific Voyage Round the World by the Corvettes Descubierta and Atrevida from 1789–94*, translated by C. Robinson (Vancouver: University of British Columbia Press, 1934), 16.
29. Ingraham, *Journal of the Brigantine Hope*, 101.
30. Lewis, *Lewis and Clark Expedition*, vol II, 532.
31. R. Cox, *The Columbia River* (Norman: University of Oklahoma Press, 1957), 226.
32. Beresford, *Voyage Round the World*, 294.
33. P. Sanday, "Toward a Theory of the Status of Women," *American Anthropologist* 75 (1973):1682–1700; E. Friedl, *Women and Men: An Anthropologist's View* (New York: Holt, Rinehart and Winston, 1975).
34. J. Jewitt, *The Adventures and Sufferings of John Jewitt Captive among the Nootka, 1903–05* (Washington: Galleon Press, 1975); Fleurie, *Voyage Round the World Performed During the Years 1790–92*, 242; Vancouver, *Voyage of Discovery*, vol. I, 347; G. Franchere, *Narrative of a Voyage to the Northwest Coast of America in the Years 1811, 12, 13, 14*, translated and edited by J. Huntington (Redfield, New York, 1854), 245.
35. G. Von Langsdorff, *Voyages and Travels in Various Parts of the World*, vol. II (New York: Da Capo Press, 1968), 132.
36. Vancouver, *Voyage of Discovery*, vol. II, 262.

37. Collins ("Growth of Class Distinctions and Political Authority among the Skagit Indians during the Contact Period," *American Anthropologist* 52 (1950)) maintains that among present-day Salish a man was labelled transvestite if he attempted any of the women's crafts. She noted that the only times there occurred cross-sexual division of labour was in the making of twine and the preparation of reef nets.
38. Espinoza, *Spanish Voyage*, 17; LaPerouse, *Voyage Round the World in the Years 1785, 6, 7, 8*, vol. I, 375.
39. Jewitt, *Adventures and Sufferings of John Jewitt*, 69.
40. LaPerouse, *Voyage Round the World in the Years 1785, 6, 7, 8*, vol. I, 370; Jewitt, *Adventures and Sufferings of John Jewitt*, 59; Beresford, *Voyage Round the World*, 187.
41. Hoskins, "Narrative of the Second Voyage of the Columbia," 265; Ingraham, *Journal of the Brigantine Hope*, 126.
42. Beresford, *Voyage Round the World*, 204.
43. Boit, "Log of the Second Voyage of the Columbia," 382; Quimper, "Diaro, 1790," 110; E. Coues, ed., *The Manuscript Journals of Alexander Henry and David Thompson*, vol. II (Minnesota: Ross and Hines, 1965), 854, 859; S. Patterson, *Narrative of the Adventures and Sufferings of Samuel Patterson* (Washington: Galleon Press, 1967), 73; Meares, *Voyage made in the Years 1788–89*, 141.
44. P. Drucker, *Indians of the Northwest Coast* (Natural History Press, 1955).
45. M. Rosaldo, "Woman, Culture, and Society: A Theoretical Overview," in *Woman, Culture, and Society*, edited by M. Rosaldo and L. Lamphere (Palo Alto, CA.: Stanford University Press, 1974); K. Sacks, "Engels Revisited: Women, the Organization of Production and Private Property," in *Woman, Culture, and Society*; Sanday, "Toward a Theory of the Status of Women."
46. S. Afonja, "Changing Modes of Production and the Sexual Division of Labour among the Yoruba," *Signs: Journal of Women in Culture and Society*, vol. 7, no. 2 (1981):299.
47. M. Etienne, "Women and Men, Cloth and Colonization: The Transformation of Production Distribution Relations among the Baule," *Cahiers d'étude africaines*, vol. 65, no. 1 (1977):41.
48. These authors maintain as well that the historical continuity of women's role in trade was a product of the gender-related ownership of household resources.

Chapter 14
Fishing is Women's Business: Changing Economic Roles of Carrier Women and Men

Jo-Anne Fiske

The colonization of indigenous peoples generally displaces women from social production, and, in the process, subordinates women to men.[1] The process dislocates women as producers, undermines their social position, and discredits their abilities as public leaders and decision makers. The impact of this process is more obvious when contrasted to known exceptions. For example, Kom women, independent farmers of Cameroon, successfully resisted state intervention into their agricultural practices. Precolonial forms of female militance mobilized women into effective widespread protests which protected their autonomy.[2] In Alaska, Tlingit women continue to enjoy beneficial employment patterns compared to men. In consequence women are effective and strong community leaders.[3] Similarly, women of the Trobriand Island improve on the male cash income through their own wealth production and ritual distribution.[4] In each case precolonial gender relations persist: high esteem for women is prevalent and social equality is the norm.

Carrier women of central British Columbia offer another exceptional situation. This paper shows how Carrier women have retained control over crucial aspects of social production and distribution. This control has grown out of the ironies of state-imposed alterations to the indigenous exploitation patterns as well as from efforts the Carrier made to diversify their economy. State intervention, combined with capital inflows and development, left salmon, the most valued resource, in the hands of women, and at the same time reduced the resources exploited primarily by men. The fact that fishing is now the work of women has altered Carrier relations to their land and changed their perceptions of resource stewardship. Appreciation of women who provide well for their families and communities has implications for women as political actors and community leaders. Today, women and men often rationalize female political actions by reference to their abilities as fisherwomen.

This analysis is based on three key arguments. First, where women control critical resources, they enjoy economic and political autonomy. Second, women's political power is a consequence of their ability to dispense patronage beyond a domestic productive unit influencing the lives of both women and men. Third, colonized women secure social and political significance by rationalizing their political actions in reference to cultural traditions which honoured female leadership, female economic autonomy, and/or cultural wisdom.

These three arguments are organized into four sections. First, an ethnographic vignette of the indigenous Carrier economy and social organization is provided. Second, the transition of the aboriginal economy from subsistence through commodity production is followed to one of subsistence and cash income with respect to gender differentiated economic opportunities. Particular attention will be paid to the role of state intervention. An analysis of women's contemporary political actions in relation to current notions of resource proprietorship and patterns of exploitation concludes the paper.

The Indigenous Economy and Social Organization

The Carrier are an Athapaskan people of central British Columbia.[5] At the time of first contact, they occupied a vast territory which stretched across the central interior plateaus from the Rocky Mountains to the Skeena watershed, and northward from the southern reaches of the Nechacko plateau to the upper arms of the Stuart Lake water system. They were subdivided into twelve groups identified by geographical features associated with their semi-permanent fishing villages. This paper refers to three of these subdivision, Stoney Creek, Nadleh, and Stellaquo. The Stoney Creek people reside on Stoney Creek, a small tributary of the Nechacko River; the Stellaquo and Nadleh bands are located, respectively, on the eastern and western shores of Fraser Lake. The Stoney Creek and the Nadleh people shared a common salmon fishing site at the Nadleh settlement.

The aboriginal Carrier subsisted on fish, primarily salmon, large and small game, and foraged berries, roots, and other vegetation. The productive unit was the extended family of bilateral membership with a patrilineal emphasis. Within the productive unit, women and men fished and trapped, while only men hunted large game, caribou, and black bear. Women gathered with the aid of children. Each family occupied a specific territory known as its *keyoh*. Resource rights were by usufruct and access was sufficiently flexible to include married men and women who resided elsewhere, according to their individual needs and productivity.

During the winter, the extended family remained within the *keyoh*. Men pursued large game and trapped small mammals. Women trapped and netted fish through the ice. The spring spawning of fresh water fish brought the extended family together at their creekside settlements where women and men trapped fish and women netted returning waterfowl. In late summer, everyone gathered at the salmon fishing sites where women and men worked on the construction of the large salmon weirs and together harvested the fish. Following the salmon run, women dispersed to their own fishing sites to net char and whitefish, and the men left to trap beaver in their home territory.

Ceremonial feasting and wealth exchange confirmed the territorial divisions of the land and acknowledged proprietorship over resources within each *keyoh*. The rights of women and men were affirmed at the *balhats* (potlatch) when the most desired or "precious" foods, berries and beaver meat, passed between persons of high status. Particular ceremony was observed in order to honour the women and men who claimed ownership of the berry grounds and beaver lodges. As these foods were distributed, the stories of their production were related; the location of harvest, the sites' owners and the workers were all identified. These ceremonies held particular relevance for women. Not only were berries "precious" due to their relative scarcity and the hard work their harvest entailed, they also symbolized female fecundity. With their ceremonial exchange, women's role as nurturers was affirmed and renewed.

Within aboriginal social organization, Carrier women and men were probably social equals. Leadership within the *keyoh* is said to have been the responsibility of two "bosses," the father and the mother of the extended family unit living there. Each "boss" was held accountable for the moral conduct, instruction, and production of the junior members of her or his gender. Within the matrilineal clans, which bound the Carrier villages together in ties of marriage, trade, and exchange, leadership parallelled that of the family units. It is said that the clans were led by a "clan father" and a "clan mother" who "stood beside each other." Leaders of either sex were noble born, that is, they were *dunzah* (true men) and *ts'kezah* (true women). They provided leadership in the co-operative use of the fishing weirs, the holding of *balhats* to confirm the heirs of *dunezah* and *tse'kezah*, and mediated disputes. They also organized the production and accumulation of clan wealth for ceremonial distribution, including harvesting resources from territories reserved for clan use.

Economic Transition and Changing Relationships to the Land

The transition of the subsistence economy to one focussed upon fur production for commercial trade altered exploitation patterns and notions of resource stewardship. Under the influence of the European traders, male clan leaders rose to paramount positions . These men, whom the traders regarded as potential or actual village chiefs, undertook the role of brokers between the trappers and traders. They received special treatment from the traders which enhanced their status and increased their wealth. Under their leadership, land use patterns were transformed. Trapping lines known as "clan" or "company" lines, shared by members of a matriclan, emerged. They might have criss-crossed an extended family territory or *keyoh*. The development of "company" lines created a two-fold system of land tenure, and with respect to resource control, a new male hierarchy.

The emergence of a two-tiered land tenure system did not seriously disrupt women's productive roles nor did it weaken their ties to the land. Like men, they trapped for trade. Married women accompanied by their children operated lines adjacent to those worked by their husbands. Young single women worked with older women, and in this way confirmed their rights to family resource areas. The extended family unit remained the independent subsistence productive unit. Within it, women continued the co-operative labour which provided fish, berries, and meat of small mammals for the family's consumption and ceremonial distribution.

In the latter third of the nineteenth century, women's subsistence production increased relative to that of men. Men had always hunted caribou during the winter months. This practice was disrupted when the men increased their winter trapping, and ceased in the 1870s with the disappearance of the caribou. Jointly these factors strengthened the role of women as the nourishers of their people, and bolstered their position as political leaders. Not only had women's subsistence production increased, women were also left in charge of community affairs during the periods when men were absent. Settlement patterns also changed. At Nadleh (Fort Fraser) and Stoney Creek, the Hudson's Bay Company had constructed trading posts. Semi-sedentary settlement near the posts led to other changes in women's subsistence production: gardening and intensification of fresh water fishing at sites near the trading posts. These practices served to reinforce women's ties to the land and the role of women as providers for their communities. In short, commodity production and increased sedentary residence did not create adverse conditions for women. Women remained significant producers in the integrated family production unit, and retained autonomous control over the distribution of their production. Their ties to the land were unbroken.

The Rise of a Capitalist Labour Market

In the 1860s, contract and wage labour altered the relations of production in a fundamental way: men gained access to cash income through contracts and individual wages while women did not. During the process of colonization, this factor alone has been sufficient to create asymmetrical gender relations *vis-à-vis* production and distribution.[6] On the surface, the situation appears no different for the Carrier. During the 1860s, the Cariboo Gold Rush attracted a surge of transient White men to Carrier territory. Gold miners, prospectors, priests, surveyors, and adventurers hired native men from Stoney Creek as packers and guides, individually on a per diem basis or by group contract for long distance travel. The men responded to this opportunity by establishing small transportation businesses. They acquired scows, barges, pack animals, and teams and wagons. By the end of the century, men were operating services which included a ferry across the Nechacko River, pack trains from Quesnel to Fort St. James, and wilderness guiding services. Similarly, men from Stellaquo and Nadleh found work guiding and serving White men arriving along the Skeena and destined for the Omineca gold fields to the north. The native men used their profits to develop other businesses, purchase livestock, and accumulate items for the *balhats*. From this new wealth and labour, successful men were able to offer new forms of economic and political patronage. Men with expanding ranches and transportation businesses could now hire others to work for them. These same men also enjoyed greater advantage in ceremonial exchange because of their increased wealth accumulation.

The trade monopoly of the Hudson's Bay Company collapsed with the Cariboo and Omineca gold rushes. Free traders followed. They hired Carrier men to bring trade goods up from the south and to return furs to a central relay point. The Carrier did not just transport goods for others, they entered into the trade independently. At Stoney Creek, the Carrier opened their own small trading posts. The free traders fell in face of this competition and soon left. With the Hudson's Bay Company in a weak position, the men of Stoney Creek experienced an advantage. Since they were situated on the trail to Quensel, they could command the trade between it and the western villages. Although these "stores" were "owned" by the men, they often were managed by women who used them to trade their own goods to personal advantage.

Men gained the most from this new labour. Where women had access to teams and wagons, they were able to offer short-term services to the White men. However, women were not free to travel great distances unless they were working with family members. They were tied to their home territory by other responsibilities. Neither were White men anxious to contract labour through women when the women were in a position to offer their services. It seems that White men favoured hiring their own sex and paid little regard to female entrepreneurs. Clearly, colonial notions of gender-appropriate behaviour favoured men.

This economic disparity, however, did not result in social subjugation. Women worked alongside the men on the pack trains. During long journeys, they hunted, snared, and fished, as did the men. As always, their labours were essential and appreciated by both women and men. In some families, women received cash and material benefits in return for their work. The women used this wealth for *balhats* contributions, and for the independent purchase of livestock, as well as the other items necessary for farming, domestic arts, clothing, and new forms of cooking. Significantly, women were never absent from the *keyoh* long enough to lose their rights to its resources; nor did prolonged stays at the growing trading post communities disrupt their food production. The distribution of surplus food production ensured their continuing prestige. Their role of patronage was also secured in a community which continued to rely upon subsistence bush foods and traditional goods for ceremonial exchange. Because of the continued value placed upon women's subsistence production, and their sustained profits from trapping, women were not dependent upon male production and cash earnings.

By the 1890s, transient White men were followed by permanent settlers who commenced farming on land adjacent to the Carrier settlements. Agricultural development brought new sources of wealth. Transportation services were in demand, and good prices could be had. Labourers were needed to clear the land, and the Carrier were the only available work force. Labour contracts were issued by the settlers through men perceived to be heads of families or through the village chiefs. These contracts did not take into account individual wages. They provided a single payment on a per acreage basis to the man holding the contract. Again, women were denied direct compensation for their labour. With other members of their families, they toiled at clearing land, caring for their young children as they did so. As before, they held responsiblity for subsistence production as they compensated for the disrupted and decreased food production of the men.

Land clearing contracts had the same social consequences as other contract labour. It provided a few men with a new form of patronage. As contractors these men could hire and fire their male peers and determine their rates of pay. With respect to women, these men could decide if they would receive any pay at all.

These patterns of contract and wage labour remained in force for the next eighty years. For example, Carrier men and women began producing railroad ties for the Grand Trunk Pacific Railway. Tie camps were established along the proposed railway route and entire families lived there from November to March. Women worked alongside the men peeling, sawing, and cutting ties. To support their families, women trapped, snared, fished, and hunted. All the domestic chores fell to women and children. When men were unable to leave the camp to trap, it was not unusual for women to go in their stead.

Whether women received cash payment for their labour in tie production depended upon the quality of their relationship with the men holding the contract. Husbands might view tie production as joint labour and its rewards as joint earnings, or they might not. In any case, women sought cash earnings elsewhere, either through trapping, or by trading their hand crafted products and food surpluses with the white settlers.

Entry into railway tie production altered traditional land use patterns. The tie camps were situated within the long established *keyoh* of the contract holder or his wife. This allowed simultaneous tie production and trapping during the winter months. However, the sedentary demands of tie production meant that these resource areas were exploited more intensely than had hitherto been necessary. At the same time, more distant areas were not used fully, for the families with established resource rights had joined the other families at the tie camps, or remained in the village while the men worked on tie production. These new residence patterns brought changes to resource exploitation: women who fished and snared, and men who operated tie camps in their own *keyoh* continued to establish resource rights by usufruct while the claims of others to resource territories ultimately were weakened with decreased usage.

This transformation in exploitation patterns altered the relations of production within and between the genders. Of considerable importance is the degree to which it separated women and men. Women left the tie camps for winter fishing at the village sites. Here they worked with other women, allocating the labour and distributing the fish throughout the community as needed. Co-operative work units remained founded on ideals of kinship but were sufficiently flexible to incorporate members according to proximity of residence or a common need predicated upon male absence. At the same time, productive relations between men altered. Co-operation within the "company" traplines was minimized by a reduction in fur bearers as well as by the shift of residence to the tie camps. Thus, while women continued to affirm their own, and their families', ties to the land and its resources through the production of the community's food, men failed to do so to the same degree.

The Impact of State Intervention

State intervention affected the Carrier economy and land use patterns in three important ways. First, it altered patterns of land ownership. Second, it set in motion a particular path of agricultural development. Third, and most significantly, it established a new regime for control over natural resources within the traditional hunting and trapping territory. In each of these instances, women and men were affected differently.

Traditional land rights based on continued usage had not created a "landed" versus "landless" gender distinction. Resources within the *keyoh* were considered to be communal property and those areas which lay elsewhere fell under the stewardship of the gender which appropriated the resource. Women "owned" berry grounds and fresh water fishing territories, and men "owned" beaver lodges. Salmon sites were communal property managed by clan and village leaders. With the establishment of Indian reserves in the 1890s, new concepts of land ownership were introduced, ones which excluded independent female ownership. Reserve lands were subdivided for nuclear family use and registered by certificates of possession in the names of male family heads. Apart from widows, women were barred from land possession. State intervention created asymmetrical gender relationships: male land owners versus landless females. This did not necessarily result in a significant gap in wealth since women continued to use land much as they had before, but it did transform male status *vis-à-vis* women.

The state was guided by its concept of the independent nuclear family in its agricultural policies as well. It allocated farm acreage on this basis, and considered the individual family as a self-sustaining economic unit by which subsidies to farmers would be granted. Tools, implements, stock and seed were portioned out to the "family head." In this way, farming was specifically designated as a male activity which required the supporting labour of women and children and which was intended to support the family.

Subsidies were not granted in a uniform fashion. At the discretion of the local Indian Agent, farmers who showed "the greatest progress"[7] received the most generous subsidies. These arbitrary distinctions also created a wealth differential among men, the more fortunate were rewarded while those experiencing difficulties were not. This situation was exacerbated by the asymmetrical distribution of cash income. Men who profited from contract labour and business enterprises were able to invest independently in their farms. The same men benefited the most from state subsidies.

Had the small-scale farming of the Carrier succeeded, a critical wealth differential between women and men would likely have occurred. This was not the case. Agriculture in the Nechacko plateau was limited by the climate with only six frost-free weeks per year, a lack of good soil within the designated reserves, and the absence of sufficient capital for expansion. Farmers needed to augment farm returns with both production *and* cash income. Moreover, subsistence still depended upon bush production, and especially salmon. Even though moose appeared in the region in the first decade of the twentieth century, game remained a supplement to the basic diet of fish and small mammals. As well, farming could not succeed without the labour of women. Significantly, women's farm production was regarded in the same manner as their bush production. Processed food was women's property to be allocated by women, and this was a key factor in the maintenance of their economic autonmomy.

The persistence of women's co-operative work organization was also important. While the state viewed farming as an individual family activity, women did not. Farm work and its proceeds were shared on the same basis as other subsistence production. The co-operative nature of women's work, and the fact that it took place without male control, meant that women continued to be socially and economically autonomous.

The production of women remained important to their social and economic position in another way: women continued to trap. Fur prices remained high and pelts were sold readily. The returns from trapping contributed to the individual's and family's living standard. They also remained central to wealth distribution, not only at the *balhats*, but in other community relations. For example, profits from fur sales contributed to the construction of the church,[8] an act which carried considerable prestige, and toward the care of orphans and elders who lacked family support.

The social and ritual distribution of property of women meant that they were not subordinated to men as a result of the economic disparity which resulted from colonization. The interdependence of the sexes was not broken. Men relied upon the participation of women in contract labour and farming, as well as upon women's independent subsistence and commodity production. Only because women entered into this wide range of economic activities were men free to pursue wage and contract labour, and to invest their earnings in capital goods and farm supplies. The integrated economy of the extended family did not disintegrate, nor had women's ties to the land and resources been eroded.

State intervention did not end with the formation of reserves and the payment of agricultural subsidies, it interfered directly with subsistence and commodity production as well. The greatest portion of the traditional resource territory fell outside of the reserve boundaries established in the 1890s. Initially this did not restrict the Carrier in their subsistence activities. However, by the turn of the century, the growing White population of the region was in direct competition with the Carrier for resources. The state sought to resolve the ensuing racial tensions by imposing strict controls on native appropriation.

The full impact of state intervention was first and most severely felt on the salmon fishery. The commercial industry on the Pacific coast had expanded rapidly and as a result a serious stock depletion occurred.[9] Racist sentiment abounded, and blame for over-exploitation was directed at the native population.[10] Traditional weirs used throughout the province were held responsible. Cannery owners and fishermen successfully petitioned the government to outlaw their use. In 1911, the government entered into formal negotiations with the Carrier to end this practice. That same year, Carrier chiefs signed the Barricade Treaty which prohibited the use of salmon weirs, and introduced a net fishery.

The transition to net fishing transformed the place of men in the relations of production. Men no longer co-operated in weir construction and operation, nor did they continue in the fishery. Men who had never netted fish now found themselves consigned to subordinate labour, while women took over the fishing. The most valued resource was now, as the Carrier say, "the business of women."

Women were soon proficient with the new technology in all its stages from the twining and repair of nets to their setting. The most skilled women quickly earned reputations as good fisherwomen which brought them respect and prestige beyond their communities. They distributed fish according to kinship obligations, and to individuals or families with whom they wished to maintain personal relationships. This allowed women to establish exchange links among themselves, and to dispense patronage to younger women and their families. The women provided for the young, elderly, and the impoverished, who were without resources or the ability to provide for themselves. As well, they provided reserve supplies for those who were engaged in wage labour elsewhere. While the practice of allocation on these bases was not new, the fact that men had been displaced from the fishery enhanced the role of women. Although women had always had the responsibility of distributing food stores, men had been in the position of allocating access to the fish at the communal weirs. This responsibility also passed into the hands of women as they decided the allotment of netting sites. What had once given rise to male patronage now provided women with an additional avenue to social esteem and the powers of obligations.

The new fishing technology also altered perceptions of resource stewardship for the Stoney Creek band. Women who had access to resource territories along the Nechacko River, either through their families or their husbands, chose to set nets there rather than fishing only at Nadleh. Thus they reinforced their independent claims to land and resources. Where netting sites fell within their husband's trapping areas and tie camps, women's fishing strengthened time honoured claims to family territories. Unlike the communal fishing sites at Nadleh, these fishing stations came to be regarded as specific personal property not to be transgressed by other women.

Fifteen years after the enforced abandonment of salmon weirs, the state imposed further restrictions upon the native economy. Because farming in the Nechacko plateau could not succeed without supplementing income, settlers had also turned to trapping. In addition, high fur prices attracted transient trappers who remained only for the trapping season. Friction arose regarding rights to the fur bearing animals, and once again the state imposed controls on native appropriation.

In 1926, the B.C. government introduced a system of registered traplines which divided Carrier territory between White and native ownership. Carrier men were assigned areas which roughly corresponded to traditional use rights associated with the family *keyoh* or the "company" lines, and were registered either for single or shared use. In the latter case, lines were designated for co-operative use within a patrilineal group rather than within the traditional matrilineal group. Rights to company areas could now be determined by government agents, and generally were restricted to men.

The registration of trapping areas put the Carrier men at a disadvantage *vis-à-vis* White men. Land and resources were wrenched from the Carrier at the discretion of state agents. Lines deemed unused or under-exploited were transferred to White trappers. The lost lines included those not utilized fully when native men had turned to tie production or wage labour, lines left for regeneration after intensive use, and those which had belonged to individuals lost in the 1918 influenza epidemic. Taken as well were vast trapping areas which state agents deemed superfluous to the Carrier's economic needs. Management rights also transferred to the state. "Tags" were issued which limited the fur harvest to amounts determined by wildlife officers. These tags were given only to men registered as line owners. Thus both women and young non-owning men were barred from the legal fur trade.

Notwithstanding the intervention of the state, women continued to trap. They travelled to the areas of male kindred where they independently worked lines and passed on their skills to younger women. Although income derived from trapping deteriorated over the years, women retained independence within the trapping economy. Often women persisted in trapping while men sought other work.

The registration of traplines destroyed the traditional land tenure system based on usufruct. Traplines became commodities for purchase and sale. This too led to a differentiation of status based on capital property. The more able trappers, farmers, or wage earners were in a position to purchase lines, usually in the name of a wife since ownership was restricted to a single line. Financial stress led some to sell their lines to Whites. Men who opted for winter wage labour suffered most, for they often lost their lines when state agents expropriated them because of lack of use.

Fishing and Contemporary Politics

When trapping eventually failed to provide a substantial return, reliance upon women's subsistence production increased. In the first three decades of this century, men lost opportunities to renew their claims to land through seasonal utilization. At the same time, the subsistence production of women remained a steady and reliable feature of the Carrier economy. A new seasonal round emerged based on women's subsistence production which has persisted to the present day. Resource depletion and state intervention have reduced Carrier access to subsistence resources. Fish, trout, suckers, whitefish, and salmon, and to a lesser extent moose meat, now provide the basic protein diet. Apart from spring gaffing of coarse fish, and the occasional line fishing of trout, men rarely participate in the fishery. Moreover, state control over moose hunting has marginalized hunting as a subsistence activity. Although moose remains an essential and significant portion of the diet, seasonal hunting has been limited by the state to a short period in the autumn. This has forced men to choose between secretive illegal hunting at other times of the year, or to restrict themselves to the state designated season. The latter choice not only reduces the ability of men to provide for others, it alienates them from the land of their forefathers.

On the other hand, women's fishing has not yet been strongly curtailed, although this practice is threatened by state control. Anxiety of White sports anglers for stocks of trout and char has resulted in a continuous and concentrated interference into women's subsistence production of all fresh water species. Similarly, salmon fishing is subject to enforced reductions. Because this is the last form of economic independence based on Carrier tradition, fishing provides women with a particular esteem and respect.

Women who annually renew their ties to the land at the salmon season experience a higher degree of autonomy and social prestige than those who do not. These women are in a position to organize the work of their daughters, nieces, and granddaughters, and to command the distribution of their communal production. Ultimately the production and distribution of salmon provides for all community members. No one is excluded from this distribution: single men, elderly widowers, and those who are incapable of self care are provided for in this manner.

The annual salmon fishery is significant in other ways which reinforce the social esteem of women. Carrier women carry on their traditional responsibility as educators of the young. Today, the time spent in close association at the fishing site can be as important as fishing itself. Travel to and from the sites allows time to renew cultural tradition through the telling of stories and legends of the cultural significance of the salmon and the women who harvest it. Elders take this time to relate personal histories which emphasize the importance of their rich and longstanding utilization of the bush to feed their families. Women's perceptions of traditional territorial divisions account for the historic use by men but stress the diverse bush activities of their grandmothers.

Women's common role as fisherwomen draws them into political unity. Continuing state intervention into their subsistence activities threatens the survival of the Carrier way of life. Women respond angrily to the threats and interference of state agents. Because fishing is their responsibility, it is up to them to speak for their rights. It is the women in the community who challenge the state's policy, engage in inter-village and inter-tribal political action, and represent their community in the dominant society around them.

Salmon fishing remains the strongest affirmation of women's rights, responsibilities, and ties to the land. It is the right of women to follow their foremothers as the owners and managers of fishing sites. It is also their responsibility to nourish their people. This entails more than the mere feeding and care of dependents and the impoverished. It calls for political actions which would seek to preserve Carrier culture, protect the environment and retain it for future generations, and to provide for others in multiple ways.

This latter responsibility draws older women into the forefront of community politics. They form voluntary associations in order to gain access to state funds for community improvement projects to provide employment for the reserve. As their foremothers of legends had advised and protected the vulnerable, they now form advisory committees to the elected band councils. Some, preferring more direct political action, are themselves councillors and chiefs.

Women's political and cultural actions are not restricted to the confines of their reserve communities. Older women are now to be found on executive committees of interracial environmental societies which oppose developments threatening the natural resources. They organize cultural events in the White community designed to alleviate prejudice. Others participate in inter-tribal programs directed toward rectifying social problems and improving educational opportunities for the young.

From their position as esteemed fisherwomen, older women commonly become strong political leaders. Having acquired autonomy through hard labour, control over resources, and by adept political skills, they have established political leadership over the young, and emerge as community leaders. The prominent elders around whom the community's politics flow are those whose ties to the bush have been the strongest.

Notes

1. Eleanor Leacock, "Women's Status in Egalitarian Society: Implications for Social Evolution," *Current Anthropology* 19 (1978):247–75; Mona Etienne and Eleanor Leacock, eds., *Women and Colonization: Anthropological Perspectives* (New York: Praeger, 1980); Maria Patricia Fernandez-Kelly, "Development and the Sexual Division of Labor: An Introduction," *Signs* 7 (1981):268–78; June Nash and Maria Patricia Fernandez-Kelly, eds., *Women, Men, and the International Division of Labor* (Albany: State University of New York Press, 1983); Heleith I.B. Saffioti, *Women in Class Society*, translated by Michael Vale (New York: Monthly Review Press, 1978).
2. Shirley Ardener, "Sexual Insult and Female Militancy," *Man* 8 (1973):422–40.
3. Laura F. Klein, "Contending with Colonization: Tlingit Men and Women in Change," in *Women and Colonization*, edited by Etienne and Leacock.
4. Annette B. Weiner, "Stability in Banana Leaves: Colonization and Women in Kirwina, Trobriand Islands," in *Women and Colonization*, edited by Etienne and Leacock.
5. The data for this paper are drawn from two periods of field-work: 1978–79 and 1983–84. The first session included interviews with women and men from these three

bands, the second consisted of ten months of study at Stoney Creek. Since my research did not extend sufficiently to other villages, my generalizations cannot be extended beyond these three bands. An earlier version of this paper was presented at the Annual CESCE Meeting in Toronto, May 1985. I am grateful to Kuldip Gill and John McMullan for their written critical comments on earlier drafts.

6. Ellice B. Gonzalez, *Changing Economic Roles for Micmac Men and Women: An Ethnohistorical Analysis*, National Museum of Man, Mercury Series (Ottawa, 1981).
7. Department of Indian Affairs, Annual Report, 1916 (Ottawa: Government of Canada); "Records of the Oblate Missions of British Columbia," from Oblate Historical Archives, St. Peters Province Holy Rosary Scholasticate, Ottawa, Microfilm. University of British Columbia Library.
8. Rolf Knight, *Indians at Work* (Vancouver: New Star Press, 1978), 247; Pat Turkki, *Burns Lake and District: A History Formal and Informal* (Burns Lake, B.C.: Burns Lake Historical Society 1973), 12, 13.
9. John L. McMullan, "State, Capital and the Salmon Fishing Industry in Pacific Canada," in *Uncommon Property: Fishing and Fish Processing Industries in British Columbia*, edited by Pat Marchack, Neil Guppy and John L. McMullan (Toronto: Methuen, forthcoming).
10. Douglas R. Hudson, "Traplines and Timber: Social and Economic Change among the Carrier Indians of British Columbia" (Ph.D. diss., University of Alberta, Edmonton, 1983) 106.

Chapter 15
The Marginalization of the Tsimshian Cultural Ecology: The Seasonal Cycle

James Andrew McDonald

Cultural ecology examines the degree to which the environment influences social and cultural processes, and the extent to which people can control their own destinies within a given environment. A considerable amount of work has been conducted on these questions, but it has become clear that such inquiries cannot treat indigenous populations in isolation. Cultural ecology has been confronted with the history of colonialism and the impact of the global expansion of capitalism. As a result, additional propositions must be formulated to determine not only what the given environment is, but also how the environment is given; and, not only how people control their destinies within a given environment, but also which people control their destinies.

Such questions apply especially to the case of the aboriginal peoples of Canada. Where these peoples were once sovereign and dominant, able to command their lives with strategies that allowed maximal ingenuity and effective responses to their complex environments, they are now marginal, both environmentally and socially. The marginalization of Indian peoples is manifest in the abysmal decline in their living conditions, especially the terrible economic problems that they experience and that we know symptomatically as unemployment, business failures, and welfare. All these are signs of maladaptation and of a breakdown of appropriate ecological relationships.[1]

In *Cultural Ecology*, Bruce Cox used his introduction to grapple with the relationship between cultural ecology and political economy. In doing so, he noted that the strategy of cultural ecology was, in outline, to examine both the technical and social processes that relate people to their environmental resources. "Hence ideology and political (and social) organization are seen as part of the process by which men gain their subsistence in a particular environment."[2] He identified two study topics as keys for opening an understanding of the relationship between culture and the human and material environment: the means by which people appropriate their resources, and the forms of property associated with those means.

In many ways, I am in agreement with Cox's general perspective at the time, although in my studies of the Tsimshian of northwestern British Columbia, I place much greater emphasis on the methods of political economy than on those of cultural ecology. This emphasis causes me to question the nature of our knowledge of the environmental relationships of the Tsimshian, especially with regard to our knowledge of the impact that capitalism has had on ecological relationships. My opinion is that, while it is not impossible to study simply the pristine, traditional, or contemporary cultural ecology of the Tsimshian, it is difficult to do so without taking into account the redefinition of their perceived resources by foreign governments (provincial and federal) for use according to the political economy of capitalism. Whatever ecological adaptations had been in place the day before the first contact, they have long since been radically altered, along with the more general political economy of Tsimshian society. The appropriation of colonial resources, the marginalization of the Tsimshian, and the consequent restructuring of Tsimshian society required rapid adjustments to the new socially defined environment.

In this paper I will attempt some of this accounting by examining a basic ecological pattern, that of the seasonal cycle. The Tsimshian of Kitsumkalum will serve as a specific case study because I am most familiar with that group as the result of several years association with them, and because they have not been described in the ethnographic literature until recently.[3]

I will then discuss three questions: what was the seasonal cycle as described by early ethnographers (the major components and structure), what effects did the new economic order have on the appropriation of the resources (tenures, legislation, and economic development), and what changes resulted in the seasonal cycle for Kitsumkalum.

The Tsimshian

The territories of the Tsimshian (sometimes referred to as the Coast Tsimshian, or the Coastal and Southern Tsimshian, or the Tsimshian proper) are in what is now northwestern British Columbia, along the lower Skeena River from Kitselas Canyon down to the coast, and throughout the adjacent archipelago of islands at its mouth, south to the Estevan Group. This area was surrounded by people sharing a similar lifestyle (Haida, Haisla, Tlingit), including some who spoke closely related languages (Gitksan, Nishga).

For most of the year, the Tsimshian distributed themselves throughout their territory to harvest the abundant resources that were necessary to maintain their complex social organization. In the winter, they consolidated themselves into the residential groups which are usually referred to as winter villages, towns, or tribes. Each of these villages was associated with a particular population and territory. Of eleven such groups on the Skeena, Kitsumkalum was the tenth village up river.

In general, the territories of Kitsumkalum were the adjacent valleys of the Zimacord and Kitsumkalum Rivers.[4] They also utilized the Skeena River valley and several marine resource sites.

Tsimshian villages were organized along matrilineal principles into lineages that lived and worked together. Of these groups, closely related lineages formed local units called houses that were led by their more important members. Each of the lineages and houses held resource property rights which were vested in the titles of their leaders. Sets of lineages and house groups that were descended from a common ancestor formed recognized clans extending beyond the villages.

There were also four matrilineal and exogamous tribal divisions or phratries: *laksgiik* (eagle), *lagybaaw* (wolf), *ganhada* (raven), *gispawadawada* (killer whale). Although these were little more than weak federations of groups of lineages and clans, the phratries did generate some sense of obligation for mutual sharing and protection among members, even among those who otherwise were strangers. This sense of obligation provided a basis for interaction between villages and neighbouring peoples that could be activated in times of practical or ceremonial need.[5]

Class was the basis for other Tsimshian sodalities of importance. To the best of our knowledge, slaves and non-titled free people had little opportunity to unite on the basis of their class, but the title holders tended to exert a pan-village influence through feasting, religious ceremonies, and the associated secret societies. Their power on such occasions depended on the strength of their titles, a strength created by their own abilities, the support of their followers, and the inheritance associated with that title. A significant part of this inheritance was the productive resources of their properties.

Kinship and the communal nature of lineage property provided the title holders with their prerogatives, but at the same time it divided them and worked against their forming stronger pan-village associations. Alliances, exemplified by mutual privileges to resources, could break down in a crisis. Title holders were not a caste, although there was a set of royal lineages; nor were they a closed class, for there was a series of graded ranks. Unfortunately, these features and the effects of colonial expropriations and depopulation have confounded anthropological analysis of Tsimshian classes.

The loss of property rights to productive resources seriously eroded the basis of the matrilineages as corporate groups. Continued occupancy and use of original resource territories safeguarded Tsimshian social principles and values to some extent, but there was a decreasing ability for the title holders and their lineages to maintain the order. They could not enforce their rights as they had done before. This applied especially to those resources that were being incorporated into the commodity economy and that were under the explicit scrutiny of the government agents.

Seasonal Cycles

The Early Pattern

Two important early descriptions of the seasonal cycle come to us from Franz Boas and his student Viola Garfield. Boas provides the earliest reconstruction of the seasonal cycle.[6]

End of winter, before river ice breaks up:	Oolachan fishing on the Nass
After oolachan run:	Return to Metlakatla (or other winter villages?)
When salmon run:	Move to salmon fishing villages on the Skeena

Fall:	Go to hunting grounds
Winter:	Some hunting, most people at winter village
Mid-winter:	Some go back to hunting ground

This information is based on a corpus of myths that were gathered mostly from 1902 to 1916, well after British Columbia's union with Canada (1871), and two decades after the arrival of resident government officers who enforced resource legislation to aid industrialization (1885). Unfortunately, Boas did not discuss what effects the changes experienced during more than a century of contact might have had on the seasonal cycle.

Garfield provides another early description of the cycle, this time based on field-work during the 1930s, not reconstructions[7] (the information in parentheses is found only in her 1939 work).

February/March:	Start of oolachan fishery
May/Late June to October:	Salmon fishing and gathering at the fish camps
(Fall):	(Hunting)
October/November to February:	Winter camp

We know that by the time Garfield's information was collected, resource laws abounded, industry and settlement were established, and some resources already were showing signs of depletion (for example, salmon stocks, halibut banks).[8] What impact did these factors have on the Tsimshian cycle? To provide an answer, additional information must be incorporated into the ethnographic record. Some of these necessary data can come from archival sources, others from the people themselves.[9] Using government archival sources, I will discuss first some of the effects the new property laws, that were introduced shortly after industrialization began, had on aboriginal activities. Then I will discuss field data concerning the resulting changes.

Effects of the New Political Economy

From the ethnographic information on the seasonal cycle, we can identify the major components of the original Tsimshian economy as being hunting, fishing, and gathering. Of course, numerous other activities also were practised, the Tsimshian are a very sophisticated people, and their ethnology reflects their diversity. Nonetheless, I will use these three activities to focus discussion, as I outline the history of contact between the industrial capitalist economy and the Tsimshian economy, on how the impact of that contact was constructed, and some parameters of its impact. I will concentrate on changes in the processes of appropriation and in associated property concepts.

Synopsis of Recent History of the Territories of the Kitsumkalum

The establishment of canneries at the mouth of the Skeena, in the 1870s, started the industrial period and began a shift in the residential patterns of the Kitsumkalum. By the twentieth century, their attention was turning away from the Kitsumkalum Valley and fixing on the coast. The occupation of their valley lands at the turn of the century by agricultural and other foreign interests further contributed to the displacement of the original popoulation.

After the 1936 flood of the Skeena River washed away significant portions of the main village at the confluence of the Kitsumkalum River, their use of Kitsumkalum Valley became intermittent and seasonal. Only two families remained permanently resident actively exploiting its resources. The others had moved to the cannery centres for work, and tended to use either the lower portions of the Skeena River or the coastal areas near Port Essington.

With the economic decline of the canneries and the way of life associated with fishing after World War II, the Kitsumkalum people moved back to Kitsumkalum Village. Since the 1960s, they have reconsolidated their residence in Kitsumkalum Valley and the surrounding area. Now their resource exploitation is concentrated again in Kitsumkalum Valley and in the nearby areas of the Skeena River.

The general reoccupation of the ancestral valleys has not yet meant a re-establishment of specific lineage land use patterns. Legal ownership is held by the Crown or private interests, according to Canadian laws, so the people of Kitsumkalum simply locate suitable sites wherever they can, with the result that families have a continued usage (usufruct) relationship to new resource locations when they hunt, fish, or gather.

Hunting

I shall use hunting as a starting point in this history and give it more detailed discussion than fishing or gathering for several reasons: the products of hunting were important to Tsimshian subsistence; this importance has often been undervalued by ethnologists because of the Tsimshian's general reputation as fishermen; and the centre of my studies, Kitsumkalum, is (and was) one of the more land-oriented of the Tsimshian villages.

The Resource

The Kitsumkalum regularly hunted a variety of land animals. Apart from the fur-bearers that they trapped, I encountered specific references to the following species: deer, elk, seals, sea lions, sea otters, mountain goats, mountain sheep, bears, porcupines, raccoons, eagles, marmots or groundhogs, caribou, moose, cougars, hares, lynx, swans, geese, ducks, and waterfowl.[10] This is, in effect, a list of all the available fauna, other than small rodents, insectivores, reptiles, and amphibians.

Foreign Appropriation

The interruption of Kitsumkalum's property relationship to the faunal resources by new uses of the land began with the arrival of large numbers of miners in the neighbourhood of Lorne Creek during the 1880s, estimated at over

200 in 1887." Next, but only shortly after, the agricultural settlers took over the hunting grounds around Kitsumkalum Lake. After the settlers, many other immigrants came to work or to set up small businesses.

These alternative land uses severely affected the original condition of Kitsumkalum's faunal resources, often in ways that were ecologically insensitive. An early and continuing problem was that all of the newcomers attempted to supplement their diets with hunting, competing with Tsimshian hunters, and depleting every game population. Some of the worst examples include the case of a small herd of caribou that was hunted nearly to extinction by the 1930s; and the once plentiful deer population that was devastated when the army stationed a large number of soldiers in Terrace for the duration of World War II. It may be only a local folktale that the soldiers used the deer for target practice, but they were known to have put heavy pressure on the resource as sports hunters, leaving deer in the area scarce to this day. Later, intensive urban development compounded these problems, especially in the years following the war when the regional population grew dramatically.

The increasing sophistication and effectiveness of hunting took its toll as well. A startling example of this, told to me by the Game Warden, is of helicopter hunting during the 1960s that seriously depleted the goat population.

Now all biological resource in the Valley may be endangered by industrial developments which have peculiar effects. New forms of pollution are being noticed, such as industrial acid rain which has hunters concerned.[12]

On the brighter side, the massive alteration of the forest by clear-cut logging after 1950 altered ecological relationships in favour of the browsing moose which replaced deer. Deer have great difficulty in the deep snow cover that results from such logging practices. I was told moose had been rare in the Valley before the war, but that within the past few decades they had become common even closer to the coast. This observation was offered to me as evidence that there had been a gradual but steady westward movement by that species in the aftermath of habitat changes. Apparently the fauna of the valley and Skeena River basin have undergone significant changes since White settlement.

Erosion of Property Rights to the Resource

Game laws, which evolved as the provincial agricultural development expanded, and which were applied against Indian food production, had a direct effect on Tsimshian hunting. Not only did these interfere with and disrupt Kitsumkalum's hunting, they further eroded Tsimshian control over the resources as a property item within Tsimshian society.

The legislation is organized under federal and provincial jurisdiction. Off the reserves, Indians must comply with provincial regulations and authorities; but on the reserves, which are federal lands, regulation is a federal matter. As a Canadian version of indirect rule, the Indian Act does not recognize the hereditary authority structure directly but instead allows the Chief Counsellor to regulate hunting activities. This elected office is defined by the Indian Act, and may or may not be filled by a hereditary leader. In Kitsumkalum, the reserve lands are too small to be used significantly for hunting, and this regulatory authority is rarely exercised, unless some safety problem (such as taking shots at small animals in the village) arises which cannot be handled through alternative social channels.

The earliest provincial Game Protection Act of significance was passed in 1887. Since then, there have been restrictions on the killing of deer, caribou, mountain goats, mountain sheep, bears, grouse, ducks, hares, and many birds. These restrictions refer to seasons in the case of big game, the age of the animal,[13] the sex,[14] and bag limits.[15] Seasonal and bag limits extend to the simple possession of parts of the animal as well as to the actual hunting of them. In addition, the killing of deer for hide was prohibited[16] as was that of mountain sheep and goats.[17]

The further constraints that these game laws put on the hunter's rights to dispose of the meat prohibits possession of game out of season,[18] and makes such possession *prima facie* evidence of illegal hunting, laying a hunter open to charges of game violation even if the meat is in storage.[19] To facilitate enforcement, processing of meat cannot destroy certain parts that indicate species, sex, and age of the animal, except at the place of consumption.[20]

In 1917, the Dominion government approved a convention signed with the government of the United States to regulate the hunting of migratory birds. Through this Migratory Birds Convention Act,[21] closed seasons and bag limits were placed on game and non-game birds. By article III, migratory game birds were under a closed season from March 10 to September 1, and it was prohibited to hunt them or even to possess them during that time. Migratory non-game birds (e.g., gulls, terns, herons, loons, grebes) were closed all year, except to Indians who could use their eggs for food or their skins for clothing, provided that no trafficking in these items occurred. Article III established a closed season on swans, shorebirds, and the whooping and sandhill cranes, without exception. This Act is still in force, keeping hunters in the double jeopardy of simultaneously violating provincial and federal laws on game birds.

Other relevant restrictions prevented hunting on enclosed land (which was defined to include any land identified for enclosement by natural or artificial landmarks), without the permission of the owners or leasees.[22] This was to protect alternative land uses, such as farming.

In the case of deer, Indians had special exemptions which allowed them to kill deer to feed their immediate families,[23] although this was curtailed by seasonal, sexual, and age limitations.[24] The sale of such kills and the clause governing killing for hides was not exempted.

Exceptions to the game laws protect aboriginal rights to a degree, but they have also been the source of frustration to Indians who resent being put into a position, *vis-à-vis* the regional population, of being permitted to break a (foreign) law. As a point of principle and justice, they would prefer a law that recognizes their aboriginal rights directly.

Thus access to Tsimshian faunal resources was curtailed very early in the Confederation period, and was just another part of the process of loss.

Maintenance of Relationships to Territory

Under the threat of police, and even military enforcement, the Skeena River Indians found it necessary to incorporate the new legal system of Canada, but they resisted the total purge of their property relationships. A good example is the association, under provincial law, of hunting areas with trapline registrations. This twentieth century innovation tranformed the ownership of certain types of territories from the corporate lineages or villages to "trapping companies," which under the Game or Wildlife Act are corporate individuals that can hold and manage a registered trapping area. Insofar as this was the understanding of trappers and field officers alike, these Indian traplines tended to be viewed in terms of the larger category of "tribal hunting grounds" and were treated accordingly, with vague deference being paid by the provincial authorities to Indian ways of organizing the use and transferral of the lines. These arrangements preserved a remnant of economic ownership over the hunting grounds and protected a small measure of the aboriginal relationships.

Before the 1960s, when trapping was still viable, the legal exclusiveness of a registration could be used to prevent or control trespass by hunters. Generally, other Indians respected this form and interpretation of ownership, but trapline registrations, being foreign, were not an effective means of internal control. Early disputes, as are reported in the archival records of the Terrace Fish and Wildlife office, which involved non-registered Indians utilizing the trapping areas registered to someone else, indicate that issues could not be resolved properly either by the defunct aboriginal system or by the fledgling provincial administration.[25] Now, as a result of the recent decline in trapping, line ownership rarely becomes a critical economic issue. Nonetheless, such lines represent aboriginal patterns critical to land claims.

Fishing

The Resource

The Tsimshian lived in an environment that was exceptionally rich in aquatic resources, and their abilities as fishermen exploiting the fish stocks provided a critical economic and symbolic base for their social formation.

The Kitsumkalum fished a variety of fresh and salt water, and anadromous fish. These included the five species of Pacific salmon, steelhead trout, oolachan, cod, halibut, herring, cuttlefish, dogfish, porpoise, bullheads, devilfish, eels, flounders, red snappers, shrimp, pilchard, occasional drift whales, trout, whitefish, suckers, chubs, and sturgeon. These resources were widespread, but many (for example, salmon, oolachan, halibut, and trout) were exploited at specific productive sites to which were attached certain property rights. Kitsumkalum concentrated its fisheries in the Kitsumkalum Valley and adjacent areas of the Skeena drainage, but the families also had property claims at maritime locations and oolachan grounds.

Redefining the Resource

A century ago, the first government Fish Guardian set up an office in residence among the Tsimshian. Under the terms of Union, the fishery laws of the Dominion were to be applied to British Columbia. This legislation was a major factor in changing seasonal patterns by outlawing many Indian fishing methods and by applying industrial standards to control the exploitation of resources.[26] The Guardian's arrival in 1885 represented the increasing pressure to redefine the Skeena fisheries and to guarantee the resource to capitalist production.

The official extension of the Dominion's Fishery Act into British Columbia, in 1874, contained the following restrictions: salmon spearing (used at Kitsumkalum Canyon) was banned except with special licence for food fishing; dip nets for oolachan required licences, but were banned for salmon[27] and trout (fished on Zimagotitz);[28] ice-fishing bags for salmon (used on Kitsumkalum Lake) were banned;[29] trawl or gill nets required licences; tidewater salmon traps were banned;[30] traps and weirs on small streams were restricted[31] and licensed;[32] angling trout was placed under seasons; and nets were required for cod. In addition, an Order-in-Council (O/C) of 26 November 1888 had banned food fishing of salmon using nets and spears, while the Provincial Fisheries Act prohibited the use of nets, shining, dragnets, and other similar devices for fishing in fresh water.[34]

During the ensuing years, salmon drag seines were prohibited,[35] as were purse seines.[36] Nets, weirs, fascine (fish weirs or traps) fisheries, and other devices which obstruct passage were prohibited in 1894; drift nets were required for tidal fishing of salmon, and explosives were banned.[37] In 1897, trout were protected in fresh water rivers and lakes under 50 square miles from explosives, poisons, seines, dragnets, and other similar devices, but hooks and lines were permitted.[38] The Provincial Fisheries Act of 1911 re-enforced the right of passage of fisheries and allowed for the instant capture and destruction of illegal seines, nets, and other such devices;[39] O/C 2 May 1904 defined the size of nets, trap locations, and prohibited their use within three miles of navigable rivers and one-half mile from salmon streams.

All these laws defined fishing technology and hindered the development of Tsimshian methods and modes of organizing fishing. Although policy toward Indians was supposedly lenient,[40] there is no documentation to demonstrate how lenient, and the general oral history in Kitsumkalum reports is that it certainly was not.

In recognition of the continuing importance of fish to Indian survival, the government developed exemptions that allowed Indians to fish for their own consumption according to permitted aboriginal methods.

This so-called food fishing required permission from the Inspector and could not be conducted with spears, traps, or pens on spawning grounds, lease areas, or propagation areas.[41] The same Order-in-Council prohibited ice fishing, the use of artifical lights, spears, or snares for trout, and restricted the herring and pilchard fishery to drift or gill nets of specified size, and only within harbours.

The Inspector also controlled food fishing with regard to where it occurred,[42] how and when,[43] which is essentially the condition of the food fishery now.

These regulations created a legal distinction between fishing for food and fishing for capital. In so doing the legislation came to restrict, in absolute amounts, the number of fish controlled by Indians relative to the canners.

Other Interferences

Another serious disruption to fishing came directly from the canners who held in contempt the established aboriginal tenure system. Immediately after the opening of the first cannery, in 1877, the Superintendent of Indian Affairs was reporting on complaints from Tsimshian that their hereditary rights to fisheries were being encroached on by the capitalist fishery.[44] For example, the Kitkatla Troubles of 1878, which led to policing by an imperial gunboat, stemmed from the invasion of fishing grounds belonging to Kitkatla people.[45] Other problems were caused by the establishment of cannery plants on top of Tsimshian shore stations or village sites.[46] Such encroachments were protected under S.C. 31V, C60, s.3.

To reduce the tensions, and ostensibly to protect Indian rights, the Fishery Inspector suggested that the reserve system be established.[47] The government's response was to commission an investigation in 1881,[48] and ten years later, to allot reserves to the Tsimshian on the Skeena.

Gathering

The Resource

The diversity of the land use area of Kitsumkalum provided the villagers with a rich storehouse of raw materials. The full range of biological resources that the Tsimshian gathered and used for food, medicines, manufactures, etc., before European contact is probably more extensive than we will ever be able to reconstruct. An indicative list includes: land flora (e.g., berries, roots, sap, crabapples, berries, mushrooms, wood), marine flora (e.g., seaweeds, kelp), aquatic fauna (e.g., fish eggs, shellfish, china slippers, sea cucumbers, sea prunes), and land fauna (e.g., bird's eggs).

The fauna are included in gathering activities because that association is made by the Kitsumkalum people. All the gathered species have the common property of being relatively immobile, unlike the species pursued in the hunt. This immobility provides a cultural characteristic important to the distinctions between the harvest activities of adult males and females.

The Question of Ownership

The establishment of the three reserves for the Kitsumkalum people, in 1891, emphatically demonstrated the legal loss of their ownership of resource sites, but the loss was not felt immediately, or practically, until the non-reserves were occupied by foreign peoples and industries.

In allotting the reserves, the Commissioner promised that the people of Kitsumkalum could "go on the mountain to hunt and gather berries as you have always done."[49] This was a simple statement, but misleading in what it assumed. The Tsimshian had a carefully organized system of tenure and use that included their gatherable resources. The details are still not systematically documented, but Garfield noted that there were "no unclaimed land or sea food resources of a kind important to the Indian's economy."[50] According to informants, such properties generally had names to identify the area and the associated packages of ownership rights.[51] Nonetheless, the Commissioner was convinced that berry grounds could not be protected by reserves because "an Indian goes where he will to hunt, or to gather berries. No survey could be made. . . ."[52]

The enactment of resource legislation such as the Forestry Act, the Fisheries Act, the Game Act, and the Migratory Bird Convention, made the Commissioner's promise a lie: the Tsimshian could not do as they always had done. In 1887, a delegation of chiefs had been told by the Premier of the province that timber on Crown lands was protected by timber lease and that people cutting trees for house construction or storage boxes could be stopped by anyone who held a lease.[53] Although legally the Tsimshian might have been able to take out provincial leases and thereby protect an aspect of their aboriginal use rights, the complicated requirements for tenure, as well as prejudice against Indian registry,[54] inhibited widespread registration of timber lands by Indians.

The appropriation of control continued into the twentieth century, and some of the old people bitterly remember how they could not take bark from the hemlock or cedar trees which was necessary for many of their manufactures. They apparently were referring to a clause in the Forestry Act which made it illegal to remove any products of the forest on Crown lands without licence.[55]

There were regulations on the other gathered resources. In the case of land fauna, the Game Protection Act of 1887 placed restrictions on collecting the eggs of the grouse, robin (an important crest animal of Kitsumkalum), blackbird, thrush, and wild ducks.[56] The Dominion's Migratory Bird Convention Act of 1917 extended these controls to include the eggs of other migratory birds, insectivorous birds, swans, shorebirds, and cranes.[57] Indians could only take the eggs of migratory non-game birds for food.[58]

With the development of the capitalist fisheries, there was an increasing number of restrictions and controls placed on marine resources by provincial and Dominion legislation. Shell fisheries were regulated when the Dominion Fisheries Act was applied to British Columbia.[59] By 1908, licences were required for clam, abalone, and crab fisheries. Abalone was closed every third year, size limits were placed on crabs, and supervision of clam beds by the local fishery officer was required.[60] Indians were to be exempt from licence requirements only.

Provincial laws were largely an extension of Dominion legislation. In 1901, the provincial Fisheries Act provided for closed seasons on fish in provincial waters, including shellfish.[61] Since 1946, licences have been required to harvest kelp and other aquatic plants.[62]

The imposition of these controls transferred sovereignty from the Tsimshian title holders to the Crown, and restructured access to the resources. Tsimshian control was as marginal as their new relationships to their old environment. Rich as most of the natural resources were, those available to the Indians were impoverished.

Massive Environmental Destruction

Besides the legal constrictions, a different kind of loss occurred: that of the destruction of resource sites by alternative land uses, especially by homesteading and forestry. Homesteading began almost immediately after the reserves were established. Within twenty years, a fair sized community existed where Terrace now is. New farms spread out across the Valley corridor from Kitimat Channel in the south, to the Nass River in the north. These farms and settlements were established strictly according to provincial, not Tsimshian, laws and tenures.

Homesteading caused considerable losses to what the government once described as the Indians' "fruit-gathering preserves" (berry bushes and fruit trees) and timber lands.[63] One woman, nearly a hundred years old, tried to explain to me where her family's berry properties had been, but she was sure I would not be able to locate the once important sites because they were overgrown with "flowers" (i.e., agricultural production). She could remember the time of their destruction at the turn of the century.

This is a sentiment I heard expressed many times and it should be emphasized: agriculture, settlement, and more recently forestry, obliterated large sections of the Tsimshian environment. Hunters, trappers, gatherers, all felt like strangers on their own territory because they could no longer find the old familiar natural landmarks, or the ancient resource sites that their lineages had groomed over the centuries.

Of course, not all the land was so changed by farming, apparently because parts were unsuitable. As a result, the children of some families could remember collecting food, even after World War II, on areas that corresponded with the hereditary properties of their phratry as listed in archives and as recognized by certain elders. Farming went into a decline in the 1940s, and was replaced by logging as the major modifier of the environment.

The enactment of new forestry laws, in 1946, lead to clear cutting by multinational companies from Terrace north, a process that is continuing today. Where this occurred, the specific old locations for harvesting different resources are obliterated. The result is that most of the aboriginal harvest now occurs along the logging roads, where the secondary growth often takes the form of berry bushes.

Tsimshian Patterns

The preceding sections outlined the drastic changes, motivated by industrial development and defined by legislation, that transformed the Tsimshian economy. Resources, technology, and even labour power were removed from Tsimshian control by the new forms of property and of resource exploitation that were established. The original Tsimshian economic order disintegrated, and the people of Kitsumkalum had to reorganize to meet the changing conditions. In this final section, I will discuss their reorganization by describing their seasonal cycles in the twentieth century. The data is based on interviews with the Kitsumkalum.

Figure 15-1 provides a summary of the early period described by Boas and Garfield, the traditional period described by elders of the Kitsumkalum, and the current period in which I have participated.

The Traditional Pattern of the Tsimshian

When the Tsimshian lost control over their economy in the nineteenth century, they were forced to exploit the resources of their territories in whatever manner and way was allowed them by the new social order. Thus, they participated in several types of economic activities, including aboriginal ones, forms of simple commodity production (notably commercial fishing, logging, and trapping), small businesses, and wage labour. Capitalist development and the evolution of the conditions that allowed these economic practices, took the Kitsumkalum through many transitions that, from their point of view, were viable adaptations to the new and changing political economy.

During the early part of the twentieth century, these changes were structured to a significant extent by simple commodity production. The oral history I collected in the 1980s suggests that, by the 1930s, a pattern with a very definite seasonal cycle, was emerging based on the use of the commercial fishing boat.

Boats gave people access to their country homes (or camps) which ideally were located where the family had its hunting territory, registered trapline, and registered logging area (for example, a timber lease). In such an ideal situation, the Indian fishing boats could be used for many purposes, if the fisherman had the gear for fishing halibut, trolling salmon, gill-netting salmon, logging, trapping, hunting, or various camp activities. These different types of gear could be placed on the boat, according to the natural or commercial season, to allow the fisherman to take advantage of a range of resources throughout the year.

Base residence in spring was the camp home where the men could shelter their boats. Typically, these were marine camps, where the family would gather seaweed, herring eggs, and shellfish, but some were along the Skeena River. In the case of the river locations, the harvest of marine resources was replaced by the planting of gardens, usually some time in May.

Figure 15.1

Sources	Jan.	Feb.	Mar.	Apr.	May	June	July	Aug.	Sept.	Oct.	Nov.	Dec.	Periods
Boas 1916		Winter Villages / Nass Oolachan					Metlakatla Salmon Fishing Villages / Salmon Fishing				Hunting Grounds		
Garfield 1939	Winter Camp										Winter Camp		EARLY
		Nass Oolachan					---------Fishing/Gathering---------		Fall Drying				
Garfield 1966	Winter Camp					Salmon Gathering			Fall Hunt				
Kitsumkalum Version A		Winter Residence: or Terrace		Pt. Essington							Winter Residence		
						Plant Gardens Canneries			Hunt/Fish/ Garden				
Version B		Log on Coast			Halibut/Gather on Coast			Commercial Fish		Dry Fish	Port Essington		TRADITIONAL
		Freeze Up					End Halibut Season		Closed Salmon		Freeze Up		
Abstract Female	----------	----------	----------	----------		Gathering	----------	----------	and Garden		----------	----------	
Male	Log and Trap	----------	----------		Gardens	----------	----------	Fish -----	Garden/Hunt	----------		Town	
Kitsumkalum	----------	----------	----------	----------	Gathering	----------	----------	----------	----------				
	----------	Oolachan	----------	----------		Salmon	----------	----------	----------	----------	----------		CURRENT
	----------	----------	----------	----------	----------		Hunt in Seasons	----------	----------	----------	----------	----------	

Figure 15-1: The Seasonal Cycles of Kitsumkalum

In the early spring, when halibut season opened (March/April to June), people who were able to do so, and who were so inclined, began commercial fishing. Of course, not every boat owner on the coast fished halibut. Some simply continued their spring logging along the coast, or beachcombing if the camps were on the Skeena River.

The end of the halibut or planting season turned attention to the June salmon fishery when whole families would move to the Port Essington area to participate. This move was important to allow the women to be near the canneries for work.

When the successive salmon seasons were over in the early fall (usually September), people dispersed back to their residences (the fall camps) until freeze-up in order to dry food/fish, hunt what they could, and harvest gardens. At this time, the boat could be converted from fishing and used for logging until spring. Beachcombers on the Skeena used their fishing boats to retrieve logs that they tied together and towed to market. On the coast legislation allowed loggers to mount a pulley system on a float and to pull the logs off the steeply sloping shores. As the fall progressed, trapping took on greater importance at the camps.

Winter caused a change in pace but it was not a slack season: trapping, hunting, and some handlogging kept many of the men busily occupied while others found part-time work in towns. Port Essington was the main winter residence to which most of the families returned, at least for short periods of a few weeks, in order to participate in Christian celebrations (notably Christmas and New Year's), and to send their children to school. If the weather conditions were poor, the men would leave their families there for slightly longer periods, and return to the traplines with their adult male partners, but these separations from the family were not popular arrangements.

The arrival of the first oolachan in March traditionally signalled the end of the winter period.

In the minds of many, this pattern is considered to be the closest to an ideal or traditional one for the Tsimshian, even though it belongs to the 20th century. There are two reasons for this perception. First, it was the way of life followed by three or four generations, with the current set of elders constituting the last generation to have participated. Second, people remember it as a lifestyle that permitted the maintenance of Tsimshian values, albeit in a highly syncretic manner. I emphasize that it is an ideal pattern because it has been romanticized somewhat as the "good old days" when the old values still applied, and because it is remembered now as the preferred way of life although not everyone could follow it. Even then there were a number of people who were so involved with wage labour, that they could not fully use the camp system. Still others did not have their own boat to engage in simple commodity production independently and, as a consequence, relied on others. Both types vacillated between camp life and wage labour.

The number of people unable to use the camp/boat system increased as people constantly were forced out of the traditional pattern by the changing capitalist economy. One change was the restructuring of the logging industry. The result of this process, which started in the 1940s, was the undermining of the abilities of handloggers to operate economically.[64] The steep economic decline in trapping, which reached a critical point in the mid-1950s, hurt another source of income. Finally, many Indian boat owners found it impossible to keep pace with the expensive technological changes that were constantly occurring in the fishing industry.[65] When very strict equipment standards were developed, "marginal" boats were forced out of the industry.[66] Many of these boats were Indian and marginal because of their year round use in the complex traditional economy.

It was the economic mixture that made their traditional way of life viable for the Kitsumkalum. Thus, the pressures on each aspect of it served to weaken and eventually, in combination, to destroy the pattern. By the 1960s the Port Essington families returned to Kitsumkalum Valley, marking the beginning of a new period in their history and in their relationship to the environment.

The Current Pattern

In the second half of this century, the present economy and seasonal cycle emerged, dominated by wage labour. Indian access to resources had been defined by new property laws. Now their time also was being defined by wage jobs, and their ability to utilize resources was sharply curtailed. The seasonal cycle that resulted, and that exists today, is simple.

Berry-collecting occurs as berries ripen from the late spring into the fall. Throughout the late spring and summer, families with access to coastal sites gather seaweeds and seafood as they become available. Other families that stay inland trade with friends or relatives on the coast for marine resources.

The hunting of small game and fowl occurs as the regulated seasons permit, or, in the case of non-regulated species, as available throughout the year. Food fishing commences with the spring oolachan runs, continues with the first salmon run in June, and ends when the people have sufficient supplies, often as early as the end of July. Some minor fishing activity always continues until the last runs of September, as people take the occasional fresh fish or coho salmon if they preferred this late running species. (Different salmon species run in different months.)

The very simplicity of the current pattern is revealing of the impact capitalist development has had, and of the many other changes that have transformed Tsimshian society. Now that the people of Kitsumkalum look to wage labour for their livelihood, the seasonal cycle that they follow stands as a monument to their determination to resist the complete transformation of their Tsimshian values.

Conclusions

Originally hunting, fishing, and gathering were the major components of the Tsimshian's system of production. These sectors provided the material basis of broader social relationships and guided the seasonality of Tsimshian life. Confederation, industrialization, and the legislation of the capitalist political economy ushered in a new era that undermined Tsimshian sovereignty, disintegrated the older order, and left Indians marginal to twentieth century development.

The transformation of the once independent and successful people of Kitsumkalum was accomplished through the various means that involved the appropriation of resources from Tsimshian production, legal attacks on their technology, and even constraints on the application of their labour. Government legislation, which redefined the property rights associated with all economic processes, restricted how, when, and where people could engage in the Tsimshian economy. The effect of all this on the seasonal cycle was the erosion of the Tsimshian ability to develop floral and faunal resources on their own terms. The seasonal cycle was one structured by the framework of the new political economy.

Partially in response to these attacks, and partially to take advantage of new opportunities, the Tsimshian added commercial activities to their seasonal rounds. In this manner, they developed new relationships to the environment that were exemplified by the simple commodity production of the fishing boat. All the forms of production, both old and new, in which the Kitsumkalum engaged, and the reorganization of their economy that was necessary to integrate each form throughout the annual cycle, eventually trapped the Kitsumkalum in capitalist production. By the twentieth century, these people, like other coastal Indians, had become dependent on the global capitalist economic formation and on the conditions that enabled that system to function.

These changes were not simply adaptations to their given environment, but accommodations to the socially defined environment that was being created under the new political economy emerging in the region. The people of Kitsumkalum no longer cut trees for trade, they work as loggers. Their fish runs have been turned into "food" and "commercial" fisheries. As capitalist production became dominant, the aboriginal Tsimshian economy was transformed into its current radically reduced state, marginal to regional economic development. Thus, the basic property arrangements governing the social economy were redefined to suit the needs of capital, and a new "cultural ecology" was founded.

Despite these pressures and changes, the Tsimshian have struggled long and hard to control and preserve their way of life, and to take their rightful position in their own development. In this struggle, Tsimshian forms of production, including those which are derived from aboriginal economic activities, have been of ultimate importance to the survival of Tsimshian society. Today, the existence of aboriginal rights protects these activities, assists the survival of aboriginal culture and society, and maintains values that could provide alternatives to those which govern capitalist societies. It is to be hoped that the future legal entrenchment of aboriginal rights in the Canadian constitution will allow aboriginal peoples the opportunity to strengthen their societies, overcome their dependency, and move out of their marginal position in Canadian society.

Notes

1. Numerous reports and books provide ample evidence for the severity of these conditions. Especially notable references are H.B. Hawthorne, C.S. Belshaw, and S. Jamieson, *Indians of British Columbia: A Study of Contemporary Social Adjustment* (Toronto: University of Toronto Press, 1958); Department of Indian Affairs and Northern Development (hereinafter DIAND), *A Survey of the Contemporary Indians of Canada. A Report on Economic, Political, and Educational Needs and Policies*, edited by H.B. Hawthorn (Ottawa: Information Canada, 1966); Department of Indian Affairs (hereinafter DIA), *Indian Conditions. A Survey* (Ottawa: The Department, 1980).
2. Bruce Cox, ed., *Cultural Ecology: Readings on the Canadian Indians and Eskimos* (Toronto: Macmillan of Canada, 1973).
3. James Andrew McDonald, "Trying to Make a Life: The Historic Political Economy of Kitsumkalum (Ph.D. diss., University of British Columbia, 1985).
4. James Andrew McDonald, "A History of the Traplines that have once been Registered by the Kitsumkalums," Kitsumkalum Social History Research Project, Report # 4 (1982).
5. Viola Garfield, "Tsimshian Clan and Society," *University of Washington Publications in Anthropology* 7 (1939):244 ff, 257 ff.
6. Franz Boas, *Tsimshian Mythology*, Annual Report of the Bureau of American Ethnology, 1909–1910 (Washington: Government Printing Office, 1916), 399.
7. Viola Garfield, "The Tsimshian and Their Neighbors," in *The Tsimshian Indians and Their Arts*, edited by Viola Garfield and Paul S. Wingert (Seattle: University of Washington Press, 1966).
8. McDonald, "Trying to Make a Life."
9. Important data still can come from elders. For example, Garfield's interpretation can still be augmented by informants who were young adults or children at the time she did her work; James Andrew McDonald, "An Historic Event in the Political Economy of the Tsimshian: Information on the Ownership of the Zimacord District," *British Columbia Studies* 57 (1983). The opportunity to expand similarly on Boas' description is probably lost now, although I have spoken with an elder who was a child in a Tsimshian village Boas visited on one of his first field-trips to the Northwest Coast and to the Tsimshian. There are other useful bits of information in ethnographic archives, such as the unpublished Beynon/Barbeau field-notes from the Skeena; John J. Cove, *A Detailed Inventory of the Barbeau Northwest Coast Files*, National Museum of Man Mercury Series, Canadian Centre for Folk Culture Studies, 54 (1985).
10. Personal communications from various Tsimshian. The earliest published reference for elk is Franz Boas, "The Indians of British Columbia: Tlingit, Haida, Tsimshian, Kotomaga," in the *Fifth Report on the Northwestern Tribes of Canada*, Report of the British Association for the Advancement of Science (London: The British Association for the Advancement of Science, 1889), 803; for eagles, Boas, *Tsimshian Mythology*, 44, 51, 52, 401, 404; for groundhogs, McDonald, "Historic Event in the Political Economy of the Tsimshian."
11. British Columbia, Sessional Papers, *Report of Conferences between the Provincial Government and Indian Delegates for Port Simpson and Nass River* (Victoria: Government Printer, 1887), 268.

12. See the Northwestern Development Conference Archives, Northwest Community College, Terrace, British Columbia.
13. Usually no immature animals less than one year old, since Revised Statutes of British Columbia (hereinafter R.S.B.C.), 1897, C88, S.3.
14. Female moose, since R.S.B.C. 1897, C88, S.3.
15. Two hundred and fifty ducks per person per season, R.S.B.C. 1897, C88, S.3; one moose, two goats, three deer of one specics or four altogether, two sheep, R.S.B.C. 1924, C94, S.10.
16. R.S.B.C. 1888, C52, S.8.
17. R.S.B.C. 1960, C160, S.16.
18. R.S.B.C. 1888, C52, S.6. 19. Statutes of British Columbia (hereinafter S.B.C.) 1966, C55, S.9.
20. S.B.C. 1966, C55, S.11.
21. Revised Statutes of Canada (hereinafter R.S.C.) 1927, C130.
22. R.S.B.C. 1911, C95, S.13.
23. R.S.B.C. 1897, C88, S.17.
24. R.S.B.C. 1911, C95, S.3.
25. McDonald, "Historic Event."
26. W.M. Ross, *Salmon Cannery Pack Statistics on the Nass and Skeena Rivers of British Columbia* (Vancouver: University of British Columbia Press, n.d.).
27. Fishery Act, 1874, C57, S.13.7.
28. *Ibid.*, S.8.
29. *Ibid.*, S.13.7.
30. *Ibid.*
31. *Ibid.*, S.13.11, S.13.14.
32. *Ibid.*, S.13.17.
33. *Ibid.*, S.3.8, clarified with regard to open season for Indian food fishing by 1889 regulations.
34. R.S.B.C. 1888, C52, S.13.
35. Order-in-Council (hereinafter O/C) 7 November 1890.
36. S.C. 1891, C44.
37. S.C. 1894, C51, S.1-3.
38. R.S.B.C. 1897, C88, S.12.
39. R.S.B.C. 1911, C89, S.17, S.45, these being a part of the 1901 legislation, S.B.C., C25, S.41.
40. See Hawthorn *et. al.*, *Indians of British Columbia*, 98.
41. O/C 12 March 1910.
42. By O/C 12 May 1910, which required food fish licences.
43. O/C 11 September 1917.
44. DIA, *Annual Report* (Ottawa: Government Printer, 1878).
45. Department of Fisheries, *Annual Narrative* (Ottawa: Government Printer, 1878), 296.
46. For example, DIAND, *Annual Reports* (Ottawa: Government Printer), 1881, 154; 1884, 277–78; 1886; 1890.
47. DIA, *Annual Report*, 1879, 134.
48. DIA, *Annual Report*, 1881, 154.
49. Public Archives of Canada, RG 10, vol. 1022, handscript of minutes.
50. Viola Garfield, "The Tsimshian and Their Neighbors," in *The Tsimshian Indians and Their Arts*, by Viola E. Garfield and Paul S. Wingert (Seattle: University of Washington Press, 1966), 23.
51. For example, see McDoanld, "Historic Event."
52. *Ibid.*
53. British Columbia, Sessional Papers, Report of Conferences, 253 ff.

54. John C. Pritchard, "Economic Development and the Disintigration of Traditional Culture Among the Haisla" (Ph.D. diss., University of British Columbia, 1977).
55. R.S.B.C. 1924, C93, S.10.1.
56. R.S.B.C. 1888, C52, S.12.
57. R.S.C. 1917, C130, Article IV.
58. R.S.C. 1917, C130, Article III.
59. S.C. 1874, C60, S.15.
60. O/C 1908, p. ccxxxi.
61. R.S.B.C. 1911, C89, S.38.
62. R.S.B.C. 1948, C125, S.30.
63. British Columbia, Sessional Papers, *Metlakatla Inquiry: Report of the Commissioners* (Victoria: Government Printer, 1885), 289; British Columbia, Sessional Papers, *Report of Conferences*, 260 ff.
64. McDonald, "Trying to Make a Life."
65. *Ibid.*, 263–66.
66. *Ibid.*, 268.

PART V
The Yukon and the Northwest Territories

In Part II we discovered that the Indians of the boreal forest made use of a "single set of social relations" within the "multi-family winter hunting group" to organize subsistence production and market production alike. In these mixed purposes, many scholars have discerned an inherent contradiction. It is, nevertheless, a contradiction which the native can manage, so long as they produce enough furs and enough food to reproduce this mixed system, contradictions and all. As we saw in Part II, this system developed over a very long time, and persists wherever it is possible to spend part of the yearly round in the bush. The contributions to Part III show natives taking part, while in the bush, in egalitarian social relations and food-sharing; this is, in short, the foraging mode of production. Here we take something of an inside view of life in the winter hunting camps, to the extent that this is possible to non-participants. Nevertheless, it is still more common to view the winter camps from the outside and in terms of their products. Viewed in this way, we may speak of the bush Indians as taking part in a "mixed economy." This is to view a process in terms only of its end results and thus to view it incompletely. Nevertheless, the term "mixed economy" is a recurring part of the debate concerning the fate of the North and mid-North, and thus must be included here, since three of the four chapters in this section deal directly with that debate. In fact, the same three chapters deal with formal public attempts to weigh the role of the native mixed economy in the future of the North. The debates on this question during the 1970s led to the call in 1977 for a ten year moratorium on megaprojects of northern development. The moratorium will have expired when this sees print, so a reassessment of the debate is long overdue. Let us begin that reassessment with a review of the first major public hearing of the 1970s to examine the role of the native mixed economy in the future of the North. Unlike later reviews, this was a trial, not a royal commission.

In April 1973, the Supreme Court of the Northwest Territories was asked to rule on an application by the Chiefs of the sixteen Indian bands of the Mackenzie drainage for a caveat on all unregistered Crown lands west of the Coronation Gulf and south of the Inuit areas on the Arctic coast. In early July of that same year, I sat in a crowded second-floor courtroom on Yellowknife's main street as the caveat came to trial. Although their caveat failed on appeal, the Mackenzie bands had the opportunity to put their case on Northern development to the public at large, a chance which had not come before. Another judge in a trial earlier that same year, Mr. Justice A.H. Malouf, found that the Cree of James Bay had "a unique concept of the land," making use of "all its fruits and products." The evidence given in Yellowknife went to establish the same point; one after another, elderly witnesses testified that they knew, used, and remembered every part of their band's territory. There was evidence given concerning food-sharing and the foraging mode of production, though not of course by that name. This came later that summer, in the testimony by Dr. June Helm, an anthropologist. Dr. Helm spoke of a "hunter ethic" which grants neighbouring bands access to needed resources. Such access was most necessary, Dr. Helm argued, as "starvation in the past had driven peoples out of their accustomed zone."[1] (Some of this is also summarized in Chapter 16.)

More on the bush economy was brought out by the two pipeline inquiries held later in the 1970s. The Yukon pipeline inquiry, in fact, strove to explain that economy to southern readers, drawing on the testimony of Clyde Blackjack of Carmacks:

> Through a judicious mix of wage employment, the trapping of fur, and the acquisition of country food, Mr. Blackjack appears to be able to produce what he needs. He is not interested in accumulation for its own sake. . . .[2]

The Mackenzie Valley Pipeline Inquiry spoke of the same subject in more general terms:

> In the North today, the lives of many native families are based on an intricate economic mix. At certain times of the year, they hunt and fish; at other times they work for wages, sometimes for government, sometimes on highway construction, sometimes for the oil and gas industry.[3]

It remains to be seen whether this "intricate mix" adds up to a single unified economy. Michael Asch, for example, argues that it does not. Following a position which we have outlined in early sections, Dr. Asch argues that northern natives operate within two modes of production, a "bush" or foraging mode, as we have called it earlier, and the capitalist mode of production. As we have already seen, the bush mode of production is based on co-operative labour, communal land tenure, and the mutual sharing of surpluses. Even during fur production for the market, the values of traditional bush life remained dominant. (A similar argument was advanced in Part II.) However, as I point out in Chapter 19, the bush economy today cannot generate enough cash to reproduce itself. That cash must come from other sources, sometimes from wage labour, as in the passage from Mr. Justice Berger's report cited above. In this connection, Michael Asch writes of "a very marked increase in the impingement of capitalist institutions and values" on the daily lives of native Northerners during the years since the Second World War. Dr. Asch points out, as I do in Chapter 19, that such needed cash often reaches the Northern villages in the form of transfer payments. We must not suppose, however, that such payments are unintrusive on the values of traditional bush life.

> Indeed, rather the contrary is the case. As in other capitalist transactions, these payments are made directly to individuals. . . . The payment of welfare to individuals and nuclear families isolated poverty and created a division between "rich" and "poor". . . . The weakness of the native economy today is not merely that it lacks capital and job opportunities but equally that its traditional

institutions and values are being eroded by the very means Native people must use to obtain essential cash.[4]

What is the remedy? Justice Berger recommends government grants to set up fur farms, tanneries, and fishing lodges. Asch correctly points out that Berger's programme, like transfer payments, would tend to reproduce capitalist relations of production. The Dene themselves are aware of this problem, and are seeking ways to organize Dene enterprises without relying on capitalist relations of production. In Chapter 19, I come down on the side of an Income Security Programme such as was put in place in Northern Quebec by the James Bay Agreement. This programme takes as its basis the "harvesting unit," making larger payments to larger units. Furthermore, the programme's payments are reduced proportionally as income from wage increases. It thus goes some way toward reducing disparities between households, and also avoids the extreme individualism on which transfer payments are predicated. Here I might point out that most native communities rely heavily on social aid paid (for status Indians) by the federal government. Putting in place an Income Security Programme (ISP) for native hunters should greatly reduce the need for such payments. This already seems to have taken place among the Cree of James Bay, who went from $846 thousand in welfare payments in 1976–77, when the ISP was put in place, to $260 thousand in 1979–80, after a few years of the programme's operation.[5] Perhaps savings sufficient to fund the programme could be realized elsewhere.

The three chapters discussed thus far deal with the survival in the North of what Michael Asch calls the bush mode of production. After all, that is the major theme of this book. Nevertheless, not all natives take part in this mode of production. Experience in Northern Quebec can give us an idea of the proportions of bush producers elsewhere. According to LaRusic,[6] over half the Cree households of James Bay are considered to be "intensive subsistence hunters," spending over half their yearly round in the bush. Experience suggests also that, without the ISP, a smaller number of households would participate intensively in subsistence production.[7] I take this to suggest that over much of the North less than half of the native households are intensively engaged in bush production. What, then, of the majority? We have so far said little about what is likely the greater proportion of native northeners, since this book is, in the main, about the bush mode of production, past and present. It is well, however, to say something about the others, those who cannot outfit themselves for a lengthy stay in the bush and must remain in the villages subsisting on part-time labour and welfare payments. Some of those who stay year-round in the Northern villages are likewise employed year-round, as Asch and I imply (see Table 19-2). Most, however, are not regularly employed, as Michael Asch makes clear. In their case, preserving a mode of production in which they cannot participate will have little effect. In their case, we can speak only of preserving language and culture. Jean-Philippe Chartrand addresses himself to that survival in the new Inuit Villages. Language is perhaps the single best predictor of cultural identity, and as such can benefit from our support. Only then will daily Inuit experience help reproduce a sense of Inuit identity.

Notes

1. June Helm, "Transcript of Testimony Given on August 20th and 21st, 1973, before Justice W.G. Morrow, Supreme Court of the N.W.T.", Yellowknife, Northwest Territories, 24.
2. K.M. Lysyk *et al.*, *Alaska Highway Pipeline Inquiry* (Ottawa: Department of Indian and Northern Affairs, 1977), 91.
3. Mr. Justice T. Berger, *Northern Frontier, Northern Homeland: The Report of the Mackenzie Valley Pipeline Inquiry*, vol. I (Ottawa: Supply and Services Canada, 1977), 122.
4. Chapter 17 of this volume.
5. Ignatius E. LaRusic, *et al.*, *Negotiating a Way of Life: Initial Cree Experience with the Administrative Structure Arising from the James Bay Agreement* (Montreal: ssDcc Inc., 1979), 91.
6. *Ibid.*, 163.
7. Colin Scott, "Production and Exchange Among Wemindji Cree: Egalitarian Ideology and Economic Base," *Culture*, vol. 2, no. 3 (1982):54.

Chapter 16
Changing Perceptions of Industrial Development in the North

Bruce Alden Cox

This paper considers some issues involved in the proposed development of energy resources in the Mackenzie region of the Canadian Northwest Territories. Since a Mackenzie petroleum pipeline is still in the picture, these issues will be taken up with the pipeline in mind, though very similar considerations would result in other sorts of resource development. A great deal has happened since I published an earlier version of this paper; in revising it for publication here I decided to emphasize events of the 1970s, particularly a native land rights case held in 1973 in the Northwest Territories. As often happens in legal cases, the land rights hearings showed in dramatic relief the different futures which the parties to the conflict held for the lands under dispute. Before examining such differing perceptions of northern resources, however, I wish to provide some background to the case.

Canada is said to have rediscovered the North and northern peoples after 1950. More particularly a re-awakened interest in Arctic energy sources came only with the discovery of substantial petroleum reserves on Alaska's Arctic slope. This is true to such an extent that a Canadian government document could say of the two decades ending in 1968: "From the standpoint of oil and gas, Canada north of 60 is virtually unexplored."[1] Such exploration as was done in the North, before Prudhoe Bay's petroleum discovery, was concentrated along the borders with Alberta and British Columbia, adjacent to producing fields in those provinces. However, this picture changed quickly when the size of the North Alaskan oil and gas reserves was discovered. Furthermore, Alaskan oil could be sent to market by tanker, but gas—without costly liquifaction—could not. Hence, a northern gas pipeline has been debated for some time now. A government report on the northern petroleum industry notes: "From the first realization of the magnitude of the Prudhoe Bay find, it has been considered likely that solution gas from the field would . . . find its way to market in the USA by a pipeline through Canada."[2] The discussion of a Canadian pipeline in turn spurred oil and gas exploration in Canada's north, since the view became widespread that economic transport to southern markets would soon be available.[3]

The discovery of gas fields in the Mackenzie Delta and northern Yukon have in themselves added to the demand for a gas pipeline. If gas reserves in the Mackenzie Delta reach "threshold" levels, the Mackenzie field would evidently be connected with a proposed Alaska-to-Chicago pipeline. (In the 1970s, pipeline companies in the Great Lakes region of the United States took options on natural gas reserves in the Mackenzie Delta region.) If the pipeline to the

Great Lakes was built, over 2,500 miles of 48-inch conduit would be required from Alaska to the international border near Emerson, Manitoba. Some 1,500 miles of conduit right-of-way would lie in the northern Yukon and the Mackenzie River drainage of the Northwest Territories. The Mackenzie River highway, constructed during the 1970s, links Fort Simpson on the upper Mackenzie with existing roads in the Mackenzie Delta. Pipeline developers would use the highway to haul construction materials, and their route would follow the road's right-of-way. (Legget denies that the same route could serve for a roadway and petroleum pipelines.[4])

The Setting

Canada north of the sixtieth parallel was inhabited in the 1970s by some 57,000 persons, 18,000 of them in the Yukon Territory, the remainder in the Northwest Territories.[5] The Indian Brotherhood of the Northwest Territories estimated that some 28,000 were native peoples, and about half were treaty Indians and Métis.[6] In the Northwest Territories, treaty Indians and Métis are nearly all found along the Mackenzie River and its tributaries. Such concentration is in large part a legacy of the fur trade when trading forts were set up a few days travel apart on the major water routes. There is also a recent tendency for native peoples to live year-round in these settlements, rather than coming there only to trade, as was done formerly.[7] Because of this concentration, there were some 4,500 native people who lived along the Mackenzie pipeline corridor and would be directly affected by it, whether for good or ill.[8]

Much of the Mackenzie region is forested, despite its northerly location. A long finger of the Canadian boreal forest reaches down the Mackenzie Plain, with the tree-line extending northward into the Mackenzie Delta. The Athabascan Indian peoples of this river and forest region—Kutchin, Hare, Dogrib, and Slavey—once relied entirely on its resources for their livelihood. For example, as recently as the mid-1960s the Corrothers Commission found two-thirds of experienced indigenous workers in the Mackenzie engaged in hunting, trapping, and fishing.[9]

Until recently, fur prices had shown a twenty-year decline from the "boom" times of the 1940s.[10] Accordingly, government policy, where it took notice of trappers at all, has been mainly oriented toward encouraging men to leave trapping for other pursuits.[11] Had I written this in the 1960s, I could hardly have faulted this policy, saving for the resultant loss of "country foods" (fish, game) and other bush resources. In the 1970s, however, fur prices were no longer low—in fact, the demand for furs appeared to be growing.[12] World fur prices rose steeply in the early 1970s bringing record prices for some fine furs.[13] Very likely substantial increases were available as well to trappers in the Mackenzie. Furthermore, the Territorial government began to make capital grants to trappers.[14] It is thus quite premature to write off trapping as a dying industry;

likely, it will remain an important part of Northern life for some time to come. This is especially so as trapping gives access to other bush resources—dog-feed, firewood, and "country foods." Many Northerners remain at least partly oriented toward the bush so as not to cut themselves off from such resources. For example, Hawthorn *et al.*[15] estimates a majority of those settlements "north of sixty" exploit bush resources in season, often in combination with casual wage labour. The risks of total commitment to industrial work are often too high for Northerners, as I argue elsewhere for another part of the North.[16] A young man in Fort Good Hope explained these risks to a committee investigating the impact of petroleum exploration in the Mackenzie region:

> If employment were available with the oil companies for several years there would be a danger that people would forget how to trap and when the seismic program ended and the people were laid off they would then have nothing to fall back on.[17]

Even for those who do not wish to remain trappers, there are possibilities for permanent employment in bush-oriented jobs. Here I have in mind opportunities in tourism, particularly in outfitting and guiding. However, these opportunities depend on the preservation of northern aesthetic values in natural landscapes, without industrial clutter. Furthermore, some sorts of tourism rely on isolation, and are inconsistent with the proposed industrial development and highways. Hans Otto Meissner, a German travel writer, comments on the sort of tourist who might be attracted by the present isolation of Mackenzie settlements: "He has no desire to pass his days in modern settlements which are more or less alike. He wants to travel the rivers by boat, to live in the forests and be always close to nature."[18]

Changing Perceptions of Development

I have cited trapping and tourism as instances in which the native interest is not identical with that of northern industrial developers. In the 1970s, it was often argued that northern energy development would benefit natives as well as White entrepreneurs, and bring "a higher standard of living for (native) northern residents."[19] It is clear that such slogans contemplated native participation in the work force required for northern projects, but not necessarily in other ways. There is evidence that this is no longer enough. James Wah-Shee, former President of the Indian Brotherhood (now the Dene Nation), said as much to a group of Northern petroleum developers: "For a pipeline to benefit us in the long run, we must be employers as well as employees from the outset."[20]

The native organizations want not only jobs, but "direct participation in development planning and decision making."[21] There is evidence that the native organizations are disturbed by the currently quickening pace of development; in fact, they consider it hostile to their fundamental interest. A position paper from the Indian Brotherhood of the Northwest Territories put their attitude quite clearly:

> With oil and seismic crews bulldozing and blasting away, and plans for pipelines and parks proceeding. . . . If the present pace of planning and development

> continues it will leave the native people without even the bargaining position to settle past grievance, let alone to realize their future.[22]

What the Indian Brotherhood wants, it seems, is what all citizens should have—a say in the projects developed, supposedly, on their behalf. Accordingly, the Brotherhood has developed legal strategies designed to give it some say in the course of northern industrial development. These strategies are considered briefly in the next section of this paper.

Before proceeding, however, it is worth noting that another sort of strategy had been taken up by the Indians of the Yukon. They have sought a legislated remedy for the problems of development. On 28 February 1972, the Chief and Councillors of the Old Crow Band in the northeastern Yukon petitioned Parliament, claiming some 66,000 square miles in the Porcupine River drainage. (The Porcupine is itself a tributary of the Yukon River.) The area claimed has been put forward as a pipeline right-of-way, as well as being a centre for petroleum exploration.[23] Subsequently, the Yukon Native Brotherhood stated an intention of negotiating a settlement of the claims of all twelve Yukon bands. Like the Mackenzie peoples, the Yukon Brotherhood expressed uneasiness at the quickening pace of industrial development:

> As each year passes, more and more land is taken away and given to the White man. Every year more mineral claims are staked. Every year more oil and gas leases are given to the oil companies. . . . This is why we need a settlement now.[24]

Accordingly, the Brotherhood is seeking a settlement consisting of mineral royalties, and land allotments for village sites and native-controlled industrial development. Participation in the benefits of this settlement will be open to people of indigenous descent certified by a committee of their own community. There will be no reliance on purely legal or administrative definitions of "Indian."[25] The band at Old Crow is given special mention; they are meant to receive title, including mineral rights, to the Crow Flats area.[26] Furthermore, legal action is proposed to protect caribou-calving grounds in the Yukon coastal plain, thus protecting the herd on which the Old Crow people depend. Recall that the Yukon coastal plain has been considered as a pipeline route, and construction activities there would likely be disruptive to caribou.[27]

The Yukon claim was based on aboriginal rights through long-term occupation. Treaties have not been signed for most of the Yukon, so there is no question here of the extinguishing of aboriginal title by means of treaty. To be sure, several bands on the Liard River in southeastern Yukon signed an adhesion to Treaty Eleven in 1922.[28] Nevertheless, these bands were apparently not the ancestors of the present-day Liard River Band.[29] So the Yukon Indians evidently have a good case. (At this writing, January 1987, negotiations are still pending between the Indians and government representatives.)

Land Rights Hearings

In April 1973, the Supreme Court of the Northwest Territories was asked to rule on an application by Chiefs of the sixteen Mackenzie drainage Indian bands for a caveat on all unregistered Crown lands west of Coronation Gulf and south of the Eskimo use areas on the Arctic coast. The Court ruled that no new land title could be recorded until the case was settled unless the new owners agreed to respect whatever interest the Indian bands might be found to have in the lands they registered. Among the first to run afoul of this order was the town of Hay River on the south shore of Great Slave Lake. The town wanted title to 1,000 acres of nearby Crown land for an industrial park.[30] The town planners were required to post a bond of $150 per acre against the possibility that the Indian bands would be found to have an interest in the site.[31] Potentially, this caveat case cast a shadow over any industrial development of Crown lands in the Mackenzie region. It seemed that the native peoples had found the tool needed to slow the quickening pace of industrial development in the Mackenzie drainage.

In late 1971, the Indian Brotherhood had put their position on development directly to the National Energy Board, when a short gas pipeline was to be built from Pointed Mountain, N.W.T. to northwestern British Columbia. Their submission to the Energy Board was to no avail; the pipeline was built as scheduled.[32] This experience doubtless prompted the search for a suitable forum in which to put the native case concerning development. The Indian Brotherhood particularly wanted its case to be heard by William Morrow, Justice of the Territorial Supreme Court. Justice Morrow's long experience with northern peoples and customs would likely make him a sympathetic listener to the Indian position.[33] The federal Department of Justice, however, attempted to keep Judge Morrow from hearing the Chiefs' application for a caveat. In June 1973, the department filed a Writ of Prohibition which would have prevented the Territorial Court's hearing the matter. In an Interim Judgement on 14 June, Judge Morrow replied in kind, maintaining the writ would "threaten the very integrity of this Court." Getting perhaps to the heart of the matter, he mused, "If I can be entrusted to adjudicate on cases involving the liberties of the subjects of the Territories permitting me to put them in gaol I should be capable of adjudicating on questions involving their property, unless of course property including land is placed on a higher plane."[34] In fact, the Crown's application for a Writ of Prohibition was dismissed on 6 July by Federal Justice Collier after hearing arguments from Douglas Sanders and other attorneys for the Indian Brotherhood. Perhaps Justice Collier was influenced as well by Judge Morrow's pointed remark (in his Interim Judgement) that government insistence on seeking a Writ of Prohibition left the impression that "Federal Court can be made to jump whenever asked by the Federal Government."[35]

The hearings on the caveat started in Yellowknife just a few days after the federal court had cleared up the matter of Judge Morrow's jurisdiction. It seemed the Mackenzie chiefs at long last had the forum they wanted. There was to be one more procedural hitch, however. Just before the hearings were to begin, the counsel for the Crown announced that he had been instructed to withdraw from the case. This "most unusual action,"[36] as Justice Morrow describes it, might have led to a judgement by default in favour of the Indian caveators. The Judge admitted considering just such a judgement, and perhaps that is what the federal government expected him to do. We must ask here, who would have been most harmed by such a resolution of the matter? I believe that the Indians would have been, since they would have lost the chance to argue for their land rights, and would gain only a judgement in default which could easily be reversed. A Yellowknife editor, writing when the hearing began, speculated about the motives behind the Justice Department's strategy. In his view, the federal government was "concerned that the Indian Brotherhood intended to take the caveat hearings as an opportunity to air the Indian Treaty and Aboriginal Rights claims,"[37] and so endeavour to prevent the proceedings. Very likely this writer was correct, and he may well have hit on the motive for Crown Counsel's withdrawing from the case.

In fact, the government's tactics did not prevent the Indians stating their case. Judge Morrow refused to give a default judgement in what was clearly "no ordinary lawsuit."[38] He appointed an attorney to act as "friend of the Court"—to assist in examining witnesses and maintaining adversarial proceedings. In the parts of the hearings which I observed, the friend of the court seemed diligent and knowledgeable in cross-examining witnesses and entering motions for the Crown. For example, he raised objections to Indian witnesses saying "what the old people told them" about Treaty negotiations, though this sort of evidence was finally admitted. The substance of these proceedings could be the subject for another presumably much longer essay. I cannot do it justice here, except to say that the Mackenzie chiefs were able to make a plausible case for their retaining title in nearly the whole of the Mackenzie drainage—some 400,000 square miles in all. As Justice Morrow put it "there is enough doubt as to whether the full aboriginal title has been extinguished . . . to justify the caveators attempting to protect the Indian position"[39] until a final court judgement could be made. At the same time, he removed the restrictions on registering new land title, although bonds already posted were to be kept by the Registrar of land title. Furthermore, he directed the Registrar to keep a record of all title registered on Crown lands, in case the Indians gained a caveat in higher court.[40] Though this finding seems modest enough, Indian organizations hailed it as a victory: "Indians Win Historic Victory—Court Supports NWT Indians' Land Claims" a headline in Edmonton's *The Native People* crowed on 14 September.[41] And perhaps they are right. At any rate, the Indians' case on Northern development had been heard, with the prospect of further hearings in higher courts.

The Indian Brotherhood treated the decision as an additional political resource. Many of its chiefs opposed the completion of the Mackenzie Valley Highway, since completed, but then scheduled to reach the Camsell Bend of the Mackenzie, some fifty miles downstream from Fort Simpson, in the fall of 1973.[42] The nearest village downstream from Camsell Bend is Wrigley, and the people of Wrigley did not want to be on a highway. In September, the Indian Brotherhood issued a statement supporting the Wrigley Settlement and Band

Council in their opposition to the Mackenzie Highway. The Brotherhood took the Morrow decision as support for its position: "The recent NWT Supreme Court decision in the caveat case confirmed the right of Indian people to this stand and the responsibility of the federal government to protect this right."[43]

Implications

I have tried to give some idea of the clash of issues over the industrial development of the Mackenzie River drainage, and of the background of this conflict of interests. In the Mackenzie, as well as the Yukon, native organizations argue for increased native control of the means of production. Nevertheless, a few questions remain. For example, how many native peoples in the remoter parts of the Mackenzie share these sentiments? On the other hand, how many Mackenzie natives wish to find jobs in massive industrial projects like the proposed natural gas pipeline? On both counts, it must be the case that some do. Nevertheless, there is a risk of over-estimating the number of Mackenzie men who are free and willing to work on such massive projects. A survey, done in 1972, found that, of 1,621 able-bodied men along the Mackenzie Valley, 700 were already employed, 254 were unwilling to accept regular wage labour, and the remainder would accept industrial jobs on a seasonal basis.[44]

Another vital question remains: what chance have the Mackenzie peoples of affecting the course of northern development? This obviously can be answered only with speculation. A variety of circumstances may influence the future, many of them not on the horizon when I first presented this paper. Here I include the priority which the U.S. government evidently puts on shipping liquified natural gas to market entirely within their national control through a trans-Alaska pipeline and on board tankers as liquified gas. This may ensure some moderation in the pace of industrial development, something the native organizations have actively sought.

But such a pause in the pace of industrial development will not in itself solve native problems. Nevertheless, there are hopeful signs here as well. It has long been noted that Canadian native communities lack capital investment. Investment in resource extraction by international corporations will not remedy this, nor is it likely that it will provide many jobs for northerners. Hawthorn, Laforet, and Jamieson concur in this view: "Only a minority of Indians and Eskimos seem likely to find long-term employment in new development—oil and gas, transportation, government administration, and accompanying industrial and commercial enterprises."[45] What can be done then? The Yukon Native Brotherhood's proposal for a negotiated settlement of claims provides a likely answer. Recall that their proposal calls for the investment of mineral royalties in local native communities. I understand that a similar proposal has been brought forward by the Dene and Mackenzie Métis. Perhaps northern development will in fact continue, though probably on very different terms from that contemplated by international petroleum corporations.

Notes

Source: *Human Organization*, vol. 34, no. 1 (Spring 1975), by permission of the Society for Applied Anthropology.

1. Department of Indian Affairs and Northern Development (hereinafter DIAND), *Oil and Gas North of 60: A Report of Activities in 1968* (Ottawa: Queen's Printer, 1969), 1.
2. DIAND, *Oil and Gas North of 60: A Report of Activities in 1969* (Ottawa: Queen's Printer, 1970), 4.
3. DIAND, *Activities in 1969*.
4. R.F. Legget, "Technology: Discussion Paper," in *Science and the North: A Seminar on Guidelines for Scientific Activities in Northern Canada* (Ottawa: Information Canada, 1973).
5. *Ibid.*, 227–28.
6. Indian Brotherhood of the Northwest Territories (hereinafter IBNWT), "The Threat to the Indian in the Northwest Territories" (Position Paper presented to the National Indian Brotherhood Meeting, Regina, July 1971, Mimeographed).
7. J. Helm and N.O. Lurie, *The Subsistence Economy of the Dogrib Indians of Lac La Martre in the Mackenzie District of the N.W.T.* (Ottawa: Northern Co-ordination and Research Centre, 1961); J.R. Wolforth, *The Mackenzie Delta—Its Economic Base and Development* (Ottawa: Northern Science Research Group, 1967).
8. R.M. Hill, "Petroleum Pipelines and Arctic Environment," *North* 18 (1971).
9. A.W.P. Corrothers, J. Beetz, and J.M. Parker, "Report of the Advisory Commission on the Development of Government in the Northwest Territories," vol. I (submitted to the Department of Northern Affairs and Natural Resources, 1966, mimeographed), 69.
10. W.A. Black, "Fur Trapping in the Mackenzie River Delta," *Geographical Bulletin* 16 (1961):62–85.
11. DIAND, "Brief to the Special Senate Committee on Poverty," in *Proceedings of the Special Senate Committee on Poverty*, no. 14, 20 January 1970 (Ottawa: Queen's Printer, 1970).
12. J. Purdie, "World Demand for Furs Reflected in Auction Prices," *Globe and Mail*, 20 March 1973.
13. *Ibid.*
14. "Grants for Trappers," *Tapwe*, 19 December 1973.
15. H.B. Hawthorne, A. Laforet, and S.M. Jamieson, "Northern People: A Discussion Paper," in *Science and the North: A Seminar on Guidelines for Scientific Activities in Northern Canada* (Ottawa: Information Canada, 1973), 37.
16. Bruce Cox, "Modernization Among the Mistassini-Waswanipi Cree: A Comment," *Canadian Review of Sociology and Anthropology* 7 (1971):212–15.
17. Mackenzie Delta Task Force, "Report No. 2" (submitted to the Department of Indian Affairs and Northern Development, 1970, mimeographed), 51.
18. T. Butters, "Visitors North: Development of a Tourist Industry in the Northwest Territories," in *Arctic Alternatives: A National Workshop on People, Resources on the Environment of '60*, edited by D.H. Pimlott, K.Vincent, and C.E. McKnight (Ottawa: Canada Arctic Resources Committee, 1973), 133.
19. J. Chretien, "Northern Development Issues in the Seventies," in *Proceedings of the Fifth Northern Development Conference, Edmonton* (Edmonton: Northern Development Conference, 1970), 133.
20. J. Wah-Shee, "Address to the Fifth International Congress of the Fondation Française d'Études Nordiques, LeHavre, May, 1973," *Northern Perspectives,* July-August (1973):5.

21. *Ibid.*
22. IBNWT, "Threat to the Indian."
23. R.F. Legget and I.C. MacFarlane, eds., *Proceedings of the Canadian Northern Pipeline Research Conference, 2–*4 February 1972, Technical Memorandum No. 104 (Ottawa: National Research Council of Canada, 1972); Yukon Native Brotherhood (hereinafter YNB), "Together Today for our Children Tomorrow: A Statement of Grievances and an Approach to Settlement by the Yukon Native People" (YNB, Whitehorse, 1973, mimeographed), 64.
24. YNB, "Together Today for our Children Tomorrow," 63.
25. *Ibid.*, 53.
26. *Ibid.*, 64.
27. U.S. Department of the Interior, *Final Environmental Impact Statement, Trans-Alaska Pipeline*, vol. V (Washington, D.C.: U.S. Government Printing Office, 1972), 147.
28. Treaty Commissioners, *Treaty No. 11 and Adhesion, with Reports, Etc.* (Ottawa: Queen's Printer, 1916), 11.
29. YNB, "Together Today for our Children Tomorrow," Appendix V.
30. "N.W.T. Indians Winning Land Battle," *The Native People*, Edomonton, 6 July 1973.
31. For the background of town-band conflict at Hay River, see B. Cox, "Land Rights of the Slavey Indians at Hay River, Northwest Territories," *Western Canadian Journal of Anthropology* 2 (1970):150–55.
32. B. Cox, "Environmental Disturbances in Northern Peoples' Lands," in *Proceedings, XL Congresso Internazionali degli Americanisti*, vol. 2 (Genova: Tilgher, 1974).
33. Personal communication, Douglas Sanders, 20 June 1973.
34. "Government Still Insists on taking Caveat Hearings Out of Territorial Court," *News of the North*, 20 June 1973.
35. *Ibid.*
36. "Morrow Arranges Legal Aid for Department of Justice," *Yellowknifer*, 11 July 1973, 5.
37. *Ibid.*, 2.
38. *Ibid.*
39. Justice W.G. Morrow, "Reasons for Judgement of the Honourable Mr. Justice W.G. Morrow in the Matter of an Application by Chief François Paulette *et al.* to Lodge a Certain Caveat with the Registrar of Titles of the Land Titles Office for the Northwest Territories" (Supreme Court of the Northwest Territories, Yellowknife, 1973, mimeographed), 49.
40. *Ibid.*, 57–58.
41. "Indians Win Historic Victory—Court Supports N.W.T. Indians' Land Claims," *The Native People*, Edmonton, 14 September 1973.
42. "Road Progress Report," *Tapwe*, 22 August 1973.
43. "Wrigley Residents Oppose Highway," *Tapwe*, 26 September 1973.
44. Legget, "Technology: Discussion Paper," 217.
45. Hawthorn, Laforet, and Jamieson, "Northern People," 39.

Chapter 17
Capital and Economic Development: A Critical Appraisal of the Recommendations of the Mackenzie Valley Pipeline Commission

Michael I. Asch

To some readers, an article criticizing the findings of Mr. Justice Berger's Mackenzie Valley Gas Pipeline Inquiry (popularly known as the Berger Inquiry) might appear to be trivial or at best of purely academic interest. In fact, nothing could be further from the truth. In finding against the construction of the pipeline in the near future, Justice Berger made specific recommendations for the future development of the Mackenzie River Valley. These recommendations now are finding support among influential Northern researchers, administrators, and government planners. Indeed, it appears that even the Government of the Northwest Territories (which once labelled Berger's report as "racist") is now looking with favour on them. In other words, Berger's findings, far from being only of historic interest, are of extreme moment for they may well become the blueprint for the economic future of the North. As such, they deserve continued critical scrutiny.

Although it urgently needs doing, a complete critique and appraisal of the Report is beyond the scope of this paper.[1] Rather, here, I will narrow my focus to the practicality of Berger's recommendations to achieve one goal: the maintenance of the Dene traditional way of life, or, as Berger styles it, "the native economy"[2] within the context of a modern northern economy.

To this end, I will first briefly outline Berger's plan for Northern development. Then, after exploring some of the main theoretical bases for this plan, I will proceed to evaluate its usefulness in achieving the stated objective. At heart my critique is that Berger's plan is founded upon an improper assessment of the native economy, and that this results in his recommending a plan which will have an effect opposite to that which he intends. Thus, if faithfully followed, his plan will lead to the destruction of the native economy, and its replacement by a renewable resource sector based on the capitalist mode of production. Therefore, his program is not useful and ought to be rejected. In my conclusion, I will offer an alternative introduced to the Inquiry by the Dene themselves but rejected by Mr. Justice Berger.[3] The nub of this alternative is the demand for political and economic self-determination by northern Natives within Confederation. This proposal is the only one which stands any chance of success to attain the goal Berger seeks.

Berger's Plan for Northern Development

In the view of the proponents of Mackenzie Valley gas pipeline, the political economy of the Mackenzie River Valley is in a period of transition from a form based on the traditional economic pursuits of hunting, fishing, and trapping to a form based on wage labour and the market. At this time, their argument goes, there is a "dual economy" in the region. This consists of a "backward" sector which utilizes traditional resources and a "modern" sector which exploits non-renewable resources. As time goes on, however, the inherent superiority of the rational industrial economy is such that it will inevitably replace the backward and irrational native economy. The pipeline is merely one further step in that inexorable process.

The view that the "traditional" or "native" economy is virtually moribund and would soon wither away was strongly and successfully refuted by the testimony of expert witnesses speaking on behalf of Native organizations and by the Native witnesses themselves. Rather, they showed a viable and dynamic economic sector which still provided much material as well as spiritual sustenance for Native peoples. This was the view of the native economy accepted by Justice Berger, and it is this acceptance that forms the basis of his proposal.

Thus, in Volume I, Berger specifically rejects the "dual economy" position and asserts rather that the traditional sector is a viable entity which forms, along with the virtually independent and equally viable "modern" sector, a unity which Berger calls "the mixed economy." The unity of this mixed economy is created by the economic activities of Native people so that:

> . . . in the north today, the lives of many native families are based on an intricate economic mix. At certain times of the year, they hunt and fish; at other times they work for wages, sometimes for government, sometimes on highway construction, sometimes for the oil and gas industry.[4]

Further, it is in their ability to synthesize two vastly different economic sectors into a single economic round that Berger finds the unique characteristic of the Native people and of the northern political economy itself.[5] And it is to the end of preserving a "mixed economy" with two viable but virtually independent sectors that Berger's proposals on Northern development are dedicated. That is, as he asserts:

> The objective of Northern development should be parallel economic sectors—large scale industrial activity where and when appropriate, co-existing with continuing development of the native economy and the renewable resource sector.[6]

At the moment, according to Berger, the main problem in the realization of this goal is that the native economy is unable under present economic conditions to provide sufficient capital and employment opportunities for Native people. As a result, many Native people, who might not otherwise do so, must seek wage employment outside the native economy. Such a process would be accelerated by the presence of a large-scale non-renewable resource-based project such as the proposed Mackenzie Valley gas pipeline, and indeed could well completely undermine the native economy. Therefore, Berger urges that the goal of Northern development should be to strengthen the native economy so that it can compete successfully with the non-renewable resource-based sector for capital and labour.

To this end, Berger specifically recommends the following. First, primary production of renewable resources traditionally associated with the native economy should be modernized and expanded so that production is increased to maximum sustainable yields. Second, to increase employment in the native economy, new industries based on the exploitation of these resources should be created. Among others, these could include fur farming and tanning. Finally, Berger recommends the expansion of the economy into new but allied fields such as tourism.[7]

Once the infrastructure needed to run such a modernized renewable resource-based economy is in place, Berger believes it will generate enough capital and employment opportunities to compete successfully for native labour with the job opportunities available on major one-time non-renewable resource-based projects such as the proposed Mackenzie Valley gas pipeline. In other words, at this point, a strong and independent native economy will have been constructed, and thus Berger's main development objective will have been realized.

Of course, before such an infrastructure can be created, much capital will be required. This capital, Native organizations argue, could come from rents, royalties, taxes, and other monies generated by non-renewable resource activities on their lands. However, Berger specifically rejected this idea, and instead proposed that:

> Until the renewable resource-based sector in the north is able to generate its own capital, government could make funds available as a matter of public policy.[8]

At the heart of the matter, it is Berger's position on this crucial point that is at issue.

Critique of Berger's Program

Broadly speaking, I am in complete agreement with Justice Berger's characterization of the contemporary "native economy." That is, I would assert that it is viable but weak. Furthermore, we both agree that a basic goal of Northern development must be the strengthening of that economy. Where we disagree fundamentally is on the remedies necessary to attain that goal. Ultimately, the basis for this disagreement can be found to lie in our theoretical stance in general and, in particular, how we each would define "economy." To Berger, an economy is defined primarily on the basis of the technical factors of production. Of these, the most important to him are the productive processes associated with the exploitation of a particular staple. In this, Berger is following one reading of Harold Innis' Staples Theory. It is based on this passage from *Empire and Communication* cited in his report:

> Concentration on the production of staples for export to more highly industrialized areas in Europe and later in the United States had broad implications for the Canadian economic, political, and social structure. Each staple in turn left its stamp, and the shift to new staples invariably produced periods of crises in which adjustments in the old structure were painfully made and a new pattern created in relation to a new staple.[10]

Using this framework, Berger defines the "native economy" as a unified entity for it consists of a complementary set of small-scale productive activities oriented around certain traditional bush staples. The weakness in this economy today, then, is attributed to the stamp of a new staple (oil, gas and minerals) on the lives of Native people and the period of crisis and adjustment which must inevitably accompany it.[11] This crisis is reflected in the relative lack of capital and job opportunities in the native economy *vis-à-vis* the sector devoted to the exploitation of the newly dominant staple. The problem and the solution to Berger is attributable to technical factors alone.

In my estimation, Berger is partially correct in this analysis, for indeed, the lack of capital and job opportunities are significant reasons for the weakness of the "native economy." Yet, this analysis is incomplete for there are urgent social and political problems tied directly to the technical problems which must be attended to with equal urgency. These can easily be seen if we switch our conceptual framework away from Berger's so as to include within our definition of economy the institutional framework of production; that is, if we move from "staples" to "mode of production."[12]

Although when examined from Berger's perspective the native economy can be defined as a unity, when institutional parameters are added such is no longer the case. Rather, we see two distinct modes of production contained within the native economy.

On the one hand, there is what I have called the bush subsistence mode of production.[13] From it, the Dene provided for themselves, through locally produced and finished goods, many of their subsistence needs. This is done within a framework in which co-operative labour, collective economic responsibility, communal land tenure, and the mutual sharing of surpluses are valued and institutionalized. It is a mode, it must be emphasized, which is not used to produce cash.

To obtain cash or trade goods, Native people participate in another mode of production: capitalism. During the fur trade era, they did this primarily in the role of small-scale commodity producers who, like the family farmer, traded a cash crop for essential goods produced by the industrialized world. Through this involvement with the fur trade, Native people came into contact with the institutional framework of capitalism with its attendant institutions and values that stress private ownership of property, individual accumulation of goods, and individual economic responsibility.

In the fur trade era, the economy operated in such a manner that the capitalist institutional framework remained subordinate in the daily life of the Dene so that they lived primarily under the influence of institutions and values associated with the traditional bush subsistence mode of production. How this was achieved is an important concern which I describe elsewhere.[14] However, the important point here is that with the collapse of fur prices, and the concomitant inflation in the price of trade goods in the period since the end of the Second World War, Native people have had to seek cash from sources other than furs. This has resulted in a very marked increase in the impingement of capitalist institutions and values on their daily lives.

That this is the case for those for whom wage labour has become the principal means of obtaining cash should be self-evident. However, for most Native people, cash income is still not derived in this way. Rather, it comes in forms such as transfer payments which do not require labour input. Yet, it does not follow that such income is therefore free from the influence of capitalist values and institutions. Indeed, the contrary is the case. As in other capitalist transactions, these payments are made directly to individuals or heads of the nuclear family. Thus, they emphasize the separateness of these units and individualize ownership of property. As a result, payments conflict with those institutions and values generated by the traditional mode of production in which emphasis is placed on the community as an indivisible economic unit and on the collectivity of property ownership. The case is particularly striking with respect to welfare. The payment of welfare to individuals and nuclear families isolated poverty and created a division between "rich" and "poor." Thus, it not only relieves the community of its traditional responsibility to share mutually, it actually provides the context for the penetration of its opposite tendency, characteristic of the capitalist mode of production: social differentiation based on relative wealth.

In other words, the weakness in the native economy today is not merely that it lacks capital and job opportunities but equally that its traditional institutions and values are being eroded by the very means Native people must use to obtain essential cash. Today, the bush subsistence mode is still dominant in the daily lives of most Native people but, even without the presence of large-scale non-renewable resource developments, is steadily losing this position as the need for cash drives Native people further and further into the institutional sphere of capitalism.

Thus, in order for Northern development to work, what is required is that the program adopted not only provides capital and jobs for the native economy, but that it does so in such a way that the impact of capitalist institutions decreases in the daily lives of Native people. Berger's plan, then, is inadequate because he fails to attend to this very real concern. As a result, it can be expected that, if his plan is adopted, traditional institutions and values will continue to lose their dominant place in the life of Native people. Furthermore, Berger's program itself may well act to accelerate the pace of erosion. Large-scale government grants, it should be clear, differ little from small-scale ones, such as transfer payments, in their institutional implications; that is, like small-scale ones, they were formulated within an economic context that assumes the institutions and values of capitalism. In the case of large grants, this fact will be reflected in the very assumptions upon which grants are given: that the grantee follow "standard business practices" or that the operation will be constructed so that it will ultimately show a "profit." As a result, it is not hard to imagine that, in order to obtain funding, Native people will be forced to develop their renewable resources within a capitalist institutional framework. In other words, in the process of developing a native economy, Native people may well be forced to transform it into a renewable resource sector of the local capitalist economy; a result which is against Berger's own stated objective.

Application to the Dene

One central problem of Northern development is to provide sufficient capital to create an infrastructure for a modern renewable resource economy in a manner that promotes traditional institutions and values rather than capitalist ones. Such a problem has no easy or certain solution. In fact, in my opinion, there is only one approach which stands any chance of success. It is the proposal presented to the Berger Inquiry by the Native Northerners themselves: the power to determine for themselves their political and economic future within Confederation, including, among other powers, the right to control and tax all economic developments undertaken in the traditional homelands of these people.

The advantages of such a solution are two-fold. In the first place, it is a practical means for raising capital sufficient to meet all the economic needs of Native Northerners. For example, as Dr. Arvin Jellis pointed out in evidence presented to the Inquiry,[15] proper and equitable taxation of non-renewable resource operations now in place on Dene lands would yield a sum of approximately $51 million per annum (in 1974 dollars). Such an income each year would easily provide the Dene with sufficient capital to service their total trade-good needs, to develop within perhaps a decade the infrastructure necessary to operate the kind of economy outlined by Berger, and to provide a cash cushion to secure the long-term sustained operation of this economy.[16]

Second, this form of capital accumulation attends well to the problem of the continued penetration of capitalist institutions. To begin with, it does not require that the Native people participate in their daily lives, or even orient any of their economic activities to capitalist institutions, for cash is generated without labour input. Furthermore, unlike government grants, these funds will be controlled and administered solely by Native people. Thus, provided the Native people can create such a development plan, these funds could easily be dispersed in a manner which promotes institutions and values of the bush subsistence mode of production. Finally, it is important to note that capital generated in this manner would be controlled by the Native community as a whole, and thus would remain consistent with their traditional framework which emphasized communal ownership of resources. This, of course, is not to say that the solution proposed by the Native people is perfect, far from it. Indeed, there are many major problems associated with it.

First, and perhaps most important, given the contemporary political situation in this country and particularly the specific rejection of this proposal by the Federal government, it is highly unlikely that such powers could be quickly or easily obtained.

Furthermore, even if these powers were granted, there is no certainty that a modern resource economy based on traditional institutions and values could be constructed. For example, it may not be possible to maintain a traditional form of egalitarianism as the division of labour shifts from its simple form in which everyone does just about the same thing, as is characteristic of the bush subsistence mode of production, to a complex form with the high degree of specialization which modernization would entail. As well, the process of development itself may lead to class divisions as some Native people gain the sophisticated knowledge necessary to oversee non-renewable resource industries, and thus become alienated from the lifestyle of other Native Northerners.

Finally, there is the ever present danger that the form of articulation with capitalist institutions envisioned in this proposal may itself act to undermine the ultimate goal. For example, it is a fact that the renewable resource sector will be dependent for a time on an economic component that is not necessarily compatible with it. As a result, Native people may be manoeuvered into a situation where their long-term objectives must be sacrificed in the interests of obtaining immediate capital. This concern is particularly real in the North for the industry with which Native Northerners must negotiate is, to say the least, not known for its sensitivity to the environmental and economic interests of local inhabitants. Also, there is the ever-present concern that, when confronted with the option, Native people may voluntarily choose short-term cash benefits rather than forgo these gains to create the capital base necessary to construct the kind of economy they say they want, and thus ensure in the process that such an economy is never built.

In the 1980s, these issues have started to come into sharper focus among the Dene. This has been due in the main to the construction of a $20 million oil pipeline south along the Mackenzie River Valley from Norman Wells, and the restart of negotiations over the outstanding aboriginal rights claim.

The Dene have responded to the challenges by beginning to flesh out in much more detail how their institutional arrangements might be adapted to a modern policy and economy. To date, most of the work has been undertaken in the political arena. It has resulted in a proposal known as *Denendeh* which calls for consensus government in the Valley based on a traditional band model which nonetheless allows within its domain provision for non-Native active participants (as equal band members) in the decision-making process once they have learned Dene culture.[17]

Although less work has been done in the economic area, it is significant to note that the Dene have not limited their concerns in this area to obtaining capital alone. Rather, Dene groups at both the national and local levels have started to work on how they might shape economic institutions in a manner consistent with decision-making principles found in the *Denendeh* document. In particular, how might a Dene-controlled enterprise handle such issues as hiring, firing, wages, profits, management-labour relations, and the relationship of such enterprises to the community they serve?

Clearly, to create such an institutional setting will be a long process. However, the fact that it is being worked on seems a clear indication that the Dene are seriously considering the option that will maximize the chance that their way of decision making and their value orientation will not be lost as development begins in earnest.

Conclusions

The nub of the problem for renewable resource development in the North is two-fold. First, it is necessary to find large sources of capital to fund the new infrastructure essential to the economic well-being of the sector. Second, a source of funds must be found which will allow maximum flexibility for the Native group to promote in the development of this infrastructure the kinds of traditional institutions and values they wish to assert.

At the Berger hearings, two proposals for obtaining these funds were put forward. The first, initiated by the Dene, called for a method which relied on obtaining rents and royalties on lands recognized as being under their jurisdiction. It is a solution which was rejected explicitly by Mr. Justice Berger when he stated:

> The various native claims proposals include provisions for the transfer of capital to native control, chiefly through royalties on non-renewable resource development. Evidence from Alaska suggests that this is not without problems: it can create rather than reduce dependence on externally controlled development. Capital transfers will not, in themselves, assure the appropriate financing of renewable resource development unless specific provisions for that purpose are incorporated in native claims settlements.[18]

In short, he rejects it because he fears that the Dene may not be able to withstand pressures to use the funds for other purposes.

As an alternative, Berger proposes the second possibility: that the Dene and other northern Native groups obtain funding through Federal government grants. This solution, as I have argued in this paper, must be rejected on the grounds that such funding carries with it a set of capitalist institutional appendages which will inexorably lead the native economy away from a traditional institutional and value framework. Failure to discuss this potential eventuality I trace in part to Mr. Justice Berger's adopting the staples theory as his analytic stance.

For myself, I see no third option. On the one hand, the capital can come directly from government either in the form suggested by Berger, or through direct cash payments, as in the case of the James Bay corporations. Or, on the other hand, it must come indirectly as through rents and royalties on lands controlled by the Native community. I share with Justice Berger the concern that the latter option may well prove problematical as the opportunity to obtain these funds and hence use them to other ends becomes more real. It is a concern which I believe remains valid, but should be tempered by the experience of the few past years.

At heart, though, there is no other option. Rents and royalties may provide temptations, but they are better than any other form of potential cash flow in that: first, they come in a form which is "collective;" second, they do not require significant labour input; and third, they are obtained on a continuing rather than a one-time basis. Each of these, I have argued, is a prerequisite if the form capital takes is to allow maximum flexibility to initiate institutional innovations. It is for these reasons that I believe it is necessary to conclude that only the proposal which the Dene have put forward offers any practical hope to ensure that a native economy consistent with Dene traditional institutions and values can become a reality.

Notes

Source: *Culture* II(3):3–10. Reprinted by permission of the Canadian Ethnology Society.

1. An earlier version of this paper was presented to the Second International Conference on Hunting-Gathering Societies, Québec City, 1980.
2. Mr. Justice T. Berger, *Northern Frontier, Northern Homeland: The Report of the Mackenzie Valley Pipeline Inquiry*, vol. I (Ottawa: Ministry of Supply and Services Canada, 1977), 122.
3. *Ibid.*, vol. II, 41.
4. *Ibid.*, vol. I, 122.
5. *Ibid.*, vol. I, 121.
6. *Ibid.*, vol. II, 4.
7. *Ibid.*, vol. II, Chapter 2.
8. *Ibid.*, vol. II, 411.
9. Harold Innis, *Empire and Communications* (Toronto: Uptown Press, 1950).
10. Berger, *Northern Frontier, Northern Homeland*, vol. I, 117.
11. *Ibid.*, vol. I, 118.
12. Michael Asch, "The Ecological-Evolutionary Model and the Concept of Mode of Production," in *Challenging Anthropology*, edited by D. Turner and G. Smith (Toronto: McGraw-Hill Ryerson, 1979).
13. Michael Asch, "The Economics of Dene Self-Determination," in *Challenging Anthropology*, edited by Turner and Smith.
14. Asch, "Economics of Dene Self-Determination."
15. Arvin Jelliss, "Economic Rents," in *Dene Nation: The Colony Within*, edited by M. Watkins (Toronto: University of Toronto Press, 1977).
16. Asch, "Economics of Dene Self-Determination."
17. Dene National Office, "Public Government for the People of the North" (Yellowknife: Dene Nation, 1981).
18. Berger, *Northern Frontier, Northern Homeland*, vol. II, 42.

Chapter 18
Survival and Adaptation of the Inuit Ethnic Identity: The Importance of Inuktitut

Jean-Philippe Chartrand

Introduction

The incorporation of previously isolated small scale societies into large industrialized states has fostered the development of new research areas in Anthropology which deal with issues of adaptation and ethnic survival. In this paper, I will examine some of the mechanisms affecting Inuit identity in Canada's North, and will place this discussion within the wider context of Inuit adaptation to modern Canadian society.

Jenness[1] has commented that the patterns of contact between Inuit and Whites can be divided into two major phases: a long period of slow acculturation when contact was essentially limited to explorers, whalers, traders, missionaries, and the R.C.M.P., followed by a short period (from 1945 on) of extremely rapid acculturation resulting from the introduction of large-scale Federal government assimilation programs. Before the late 1940s, Inuit society had been profoundly modified by external agents. In pre-contact days, the Inuit mode of production, as in most foraging societies, was subsistence-based and organized along kinship lines.[2] By the late 1920s, the subsistence mode of production had became articulated with capitalism through trade.[3] This shift not only fostered a growing dependency on traders, but also modified the way in which hunting activities were carried out. They became more individualized, producing substantial modifications in the social structure and residence patterns of the Inuit.[4] Traditional Inuit cosmology was gradually forgotten through conversion by missionaries. It seems from the general literature that the Inuktitut language may be the only feature of pre-contact culture to emerge almost unscathed from this "slow phase" of acculturation.

Even this element of traditional culture has been under severe pressure since the late 1940s. Federal policy during that period responded to several factors: first, the collapse of the fur trade as a viable economic support structure;[5] second, widespread famines and severe health problems;[6] third, the knowledge of the existence of valuable resources in the north; and fourth, international geopolitical interest in the face of the Cold War.[7] The Federal government, feeling a need to affirm its claim of sovereignty over the Arctic, announced a policy of:

> . . . incorporating the Eskimos into the mainstream of Canadian life and providing them with the benefits already being received by other Canadians.[8]

The two major components of this assimilation policy were a massive population relocation program in which Inuit were encouraged to live in government built-and-controlled permanent settlements,[9] and the development of a formal southern Canadian education system that was to involve residential as well as day schools and that would infuse Inuit children with White values and norms. It was recognized at the time a major obstacle for assimilation was the fact that very few Inuit possessed a working knowledge of English. Therefore, English usage not only had to be enforced in schools, but in all social spheres in which Inuit interacted with Whites. H.A. Young, the Commissioner of the Northwest Territories in 1950, stated that:

> We hope that all the White people in the north, regardless of occupation, will take keen and active interest in encouraging the use of English by natives and will make the teaching of English a personal project.[10]

The exclusive use of English in education lasted until the early 1960s in Quebec, the early 1970s in the Northwest Territories and the mid-1970s in Labrador.[11] Northern life was characterized by a virtually total disregard of Inuktitut in the media until roughly the mid-1970s.[12] These were extreme pressures on what may be the major remaining feature of traditional culture (excluding hunting). They have prompted my research, which relies heavily on a comparison of 1971 and 1981 census data. These data will reveal that while usage has declined significantly between 1971 and 1981,[13] the Inuit language (Inuktitut) still remains very strong, particularly in northern Quebec and the eastern Arctic.

Berreman and Hechter,[14] and others, have sought to account for the global resurgence of ethnic identity. It is not as a phenomenon that occurs in spite of pressures to conform to the values and norms of the dominant groups in modern industrial societies, but a phenomenon which occurs because of those pressures.

For the Inuit, dependency, within a general situation of internal colonialism, has played a key role in the maintenance of a distinctive identity. Maintaining such an identity binds individuals to a group,[15] permitting an organizational basis for political activity in which a dependent minority group can attempt to redefine its political and economic position within the wider society.[16]

The retention of Inuktitut can play a significant role in the struggle for identity maintenance. It is no accident that the major Inuit political organization, the Inuit Tapirisat of Canada, sees the promotion of Inuktitut as one of the key vehicles for fostering dignity and pride in Inuit heritage.[17]

General Demographic Features

It is extremely difficult to provide a precise estimate of the pre-contact Inuit population; Crowe and Bone suggest that some twenty-five to thirty thousand Inuit may have inhabited the Canadian Arctic.[18] Both authors agree that this population was severely reduced in number after contact with Europeans. Crowe estimates that by 1900, disease had reduced the Inuit population by one-third.[19] While all Inuit groups were affected by European-imported diseases, one group, the Sadlik Inuit, was entirely wiped out by 1948.[20] The Mackenzie Inuit, originally numbering some twenty-five hundred people, were reduced to four hundred in 1900, to one hundred and thirty by 1910,[21] and were virtually extinct by the 1920s.[22] Any remaining individuals were incorporated into Alaskan Inuit groups who migrated to the Delta in order to take part in the then booming fur trade.[23] Nevertheless, through the provision of health services in the twentieth century, the Inuit population increased dramatically.[24]

Table 18-1 shows that the Inuit population is very small when compared to the national population. In 1981, the Inuit made up slightly less than 0.1 percent of the total Canadian population. Nevertheless, their numbers are increasing very rapidly. Between 1971 and 1981, there was an increase of approximately 32 percent at the national level. Table 18-1 also shows uneven distribution of Inuit across the major regions. Newfoundland (Labrador) possesses the smallest number of Inuit. In Quebec, there are over three times as many. The overwhelming majority of Inuit, 66 percent, reside in the N.W.T. The Inuit living in the rest of Canada have the lowest proportion of increase. They are dispersed throughout all the provinces, and are highly exposed to racial intermarriage.

Rapid population growth in all other areas reflects high fertility rates, twice the rates of non-native women.[25] The Inuit population is also very young. Nationally, 43 percent of Inuit are under 15 years of age, while only 3 percent are 65 years and over.[26] While the rates of population growth have been decreasing for some time,[27] the overall youth of the population is a good indicator that it is likely to continue to grow much more rapidly than the non-native population.

Inuktitut Retention, 1971 and 1981

Language retention ratios fall into two main types. Ancestral retention ratios (ARR) represent the proportion of the population which has Inuktitut as its mother tongue. Since individuals are unlikely to report changes in their mother

Table 18-1 Ethnic Origin Data, 1971 and 1981

Inuit Population	Canada	Newfoundland (Labrador)	Quebec	Northwest Territories	Rest of Canada
1971 Total	17,550	1,055	3,755	11,400	1,340
1981 Total	23,200	1,365	4,775	15,495	1,565
Increase	5,650	310	1,020	4,095	225
percent	(32.2)	(29.4)	(27.2)	(35.9)	(16.7)

Source: Statistics Canada, Census of Canada, Population: Ethnic groups, Table 2; Census of Canada, Population: Ethnic Origin, Table 1.

Note: The 1981 ethnic origin data concerns only single ethnic origin responses in order to provide a more valid comparison with 1971 data. The 1971 census reported ethnic origin responses from only the paternal line, while the 1981 census permitted to trace one's ancestry from both maternal and paternal lines, thus providing multiple ethnic origin.

tongue during the course of their lifetime, ARRs are fairly stable indicators over time. Current retention ratio (CRR) represents the number of persons using Inuktitut as a home language, expressed as a percentage of those who report Inuktitut as their mother tongue. The home language can easily change in an individual's lifetime. CRRs consequently tend to be less stable over time than ARRs.[28] Table 18-2 provides the ARRs for the major regions introduced in Table 18-1.

For Canada in 1971, 87 percent of all Inuit reported Inuktitut as their mother tongue, of which 41 percent were bilingual, and 46 percent unilingual Inuktitut speakers. Ten years later, 81 percent of the Inuit population reported Inuktitut as their mother tongue of which 45 percent were bilingual and 37 percent unilingual. A regional breakdown shows that the Inuit in the rest of Canada have the smallest proportion of individuals with an Inuktitut mother tongue. The data presented in Table 18-2 provide our first general trends in Inuktitut retention. The Inuit language appears to be strongest in Quebec, followed by the Northwest Territories; however, in Quebec, there appears to be a language shift toward unilingualism, while in the Northwest Territories there is a trend toward bilingualism. Inuktitut usage appears to have weakened considerably in

Table 18-2 Ancestral Retention Ratios of Inuit, 1971 and 1981

Region	Year	% whose mother tongue is Inuktitut	% fluent in English, French, or both, whose mother tongue is Inuktitut	% Inuktitut unilingual
Canada	1971	87.1	41.3	45.8
	1981	80.9	44.9	36.7
Newfoundland	1971	91.5	73.9	17.0
	1981	58.6	50.9	7.7
Quebec	1971	91.2	34.4	57.2
	1981	95.0[a]	25.3	69.5[a]
Northwest Territories	1971	90.8	41.7	49.0
	1981	85.0	52.2	32.8
Rest of Canada	1971	23.1	16.1	7.0
	1981	16.6	16.3	0.3

Source: Statistics Canada, 1971a,b and 1981a,c.

Note: The ratios were obtained by dividing the number of Inuit reporting Inuktitut as mother tongue by the number of individuals reporting on Inuit ethnic origin in Table 18-1, and multiplying the result by 100. This procedure was carried out for all major regions. These results are provided in the first column of Table 18-2. The other two columns reflect a breakdown of the ratios in the first column, in terms of bilingual and unilingual Inuktitut speakers.

a. Smith (1985, personal communication) suggested that part of this increase in the proportion of unilingual Inuktitut speakers may be due to the decrease in bilingual speakers, who left the province after a transfer of responsibility for education took place in the 1970s.

Labrador, and is very weak in the rest of Canada. In these two regions, the data seem to indicate that as the older generations are dying, so is Inuktitut. Most Inuit children are brought up with English as their mother tongue.

However, ARRs can only provide approximations as to the actual usage of Inuktitut. Table 18-3 lists the CRRs for our five main regions, that is, the proportions of Inuit with Inuktitut as their mother tongue also using Inuktitut as their home language. Table 18-3 reveals similar trends to those found in Table 18-2. The difference is that the ratios are usually greater in this case. This means

Table 18-3 Current Retention Ratios, 1971 and 1981

Region	Year	% of Inuit for whom Inuktitut is mother tongue	% of Inuit for whom Inuktitut is home language	% of Inuit who use Inuktitut as home language	% of Inuit who only speak Inuktitut
Canada	**1971**	**90.0**	**84.2**	**78.5**	**45.8**
	1981	**89.5**	**80.7**	**72.3**	**36.7**
Newfoundland	**1971**	**78.7**	**75.0**	**72.0**	**17.0**
	1981	**63.7**	**57.5**	**37.3**	**7.7**
Quebec	**1971**	**97.8**	**94.9**	**87.9**	**57.2**
	1981	**97.7**	**92.1**	**92.7**	**69.5**
Northwest Territories	**1971**	**92.0**	**82.7**	**83.6**	**49.0**
	1981	**89.8**	**83.7**	**76.3**	**32.8**
Rest of Canada	**1971**	**35.5**	—	—	**8.2**
	1981	**5.7**	—	—	**0.9**

Source: Statistics Canada, Census of Canada. Special Publications: Population, 1971, Table 2; Census of Canada, Population, Ethnic Origin, Table 1.

Note: These ratios were obtained in very much the same way as those for Table 2. The general method consisted in dividing the number of individuals reporting Inuktitut as home language by the number reporting Inuktitut as mother tongue, for a particular region, and multiplying the result by 100. The reader should note that the second column in Table 3 is not a breakdown of the first column. Instead, it provides an indication of the home language. J.P Chartrand, "Inuktitut Language Retention in the Canadian North: An Analysis of 1971 and 1981 Census Data," Centre for Research on Ethnic Minorities, Working Paper # 6 (Ottawa: Carleton University, Department of Sociology and Anthropology, 1985.

that when reporting Inuktitut as the mother tongue, there is a good chance that the individual also uses it as the home language. Again, Inuktitut usage is strongest in Quebec, with no significant decline between 1971 and 1981. The language is also very strong in the Northwest Territories, although it is somewhat weaker than in Quebec. Between 1971 and 1981, Newfoundland (Labrador) witnessed a drop in the proportion of individuals using Inuktitut as home language. More alarming is the very severe decline in the proportion of Inuit (irrespective of mother tongue) using Inuktitut as home language. While this ratio drops slightly for all regions (except Quebec), in Labrador it tumbles from 72 percent to 37 percent. Table 18-3 furthermore confirms that Inuktitut usage is disappearing outside Quebec, the Northwest Territories, and Newfoundland.

Finally, the second column in Table 18-3 is worthy of comment. This column represents the internal CRR of the bilingual Inuit population. This provides a crude indication of the risk of switching from Inuktitut to English as a home language. This risk can be evaluated by comparing the percentages in column one with those in column two: all percentages in column two are lower, indicating that bilingual individuals will tend to switch to English as their home language. But this generalization may conceal the complexity of the language shift process. It is possible that a reverse shift occurred in some households. Some Inuit with English as their mother tongue may have switched to Inuktitut as their home language, as a result of political activity reinforcing pride in Inuit identity. However, the predominance of the opposite type of shift is undoubtedly a consequence of the intensive assimilation pressures that exist in the North.

So far this linguistic analysis has considered all of the N.W.T. Inuit as a homogeneous group. However, previous studies show that Inuktitut retention is

Table 18-4 Retention Ratios by N.W.T. Census Divisions, 1981

		Mother Tongue		Home Language	
Region	**Ethnic Origin**	**Inuktitut**	**English**	**Inuktitut**	**English**
N.W.T.	15,910	13,150	2,730	11,935	3,955
Baffin	6,945	6,815	110	6,700	240
Keewatin	3,815	3,665	145	3,495	320
Central Arctic	2,875	2,060	815	1,500	1,370
Inuvik/Fort Smith	2,280	615	1,655	260	2,030

	N.W.T.	**Baffin**	**Keewatin**	**Central Arctic**	**Inuvik/Fort Smith**
ARR	82.6	98.1	96.0	71.6	26.9
CRR	90.7	98.3	95.3	72.8	42.2
HL/EO	75.0	96.5	91.6	52.2	11.4

Source: Statistics Canada, Census of Canada. Native People's Tape, Table SDN81B81, Population (6) by Mother Tongue (20), 1981; Table SDN81B91, Population (6) by Home Language (20), 1981.

much lower in the western Arctic than in the eastern Arctic.[29] Furthermore, language patterns in the western Arctic may provide interesting parallels to those in Labrador. In both regions (as opposed to northern Quebec and the eastern Arctic), the Inuit live among other ethnic groups sharing similar socio-economic status within a broader cultural division of labour. Fortunately, the 1981 census contains sufficiently detailed data on Inuktitut retention and Inuit population distribution to permit an east to west comparison. Table 18-4 clearly demonstrates that Inuktitut retention is extremely high in the eastern Arctic, where over 90 percent of all Inuit use their native language at home. Inuktitut retention is significantly lower in the central Arctic, where 71 percent of Inuit report Inuktitut as their mother tongue and where 72 percent of this group uses it as their home language. Finally, Inuktitut retention is extremely low in the western Arctic. While the CRR is fairly high (42 percent), this figure is misleading since only 27 percent of Inuit report Inuktitut as their mother tongue.

In summary, Tables 18-3 and 18-4 show that the Inuktitut language is strongest in the Baffin and Keewatin regions of the Northwest Territories, and in northern Quebec. In fact, it seems that Inuktitut usage could scarcely be greater now than it was in those areas in 1981. But in Labrador, Inuktitut has weakened considerably. The magnitude of this decline since 1971 appears to suggest that its usage will continue to drop. Finally, it is very weak in the western Arctic, and virtually dead in the rest of Canada. In the following sections of the paper, these findings will be explained in terms of a model of ethnic identity.

Ethnic Identity and Inuktitut Retention in the Canadian North

In order to understand how the retention of Inuktitut has come to vary to such an extent between regions, we must return to the nineteenth century colonialization patterns of White settlers and traders in the Canadian North. The Inuit living in Labrador were exposed to intensive inter-ethnic relationships with Whites much earlier than Inuit elsewhere in Canada.[30]

The Moravian missionaries who settled along the Labrador coast as early as 1771 had established permanent settlements that would gradually prepare the Inuit to take part in an emerging industrial world.[31] The Moravians were in fact both missionaries and traders and sought to sustain the economics of their conversion work through their control of trading stations.[32] However, from the early 1800s, Labrador was the destination of employee immigrants from British, Scottish, and Norwegian trading companies who eventually married native women. Kleivan states that between 1830 and 1870, extensive cultural borrowing took place as a result of the intermarriage between Inuit and these Settlers. Seal hunting techniques and Inuit terminology, for example, became part of the emerging Settler culture. Settlers adopted a subsistence mode of production that parallelled that of the Inuit, and they were subsequently incorporated into the Moravian settlements.[34]

Despite a relative equality of social status, and considerable racial intermarriage, Inuit and Settler ethnic identities did not completely fuse together. Their distinct identities were sustained by the Moravians, who believed that the welfare of their Inuit protégés necessitated the maintenance of a basic Inuit identity.[35] In fact, the Moravian Mission preserved what it saw as being essential to Inuit culture: a traditional diet, a hunting mode of production altered to accommodate a trading economy, and Inuktitut, which became the official language of instruction in settlement schools.[36] So while Settlers developed an identity based on bicultural and bilingual features, the Inuit identity was characterized by the retention of key aspects of their traditional culture, and by the acquisition of some power over the Settlers through their control of rudimentary political offices created by the Moravians.[37] In 1926, declining profits forced the Moravians to lease their trading rights to the Hudson's Bay Company,[38] but they remained in charge of the churches and schools until Newfoundland joined Confederation in 1949.[39]

Fur prices collapsed in the 1930s,[40] and since by then most Inuit had become heavily dependent on trading, the closure of many outposts brought about unprecedented misery and famine.[41] By the 1940s, virtually all Inuit were dependent on the wider Canadian society.[42] This defines an ongoing situation of unequal power relations in which:

> Whites in the North have always been intent on causing change; in realizing these changes they have dominated the Eskimos, and they continue to do so . . . it is they who decide what the Eskimos need or should need, and it is they who decide how these needs are to be met.[43]

The large-scale Federal assimilation programs started in the late 1940s were no exception to this pattern, which Hechter calls internal colonialism.[44] Hechter furthermore asserts that within the internal colony, the relations of production will be structured in terms of a cultural division of labour: "a system of stratification where objective cultural distinctions are superimposed upon class lines."[45]

The evidence supporting this claim throughout the North is overwhelming. Governments are by far the largest employer in the North.[46] Writing about employment in government during the 1970s Paine comments that:

> In the early '70's, the number of federal employees in permanent jobs, actually located in the N.W.T., approached 1,500; but no more than 8 percent of these were filled by Inuit. A number of key departments [for example, Indian Affairs and Northern Development] were . . . without any Inuit on their permanent staff in the N.W.T.[47]

The 1981 census data on labour force participation shows a two-level cultural division of labour: first, throughout the North, 52 percent of adult Inuit are not in the labour force.[48] Second, in the labour force itself, there exists a systematic over-representation of non-natives in key management and administration positions.[49]

The creation of this cultural division of labour was, and is, part of a general programme that espoused the "culture of poverty" model of social development. This model[50] stipulates that the modernization of "primitives" can only occur if they give up their traditional culture and adopt the values of the dominant society. Since the "primitives" lack the skills to occupy key political and economic roles, members of the "superior" culture must fill these so that by their very presence, they can demonstrate the benefits that result from adopting the values of their culture. Brody confirms this as the underlying reasoning of many Whites that are involved with the North.[51] The basic fallacy in this approach is that Whites will tend to inherit positions from Whites, and the Inuit population will remain economically and socially marginal and dependent.[52]

The major tool for assimilating the Inuit was the development, by the Federal government, of a formal centralized southern-style education system that was ultimately controlled by the Department of Indian Affairs and Northern Development (DIAND) in Ottawa. While only 110 Inuit children attended school full-time in 1950, by the end of that decade, their enrollment had increased to 1,165.[53] During the period of Federal control, English was the only language of instruction. This remained unaltered until the early 1960s in Quebec, the early 1970s in the Northwest Territories, and the mid-1970s in Labrador.[54] The education system imposed severe pressures on Inuktitut. Young children who often could only speak this language were taught entirely in English and were often forbidden to speak their mother tongue in school.[55] Most Federal teachers came from southern Canada, half of of them were under 30 years of age and the teaching force had a 33 percent turnover.[56] Children were not taught by individuals who were sensitive to their lifestyle. But the education system did much more than exert strong pressures on Inuktitut. It contributed to the development of an intergenerational culture gap in northern communities:

> Most young people who went to school between 1950 and 1970 have suffered from the "in-between" feeling, not able to fit into native life or [modern life]. . . .[57]

Northern education produced considerable acculturation, but not assimilation. In order to understand why this is the case we must return to Hechter's model of internal colonialism. According to Hechter,[58] the existence of a cultural division of labour permits the maintenance of distinct identities within each ethnic group. The maintenance of distinct identities occurs since "actors come to categorize themselves and others according to the range of roles each may be expected to play."[59] The division of labour produces further social consequences. Since Whites hold the best jobs, they are able to obtain the best housing[60] and can enjoy luxuries that the Inuit cannot obtain. Day-to-day experiences constantly reinforce a sense of difference between the two groups.[61] While the nature of Inuit identity has unquestionably changed since pre-contact days, this does not necessarily imply that the Inuit do not have a distinct identity from that of Whites in the North. In fact, dependency tends to alienate Inuit from their traditional identity, and prevents the development of an identity similar to that of the economically and politically dominant White population.[62]

The existence of a cultural division of labour can permit the retention of some features of the traditional culture, since the resulting socio-economic "segregation" forces the ethnic group at the bottom of the strata to rely partly on itself for its subsistence. In the case of the Inuit, this is supported by the existence of an articulation of modes of production,[63] a reliance on several sources for their subsistence: welfare, wages, handicrafts, and hunting. Within this set of economic resources, the hunting mode of production is the persisting feature from the traditional culture. Furthermore, Graburn reports that another feature of traditional culture, namely strong kinship relations, persists in modern settlements (albeit in a somewhat modified form).[64] Finally, of course, there is Inuktitut.

It seems that the magnitude of language retention far exceeds the magnitude of retention of other features of traditional culture, at least in northern Quebec and the eastern Arctic. There are other reasons why language retention may be playing a key role in the maintenance of a distinct Inuit identity. First, it contributes to the maintenance of a boundary between Inuit and Whites. As a mode of communication, it is a particularly penetrating feature, a system of meaningful signs that represent and influence the concept of the world.[65] Perhaps more than any other feature of traditional culture, language can provide a positive feedback on identity. In a comprehensive survey (that did not include Inuit),[66] Reitz sought to establish which of several variables correlated most strongly with in-group interaction and ethnic identification. His analysis led Reitz to conclude that: "Language retention is the cultural characteristic that best reflects current and continued ethnic cohesion; it is perhaps the most distinctively ethnic activity."[67]

If this is the case, then one may reasonably ask why Inuktitut retention should have dropped so significantly in Labrador and in the western Arctic. In order to properly address this matter, we must consider the differences that separate, on the one hand, the eastern Arctic and northern Quebec from, on the other hand, Labrador and the western Arctic. In the latter regions, Inuit co-exist with other ethnic groups (Dene and Métis in the western Arctic, Settlers in Labrador). The cultural division of labour in these regions separates Whites from all other ethnic groups.[68] Common conditions of dependency *vis-à-vis* Whites, and the resulting similarity of day-to-day experiences between Inuit, Dene, and Métis in the western Arctic (and between Inuit and Settlers in Labrador), tend to impart a common identity. Paine confirms that this is occurring in part in Labrador, but further states that the development of a common identity is fostered by the mutual recognition of Inuit and Settlers of their need for one another in political negotiations of land claims and self-government.[69] While there is less evidence concerning this matter in the western Arctic, Smith argues that Inuit in the Delta feel closer ties to other native ethnic groups in this region than they do with fellow Inuit in the eastern Arctic.[70] However, the Land Claim Settlement, ratified by the Committee for the Original Peoples' Entitlement in 1984, may enhance feelings of difference between the Inuvialuit (the western Arctic Inuit) and the other native peoples in the western Arctic, since the former now possess distinct political relations with the wider society.[71]

The development of a common identity between several ethnic groups under the cultural division of labour would result in a tendency to downplay cultural features of difference between these groups. In the western Arctic, Inuktitut is precisely such a feature. In Labrador, it historically was not, since Settlers were bilingual.[72] Since the introduction of federal programs, a small shift of power has taken place in local communities, as Settlers, by virtue of their bicultural bilingual characteristics, are now somewhat preferred as employees in White agencies[73]—although in overall terms they share a similar socio-economic status with Inuit. Under such conditions, the English language would tend to be perceived as a language of prestige.[74] Due to the mutual needs of Inuit and Settlers for one another in political spheres, a downplaying of cultural features that differentiate the ethnic groups in the lower stratum of the cultural division of labour may be occurring. These developments took place in the 1970s, the time period in which Inuktitut usage dropped significantly, at least in Labrador. In northern Quebec and in the eastern Arctic, the cultural division of labour involves only two ethnic groups: Whites and Inuit, the latter forming an overwhelming demographic majority. In those regions, Inuktitut can only serve as a positive unifying source of identity and solidarity.

Conclusion

Much of traditional culture of the Inuit people has been lost. In the light of the drastic changes that the Inuit have been through, it is astounding to witness the patience and tolerance with which these people have sought to redefine their social, political, and economic position in modern Canadian society. This analysis of Inuktitut retention has shown that the Inuit language is extremely strong in the eastern Arctic and in northern Quebec. These are the areas where the vast majority of Inuit live, and where the cultural division of labour only involves two ethnic groups. The overall decline in Inuktitut retention between 1971 and 1981 can be attributed to declines in areas involving other ethnic groups.

Labrador and the western Arctic are regions in which a purely traditional Inuit identity appears to have been undermined more intensively and for a longer period than in the eastern Arctic and northern Quebec. However, this does not imply that Inuit in these regions are more assimilated than Inuit living in areas of high language retention. I have argued that where there are several ethnic groups besides Whites, the cultural division of labour would tend to foster the development of a common identity between these groups. This development may result in a downplaying of traditional cultural features that would reinforce a sense of difference between these groups, since they may likely need each other in terms of political negotiations that would seek to redefine their relations with the wider society. Such appears to be the case in Labrador, although additional factors may have shaped ethnopolitical developments in the western Arctic.

In northern Quebec and the eastern Arctic, the cultural division of labour would encourage the retention of some key features of traditional culture. The

Inuit in these areas have also made a grassroots commitment to Inuktitut,[75] which further reinforces pride in cultural roots and group solidarity.

The maintenance of Inuktitut may be a phenomenon that has occurred because of wider pressures of sociocultural assimilation, not despite them. However, it would be misleading to conclude from this that Inuktitut usage will continue indefinitely to remain as strong as it was in 1981. The pace of social change continues to increase in northern communities. In recent years, northern lifestyles have been radically altered by the communications revolution:

> Which now offers: 4 TV stations from southern cities, 7 radio stations from across Canada . . . 7 pay television channels, 2 educational services and even programming packaged in France, providing 18 services available on satellites in 1983.[76]

Fortunately, the Inuit Broadcasting Corporation (IBC) was established in 1981, with a mandate to broadcast in Inuktitut. There is an urgent need for more funding for IBC so that it can expand its programming to provide Inuktitut programs dealing with contemporary issues as well as traditional Inuit culture, and particularly so it can develop children's programming.[77] As the organization has asserted:

> . . . no single feature of southern culture was as profound in its effects on the Inuit way of life as television. It destroyed old habits and social behaviours; it imported new values and attitudes. It became an alternative way of life, particularly for the young.[78]

If the Inuit language is to remain strong in the eastern Arctic and northern Quebec, it is absolutely essential that policies and measures be taken to develop its usage in emerging social institutions, as well as more traditional ones like education. Only then will individuals receive the necessary feedback from everyday experience to feel the positive effects of cultural continuity.[79] Only with the maintenance of a distinct identity do Inuit have the chance of altering the wider conditions of social and economic dependency which presently characterize so much of their lives.

Acknowledgements

This work was made possible, and was later substantially improved, through comments and suggestions made by several scholars. Professor Bruce Cox of the Department of Sociology and Anthropology at Carleton University, first suggested that I examine census data on Inuktitut. Professors J. Iain Prattis and Derek G. Smith, of the same department, provided valuable comments regarding my analysis. Professor John deVries, also from Carleton University, guided the entire project. Finally, Wally Boxhill and Luc Albert of Statistics Canada helped me to locate more detailed data on Inuktitut retention. I also wish to thank my friend Nicole Richer for typing a lengthy earlier version of this article.

Notes

1. D. Jenness, *Eskimo Administration: II. Canada*, Arctic Institute of North America, Technical Paper #14 (Montreal: McGill-Queen's University Press, 1964).
2. N. Graburn, *Eskimos without Igloos: Social and Economic Development in Sugluk* (Boston: Little, Brown and Co., 1969), 56–70.
3. C. Hughes, "Under Four Flags: Recent Culture Change Among the Eskimos," *Current Anthropology*, vol. 6, no. 1 (1965):17.
4. *Ibid.*, 17–18.
5. Jenness, *Eskimo Administration: II. Canada*, 65.
6. K. Crowe, *A History of the Original Peoples of Northern Canada* (Montreal: McGill-Queen's University Press, 1974), 114–15; Graburn, Eskimos without Igloos, 120–44.
7. R. Paine, ed., *The White Arctic: Anthropological Essays on Tutelage and Ethnicity* (Toronto: University of Toronto Press, 1977), 12.
8. Department of Indian and Northern Affairs (hereinafter DINA), *The Inuit* (Ottawa: North of 60° Publication, 1978), 6.
9. D. Smith, *Natives and Outsiders: Pluralism in the Mackenzie Delta* (Ottawa: Department of Indian Affairs and Northern Development, 1975), 132; Paine, *The White Arctic*, 34–35.
10. H. Young, *Elementary English for the Eskimo* (Ottawa: Ministry of Resources and Development, 1950).
11. DINA, *The Inuit*, 15; K. Harper, *Writing in Inuktitut: An Historical Perspective* (Ottawa: Department of Indian Affairs and Northern Development, 1983), 28.
12. J.I. Prattis and J.P. Chartrand, *System and Process: Inuktitut-English Bilingualism in the Northwest Territories of Canada*, Centre for Research on Ethnic Minorities, Working Paper #5 (Ottawa: Carleton University, Department of Sociology and Anthropology, 1985); P. Welsman, "Education of Native People in the Northwest Territories: A Northern Model," in *The North in Transition*, edited by N. Orvic and K. Patterson (Kingston: McGill-Queen's University Press, 1976), 37.
13. The reader should be aware of the fact that the data in this paper present several problems. The reader should keep in mind the fact that the 1981 census was taken during the summer—the time period when Inuit leave settlements for summer camps. While this would tend to affect all data relatively equally (i.e., there is no reason why only bilingual Inuit would leave for summer camps), segments of the population may have been missed, possibly affecting the data in this paper (Metcalfe 1985). Furthermore, part of the high 1981 retention ratios in Quebec and in the eastern Arctic may be the result of political activity that has occurred in these areas since the early 1970s. In other words, part of the reason for the increase in awareness and relevance of ethnic identity may result from political activity. On the other hand, the major advantage of this piece of work is that to my knowledge, for the first time, compatible data on Inuktitut retention are presented and compared with the same methodological procedures.
14. M. Hechter, *Internal Colonialism* (Los Angeles: University of California Press, 1975; G. Berreman, *Caste and Other Inequities* (Vatuk: Meerut, 1979). 15. F. Barth, *Ethnic Groups and Boundaries* (Boston: Little, Brown and Co., 1969).
16. E. Enloe, *Ethnic Conflict and Political Development* (Boston: Little, Brown and Co., 1973); E. Enloe, "Multinational Corporations and the Making and the Unmaking of Ethnic Groups," in *Ethnonationalism, Multinational Corporations and the Modern State* by Grant Ronald and E.S. Wellhoffer, Monograph, Science and World Affairs, vol. 1, no. 15, bk. 4 (Denver: University of Denver, 1979).
17. Paine, *The White Arctic*, 235; Inuit Tapirisat of Canada (hereinafter ITC), *Annual Report, 1979–1980* (Ottawa: Information Services of Inuit Tapirisat of Canada, 1980); "Nunavut—Our Land," in *Two Nations, Many Cultures: Ethnic Groups in Canada*, by J. Elliott (Scarborough: Prentice-Hall Inc., 1983).

18. Crowe, *Original Peoples of Northern Canada*, 20; Robert M. Bone, "The Number of Eskimos: An Arctic Enigma," *Polar Record*, vol. 16, no. 103 (1973):554.
19. Crowe, *Original Peoples of Northern Canada*, 108.
20. *Ibid.*, 59.
21. *Ibid.*, 110, 128.
22. R. McGhee, *Beluga Hunters: An Archaeological Reconstruction of the Mackenzie Delta Kittegaryumiut* (St. John's: Memorial University of Newfoundland, Institute of Social and Economic Resources, 1974), 5–6.
23. D. Smith, "Mackenzie Delta Eskimos," in *Handbook of North American Indians*, vol. 5, edited by W.C. Sturtevant, volume edited by D. Damas (Washington: Smithsonian Institute, 1984), 356.
24. Robert M. Bone, "The Number of Eskimos: An Arctic Enigma," *Polar Record*, vol. 16, no. 103 (1973):555.
25. Statistics Canada, *Census of Canada, Canada's Native People* (1981), Table 2.
26. *Ibid.*, Table 2.
27. Bone, "Number of Eskimos."
28. The ratio of Inuit who speak Inuktitut is likely larger than that reported here.
29. M. Barrados and M.B. van Dine, *Multilingualism of Natives in the Mackenzie District* (Ottawa: Department of Indian Affairs and Northern Development, North of 60° Publications, 1977); L. Osgood, "Forward," in Basic Kangiryuarmiut Eskimo Dictionary (Inuvik: Committee for the Original People's Entitlement, 1983), ix.
30. Crowe, *Original Peoples of Northern Canada*, 110–11.
31. J. Kennedy, "Northern Labrador: An Ethnohistorical Account," in *The White Arctic: Anthropological Essays on Tutelage and Ethnicity*, edited by R. Paine (Toronto: University of Toronto Press, 1977), 267.
32. *Ibid.*, 269.
33. H. Kleivan, *The Eskimos of Northeast Labrador: A History of Eskimo-White Relations, 1771–1995* (Oslo: Norsk Polarinstitutt Skrifter 139, 1966).
34. Kennedy, "Northern Labrador," 275.
35. T. Brantenberg, "Ethnic Commitments in Local Government in Nain, 1969–76," in *The White Arctic*, edited by Paine, 383.
36. Kennedy, "Northern Labrador," 272; A. Brantenberg, "The Marginal School and the Children of Nain," in *The White Arctic*, edited by Paine, 345.
37. Kennedy, "Northern Labrador," 271.
38. A. Brantenberg and T. Brantenberg, "Coastal Labrador After 1950," in *The White Arctic*, edited by Paine, 689.
39. Harper, *Writing in Inuktitut*, 28.
40. Jenness, *Eskimo Administration, II Canada*, 65.
41. Jenness, *Eskimo Administration, II Canada*; Graburn, *Eskimos Without Igloos*, 120.
42. H. Brody, *The People's Land: Whites and the Eastern Arctic* (New York: Penguin Books, 1975); J.I. Prattis, *The Structure of Resource Development in the Canadian North* (Ottawa: Carleton University, Department of Sociology and Anthropology, Working Paper 80-6, 1980); J.I. Prattis, *The Political Economy of Native Land Claims in the Canadian North* (Ottawa: Unpublished manuscript, 1983); K. Rea, *The Political Economy of Northern Development* (Ottawa: Science Council of Canada, 1976); G. Valaskakis, "Communications and Control in the North: The Potential of Interactive Satellites," *Etudes Inuit Studies* 6 (1982):19–28.
43. Brody, *People's Land*, 31.
44. Hechter, *Internal Colonialism*.
45. *Ibid.*, 30.
46. Paine, *The White Arctic*, 17.
47. *Ibid.*, 34–35.

48. N. Robitaille and R. Choinière, *An Overview of Demographic and Socio-Economic Conditions of the Inuit in Canada* (Ottawa: Department of Indian Affairs and Northern Development, 1985), 40.
49. Statistics Canada, *Census of Canada, Native People's Tape*, Table SDN81BG1, Population 15 years and over by Labour Force Activity (5) (1981); Statistics Canada, Census of Canada, Native People's Tape, Table SDN81BI1, Labour Force 15 years and over by Occupation Major Groups (15) (1981).
50. For example, O. Lewis, *La Vida* (New York: Random House, 1966); and I. Honigman and J. Honigman, *Eskimo Townsmen* (Ottawa: Canadian Research Center for Anthropology, Saint Paul University, 1965).
51. Brody, *People's Land*; H. Brody, "The Settlement Managers: Ambivalence in Patronage," in *The White Arctic*, edited by Paine.
52. Paine, *The White Arctic*, 17–21.
53. *Department of Northern Affairs and Natural Resources (herinafter DNANR), Northern Education: Ten Years of Progress* (Ottawa: The Department, 1961).
54. DINA, *The Inuit*, 15; Harper, *Writing in Inuktitut*, 28.
55. B. Fraser, "Why Nanook of the North Still Can't Read" (Ottawa: DNANR, 1967), David O. Born, *Eskimo Education and the Trauma of Social Change* (Ottawa: Northern Science Research Group, 1970); Graburn, *Eskimos Without Igloos*, 201.
56. DNANR, *Northern Education.*
57. Crowe, *Original Peoples of Northern Canada*, 198.
58. Hechter, *Internal Colonialism*, 30–40.
59. *Ibid.*, 40.
60. Paine, *The White Arctic*, 20.
61. Berreman, *Caste and Other Inequities*; Barth, *Ethnic Groups and Boundaries.*
62. Berreman, *Caste and Other Inequities*; Hechter, *Internal Colonialism.*
63. Smith, *Natives and Outsiders.*
64. Graburn, *Eskimos Without Igloos*, 225.
65. W. Lambert, "The Effects of Bilingualism on the Individual: Cognitive and Sociocultural Consequences," in *Bilingualism: Psychological, Social and Educational Implications*, edited by P.A. Hornby (New York: Academic Press, 1977).
66. J. Reitz, *The Survival of Ethnic Groups* (Toronto: McGraw-Hill Ryerson Ltd., 1980). Analysis revealed that language retention had a correlation coefficient of 0.64 with in-group interaction, and 0.53 with identification. The other variables had significantly lower coefficients.
67. Reitz, *Survival of Ethnic Groups*, 117.
68. Statistics Canada, *Census of Canada, Native People's Tape*, Table SDN81BG1, Table SDN81BI1.
69. Paine, *The White Arctic*, 249–67.
70. Smith, *Natives and Outsiders.*
71. T. Berger, *Caste and Other Inequities* (Vatuk: Meerut, 1985), 47, 164.
72. Kennedy, "Northern Labrador."
73. Brantenberg and Brantenberg, "Coastal Labrador After 1950."
74. J. Chambers and P. Trudgill, *Dialectology* (New York: Cambridge University Press, 1980).
75. Inuit Cultural Institute (hereinafter ICI), *Annual Report, 1979–1980* (Ottawa: Information Services of Inuit Tapirisat of Canada, 1978).
76. Prattis and Chartrand, *System and Process*, 21.
77. Inuit Broadcasting Corporation (hereinafter IBC), *Proposal for Inuit Children's Educational Television*, IBC July (1982); IBC, *Position on Northern Broadcasting*, IBC August (1982).
78. IBC, *Position on Northern Broadcasting*, i.
79. Barth, *Ethnic Groups and Boundaries*; Prattis and Chartrand, *System and Process*, 9.

Chapter 19
Prospects for the Northern Canadian Native Economy

Bruce Alden Cox

Much ink has been spilled concerning the future prospects of a Northern native economy based on a mix of hunting, trapping, and wage work. A great deal of information on this mixed economy was generated during the debates over Northern pipeline development which raged during the 1970s. (These debates ended with the call, in 1977, for a ten-year moratorium on all such megaprojects.) Although the native lifestyle came under close scrutiny during that period, skeptics remain unconvinced of the very existence, let alone the viability, of a native mixed economy. In the skeptics' view, a way of life based on harvesting "country foods" is moribund, and ought to give place to a full-fledged wage economy as soon as is decently possible. Moreover, those who think otherwise, including the authors of the pipeline Inquiries, are misguided romantics. This paper re-examines the debates over the prospects for a native hunting economy on the eve of the expiration of Justice Berger's ten-year moratorium on Northern pipeline developments. I will conclude that, given proper institutional support, a mixed economy should persist into the next century. Furthermore, I hope to show that the critics of the bush economy have underestimated its contribution to the welfare of Northern natives.

Native Economy

Peter Usher maintains that "the North may well be the only place where a poor man's table is laden with meat."[1] This essay speculates about how long native tables in the Canadian North can continue to be laden with fresh-killed meat. Thus we will examine the prospects for survival of a way of life based on "country foods" and other resources of bush and northern waters. As is now well understood, this way of life derives ultimately from native adaptations to the needs of early European fur-trading posts. It is now clear that the early customers of the trading posts were participating in what we would call a "mixed economy." That is, their way of life combined limited participation in a market economy with a non-monetary subsistence economy.[2] Such a way of life has long been part of native tradition, but what are its prospects for the future? That is, what are the prospects for the persistence of a way of life based on harvesting country foods and other products of bush, tundra, and northern waters? The data which speak to this question come from the Yukon and the Northwest

Territories. Nevertheless, the lessons we take from the area can probably be applied to Indian communities throughout the Canadian subarctic.

In the last decade, much new information has appeared on the native peoples of the North and the prospects for their way of life. In 1977, for example, the Mackenzie Valley Pipeline Inquiry brought down its Report under the authorship of Justice Thomas Berger. The Commission's Report was based on extensive staff work, and on hearings in "every city and town, village and settlement in the Mackenzie Valley and the Western Arctic."[3] As such, the Inquiry was seen as a model of community participation, although not by everyone. Critics like Ritchie wrote of "an unhealthy politicisation, of the [inquiry] process."[4] On the other hand, supporters pointed out that a debate on the effects of large-scale industrial projects of this kind could hardly eschew political considerations. Fuller expressed the view pithily: "Judge Berger's mandate was to fiddle with rules, he was pilloried because he questioned outcomes."[5]

Not all Northern Inquiries seem to have closely questioned outcomes, however. Members of the Lysyk Inquiry were led by the press of events in the 1970s to believe that construction might soon begin on the Alaskan Highway Pipeline. In this era of low oil prices the Yukon line seems moribund, and the proposed Mackenzie Valley line at least dormant. The reports of the Yukon and Mackenzie Inquiries are mainly useful here, however, as a source of information on the mixed economy of Northern native communities. The Lysyk report, in fact, speaks directly to the subject of a mixed economy. The Report describes a way of life based on a mixed economy, drawing on the testimony of Mr. Clyde Blackjack of Carmacks at Mile 103 on the Klondike Highway:

> Through a judicious mix of wage employment, the trapping of fur, and the acquisition of country food, Mr. Blackjack appears to be able to produce what he needs. He is not interested in accumulation for its own sake, of being "carried away" with production solely for material gain.[6]

Unfortunately, the Alaska Highway Pipeline Inquiry was unable to say how many of the 6,000 Yukon Indians and Métis took part in a mixed economy. Moreover, the Report urged caution in making such estimates, judging from the experience of Quebec's James Bay hydroelectric project:

> The Quebec government (wrongly) assumed that the lifestyle and activities of the Cree Indians near James Bay were already so modified and so directed toward wage employment that the proposed hydroelectric project would not significantly affect them.[7]

The Inquiry's Report goes on to speculate that further research in the Yukon, as in Quebec, might well support native claims about the extent of the mixed economy. In any case, public policy should aim to create "an economic framework that will allow Indian people a choice among the various possibilities of a mixed economy."[8] We will return a little later to the question of how natives can be guaranteed the right to take part in a mixed economy. Let us remain for the moment, however, with the Mackenzie Valley Pipeline Inquiry, which made a serious attempt to gauge native participation in a mixed economy during the 1970s.

Previous investigators had misconstrued the native mixed economies and sold short the contribution of country foods to native welfare. Not so the Berger Commission. For Volume II of their Report, the Commission's staff collected a wealth of figures on hunting and trapping throughout the Mackenzie region and Northern Yukon for 1970–75. They found that an annual average of nearly 2,210 metric tonnes of edible meat were taken, in the form of big game, beaver, whales, seals, ducks, geese, fish, and hares. This included, however, over 707 tonnes of dogmeat, in the form of fur-bearers, marine mammals, and especially fish. This left just over 1,502 tonnes of country foods annually to support the region's Inuit, Métis, and Indian people.[9] The annual harvest averaged 2,209,818.5 kilograms, with 707,549.9 kilograms fed to dogs, and 1,502,268.6 kilograms eaten by natives. Using Berger's figures to compute the daily portion of the 15,000 natives who then lived in the Mackenzie Valley and Northern Yukon,[10] we see in Table 19-1 that an individual share of the region's annual harvest of country foods amounts to 100 kilograms. This works out as a daily portion of about 275 grams for each native person.

Critics complain that 275 grams are not enough. Bliss, for example, argues that some 1.4 kilograms of country foods would be needed each day by anyone eating "off the land." In fact, he denies Judge Berger's claim that "most native people already eat well off the land."[12] Taking up the question of the quality of native diet, we must re-examine the notion of "eating off the land." If this means getting all one's energy from country foods, then much will be needed. In theory, 575 grams of protein would be sufficient to provide 2,500 large calories. In fact, the net energy available from those 575 grams of country provisions might be a fraction of the 2,500 large calories required daily by an adult.[13] Bliss may have it about right when he reckons that an adult eating only country foods would need nearly one-and-one-half kilograms of them daily. Nevertheless, it has probably been some time since anyone in the Northwest Territories derived all their dietary energy from country provisions. Even in the 1700s, trading posts gave

Table 19-1 The Production of Country Foods in the North

	Region	Native population	kg/person/yr	g/person/day	% Fish
1975	Mackenzie Valley and Northern Yukon	15,000	100[a]	274[b]	27
2001	Northwest Territories	53,000	51[a]	140[b]	77

Source: Berger, *Northern Frontier, Northern Homeland*, vol. I, 146–47, vol. II, 32–34; Fuller and Hubert, "Fish, Fur and Game," 14, 17–21.

a. To the nearest kilogram.

b. The 1975 figures are based on "edible weight," while the figures for 2001 are expressed as "available protein," a more conservative measure.

out porridge oats to Indian hunters who were down on their luck. Cereal grains have thus formed some part of the boreal forest diet for centuries. To insist otherwise is to ignore a large part of the boreal forest history, harking back to an aboriginal Eden where nobody ate porridge!

An alternative approach is to see what boreal forest people actually eat, something that the Pipeline Inquiries did not tell us. Kristen Borré, a nutritionist, studied the Severn River Band's diet during 1975, concluding that imported foods served an important function in this bush community in the James Bay drainage:

> Imported foods help relieve the risk of winter starvation, which once was a common hazard for sub-Arctic populations. They also provide the necessary carbohydrate which allows dietary protein to be used for protein and not energy. . . .[14]

Accordingly, Borré and Winterhalder found that fully 81 percent of the energy in the Severn Band's diet came from imported foods and garden potatoes, with only 19 percent, on average, coming from country foods.[15] Protein, on the other hand, came predominantly from country foods; 69 percent over the year, running 84 percent throughout September, October, and November.[16] Very likely the diet of other boreal forest communities would show similar proportions, although we cannot know that for a certainty. In any case, Borré's main point stands: cereal products and country foods complement each other in the native diet. Both are necessary, and are likely to remain so.

Such seems to be the assumption also of Fuller and Hubert who admit that their figures and forecasts would remain insufficient to someone living on country foods alone.[17] Fuller and Hubert cast a wider net than the Pipeline Inquiries did. They take the whole Northwest Territories for their subject, and they hazard guesses about the future as well. Table 19-1 sets out their findings on native diet alongside those from the Mackenzie Valley Pipeline Inquiry. Unfortunately, Fuller and Hubert left the Métis and other unregistered natives out of their reckoning.[18] To correct this omission we must draw on the census, which in 1981 covered status and non-status Indians, Métis, and Inuit. Doubling the census figure of 26,430 native people for 1981[19] brings us to a generous estimate of 53,000 Métis, Inuit, and Indians in the year 2001 subsisting on a possible future supply of 2,707 tonnes of protein from fish and game.[20] Most of the increase would come in the form of fish, shrimp, and other marine invertebrates. According to Fuller and Hubert, Northerners would be eating more marine products in the year 2001, more perhaps than they wanted.[21] Still, this ought to be enough. If we suppose that 55 grams of protein are needed by adults daily, then this requirement is met, and more.[22]

In a general way then, Table 19-1 supports the findings of Commissioner Berger, who held that "most native people already eat well off the land." Furthermore, they should continue to do so.

> Can the land support a larger native population? . . . In aboriginal times the land supported a larger native population than it does today. In fact, there is little

evidence that native people are over-exploiting their resources at present, and there is much evidence that overall yields could be increased.[23]

The Cost of Maintaining a Mixed Economy

Thus far we have ordered a meal for the native people, quibbling somewhat over portions, without once glancing at the right-hand column of the menu. That is always a risky thing to do, as Bliss, for example, hastens to remind us. In fact, Bliss maintains that most native families cannot meet the costs of harvesting country foods, that there is "not enough cash flow from the sale of furs to cover their hunting and trapping costs."[24] This is clearly a serious charge, one which must be examined closely. Bliss recomputes Justice Berger's figures[25] to arrive at average yearly harvesting expenses of $3,500,000 for the native hunters of the Mackenzie and Western Arctic during 1970–75. Thus, a hefty bill must be settled yearly for the meal of country foods, even if it is divided among the 3,000 native men who were active in the bush at that time.[26] Furthermore, in whatever way this bill be divided, it remains larger than the $1,200,000 in average yearly fur sales over the same period.[27] How can we explain this anomaly?

Those who are skeptical about the prospects of a mixed economy would claim that these figures prove that the traditional native economy is moribund. In fact, that is exactly the construction which Bliss, for one, puts on the figures for harvesting costs. The economist J.C. Stabler[28] argues as well against Justice Berger's contention that "hunting and trapping produce, not five percent, but more like 50 percent of native income."[29] Stabler goes on to maintain that most trappers earn too little money from trapping to renew their equipment, and that most are dependent on wage employment to obtain trapping "grubstakes" and maintain their trapping outfit.[30] We shall see that Stabler here fails to do justice to the position of native trappers. Let us grant that many trappers may use wages from seasonal employment to maintain their trapping equipment. Nevertheless, this need not support Stabler's conclusion that wage employment predominates over hunting and trapping in the Northern economy. In order to illustrate what I mean here, figures for cash income will be compared with data on country foods drawn from the Berger Commission's Report. Figures for cash income come from Meldrum and Helman's summary of the Northern Manpower survey.[31] (See Table 19-2).

The Northern Manpower Survey visited communities in the Mackenzie Valley in the fall of 1970 and the Northern Yukon in late fall of 1971. Meldrum and Helman report family income in the Mackenzie Valley for 1969–70 and the Yukon for 1970–71.[32] In Table 19-2, these figures are arranged to compare with estimates of the substitution value of country foods harvested.[33]

Table 19-2 should give a good idea of how the native mixed economy works. Stabler is right in supposing that fur sales account for only a small part of the native domestic economy. Nevertheless, trapping remains of overwhelming importance since it puts the trapper in the way of quantities of country

Table 19-2 The Contribution of Country Foods to Family Incomes in the Mackenzie Valley and Northern Yukon, 1969-71

Region and group	Average cash income per family (dollars)	Potential value of country foods, family of 5 (dollars)	Country food as % of family income (percent)
Mackenzie Indians	2,106	3,630	63
Mackenzie Métis	4,519	3,630	44
Mackenzie Inuit	4,380	3,660	45
Northern Yukon Indians	3,574	3,630	50
Northern Yukon Métis	6,431	3,660	36

Source: Meldrum and Helman, *D.I.A.N.D. Northern Manpower Survey*, 78, 141; Berger, *Northern Frontier, Northern Homeland*, vol. II, 33.

provisions. As such, it may be necessary to subsidize his visits to the bush with income from jobs in the settlements, pensions, or indeed from any source available.

This is not to say that wage work is only esteemed because it provides the wherewithal to renew hunting equipment. Some Northern natives would doubtless welcome regular employment. Nevertheless, such employment would have to be very regular indeed in order to represent a net gain. Since, in Table 19-2, nearly two-thirds of Mackenzie Indian family income is gained from the bush, wage income would need to double in order for wages to replace hunting and trapping. Incomes of this order are probably not attainable in the smaller settlements; this may explain as well why young Northerners often express a preference for work outside these settlements.[34]

Table 19-2 shows that a mixed economy is not a subsistence economy, as Justice Berger pointed out as well.[35] Cash is needed to keep it going, to renew harvesting equipment, to pay for transport into the bush, and so on. This is by no means a new problem, as the captain of Eastmain's Post hunters explained to Joseph Isbister in the fall of 1739. Isbister wrote in the post journal:

> He Answard and sead . . . they must be soplied with Neceserys to Catch them withall or Else Theire wold be but Letle Trade, so I trusted ye Capt and some of his Gaurd a Small Matter as Much as I though they Culd well pay an no mor.[36]

From Isbister's day on, trapping has depended on outside sources of cash or credit, whether from the manager of a trading post, seasonal employers, or the Social Security administrator. The amounts so received may be inadequate, and paid out as grudgingly as Joseph Isbister did. In some few communities where more cash is available, winter trapping may increase apace. This is particularly so where work schedules are arranged to include a "long break," a week or more off work after a period on the job. Charles Hobart reports on such a case at

Coppermine, N.W.T., and in other Arctic communities, where there has been a substantial increase in pay packets from frontier mineral exploration.[37] Trapping did not suffer accordingly, however. In fact, Hobart reports "Increased trapping in the years after the employment became available." So also did harvests of country foods increase, aided by new harvesting equipment such as "motor toboggans, boats, outboard motors, guns, tents."[39]

Motor toboggans, boats, and outboard motors, however, cannot always be financed by wages from industrial activity, as the people of Coppermine must know very well. The Canadian North is surely a large place, and not all of it will be subject to industrial development. (Amen to that, some might add.) Before closing, then, let us consider a case in which the capital costs of bush production come from another source. Here I have in mind the Income Security Programme for trappers, established in 1976 by the James Bay Agreement.[40] This programme provides payments of up to $2,400 per year for each adult in a harvesting unit, calculated in constant (indexed) dollars. This sum is compounded of "an amount of $10.00 . . . for every day spent in the bush by each adult" in the harvesting unit, and $2.00 per day "for every day not spent in the bush" and not receiving other income. This programme seems predicated on a mixed economy. It reduces payments by 40 percent of "other income"—income not derived from trapping—and it requires that the beneficiaries derive "the greater part of their earnings from the bush," or spend "more time conducting harvesting or related activities than time spent in salary or wage employment."[41] The Province of Québec pays these sums quarterly with the first available in September. Those who need a "grubstake" for a long stay in the bush can get one-half of the amount which is coming to them in the fall.[42]

The Québec programme is not unique; limited support is available to trappers in the Northwest Territories. (Not, however, in any province outside Québec, despite the prevalence of a native bush-oriented economy throughout the Canadian subarctic.) The Québec programme is cited here simply to show what might be done to strengthen the native mixed economy throughout the forested regions of Canada. It is possible to quibble with the figures of Table 19-2, but their general import is inescapable: native Northerners derive much of their income in the form of country provisions, and anything which reduces their harvest reduces their general standard of living. Efforts to improve native life must, in areas where this is possible, be directed toward strengthening the bush economy. This conclusion does not grow out of nostalgia for a vanishing way of life, it is simply based on an appreciation of the position of those natives who still have access to country produce. This appreciation rests on the assumption that whatever industrial projects may be sited in the boreal forest and beyond, the native communities will remain largely marginal to them. I see nothing in the recent history of northern industrial projects which contradicts this assumption: not in the James Bay project, and certainly not in the so-far hypothetical northern pipeline. Industrial projects may bring welcome cash to the natives, but they are unlikely to endure long enough to replace the bush economy.

But what if we are wrong in making these assumptions? If industrial projects become a permanent feature of life in the bush, and if natives cease to be marginal to such projects, what then? If they should, and natives all get steady jobs, an Income Security Programme would cost nothing. The programme's beneficiaries must derive the major part of their sustenance from the bush, and its benefits are reduced in proportion to other income received. There is thus no risk in putting such a programme in place; if it should not be needed, it will cost nothing.

We began this chapter with Peter Usher's musings on the diet of Northern natives. Usher speculated that Northern Canada may be the only place where a poor man's table is laden with meat. We can make this observation without taking any joy from the fact of their poverty. Nevertheless, any remedy for their state of poverty must take account of the amenities of northern life. We have seen that the bush can provide, and will continue to provide, an adequate diet. Natives thus will not thank us if attempts at mitigating their poverty wreak their harvest of country provisions. This is not a matter of harking back to some dimly glowing scene from an Arcadian past. It is now a mixed economy which must be preserved, but nonetheless worthy of preservation for that. It is an economy which provides only a modest subsistence, make no mistake. But it is not, after all, nostalgia which makes natives want to hold on to what they have, however modest. There is a sense, after all, in which a bird from the bush, but well in hand, is worth two score which are expected one day from the south.

Notes

Source: Revised from an article in *Polar Record*, vol. 22, no. 139 (1985):393–400, by permission of the publishers and editor.

1. P.J. Usher, "Evaluating Country Food in the Northern Native Economy," *Arctic*, vol. 29, no. 2 (1976):119.
2. H. Brody, *The People's Land: Eskimos and Whites in the Eastern Arctic* (Harmondsworth: Penguin Books, 1975), 214.
3. Mr. Justice T. Berger, *Northern Frontier, Northern Homeland: The Report of the Mackenzie Valley Pipeline Inquiry*, vol. I (Ottawa: Ministry of Supply and Services Canada, 1977), vii.
4. J.C. Ritchie, "Northern Fiction—Northern Homage," *Arctic*, vol. 31, no. 2 (1978):73.
5. W.A. Fuller, "Of Conservation and Mysticism, Democracy and Things," *Arctic*, vol 390, no. 1 (1979):184.
6. K.M. Lysyk, *et al.*, *Alaska Highway Pipeline Inquiry* (Ottawa: Department of Indian and Northern Affairs, 1977), 91.
7. *Ibid.*
8. *Ibid.*, 92.
9. Berger, *Northern Frontier, Northern Homeland*, vol. II, 31.
10. *Ibid.*, vol. I, 185.
11. L.C. Bliss, "Report of the Mackenzie Valley Pipeline Inquiry, Volume Two: An Environmental Critique," *Musk-ox* 21 (1978):36.
12. Berger, *Northern Frontier, Northern Homeland*, vol. II, 38.
13. W.A. Fuller and B.A. Hubert, "Fish, Fur and Game in the Northwest Territories:

Some Problems of, and Prospects for Increased Harvest," in *Proceedings: First International Symposium on Renewable Resources and the Economy of the North*, edited by M.R. Freeman (Ottawa: Association of Canadian Universities for Northern Studies, 1981), 21.

14. K. Borré and B. Winterhalder, "Cost-Effectiveness of Local and Imported Foods in a Boreal Forest Community" (1983, unpublished paper), 26.
15. *Ibid.*, Table V.
16. *Ibid.*
17. Fuller and Hubert, "Fish, Fur and Game," 21.
18. *Ibid.*, 14.
19. Walton O. Boxhill, "1981 Census Data on the Native Peoples of Canada," *Canadian Statistical Review*, vol. 60, no. 2 (1985):vii.
20. Fuller and Hubert, "Fish, Fur and Game," 18.
21. *Ibid.*, 21.
22. *Ibid.* Fuller and Hubert evidently use this standard in their Table 3, p.20.
23. Berger, *Northern Frontier, Northern Homeland*, vol. I, 185.
24. Bliss, "Mackenzie Valley Pipeline Inquiry," 36.
25. Berger, *Northern Frontier, Northern Homeland*, vol. II, 14, 32. Berger himself reports harvesting costs of $3,440,000.
26. *Ibid.*, 18.
27. *Ibid.*, 32.
28. J.C. Stabler, "The Report of the Mackenzie Valley Pipeline Inquiry, Volume I: A Socio-Economic Critique," *Musk-ox* 20 (1977).
29. Berger, *Northern Frontier, Northern Homeland*, vol. I, 108.
30. Stabler, "Mackenzie Valley Pipeline Inquiry," 61.
31. Sheila Meldrum and Marion Helman, *Summary of the Statistical Data from the D.I.A.N.D. Northern Manpower Survey Program in the Yukon and Northwest Territories, 1969–1971* (Ottawa: Department of Indian and Northern Affairs, 1975).
32. *Ibid.*, 78, 141.
33. That is, the cost if they had eaten imported meat; see Berger, *Northern Frontier, Northern Homeland*, vol. II, 25, 33; Usher, *Evaluating Country Food.* This value for country foods was set at just over $3.00 per pound; this may be inflated in terms of 1969–71 prices.
34. Stabler, "Mackenzie Valley Pipeline Inquiry," 63.
35. Berger, *Northern Frontier, Northern Homeland*, vol. II, 338.
36. Cited in T. Morantz, *An Ethnohistoric Study of Eastern James Bay Cree Social Organization, 1700–1850* (Ottawa: National Museum of Man, 1833), 42–43.
37. C.W. Hobart, "Impacts of Industrial Employment on Hunting and Trapping Among Canadian Inuit," in *Proceedings: First International Symposium of Renewable Resources and the Economy of the North*, edited by M.R. Freeman.
38. *Ibid.*, 207.
39. *Ibid.*, 214.
40. Harvey A. Feit, "Negotiating Recognition of Aboriginal Rights," *Canadian Journal of Anthropology* 12 (1980).
41. Québec, *The James Bay and Northern Québec Agreement* (Québec City: National Library, 1976), 440–441.
42. *Ibid.*, 438, 444.

PART VI
Suggestions for Further Study

Chapter 20
Recent Publications in Canadian Native Studies

John A. Price

In the early 1960s Canada was producing only about a dozen Native studies books, monographs, and graduate theses per year. These were largely concentrated in archaeology and cultural anthropology. References cited in the 1973 edition of *Cultural Ecology*, for example, had a relatively early median average publication date of 1955, only 18 percent of the items were published in Canada, and only 1 percent were written by women. Since then, there has been a large scale increase in Canadian Native studies: most are now produced in Canada, and authorship of these works by women currently runs at about 28 percent.

Today about 75 books and technical monographs and about 40 graduate theses are produced each year in the burgeoning field of Canadian Native studies. There is a rough correlation between the amount of publication (and audio-visual coverage) on a Native society and that society's population, except that the Inuit are over-represented and the Métis under-represented. Archaeology and cultural anthropology are important today, as they were in the 1960s, but many new specializations are also doing well. Table 20-2 shows the distribution of 1,197 books, monographs, and graduate theses produced in Canada in Native studies over ten years by specialization.

Journals

The *American Anthropologist* used to be the major academic forum on Native peoples of the Western Hemisphere. From its start in 1888 through the 1930s around 62 percent of its articles concerned Native peoples. Nevertheless, this proportion fell progressively over the years, until it was only 14 percent in the 1980s. It has tended to remain conservatively in traditional anthropology, rather than, for example, exploring practical issues, as is the case of *Human Organization*, the journal of the Society of Applied Anthropology, or the intersection with history, as in *Ethnohistory*, which also often has articles on Native studies.

There are four Native studies journals with a general coverage: *America Indigena*, in Spanish from Mexico City; *The American Indian Quarterly*, with an arts and social science orientation, from University of California, Berkeley; *American Indian Culture and Research Journal*, with an arts and humanities orientation, from University of California, Los Angeles (UCLA); and *The Canadian Journal of Native Studies*, with an applied social science orientation, from Brandon University in Brandon, Manitoba. *Abstracts of Native Studies* has also been recently started at Brandon University.

Table 20-1 Recent Books, Monographs and Theses Produced in Canada

	Percent		Percent
Archaeology	24	Linguistics	4
History, Ethnohistory	13	Physical Anthropology	4
Cultural Anthropology	12	Economics, Econ. Anth.	3
Literature	9	Religion, Philosophy	3
Art, Dance and Music	8	Sociology, Social Work	3
Politics, Law	8	Medicine, Psychology	1
Education, Texts	6		

In Canada, there are four general anthropology journals: *Anthropologica*, with 33 percent Native studies articles in the last several volumes, from Laurentian University; *Culture* with 30 percent in Native studies, from the Canadian Ethnology Society; *Canadian Journal of Anthropology* (formerly the *Western Canadian Journal of Anthropology*), in which Native studies articles predominate, from the University of Alberta; and *Anthropologies et Sociétés* with only 6 percent Native studies articles, from Laval University, Quebec City. *Anthropologica* is the only one of the four with a really deep backlog of Native studies articles, since it started in 1955 exclusively as a Native studies journal, sponsored by the Canadian Research Center for Amerindian Anthropology at the University of Ottawa.

Although their funding sources are weak and their publication irregular, Canada now has six major specialized Native studies journals: (1) *Canadian Journal of Archaeology*, from the University of Victoria; (2) *Canadian Journalof Native Education*, now at the University of Alberta; (3) *Etudes/Inuit/Studies*, from Laval University; (4) *Native Studies Review*, concerning the Prairies and the Métis, from the University of Saskatchewan; (5) *Papers of the Algonquian Conference*, an excellent annual on speakers of Algonquian, Abenaki, Blackfoot, Cree, Ojibwa, Malecite, Montagnais, Micmac, and so on, from Carleton University, Ottawa; and (6) *Recherches Amérindiennes au Québec,* with an orientation toward Quebec, from the University of Montreal. *Arctic Anthropology* from the University of Wisconsin also has a great deal of Canadian content.

Theses

For those interested in technical research, the pool of knowledge of graduate theses in Canadian Native studies has become vast. My list for theses produced at universities in Canada for the years 1975–84 has 429 titles. The basic source of these theses for the researcher is by purchase from

Canadian Theses on Microfiche Service,
National Library of Canada,
Ottawa, K1A 0M4.

This service publishes an annual list and a five year summary, which are both available in most university libraries. Also see the bibliography of theses listed below by Gadacz and Asch.

Monographs of the Canadian Museum of Civilisation

Another important source of technical publication in Canadian Native studies is the Canadian Museum of Civilisation in Ottawa, particularly the monograph series called *Archaeological Survey*, which includes physical anthropology studies, and *Canadian Ethnology Service* (CES), which includes linguistic studies. There are now more than 100 volumes in each of these series.

Pioneers

Before we present a bibliography of recent books, consider this list of fifty of the most prominent pioneers of Canadian Native studies selected on the basis of the frequency with which their works are cited. Anyone who published a book or monograph in Canadian Native studies prior to 1966 can be considered to be a pioneer in the field. After this, a modern period in the discipline began, the rate of publication increased markedly, and the field opened up to the whole range of academic disciplines. The following list is just a selection of these pioneers. They are arranged first by the Native culture areas where they did most of their work, and secondly, in sequence of time when they published. The Native societies they wrote about are also indicated. These scholars came largely from the United States and British Commonwealth countries to do their research. Many of them were important in founding anthropology, both internationally and in Canada. This list should help the reader track down early publications concerning particular Native societies.

Fifty Pioneers in Canadian Native Studies

General

Franz Boas	Inuit, Kwakiutl, Tsimshian
Edward Sapir	Lingistics, Nootka
C. Marius Barbeau	Haida, Huron, Iroquois
Frances Densmore	Ojibwa, Nootka, music
Diamond Jenness	Carrier, Inuit, Ojibwa, Sarcee, Sekani
Frank G. Speck	Beothuk, Iroquois, Micmac, Montagnais, Naskapi, Penobscot
Gertrude Kurath	Music, dance
Richard S. MacNeish	Archaeology

Pacific

Edward S. Curtis	Salish, Kwakiutl, Nootka, Haida
John R. Swanton	Haida, Tlingit

Erna Gunther	Klallam
James Teit	Lillooet, Shuswap, Tahltan, Thompson
Viola E. Garfield	Tsimshian
George P. Murdock	Haida
Irving Goldman	Carrier, Kwakiutl
Thomas McIlwriath	Bella Coola
Ronald L. Olson	Haisla
Helen Codere	Kwakiutl
Philip Drucker	Nootka, Kwakiutl
Homer G. Barnett	Salish
Harry B. Hawthorn	British Columbia
Wilson Duff	British Columbia

Prairies

George B. Grinnell	Blackfoot
Robert H. Lowie	Assiniboine
Clark Wissler	Blackfoot
John C. Ewers	Blackfoot
H.H. Turney-High	Kutenai
David Mandlebaum	Plains Cree

Iroquoia

Louis H. Morgan	Iroquois
Arthur C. Parker	Iroquois
William N. Fenton	Iroquois
Bruce G. Trigger	Huron

Subarctic

Emile Petitot	Chipewyan, Hare, Inuit, Kutchin
Pliny E. Goddard	Beaver, Chipewyan, British Columbia
John Cooper	Northern Algonquians
Leonard Bloomfield	Cree
Regina Flannery	Eastern Cree
Cornelius G. Osgood	Han, Ingalik, Kitchin, Tanaina
Irving A. Hallowel	Abenaki, Ojibwa, Saulteaux
Ruth Landes	Ojibway, Potawatomi
John Honigmann	Inuit, Kaska, Slave
Eleanor Leacock	Montagnais
Wilson D. Wallis	Micmac, Malecite
Robert W. Dunning	Ojibwa
Edward S. Rogers	Ojibwa, Cree
June Helm	Dogrib

Arctic

Knud Rasmussen	Inuit
Kaj Birkett-Smith	Inuit
David Damas	Inuit

The bibliography which follows is a selection of about 300 titles from a long list of books and monographs published since 1966, a year that represents something of a beginning of modern Native studies publication. The selection was made on such grounds as a wide availability in the university libraries, comprehensive coverage for an introduction to Canadian Native studies in all its diversity, and good quality within a sub-field of Native studies. Some of these books themselves, of course, make reference to the early works of the pioneers in Canadian Native studies.

The topical organization of this bibliograhy is as follows:

Bibliographies
General
Native Authors
Archaeology
Art
Cultural Anthropology
Economics
Education
History
Linguistics
Medicine
Politics, Law
Religion
Sociology, Social Work

Bibliographies

Bradley, Ian L. and Patricia Bradley. *A Bibliography of Canadian Native Arts*. Victoria: GLC Publishers, 1977

Buller, Edward. *Indigenous Performing and Ceremonial Arts in Canada: A Bibliography*. Toronto: Association for Native Development in the Performing and Visual Arts, 1981.

Corley, Nora T. *Resources for Native Peoples Studies*. Ottawa: The National Library of Canada, 1984. (Data on 356 Canadian libraries and collections, including periodicals.)

Gadacz, Rene R. and Michael I. Asch. *Theses and Dissertation Titles and Abstracts on the Anthropology of Canadian Indians, Inuit and Métis from Canadian Universities, 1970–1982*. Ottawa: CES 95, 1984.

Murdock, George P. and T.J. O'Leary, eds. *Ethnographic Bibliography of North America*, 4th ed., 5 vols. New Haven: HRAF Press, 1975. (Detailed bibliographies by society.)

Rothwell, Stephen J. *Multi-media on Indians and Inuit of North America, 1965–1980*. Ottawa: Department of Indian Affairs and Northern Development, 1981.

General

Cox, Bruce, ed. *Cultural Ecology: Readings on the Canadian Indians and Eskimos*. Toronto: McClelland and Stewart, 1973.

Department of Indian Affairs and Northern Development. *Linguistic and Cultural Affiliations of Canadian Indian Bands*. Ottawa: The Department, 1980.

Driver, Harold E. *Indians of North America*. 2nd ed. Chicago: University of Chicago Press, 1969.

Frideres, James S. *Native People in Canada: Contemporary Conflicts*. 2nd ed. Scarborough: Prentice-Hall Canada, 1983.

Jenness, Diamond. *The Indians of Canada*. Toronto: University of Toronto Press, 1977 (Originally published in 1932 by the National Museum.)

Marsh, James H., ed. *The Canadian Encyclopedia*. 3 volumes. Edmonton: Hurtig, 1985. (Sketches of all Native societies in Canada, biographies of prominent Native people, and analytical articles on Native art, communications, demography, economy, law, languages, religion, politics, etc.)

Morrison, R. Bruce and C. Roderick Wilson, eds. *The Native Peoples: The Canadian Experience*. Toronto: McClelland and Stewart, 1986.

Price, John A. *Indians of Canada: Cultural Dynamics*. Scarborough: Prentice-Hall Canada, 1978.

———. *Native Studies: American and Canadian Indians*. Scarborough: McGraw-Hill Ryerson, 1979.

Sturtevant, William C., general ed. *Handbook of North American Indians*. 20 volumes. Washington, D.C.: Smithsonian Institution, 1978 ff. (*Arctic* volume edited by David Damas, *Subarctic* by June Helm, and *Northeast* by Bruce Trigger.)

Statistics Canada. *Canada's Native People*. Ottawa: Department of Supply and Services, Canada, 1984.

Native Authors

Adams, Howard. *Prison of Grass: Canada From the Native Point of View*. Toronto: New Press, 1975. (Educator)

Ahenakew, Edward. *Voices of Plains Cree*. Toronto: McClelland & Stewart, 1973.

Ahenakew, Freda. *Stories of the House of People*. Winnipeg: University of Manitoba, 1983.

Allen, Robert S. *Native Studies in Canada: A Research Guide*. Ottawa: Department of Indian Affairs and Northern Development, 1982. (Lists of programs, associations, and centres.)

Boulanger, Tom. *An Indian Remembers: My Life as a Trapper in Northern Manitoba*. Winnipeg: Pegais (Cree), 1971.

Campbell, Maria. *Halfbreed*. Toronto: McClelland & Stewart, 1973.

Cardinal, Harold. *The Unjust Society: The Tragedy of Canada's Indians*. Edmonton: Hurtig, 1969.

———. *The Rebirth of Canada's Indians*. Edmonton: Hurtig, 1977. (Cree politician.)

Clutesi, George. *Son of Raven, Son of Deer: Fables of the Tse-shaht People*. Sidney, B.C.: Gray's, 1975. (Nootka writer.)

Daniels, Harry W. *The Forgotten People: Métis and Non-Status Indian Land Claims*. Ottawa: Native Council of Canada, 1979.

Dion, Joseph F. *My Tribe, The Crees*. Calgary: Glenbow-Alberta Institute, 1979.

Gedaloff, Robin, ed. *Paper Stays Put: A Collection of Inuit Writing*. Edmonton: Hurtig, 1980.

George, Chief Dan and Helmut Hirnschall. *My Spirit Soars*. Surrey, B.C.: Hancock House, 1982. (Former Shuswap chief and professional actor.)

Greene, Alma. *Tales of the Mohawks*. Toronto: J.M. Dent, 1975.

Gros-Louis, Max. *First Among the Hurons*. Montreal: Harvest House, 1973.

Handsome Lake. *The Code of Handsome Lake*. Osweken, Ont.: Iroqrafts, 1983. (Early Iroquois religious leader.)

Harper, Vern. *Following the Red Path: The Native People's Caravan*. Toronto: N.C. Press, 1979. (Toronto educator)

Johnston, Basil. *Ojibway Heritage*. Toronto: McClelland & Stewart, 1976.

_________. *Moose Meat and Wild Rice*. Toronto: McClelland & Stewart, 1978.

_________. *Tales the Elders Told: Ojibway Legends*. Toronto: Royal Ontario Museum, 1981. (Royal Ontario Museum curator and linguist.)

Kinsella, W.P. *The Moccasin Telegram and Other Stories*. Markham, Ont.: Penguin, 1983.

Little Bear, Leroy *et al.*, eds. *Pathways to Determination: Canadian Indians and the Canadian State*. Toronto: University of Toronto, 1983.

Manuel, George and M. Poslums. *The Fourth World: An Indian Reality*. Toronto: Collier-Macmillan, 1974.

Martin, Mungo. *Mungo Martin, Man of Two Cultures*. Sidney, B.C.: Gray's, 1982.

Nowell, Charles J. *Smoke From Their Fires: The Life of a Kwakiutl Chief*. Edited by C.S. Ford. Hamden, Conn.: Archon, 1968.

Nuligak. *I, Nuligak*. Translated by Maurice Meteyer. Toronto: Peter Martin, 1968.

Overvold, Joanne, ed. *Our Métis Heritage: A Portrayal*. Yellowknife: Métis Association of the Northwest Territories, 1976.

Pitseolak, Peter and Dorothy Eber. *People From Our Side: An Inuit Record of Seekooseelak*. Edmonton: Hurtig, 1975.

Redbird, Duke. *We are Métis: A Métis View of the Development of a Native People*. Willowdale: Ontario Métis and Non-Status Indian Association, 1980.

Spradley, James P., ed. *Guests Never Leave Hungry: The Autobiography of James Sewid, a Kwakiutl Indian*. Toronto: Samuel Stevens, 1969.

Tetson, John. *Trapping is My Life*. Toronto: Peter Martin, 1970. (Slavey)

Thompson, Albert E. *Chief Peguis and His Descendants*. Winnipeg: Peguis Publishers, 1973. (Ojibwa)

Thrasher, Anthony A. *Thrasher: Skid Row Eskimo*. Toronto: Griffith House, 1976.

Warner, John A. and Allan Sapp. *A Cree Life: The Art of Alan Sapp*. Vancouver: Douglas & Vancouver, 1977.

Waubageshig (Harvey McCue), ed. *The Only Good Indian: Essays by Canadian Indians*. Toronto: New Press, 1970. (Primarily by Ontario Ojibwa.)

Wuttunnee, William. *Ruffled Feathers: Indians in Canadian Society*. Calgary: Bell Books, 1972. (Businessman)

Archaeology

Fladmark, Knut R., ed. *Fragments of the Past: British Columbia Archaeology in the 1970's*. B.C. Studies, 1981.

MacDonald, George F. and Richard Inglis. *The Dig: An Archaeological Reconstruction of a West Coast Village*. Ottawa: National Museum, 1976.

_________. *Ninstints: Haida World Heritage Site*. Vancouver: University of British Columbia Press, 1983.

McGhee, Robert. *Canadian Arctic Prehistory*. Ottawa: National Museum, 1978.

_________. *The Tuniit: First Explorers of the High Arctic*. Ottawa: National Museum, 1981.

McKay, Alexander G., ed. *New Perspectives in Canadian Archaeology*. Ottawa: The Royal Society of Canada, 1977.

Pettipas, L.F., ed. *Directions in Manitoba Prehistory*. Winnipeg: Association of Manitoba Archaeologists, 1981.

Storck, Peter L. *Ontario Prehistory* (rev. ed.). Toronto: Royal Ontario Museum, 1981.

Tuck, James A. *Newfoundland and Labrador Prehistory*. Ottawa: National Museum, 1976.

_________. *Maritime Provinces Prehistory*. Ottawa: National Museum, 1984.

Wright, James V. *Six Chapters of Canada's Prehistory*. Ottawa: National Museum, 1976.

_________. *Quebec Prehistory*. Ottawa: Van Nostrand Reinhold, 1979.

Art

Ashwell, Reg. *Coast Salish: Their Art, Culture and Legends*. Vancouver: Hancock House, 1981.

Barbeau, Marius. *Art of the Totem*. Vancouver: Hancock House, 1983.

Brodsky, Anne T. *et al.*, eds. *Stone, Bones and Skin: Ritual and Shamanic Art*. Toronto: Artscanada, 1977.

Crumrine, N. Ross and Marjorie M. Halpin. *The Power of Symbols: Masks and Masquerade in the Americas*. Vancouver: University of British Columbia, 1983.

Duff, Wilson. *Images: Stone: B.C.* Toronto: Oxford College, 1975.

Ewers, John C. *Blackfeet: Their Art and Culture*. Vancouver: Hancock House, 1983.

Garfield, Viola and Paul Wingert. *The Tsimshian Indians and Their Arts*. Vancouver: Douglas & McIntyre, 1980.

Gustafson, Paula. *Salish Weaving*. Vancouver: Douglas & McIntyre, 1980.

Halpin, Marjorie. *Totem Poles: An Illustrated Guide*. Vancouver: University of British Columbia, 1981.

Holm, Bill. *Northwest Coast Indian Art: Analysis of Form*. Vancouver: Douglas & McIntyre, 1978.

Kane, Paul. *Wanderings of an Artist Among the Indians*. Edmonton: Hurtig, 1968. (First published in 1859.)

Patterson, Nancy-Lou. *Canadian Art*. Don Mills: Collier-Macmillan, 1972.

Sinclair, Lister and Jack Pollack. *The Art of Norval Morrisseau*. Toronto: Methuen, 1979.

Stewart, Hillary. *Looking at Indian Art of the Northwest Coast*. Vancouver: Douglas & McIntyre, 1979.

Swinton, George. *Sculpture of the Eskimo*. Toronto: McClelland & Stewart, 1982.

Witmer, Robert. *The Musical Life of the Blood Indians*. Ottawa: CES 86, 1982.

Wyatt, Victoria. *Shapes of Their Thoughts: Reflections of Culture Contact in Northwest Coast Indian Art*. Normal: University of Oklahoma, 1984.

Cultural Anthropology

Adams, John. *The Gitskan Potlatch*. Toronto: Holt, Rinehart & Winston, 1973.

Axtell, James, ed. *The Indian Peoples of Eastern America: A Documentary History of the Sexes*. New York: Oxford University, 1981.

Baliksi, Asen. *The Netsilik Eskimo*. Garden City, N.Y.: Natural History, 1970.

Barnett, Homer G. *The Nature and Function of the Potlatch*. Eugene: University of Oregon, 1968.

Boas, Franz. *Kwakiutl Ethnography*. Edited by H. Codere. Chicago: University of Chicago, 1966.

Bock, Philip K. *The Micmac Indians of Restigouche: History and Contemporary Description*. Ottawa: National Museum, 1966.

Briggs, Jean L. *Never in Anger: Portrait of an Eskimo Family*. Cambridge: Harvard University, 1970.

Brody, Hugh. *The People's Land: Eskimo and Whites—The Eastern Arctic*. Markham: Penguin, 1975.

__________. *Maps and Dreams: Indians and the British Columbia Frontier*. Vancouver: Douglas & McIntyre, 1981.

Chance, Norman A., ed. *Conflict in Culture: Problems of Developmental Change Among the Cree*. Ottawa: Saint Paul University, 1968.

Cruikshank, Julie. *Athapaskan Women: Lives and Legends*. Ottawa: CES 57, 1979.

Drucker, Philip and Robert F. Heizer. *To Make My Name Good: A Reexamination of the Southern Kwakiutl Potlatch*. Berkeley: University of California, 1967.

Elias, Peter D. *Metropolis and Hinterland in Northern Manitoba*. Winnipeg: Manitoba Museum of Man and Nature, 1975.

Fenton, William N., ed. *Parker on the Iroquois*. Syracuse, N.Y.: Syracuse University, 1968.

Freeman, Milton, ed. *Inuit Land Use and Occupancy Project*. 3 volumes. Ottawa: Department of Supply and Services, Canada, 1976.

Graburn, Nelson H. *Eskimos of Northern Canada*. 2 volumes. New Haven, Conn.: HRAF Press, 1972.

Guedon, Marie-Françoise. *People of Tetlin, Why are You Singing?* Ottawa: CES 9, 1974.

Gunther, Erna. *Indian Life on the Northwest Coast of North America, as Seen by the Earliest Explorers and Fur Traders*. Chicago: University of Chicago, 1972.

Hawthorn, Harry B., ed. *A Survey of the Contemporary Indians of Canada*. 2 volumes. Ottawa: Department of Indian Affairs and Northern Development, 1966.

Henrikson, George. *Hunters in the Barrens: The Naskapi on the Edge of the White Man's World*. St. John's: Memorial University, 1973.

Hill-Tout, Charles. *The Salish People*. Vancouver: Talonbooks, 1978.

Kenyon, Susan M. *The Kyuquot Way: Nootka*. Ottawa: CES 61, 1981.

Knight, Rolf. *Ecological Factors in Changing Economy and Social Organization Among Rupert House Cree*. Ottawa: National Museum, 1968.

Krause, Aurel. *The Tlingit Indians*. Vancouver: Douglas & McIntyre, 1979.

Landes, Ruth. *The Ojibwa Woman*. New York: W.W. Norton, 1971.

Lafitau, Joseph. *Customs of the American Indians (1724)*. Toronto: The Champlain Society, 1977.

Lithman, Yngve G. *The Community Apart: A Case Study of a Canadian Indian Reserve Community*. Winnipeg: University of Manitoba, 1983.

Mandelbaum, David G. *The Plains Cree*. Regina: Canadian Plains Research Centre, 1979. (First published in 1936.)

McClellan, Catherine. *My Old People Say: An Ethnographic Survey of Southern Yukon Territory*. Ottawa: National Museum, 1975.

McFeat, Tom. *Indians of the North Pacific Coast*. Toronto: McClelland & Stewart, 1966.

McGee, Harold F., ed. *The Native Peoples of Atlantic Canada*. Toronto: McClelland & Stewart, 1974.

Miller, J. and Charles Eastman, ed. *The Tsimshian and their Neighbours on the North Pacific Coast*. Seattle: University of Washington, 1984.

Mozino, Jose Mariano. *Noticias de Nutka: An Account of Nootka Sound in 1792*. Seattle: University of Washington, 1970.

Oberg, Kalvero. *The Social Economy of the Tlingit Indians*. Vancouver: Douglas & McIntyre, 1980.

Osgood, Cornelius. *The Han Indians*. New Haven: Yale University, 1971.

Roberts, Kenneth and Philip Shackleton. *The Canoe: A History of the Craft from Panama to the Arctic*. Toronto: Macmillan, 1983.

Rogers, Edward S. *The Quest for Food and Furs: The Mistassini Cree, 1953–1954*. Ottawa: National Museum, 1973.

Rohner, Ronald P. and Evelyn C. Rohner. *The Kwakiutl Indians of British Columbia*. New York: Hold, Rinehart & Winston, 1970.

Sawchuk, Joe. *The Métis of Manitoba: Reformulation of an Ethnic Identity*. Toronto: Peter Martin, 1978.

Slobodin, Richard. *Métis of the Mackenzie District*. Ottawa: Saint Paul University, 1966.

Smith, Derek G. *Natives and Outsiders: Pluralism in the Mackenzie River Delta, Northwest Territories*. Ottawa: Department of Indian Affairs and Northern Development, 1975.

Stearns, Mary Lee. *Haida Culture in Custody—The Masset Band*. Vancouver: Douglas & McIntyre, 1981.

Stewart, Hilary. *Indian Fishing: Early Methods on the Northwest Coast*. Vancouver: J.J. Douglas, 1977.

__________. *Artifacts of the Northwest Coast Indians*. Rev. ed. Vancouver: Hancock House, 1980.

Stymeist, David H. *Ethnic and Indians: Social Relations in a Northwestern Ontario Town*. Toronto: Peter Martin, 1975.

Tarasoff, Koozma J. *Persistent Ceremonialism: The Plains Cree and Saulteau*. Ottawa: CES 69, 1980.

Tooker, Elizabeth. *An Ethnography of the Huron Indians, 1615–1649*. Midland, Ont.: Huron Historical Development Council, 1967.

Tremblay, Marc-Adelard, ed. *Les Facettes de l'Identité Amérindienne*. Québec: Université Laval, 1976.

Trigger, Bruce G. *The Huron: Farmers of the North*. New York: Holt, Rinehart & Winston, 1969.

Valentine, Victor and Frank G. Vallee, eds. *Eskimo of the Canadian Arctic*. Toronto: McClelland & Stewart, 1968.

Van Stone, James W. *Athapaskan Adaptations: Hunters and Fisherman of Subarctic Forests*. Chicago: Aldine, 1974.

Economics

Bishop, Charles A. *The Northern Ojibwa and the Fur Trade: A Historical and Ecological Study*. Toronto: Holt, Rinehart & Winston, 1974.

Clatworthy, Stewart and Jonathan P. Gunn. *Economic Circumstances of Native People in Selected Metropolitan Centre in Western Canada*. Winnipeg: University of Winnipeg, 1981.

Clatworthy, Stewart and Jeremy Hull. *Native Economic Conditions in Regina and Saskatchewan*. Winnipeg: University of Winnipeg, 1983.

Fields, D. and William Stanbury. *The Economic Impact of the Public Sector Upon the Indian of British Columbia*. Vancouver: University of British Columbia, 1975.

Gonzalez, Ellice B. *Changing Economic Roles of Micmac Men and Women: An Ethnohistorical Analysis*. Canadian Ethnology Service, No. 72. Ottawa: National Museum of Man, 1981.

Grant, Gail. *The Concrete Reserve: Corporate Programs for Indians in the Urban Workplace*. Montreal: Institute for Research on Public Policy, 1983.

Jansen, William H. *Eskimo Economics: Rankin Inlet*. Canadian Ethnology Service, No. 46. Ottawa: National Museum of Man, 1979.

Judd, Carol and Arthur J. Ray, eds. *Old Trails and New Directions: Papers of the Third North American Fur Trade Conference*. Toronto: University of Toronto, 1980.

Knight, Rolf. *Indians at Work: An Informal History of Native Labour in British Columbia, 1858–1930*. Vancouver: New Star, 1978.

Lithman, Yngve G. *The Practice of Under-development and the Theory of Development: the Canadian Indian Case*. Stockholm: University of Stockholm, Anthropology, 1983.

Ray, Arthur J. *Indians in the Fur Trade*. Toronto: University of Toronto, 1974.

Ray, Arthur J. and Donald Freeman. *"Give Us Good Measure": An Economic Analysis of Relations Between the Indians and the Hudson's Bay Company Before 1763*. Toronto: University of Toronto, 1978.

Wills, Richard H. *Conflicting Perceptions: Western Economics and the Great Whale River Cree*. Chicago: Tutorial Press, 1985.

Education

Barman, Jean *et al.*, eds. *Indian Education in Canada: The Legacy*. Vancouver: University of British Columbia Press, 1986.

King, Richard A. *The School at Mopass: The Problem of Identity*. Toronto: Holt, Rinehart & Winston, 1970.

_________. *Native Indians and Schooling in British Columbia: A Handbook for Teachers*. Victoria: University of Victoria, Faculty of Education, 1978. King, C. *The Education of Our Native Children*. Saskatoon: University of Saskatchewan, Indian and Northern Education, 1976.

Ridington, Jillian. *Education of Native People in Manitoba*. Winnipeg: University of Manitoba, Monographs in Education, 1980.

Vincent, Sylvie and Bernard Arcand. *L'image de l'Amérindien dans les manuels scolaires du Québec ou Comment les Québecois ne sont pas des sauvages*. Montréal: Cahiers du Québec/Hetubise HMH, 1979.

Wolcott, Harry T. *A Kwakiutl Village and School*. Toronto: Holt, Rinehart & Winston, 1967.

History

Bailey, Alfred G. *The Conflict of European and Eastern Algonkian Cultures, 1504–1700*. Toronto: University of Toronto, 1969.

Bechard, Henri. *L'Heroique indienne Kateri Takawitha*. Montréal: Fides, 1980.

Chamberlain, J.E. *The Harrowing of Eden: White Attitudes Toward North American Natives*. Toronto: Fitzhenry & Whiteside, 1975.

Crowe, Keith J. *A History of the Original Peoples of Northern Canada*. Montreal: McGill-Queen's University Press, 1974.

Dempsey, Hugh A. *Crowfoot of the Blackfeet*. Edmonton: Hurtig, 1972.

________. *Charcoal's World*. Saskatoon: Prairie Books, 1978.

________. *Red Crow: Warrior Chief*. Saskatoon: Western Prairie Producer Books, 1980.

________. *The Gentle Persuader: A Biography of James Gladstone, Indian Senator*. Saskatoon: Western Producer Prairie Books, 1986.

de Tremaudan, August-H. *Hold High Your Heads: History of the Métis Nation in Western Canada*. Winnipeg: Pemmican, 1982.

Dickason, Olive P. *Louisbourg and the Indians: A Study of Imperial Race Relations*. Ottawa: National Museum, 1976.

________. *The Myth of the Savage and the Beginnings of French Colonialism in the Americas*. Edmonton: University of Alberta, 1984.

Douville, Raymond and Jacques-Donat Casanova. *La Vie quotidienne des Indiens du Canada à l'époque de la colonization française*. Montreal: LRP, 1982.

Fisher, Robin. *Contact and Conflict: Indian-European Relations in British Columbia, 1774–1890*. Vancouver: University of British Columbia, 1977.

Flanagan, Thomas. *Riel and the Rebellion: 1885 Reconsidered*. Saskatoon: Western Producer Prairie Books, 1983.

Francis, Daniel and Toby Morantz. *Partners in Furs: A History of the Fur Trade in Eastern James Bay*. Ottawa: National Museum, 1983.

Fredrickson, N. Jaye and Sandra Gibb. *The Covenant Chain: Indian Ceremonial and Indian Trade Silver*. Ottawa: National Museum, 1980.

Fumoleau, Rene. *As Long as this Land Shall Last: A History of Treaty 8 and Treaty 11, 1870–1939*. Toronto: McClelland & Stewart, 1975.

Gagnon, François-Marc. *Ces hommes dits sauvages: l'Histoire fascinante d'un préjuge qui remonte aux premiers découvreurs du Canada*. Montreal: Libre Expression, 1984.

Getty, Ian and A.S. Lussier, eds. *As Long as the Sun Shines and Water Flows: A Reader in Canadian Native Studies*. Vancouver: University of British Columbia, 1983.

Getty, Ian and Donald B. Smith, eds. *One Century Later: Western Canadian Reserve Indians Since Treaty 7*. Vancouver: University of British Columbia, 1978.

Gough, Barry M. *Gunboat Frontier: British Maritime Authority and Northwest Coast Indians, 1846–1890*. Vancouver: University of British Columbia, 1983.

Graham, Elizabeth. *Medicine Man to Missionary: Missionaries as Agents of Change Among the Indians of Southern Ontario, 1784–1867*. Toronto: Peter Martin, 1975.

Grant, John. *Moon of Wintertime: Missionaries and the Indians of Canada in Encounter since 1534*. Toronto: University of Toronto, 1984.

Hantzsch, Bernard A. *My Life Among the Eskimos: The Baffin Journals, 1909–11*. Saskatoon: University of Saskatchewan, 1977.

Heard, J. Norman. *White into Red: A Study of the Assimilation of White Persons Captured by Indians*. Metuchen, N.J.: Scarecrow, 1973.

Heidenreich, Conrad. *Huronia: A History and Geography of the Huron Indians, 1600–1650*. Toronto: McClelland & Stewart, 1971.

Jaenen, Cornelius J. *Friend and Foe: Aspects of French-Amerindian Cultural Contact in the Sixteenth and Seventeenth Centuries*. Toronto: McClelland & Stewart, 1976.

Keller, Betty. *Pauline: A Biography of Pauline Johnson*. Vancouver: Douglas & McIntyre, 1981.

Kidd, Bruce. *Tom Longboat*. Don Mills: Fitzhenry & Whiteside, 1980.

LaViolette, F.E. *The Struggle for Survival: Indian Cultures and the Protestant Ethnic in British Columbia*. Toronto: University of Toronto, 1973.

Leacock, Eleanor and Nancy O. Lurie, eds. *North American Indians in Historical Perspective*. New York: Random House, 1971.

Lillard, Charles. *Warriors of the North Pacific Coast: Missionary Accounts of the Northwest Coast . . . 1829–1900*. Victoria: Sono Nis Press, 1984.

Lussier, Antoine S. and D. Bruce Sealey, eds. *The Other Native: The Métis*. 3 volumes. Winnipeg: Métis Federation Press, 1978.

MacEwan, Grant. *Tatanga Mani: Walking Buffalo of the Stonies*. Edmonton: Hurtig, 1969.

_________. *Sitting Bull: Ten Years in Canada*. Edmonton: Hurtig, 1973.

_________. *Métis Makers of History*. Saskatoon: Western Producer Prairie Books, 1981.

McGee, H.H. *The Native Peoples of Canada: A History of Indian-European Relations*. Ottawa: Carleton University, 1983.

Morantz, Toby. *An Ethnohistorical Study of Eastern James Bay, Cree Social Organization, 1700–1850*. Ottawa: CES 88, 1983.

Muise, D.A., ed. *Approaches to Native History in Canada*. Ottawa: National Museum, History Division, 1977.

Patterson, E. Palmer. *The Canadian Indian: A History Since 1500*. Don Mills: Collier-MacMillan, 1972.

Pendergast, James F. and Bruce G. Trigger. *Cartier's Hochelaga and the Dawson Site*. Montreal: McGill-Queen's University Press, 1972.

Ross, W Gillies. *Whaling and Eskimos: Hudson Bay 1860–1915*. Ottawa: CES10, 1975.

Rowe, Frederick W.. *Extinction: The Beothuks of Newfoundland*. Toronto: University of Toronto, 1977.

Sealey, D. Bruce and Antoine S. Lussier. *The Métis: Canada's Forgotten People*. Winnipeg: Manitoba Métis Federation Press, 1975.

Smith, D.B. *Le Sauvage: The Native People in Quebec Historical Writing on the Heroic Period (1534–1663) of New France*. Ottawa: National Museum, History Division, 1974.

Sprague, D.M. and R.P. Frye. *The Genealogy of the First Métis Nation: The Development and Dispersal of the Red River Settlement, 1820–1900*. Winnipeg: Pemmican Publications, 1974.

Such, Peter. *Vanished Peoples: The Archaic, Dorset and Beothuk People of Newfoundland*. Toronto: NC Press, 1978.

Trigger, Bruce G. *The Children of the Aataensic: A History of the Huron People to 1660*. 2 volumes. Montreal: McGill-Queen's University, 1976.

_________. *Natives and Newcomers: Canada's Heroic Age Reconsidered*. Kingston: McGill-Queen's University Press, 1985.

Turner, C. Frank. *Across the Medicine Line: The Epic Confrontation Between Sitting Bull and North-West Mounted Police*. Toronto: McClelland & Stewart, 1977.

Upton, Leslie. *Micmacs and Colonialists: Indian-White Relations in the Maritime Provinces, 1713–1867*. Vancouver: University of British Columbia, 1979.

Van Den Brink, J.H. *The Haida Indians: Cultural Change Mainly Between 1876–1970*. Leiden: E.J. Brill, 1974.

Van Kirk, Sylvia. *Many Tender Ties: Women in Fur-Trade Society, 1670–1870*. Winnipeg: Watson & Dwyer, 1980.

Walker, Alexander. *An Account of a Voyage to the Northwest Coast of North America in 1785 and 1786*. Vancouver: Douglas & McIntyre, 1982.

Woodcock, George. *Gabriel Dumont*. Don Mills: Fitzhenry & Whiteside, 1978.

Linguistics, Literature

Burnaby, Barbara. *Languages and their Roles in Educating Native Children*. Toronto: OISE, 1980.

———. *Language in Education Among Canadian Native Peoples*. Toronto: OISE, 1982.

Christian, Jane and Peter M. Gardner. *The Individual in Northern Dene Thought and Communication*. Canada Ethnology Service, No. 35. Ottawa: National Museum of Man, 1977.

Clark, George. *Indian Legends of Canada*. Toronto: McClelland & Stewart, 1977.

Coatsworth, Emerson S. and David Coatsworth, eds. *The Adventures of Nanabush: Ojibway Indian Tales*. Toronto: Doubleday, 1979.

Colombo, John Robert, ed. *Poems of the Inuit*. Ottawa: Oberon Press, 1981.

———. *Windigo: An Anthology of Fact and Fantastic Fiction*. Saskatoon: Western Producer Prairie Books, 1982.

———. *Songs of the Indian*. Ottawa: Oberon Press, 1983.

Cook, Eung-Do and Jonathan Kaye, eds. *Linguistic Studies of Native Canada*. Vancouver: University of British Columbia, 1978.

Cooke, Katie. *Images of Indians Held by Non-Indians: A Review of Current Canadian Research*. Ottawa: Department of Indian Affairs and Northern Development, 1984.

MacDonald, George F. *In the Shadow of the Raven: The Raven Myth in Polar Cultures*. Vancouver: University of British Columbia, 1983.

Maud, Ralph. *A Guide to B.C. Indian Myth and Legend*. Vancouver: Talonbooks, 1982.

McGrath, Robin. *Canadian Inuit Literature*. Ottawa: CES 94, 1984.

Michelson, Karin. *Three Stories in Oneida*. Ottawa: CES 73, 1981.

Monkman, Leslie. *A Native Heritage: Images of the Indian in English-Canadian Literature*. Toronto: University of Toronto, 1981.

Mowat, William and Christine Mowat, eds. *Native Peoples in Canadian Literature*. Toronto: Gage, 1975.

Nelson, Richard K. *Shadow of the Hunter: Stories of Eskimo Life*. Toronto: University of Toronto, 1980.

Niatum, Duane, ed. *Carriers of the Dream Wheel: Contemporary Native American Poetry*. Toronto: Fitzhenry & Whiteside, 1981.

Petrone, Penny, ed. *First People, First Voices*. Toronto: University of Toronto, 1983.

Preston, Richard J. *Cree Narrative: Expressing the Personal Meanings of Events*. Canadian Ethnology Service, No. 30. Ottawa: National Museum of Man, 1975.

Rothenberg, James, ed. *Shaking the Pumpkin: Traditional Poetry of the Indian North Americans*. Garden City, N.Y.: Doubleday, 1972.

Scollon, Ronald. *The Context of the Informant Narrative Performance: Fort Chipewyan, Alberta*. Canadian Ethnology Services, No. 52. Ottawa: National Museum of Man, 1979.

Wood, Marion. *Spirits, Heroes and Hunters from North American Indian Mythology*. Vancouver: Douglas & McIntyre, 1983.

Medicine

Bureau of Nutritional Sciences. *Nutrition Canada: The Indian Survey Report*. Ottawa: Health and Welfare, 1975.

Jilek, Wolfgang G. *Indian Healing: Shamanic Ceremonialism in the Pacific Northwest Today*. Surrey, B.C.: Hancock House, 1982.

Large, Richard G. *Drums and Scalpel: From Native Healers to Physicians on the Northwest Coast*. Vancouver: Mitchell Press, 1968.

Shephard, R.J. and S. Itoh, eds. *Circumpolar Health*. Toronto: University of Toronto, 1976.

Vogel, Virgil J. *American Indian Medicine*. New York: Ballantine Books, 1975.

Politics, Law

Asch, Michael. *Home and Native Land: Aboriginal Rights and the Canadian Constitution*. Toronto: Methuen, 1984.

Bartlett, Richard. *Indians and Taxation in Canada*. Saskatoon: University of Saskatchewan, 1980.

Berger, Mr. Justice Thomas R. *Northern Frontier, Northern Homeland: The Report of the Mackenzie Valley Pipeline Inquiry*. 2 volumes. Ottawa: Department of Supply and Services, Canada, 1977.

Burke, James. *Paper Tomahawks: From Red Tape to Red Power*. Winnipeg: Queenston House, 1976. (Manitoba Indian Politics)

Cumming, Peter A. and Neil H. Mickenberg. *Native Rights in Canada*. Toronto: CASNP, 1980.

Daniel, R. *A History of Native Claims and Processes in Canada*. Ottawa: Department of Indian Affairs and Northern Development, 1980.

Dosman, Edgar. *The National Interest: The Politics of Northern Development, 1968–75*. Toronto: McClelland & Stewart, 1975.

Driben, Paul and Robert S. Trudeau. *When Freedom is Lost: The Dark Side of the Relationship between Government and the Fort Hope Band*. Toronto: University of Toronto, 1983.

Dyck, Noel, ed. *Indigenous Peoples and the Nation State: Fourth-World Politics in Canada, Australia and Norway*. St. John's: Memorial University, 1984.

Gagnon, JoAnn. *Le régime de chasse, de pêche et de trappage et les conventions du Quebec nordique*. Quebec City: Laval University, 1982.

Hawley, Donna Lea. *The Indian Act Annotated: Indian Law in Canada*. Agincourt, Ont.: Carswell, 1984.

House of Commons. *Indian Self-Government in Canada*. Ottawa, 1983.

La Rusic, Ignatius E. *et al. Negotiating a Way of Life: Initial Cree Experience with the Administrative Structure Arising from the James Bay Agreement*. Ottawa: Department of Indian Affairs and Northern Development, 1979.

McCardle, Bennett E. *Indian History and Claims: A Research Handbook*. Ottawa: Department of Indian Affairs and Northern Development, 1982.

McCullum, Hugh *et al. This Land is Not for Sale*. Toronto: Anglican Book Centre, 1977.

_________. *Moratorium: Justice, Energy, the North, and the Native People*. Toronto: Anglican Book Centre, 1977.

McNell, Kent. *Indian Hunting, Trapping and Fishing Rights in The Prairie Provinces of Canada*. Saskatoon: University of Saskatchewan, Native Law Centre, 1983.

Miller, Kahn-Tineta and Robert Lerchs. *Historical Development of the Indian Act*. Ottawa: Department of Indian Affairs and Northern Development, 1975.

Ministry of the Solicitor General. *Native Peoples and Justice: Reports on the National Conference*. Ottawa: Information Canada, 1975.

Morrison, William R. *A Survey of the History and Claims of the Native Peoples of Northern Canada*. Ottawa: Department of Indian Affairs and Northern Development, 1983.

Morse, Bradford W. *Indian Tribal Courts in the United States: A Model for Canada?* Saskatoon: University of Saskatchewan, Native Law Centre, 1980.

_________. *Aboriginal Peoples and the Law: Indian, Métis and Inuit Rights in Canada*. Ottawa: Carleton University Press, 1985.

O'Malley, Martin. *The Past and Future Land: An Account of the Berger Inquiry into the Mackenzie Valley Pipeline*. Toronto: Peter Martin, 1976.

Ponting, J. Rick and Roger Gibbons. *Out of Irrelevance: A Socio-political Introduction to Indian Affairs in Canada*. Toronto: Butterworths, 1980.

_________. *Arduous Journey: Canadian Indians and Decolonization*. Toronto: McClelland and Stewart, 1986.

Price, Richard, ed. *The Spirit of the Alberta Indian Treaties*. Edmonton: Institute for Research on Public Policy, 1979.

Richardson, Boyce. *James Bay: The Plot to Drown the North Woods*. San Francisco: Sierra Club, 1972.

_________ . *Strangers Devour the Land: The Cree Hunters of the James Bay Area Versus Premier Bourassa and the James Bay Development Corporation*. New York: Alfred A. Knopf, 1975.

Ryan, Joan. *Wall of Words: The Betrayal of the Urban Indian*. Toronto: Peter Martin, 1979.

Savard, Remi and Jean-Rene Proulx. *Canada derrière l'épopée, les autochtones*. Montreal: L'hexagone, 1982.

Slattery, Brian. *Ancestral Lands, Alien Laws: Judicial Perspectives on Aboriginal Title*. Saskatoon: University of Saskatchewan, Native Law Centre, 1983.

Smith, Derek G., ed. *Canadian Indians and the Law: Selected Documents, 1663–1972*. Toronto: McClelland & Stewart, 1975.

Tanner, Adrian, ed. *The Politics of Indianness: Case Studies of Native Ethnopolitics in Canada*. St. John's: Memorial University, 1983.

Weaver, Sally M. *Medicine and Politics Among the Grand River Iroquois*. Ontario: National Museums, 1972.

_________ . *Making Indian Policy: The Hidden Agenda, 1968–1970*. Toronto: University of Toronto press, 1981.

Zlotkin, Norman K. *Unfinished Business: Aboriginal Peoples and the 1983 Constitutional Conference*. Kingston: Queen's University, Institute of Intergovernmental Relations, 1983.

Religion

Dewdney, Selwyn H. *The Sacred Scrolls of the Southern Ojibway*. Toronto: University of Toronto Press, 1975.

Fenton, William N. *Masked Medicine Societies of the Iroquois*. Osweken, Ont.: Iroqrafts, 1984.

Goldman, Irving. *The Mouth of Heaven: Introduction to Kwakiutl Religious Thought*. New York: John Wiley & Sons, 1975.

Landes, Ruth. *Ojibwa Religion and the Midewiwin*. Madison: University of Wisconsin, 1968.

Schaeffer, Claude E. *Blackfoot Shaking Tent*. Calgary: Glenbow-Alberta Institute, 1969.

Tanner, Adrian. *Bringing Home Animals: Religious Ideology and Mode of Production of the Mistassini Cree Hunters*. St. John's: Memorial University, 1979.

Tedlock, Dennis and Barbara Tedlock, eds. *Teachings from the American Earth: Indian Religion and Philosophy*. New York: Liveright.

Vecsey, Christopher. *Traditional Ojibwa Religion and its Historical Changes*. Philadelphia: American Philosophical Society, 1983.

Walens, Stanley. *Feasting with Cannibals: An Essay on Kwakiutl Cosmology*. Princeton: University of Princeton Press, 1981.

Wallace, Anthony F. *The Death and Rebirth of the Seneca*. Toronto: Random House, 1972.

Waugh, Earle H. and H.D. Prithibul, eds. *Native Religious Traditions*. Waterloo: Wilfrid Laurier, 1979.

Sociology, Social Work

Birkenmayer, A.C. and Stan Jolly. *The Native Inmate in Ontario*. Toronto: Ministry of Correctional Services, 1981.

Braroe, Niels W. *Indian and White: Self-Image and Interaction in a Canadian Plains Community*. Stanford: Stanford University, 1975.

Breton, Raymond and Gail Grant, eds. *The Dynamics of Government Programs for Urban Indians in the Prairie Provinces*. Montreal: Institute for Research on Public Policy, 1984.

Brody, Hugh. *Indians on Skid Row*. Ottawa: Information Canada, 1971. (Edmonton)

Dosman, Edgar J. *Indians: The Urban Dilemma*. Toronto: McClelland & Stewart, 1972. (Saskatoon)

Elliot, Jean L., ed. *Minority Canadians: Native Peoples*. Scarborough: Prentice-Hall of Canada, 1971.

Guillemin, Jeanne. *Urban Renegades: The Cultural Strategy of American Indians*. New York: Columbia University Press, 1975. (Micmacs in Boston)

Hornby, Roger and Richard H. Dana, Jr., eds. *Mni Wakan and the Sioux: Respite, Release and Recreation*. Brandon, Man.: Justin, 1984. (Alcoholism)

Johnston, Patrick. *Native Children and the Child Welfare System*. Toronto: James Lorimer, 1983.

Lewis, Claudia. *Indian Families of the Northwest Coast: The Impact of Change*. Toronto: McClelland & Stewart, 1970.

Ministry of Culture and Recreation. *Métis and Non-Status Indians of Ontario*. 2 volumes. Toronto: The Ministry, 1980.

Nagler, Mark. *Indians in the City*. Ottawa: Saint Paul University, 1971. (Toronto)

Robertson, Heather. *Reservations Are for Indians*. Toronto: James Lewis & Samuel, 1970.

Stanbury, William T. and Siegel. *Success and Failure: Indians in Urban Society*. Vancouver: University of British Columbia, 1975.

Vincent, David. *An Evaluation of the Indian-Métis Urban Problem*. Winnipeg: University of Winnipeg, 1970.

List of Contributors

Michael Asch formerly chaired the Department of Anthropology, University of Alberta, where he teaches Anthropology.

Dennis Bartels teaches Anthropology at Sir Wilfred Grenfell College of the Memorial University of Newfoundland, where he and Alice Bartels have been active in the Micmac struggle for recognition.

Jennifer S.H. Brown is an Anthropologist who teaches History at the University of Winnipeg. She is the author of *Strangers in Blood* and editor, with Jacqueline Peterson, of *The New Peoples.*

Jean-Philippe Chartrand is a postgraduate student of Anthropology at McMaster University.

Leland Donald chairs the Department of Anthropology, University of Victoria where, with Donald Mitchell, he has conducted a long-term study of stratification among indigenous societies of the North Pacific Coast.

Harvey Feit is the author of numerous studies of the Cree of Northern Quebec; he teaches Anthropology at McMaster University.

Jo-Anne Fiske teaches Anthropology at Mount Saint Vincent University.

John E. Foster is the author of numerous studies of relationships between Indians and fur-trading companies. He teaches History at the University of Alberta.

Brian Given is an Anthropologist who teaches at Carleton University.

Harriet Gorham has just completed a study of the "Mixed Bloods" of the Great Lakes region.

Susan Johnston is a past President of the Ontario Archaeological Society; she resides in Ottawa.

Loraine Littlefield is a postgraduate student of Anthropology at the University of British Columbia; she resides in Richmond, British Columbia.

Eleanor Leacock died in the spring of 1987. She was a professor of Anthropology at the City College of the City University of New York, and the author of *Myths of Male Dominance*, and (with Richard Lee) the editor of *Politics and History in Band Societies*, in which there is more on the Innu of Labrador.

James Andrew McDonald is Assistant Curator in the Department of Ethnology of the Royal Ontario Museum; he resides in Toronto.

John A. Price taught Anthropology and Native Studies at York University, and founded the Canadian Society for Applied Anthropology. He died in 1988.

George Herman Sprenger is a freelance Anthropologist based in Edmonton. He has taught at several universities in Western Canada, including Brandon University, Athabasca University, and the University of Manitoba.

Adrian Tanner teaches Anthropology at the Memorial University of Newfoundland, in St. John's. Like the Bartels, he has been active in the Micmac struggle for recognition as indigenous to Newfoundland. With Harvey Feit and Eleanor Leacock, he contributed to *Cultural Ecology*, a precursor of this volume.

John L. Tobias teaches History at Red Deer College, where he is Dean of the Liberal and Applied Arts Division of the College.

Bibliography

Afonja, S. "Changing Modes of Production and the Sexual Division of Labour among the Yoruba." *Signs: Journal of Woman in Culture and Society*, vol. 7, no. 2, 1981.

Anger, Dorothy C. "The Micmacs of Newfoundland: A Resurgent Culture." *Culture*, vol. 2, no. 1, 1981.

Annales de l'Association de la Propagation de la Foi. Paris: La Librairie Ecclesiastique du Rusand, n.d.

Ardener, Shirley. "Sexual Insult and Female Militancy." *Man* 8, 1973.

Barrados, M. and M.B. von Dine. *Multilingualism of Natives in the Mackenzie District.* Ottawa: Department of Indian Affairs and Northern Development, North of 60° Publications, 1977.

Bartels, Dennis. "Time Immemorial? A Research Note on Micmacs in Newfoundland." *Newfoundland Quarterly*, vol. 75, no. 3, 1979.

Barth, Fredrik. *Models of Social Organization.* Occasional Paper No. 23. Royal Anthropological Institute of Great Britain and Ireland, 1966.

_________. *Ethnic Groups and Boundaries.* Boston: Little, Brown and Co., 1969.

Bayley, Denis. *A Londoner in Rupert's Land; Thomas Bunn of the Hudson's Bay Company.* Sussex, England: Moore and Tillyer, 1969.

Beal, Bob and Rod MacLeod. *Prairie Fire: The 1885 North-West Rebellion.* Edmonton: Hurtig Press, 1984.

Bell, E. *A New Vancouver Journal on the Discovery of Puget Sound by a Member of the Chatham's Crew.* Edited by E. Meany. Seattle, 1915.

Beresford, W. *A Voyage Round the World: But More Particularly to the Northwest Coast of America; Performed in 1785–88.* Edited by Capt. Dixon and Capt. Portlock. London, 1789.

Berger, Mr. Justice T. *Northern Frontier, Northern Homeland: The Report of the Mackenzie Valley Pipeline Inquiry*, Vol. I and II. Ottawa: Ministry of Supply and Services Canada, 1977.

Bieder, Robert E. "Scientific Attitudes toward Indian Mixed-bloods in Early Nineteenth Century America." *Journal in Ethnic Studies*, vol. 8, no. 7, 1980.

Bishop, C. *The Journal and Letters of Capt. Charles Bishop on the Northwest Coast of America, in the Pacific and in the New South Wales 1794–1799.* Edited by M. Rowe. Cambridge: Hakluyt Society, 1967.

Black, F.L., F. De Pinheiro, W.J. Hierholzer, and R.V. Lee. "Epidemiology of Infectious Disease: The Example of Measles." *CIBA Foundation Symposium* 49, new series, 1976.

Black, W.A. "Fur Trapping in the Mackenzie River Delta." *Geographical Bulletin* 16, 1961.

Bliss, L.C. "Report of the Mackenzie Valley Pipeline Inquiry, Volume Two: An Environmental Critique." *Musk-ox* 21, 1978.

Boas, Franz. Fifth *Report on the Northwestern Tribes of Canada.* Report of the British Association for the Advancement of Science. London: The British Association for the Advancement of Science, 1889.

_________. *Tsimshian Mythology.* Annual Report of the Bureau of American Ethnology, 1909–1910. Washington: Government Printing Office, 1916.

_________. *Kwakiutl Ethnography.* Edited by Helen Codere. Chicago: University of Chicago Press, 1966.

Bone, Robert M. "The Number of Eskimos: An Arctic Enigma." *Polar Record*, vol. 16, no. 103, 1973.

Boone, Nicholas. *Military Discipline*. Boston, 1701.

Born, David O. *Eskimo Education and the Trauma of Social Change*. Ottawa: Northern Science Research Group, 1970.

Borré, K. and B. Winterhalder. "Cost-Effectiveness of Local and Imported Foods in a Boreal Forest Community." 1983, unpublished paper.

Bouton, N. *et al. New Hampshire State Papers*. 40 volumes. Manchester, N.H., 1867–1941.

Boxhill, Walton O. "1981 Census Data on the Native Peoples of Canada." *Canadian Statistical Review*, vol. 60, no. 2, 1985.

Bradford, Wm. and E. Winslow. *Mourt's Relation or Journal of the Plantation at Plymouth, 1622*. Reprint. New York: Garret Press, 1969.

British Columbia. Sessional Papers. *Metlakatla Inquiry: Report of the Commissioners*. Victoria: Government Printer, 1885.

British Columbia. Sessional Papers. *Report of Conferences between the Provincial Government and Indian Delegates for Port Simpson and Nass River*. Victoria: Government Printer, 1887.

Brody, H. *The People's Land: Eskimos and Whites in the Eastern Arctic*. Harmondsworth: Penguin Books, 1975.

Brown, Alexander. *The Genesis of the United States*. Vol. II. Boston, 1890.

Brown, Jennifer S.H. *Strangers in Blood: Fur Trade Company Families in Indian Country*. Vancouver: University of British Columbia Press, 1980.

________. "Woman as Centre and Symbol in the Emergence of Métis Communities." *Canadian Journal of Native Studies*, vol 3, no. 1, 1983.

Brown, Judith. "Economic Organization and the Position of Women Among the Iroquois." *Ethnohistory* 17, 1970.

Bryce, P.H. *Report on the Indian Schools of Manitoba and North-West Territories*. Ottawa: Department of the Interior, 1907.

Butler, William Francis. *The Great Lone Land*. Vermont: Rutledge, 1970.

Caamano, J. "Extracto Del Diario, 1792." *British Columbia Historical Quarterly* 2, 1938.

Campbell, Maria. *Halfbreed*. Toronto: McClelland and Stewart, 1973.

The Canadian Encyclopedia. Edmonton: Hurtig, 1985.

Canadian Journal of Native Studies, vol. 3, no. 1, 1983. Appeared as a special issue on the Métis since 1870, and contains useful articles on Métis history, claims, language, and other topics.

Carver, Jonathan. *Travels Through the Interior Parts of North America in the Years 1766, 1767, and 1768*. Minneapolis: Ross & Hines, 1956.

Chambers, J and P. Trudgill. *Dialectology*. New York: Cambridge University Press, 1980.

Chaput, Donald. "The 'Misses Nolin' of Red River." *The Beaver* 306, 1975.

Charlevoix, P.F.X *History and General Description of New France*. Translated by Dr. J.G. Shea, 2 volumes. London: Francis Edwards, 1902.

Clifton, James A. "Personal and Ethnic Identity on the Great Lakes Frontier: The Case of Billy Caldwell, Anglo-Canadian." *Ethnohistory* 25, 1978.

Codere, Helen. *Fighting with Property, A Study of Kwakiutl Potlatching and Warfare 1792–1930*. Monograph of the American Ethnological Society 18. Seattle and London: University of Washington Press, 1950.

Coles, John. *Archaeology by Experiment*. London: Hutchinson University Library, 1973.

Collins, J. "Growth of Class Distinctions and Political Authority among the Skagit Indians during the Contact Period." *American Anthropologist* 52, 1950.

Colson, Elizabeth. *The Makah Indians*. Manchester: Manchester University Press, 1953.

Cook, J. *A Voyage to the Pacific Ocean Performed Under the Direction of Captains Cooke, Clerke and Gore, in His Majesty's Ships the Resolution and the Discovery in the Years 1776, 1777, 1778, 1779, and 1780*. 3 volumes. London, 1784.

Cook, S.F. "The Significance of Disease in the Extinction of New England Indians." *Human Biology*, vol. 45, no. 173 (n.d.).

Corrothers, A.W.P., J. Beetz, and J.M. Parker. "Report of the Advisory Commission on the Development of Government." Vol. I. Submitted to the Department of Northern Affairs and Natural Resources, 1966. Mimeographed.

Coues, E., ed. *The Manuscript Journals of Alexander Henry and David Thompson*. Vol. II. Minnesota: Ross and Hines, 1965.

Cox, Bruce. "Land Rights of the Slavey Indians at Hay River, Northwest Territories." *Western Canadian Journal of Anthropology* 2, 1970.

________. "Modernization Among the Mistassini-Waswanipi Cree: A Comment." *Canadian Review of Sociology and Anthropology* 7, 1971.

________. *Cultural Ecology: Readings on the Canadian Indians and Eskimos*. Toronto: Macmillan Company of Canada, 1978.

________. "Comments on Optimal Foraging Theory in Anthropology." *Current Anthropology* 24, 1983.

Cox, R. *The Columbia River*. Norman: University of Oklahoma Press, 1957.

Crespi, J.M. *Missionary Explorer on the Pacific Coast 1769-74*. Edited by H.E. Bolton. Berkeley: University of California Press, 1927.

Crosby, A.W. "Virgin Soil Epidemics as a Factor in the Aboriginal Depopulation in America." *William and Mary Quarterly* 33, 1976.

Crowe, K. *A History of the Original Peoples of Northern Canada*. Montreal: McGill-Queen's University Press, 1974.

Culleton, Beatrice. *In Search of April Raintree*. Winnipeg: Pemmican Publications, 1983.

Davies, K.G., ed. *Letters from Hudson's Bay, 1703–40*. London, 1965.

de la Pena, Fray Tomas. *Diary of Fray Tomas de la Pena kept during the voyage of the Santiago—dated 28 August 1774*. Edited by G.B. Griffin. The Sutro Collection, Historical Society of California. Los Angeles: Franklin Press, 1891.

Dene National Office. "Public Government for the People of the North." Yellowknife: Dene Nation, 1981.

Department of Fisheries. *Annual Narrative*. Ottawa: Government Printer, 1878.

Department of Indian Affairs. *Indian Conditions. A Survey*. Ottawa: The Department, 1980.

Department of Indian Affairs and Northern Development. *A Survey of the Contemporary Indians of Canada. A Report on Economic, Political, and Educational Needs and Policies*. Edited by H.B. Hawthorn. Ottawa: Information Canada, 1966.

Department of Indian Affairs and Northern Development. *Oil and Gas North of 60: A Report of Activities in 1968*. Ottawa: Queen's Printer, 1969.

Department of Indian Affairs and Northern Development. *Oil and Gas North of 60: A Report of Activities in 1969*. Ottawa: Queen's Printer, 1970.

Department of Indian Affairs and Northern Development. "Brief to the Special Senate Committee on Poverty." In *Proceedings of the Special Senate Committee on Poverty*. No. 14, 20 January 1970. Ottawa: Queen's Printer, 1970.

Department of Indian and Northern Affairs. *The Inuit*. Ottawa: North of 60° Publication, 1970.

Department of Northern Affairs and Natural Resources. *Northern Education: Ten Years of Progress*. Ottawa: The Department, 1961.

de Tremaudan, A.-H. *Hold High Your Heads*. Translated by Elizabeth Maguet. Originally published as *History of the Métis Nation in Western Canada*, 1936. Winnipeg: Pemmican Publication, 1982.

de Widersprach-Thor, Martine. "The Equation of Copper." *Papers from the Sixth Annual Congress, 1979, Canadian Ethnology Society*. National Museum of Man Mercury Series. Canadian Ethnology Service, 78, 1981.

Dixon, C.W. *Smallpox*. London: 1962.
Dobbin, Murray. *The One-and-a-half-Men: The Story of Jim Brady and Malcolm Norris*. Vancouver: New Star Books, 1981.
Dobyns, H.F. "Estimating Aboriginal Population. 1. An Appraisal of Techniques with a New Hemisphere Estimate." *Current Anthropology* 7, 1966.
Donald, Leland. "Was Nuu-chah-nulth-aht (Nootka) Society Based on Slave Labour?" In *The Development of Political Organization in Native North America; 1979 Proceedings of the American Ethnology Society*, Elizabeth Tooker Edition. Washington, D.C.: American Ethnological Society, 1983.
________. "Captive or Slave? A Comparison of Northeastern and Northwestern North America by Means of Captivity Narratives." *Culture* V, 1985.
Douaud, Patrick C. *Ethnolinguistic Profile of the Canadian Métis*. National Museum of Man, Mercury Series, Canadian Ethnology Service Paper, no. 99. Ottawa, 1985.
Drucker, Philip. *Indians of the Northwest Coast*. Natural History Press, 1955.
________. *Cultures of the North Pacific Coast*. Scranton, PA: Chandler Publishing Company, 1965.
Dunning, Robert W. *Social and Economic Change among the Northern Ojibwa*. Toronto: University of Toronto Press, 1959.
Eggan, F., ed. *Social Anthropology of North American Tribes*. Chicago: University of Chicago Press, 1955.
Enloe, E. *Ethnic Conflict and Political Development*. Boston: Little, Brown and Co., 1973.
Erickson, Kai T. *Wayward Puritans: A Study in the Sociology of Deviance*. New York: John Wiley & Sons, 1966.
Espinoza, J. *A Spanish Voyage to Vancouver and the Northwest Coast in the Year 1792 by the Schooner 'Sutil' and 'Mexicane' to Explore the Strait of Fuca*. Translated by C. Jane. London: Argonaut Press, 1930.
Etienne, M. "Women and Men, Cloth and Colonization: The Transformation of Production Distribution Relations among the Baule." *Cahiers d'etude africaines*, vol. 65, no. 1, 1977.
Etienne, Mona and E. Leacock, eds. *Women and Colonization: Anthropological Perspectives*. New York: Praeger, 1980.
Ewers, J.C. "The Influence of Epidemics on the Indian Populations and Cultures of Texas." *Plains Anthropology* 18, 1973.
Feit, Harvey A. "Negotiating Recognition of Aboriginal Rights." *Canadian Journal of Anthropology* 12, 1980.
Ferguson, R.B., ed. *Warfare, Culture and Environment*. New York: Academic Press, 1984.
Fernandez-Kelly, M.P. "Development and the Sexual Division of Labor: An Introduction." *Signs* 7, 1981.
Flanagan, Thomas. *Riel and the Rebellion: 1885 Reconsidered*. Saskatoon: Western Producer Prairie Books, 1983.
Fleurie, C. *A Voyage Round the World Performed During the Years 1790–92 by Etienne Marchand*. Vol. 2. London, 1801.
Foster, John E., ed. *The Developing West*. Edmonton: University of Alberta Press, 1983.
Franchere, G. *Narrative of a Voyage to the Northwest Coast of America in the Years 1811, 12, 13, 14*. Translated and edited by J. Huntington. Redfield, N.Y., 1854.
Francis, Daniel and Toby Morantz. *Partners in Furs: A History of the Fur Trade in Eastern James Bay 1600–1870*. Kingston and Montreal: McGill-Queen's University Press, 1983.
Franklin, J. ed. *Narratives of New Netherlands 1609–1664*. New York, 1909.
Fraser, B. "Why Nanook of the North Still Can't Read." Ottawa: Department of Northern Affairs and Natural Resources, 1967.

Freeman, M.R., ed. *Proceedings: First International Symposium on Renewable Resources and the Economy of the North.* Ottawa: Association of Canadian Universities for Northern Studies, 1981.

Friedl, E. *Women and Men: An Anthropologist's View.* New York: Holt, Rinehart and Winston, 1975.

Friesen, John W. and Terry Lusty. *The Métis of Canada: An Annotated Bibliography.* Toronto: OISE Press, 1980.

Fuller, W.A. "Of Conservation and Mysticism, Democracy and Things." *Arctic*, vol. 39, no. 1, 1979.

Fumoleau, René. *As Long as this Land Shall Last: A History of Treaty 8 and Treaty 11, 1870–1939.* Toronto: McClelland and Stewart, 1974.

Garfield, Viola. "Tsimshian Clan and Society." *University of Washington Publications in Anthropology* 7, 1939.

Garfield, Viola and Paul S. Wingert, eds. *The Tsimshian Indians and Their Arts.* Seattle: University of Washington Press, 1966.

Gates, Charles M. and Grace Lee Nute, eds. *Five Fur Traders of the Northwest.* 1933. Reprint. St. Paul: Minnesota Historical Society, 1965.

Getty, I.A.L. and A.S. Lussier, eds. *As Long as the Sun Shines and Water Flows.* Vancouver, 1983.

Giraud, Marcel. *Métis in the Canadian West.* Translated by George Woodcock. Edmonton: University of Alberta, 1986.

Given, Brian J. " A Study of European Weapons Technology as a Locus of Native Trade Dependence Prior to the Iroquois Defeat of the Huron, 1648–52." M.A. thesis, Carleton University, Ottawa, 1979.

Glueck, Alvin C. *Minnesota and the Manifest Destiny of the Canadian Northwest; a Study in Canadian-American Relations.* Toronto: University of Toronto Press, 1965.

Godelier, Maurice. *Perspectives in Marxist Anthropology.* Translated by Robert Brain. Cambridge: Cambridge University Press, 1977.

Goldstein, R. *French-Iroquois Diplomatic and Military Relations, 1609–1701.* The Hague: Mouton & Co., 1969.

Gonzalez, Ellice B. *Changing Economic Roles for Micmac Men and Women: An Ethnohistorical Analysis.* National Museum of Man, Mercury Series. Ottawa, 1981.

Gooding, S.J. *The Canadian Gunsmiths, 1608–1900.* West Hill, Ontario: Museum Restoration Service, 1962.

Government of Newfoundland and Labrador. *Assessment and Analysis of the Micmac Land Claim in Newfoundland.* St. John's Newfoundland, 1982.

Graburn, N. *Eskimos without Igloos: Social and Economic Development in Sugluk.* Boston: Little, Brown and Co., 1969.

Hanley, Thomas O'Brien, ed. *The John Caroll Papers.* 3 volumes. Notre Dame: University of Notre Dame Press, 1976.

Hargrave, James. *The Hargrave Correspondence 1821–1843.* Edited by G.P. de T. Glazebrook. Toronto: Champlain Society, 1938.

Harner, Michael J. "Population Pressure and the Social Evolution of Agriculturalists." *Southwestern Journal of Anthropology*, vol. 26, no. 1, 1970.

Harper, K. *Writing in Inuktitut: An Historical Perspective.* Ottawa: Department of Indian Affairs and Northern Development, 1983.

Harris, Leslie. *Newfoundland and Labrador, a Brief History.* J.M. Dent & Sons (Canada) Ltd., 1968.

Harris, Marvin. *The Rise of Anthropological Theory: A History of Theories of Culture.* New York: Thomas Crowell, 1986.

Hart, C.W.M. and A.R. Pilling. *The Tiwi of North Australia.* New York: Holt, Rinehart and Winston, 1962.

Hartwig, G.W. and K.D. Patterson, eds. *Disease in African History.* Durham, N.C.: Duke University Press, 1978.

Hawthorn, H.B., C.S. Belshaw, and S. Jamieson. *Indians of British Columbia: A Study of Contemporary Social Adjustment*. Toronto: University of Toronto Press, 1958.

Hawthorne, H.B., A. Laforet, and S.M. Jamieson. "Northern People: A Discussion Paper." In *Science and the North: A Seminar on Guidelines for Scientific Activities in Northern Canada*. Ottawa: Information Canada, 1973.

Hechter, M. *Internal Colonialism*. Los Angeles: University of California Press, 1975.

________. "Ethnicity and Industrialization: On the Proliferation of the Cultural Division of Labor." *Ethnicity* 3, 1976.

________. "Group Formation and the Cultural Division of Labor." *American Journal of Sociology* 84, 1978.

Heidenreich, C.E. *Huronia: A History and Geography of the Huron Indians, 1600*–1650. Toronto: McClelland and Stewart, 1971.

Held, Robert. *The Age of Firearms*. Northfield: The Gun Digest Co., 1957.

Helm, J. and N.O. Lurie. *The Subsistence Economy of the Dogrib Indians of Lac La Martre in the Mackenzie District of the N.W.T.* Ottawa: Northern Co-ordination and Research Centre, 1961.

Hickerson, H. "Some Implications of the Theory of the Particularity, or Atomism, of Northern Algonkians." *Current Anthropology*, vol. 8, no. 2, 1967.

Hill, R.M. "Petroleum Pipelines and Arctic Environment." *North* 18, 1971.

Hind, H.Y. *Explorations in the Interior of the Labrador Peninsula*. London: Longman, Green and Co., 1863.

Hind, Youle A. "Red River Settlement and the Half-breed Buffalo Hunters." *Canadian Merchants Magazine and Commercial Review* 3, 1958.

Hines, J. *The Red Indians of the Plains: Thirty Years Missionary Experience in Saskatchewan*. Toronto: MacLean, Roger & Co., 1916.

Honigman, I and J. Honigman. *Eskimo Townsmen*. Ottawa: Canadian Research Center for Anthropology, Saint Paul University, 1965.

Hornby, P.A. *Bilingualism, Psychological, Social and Educational Implications*. New York: Academic Press, 1977.

Horsmand, Reginald. *Race and Manifest Destiny*. Cambridge, Mass.: Harvard University Press, 1981.

Howay, F.W. "A List of Trading Vessels in the Maritime Fur Trade, 1785–94." *Transactions of the Royal Society of Canada*, 3d series 24, section 2, 1930.

Howay, F.W., ed. *Voyages of the Columbia*. Boston, MA.: Historical Society, 1940.

Hudson, D.R. "Traplines and Timber: Social and Economic Change among the Carrier Indians of British Columbia." Ph.D. diss., University of Alberta, Edmonton, 1983.

Hughes, C. "Under Four Flags: Recent Culture Change Among the Eskimos." *Current Anthropology*, vol. 6, no. 1, 1965.

Hunt, George T. *The Wars of the Iroquois: A Study in Intertribal Relations*. Madison: University of Wisconsin Press, 1940.

Hyde, G.E. *Indians of the Woodlands, from Prehistoric Times to 1725*. Norman: University of Oklahoma Press, 1962.

Indian Brotherhood of the Northwest Territories. "The Threat to the Indian in the Northwest Territories." Position Paper presented to the National Indian Brotherhood Meeting, Regina, July 1971. Mimeographed.

Indian and Inuit Support Group of Newfoundland and Labrador. "The Newfoundland Government's Rejection of the Micmac Land Claim." St. John's, Newfoundland, 1982. Unpublished position paper.

Ingraham, J. *Journal of the Brigantine Hope on a Voyage to the Northwest Coast of North America 1790–92*. Edited by M.D. Kaplanoff. Massachusetts: Imprint Society, 1971.

Innis, Harold A. *Empire and Communications*. Toronto: Uptown Press, 1950.

________. *The Fur Trade in Canada; An Introduction to Canadian Economic History*. Toronto: University of Toronto Press, 1962.

Inuit Broadcasting Corporation. *Proposal for Inuit Children's Educational Television*. IBC July 1982.

Inuit Broadcasting Corporation. *Position on Northern Broadcasting*. IBC August 1982.

Inuit Cultural Institute. *Annual Report, 1979–1980*. Ottawa: Information Services of Inuit Tapirisat of Canada, 1978.

Inuit Tapirisat of Canada. *Annual Report, 1979–1980*. Ottawa: Information Services of Inuit Tapirisat of Canada, 1980.

Inuit Tapirisat of Canada. "Nunavut—Our Land." In *Two Nations, Many Cultures: Ethnic Groups in Canada*. By J. Elliott. Scarborough: Prentice-Hall, Inc., 1983.

Jaeren, Cornelius. *The French Relationship with the Native Peoples of New France and Acadia*. Ottawa: Indian and Northern Affairs, 1984.

Jenness, D. Eskimo *Administration: II. Canada*. Arctic Institute of North America, Technical Paper 14. Montreal: McGill-Queen's University Press, 1964.

Jennings, Francis. *The Invasion of America: Indians, Colonialism and the Cant of Conquest*. Chapel Hill: University of North Carolina Press, 1975.

Jewitt, John R. *Narrative of the Adventures and Sufferings of John R. Jewitt While Held as a Captive of the Nootka Indians of Vancouver Island, 1803 to 1805*. Edited by Robert F. Heizer. Ballena Press Publications in Archaeology, Ethnology and History, No. 5, 1975.

Johnson, S.M. "Epidemic Effects as Causes of Warfare in the Northeast after 1640." M.A. thesis, Carleton University, 1982.

Judd, C.M. "Native Labour and Social Stratification in the Hudson's Bay Company's Northern Department, 1770–1870." *Canadian Review of Sociology and Anthropology*, vol. 17, no. 4, 1980.

Judd, C.M. and A.J. Ray, eds. *Old Trails and New Directions: Papers of the Third North American Fur Trade Conference*. Toronto: University of Toronto Press, 1980.

Kane, Paul. *Wanderings of an Artist among the Indians of North America, from Canada to Vancouver's Island and Oregon Through the Hudson's Bay Company's Territory and Back Again*. 1859. Reprint. Edmonton: Hurtig, 1968.

Keating, William H. *Narrative of an Expedition to the Source of St. Peter's River, Lake Winnepeek, Lake of the Woods, etc. Performed in the Year 1823*. Reprint. Minneapolis: Ross & Haines, 1959.

Keesing, Felix M. *The Menomini Indians of Wisconsin*. Philadelphia: The American Philosophical Society, 1939.

Keyes, Charles F. "Towards a New Formation of the Concept of Ethnic Groups." *Ethnicity* 3, 1976.

Kinietz, W. Vernon. *The Indians of the Western Great Lakes, 1615–1760*. Ann Arbor: University of Michigan Press, 1965.

Kleivan, H. *The Eskimos of Northeast Labrador: A History of Eskimo White Relations, 1771–1995*. Oslo: Norsk Polarinstitutt Skrifter 139, 1966.

Knight, Rolf. *Ecological Factors in Changing Economy and Social Organization among the Rupert House Cree*. National Museum of Man, Anthropological Papers No. 15. Ottawa, 1968.

_________. "Grey Owl's Return: Cultural Ecology and Canadian Indigenous Peoples." *Reviews in Anthropology* 1, 1974.

_________. *Indians at Work*. Vancouver: New Star Press, 1978.

Ktaqamkuk Ilnui Saqimawoutic and the Conne River Indian Band Council. *Freedom to Live Our Own Way in Our Own Land*. Conne River, Newfoundland: Ktaqamkuk Ilnui Saqimawoutic and the Conne River Band Council, 1982.

Lagassé, Jean H., Director. *The People of Indian Ancestry in Manitoba*. 3 volumes. Winnipeg: Department of Agriculture and Immigration, 1959.

LaPerouse, J. *A Voyage Round the World in the Years 1785, 6, 7, 8*. 3 volumes. Edited by M. Milet-Mareau. London, 1798.

LaRocque, Emma. "The Métis in English Literature." *Canadian Journal of Native Studies*, vol. 3, no. 1, 1983.

LaRusic, Ignatius E. *et al. Negotiating a Way of Life: Initial Cree Experience with the Administrative Structure Arising from the James Bay Agreement*. Montreal: ssDoc Inc., 1979.

La Sierra. *Diaries of Benito de la Sierra and Padre Miguel de la Campa made on Board the Frigate Santiago 1775*. Mexico: D.F., 1929.

Laverdure, Patline and Ida Rose Allard. *The Michif Dictionary: Turtle Mountain Chippewa Cree*. Edited by John Crawford. Winnipeg: Pemmican Publications, 1983.

Leach, Douglas Edward. *Flintlock and Tomahawk: New England in King Philip's War*. New York: Macmillan Co., 1958.

Leacock, E. *The Montagnais "Hunting Territory" and the Fur Trade*. Memoir No. 78 of the American Anthropological Association, 1954.

________. "Matrilocality in a Simple Hunting Economy (Montagnais-Naskapi)." *Southwestern Journal of Anthropology*, 1955.

________. "Women's Status in Egalitarian Society: Implications for Social Evolution." *Current Anthropology* 19, 1978.

Leacock, E.B. and N.O. Lurie, eds. *North American Indians in Historical Perspective*. New York: Random House Inc., 1971.

Lee, Richard B. "Is There a Foraging Mode of Production?" *Canadian Journal of Anthropology*, vol, 2, no. 1, 1981.

Legget, R.F. "Technology: Discussion Paper." In *Science and the North: A Seminar on Guidelines for Scientific Activities in Northern Canada*. Ottawa: Information Canada, 1973.

Legget, R.F. and I.C. MacFarlane, eds. *Proceedings of the Canadian Northern Pipeline Research Conference, 2-4 February 1972*. Technical Memorandum No. 104. Ottawa: National Research Council of Canada, 1972.

Legros, Dominique. "Chance, Necessity and Mode of Production: A Marxist Critique of Cultural Evolutionism." *American Anthropologist*, vol. 79, no. 1, 1977.

________. "Reflexion sur l'origine des inégalités sociales à partis du cas des Athapaskan tutchone." *Culture*, vol. 2, no. 3, 1982.

Lewis, M. *The Lewis and Clark Expedition*. Volume II. Philadelphia and New York: Lippincott Co., 1961.

Lewis, O. *La Vida*. New York: Random House, 1966.

Lips, J. "Public Opinion and Mutual Assistance Among the Montagnais-Naskapi." *American Anthropologist* 39, 1937.

________. "Naskapi Law." *Transactions of the American Philosophical Society* 37, 1947.

Lysyk, K.M. et al. *Alaska Highway Pipeline Inquiry*. Ottawa: Department of Indian and Northern Affairs, 1977.

MacDonald, Graham A. "Commerce, Civility and Old Sault Ste. Marie." *The Beaver* 312, 1981.

MacDougall, John. *Opening of the Great West—Experience of a Missionary in 1875–1876*. Calgary: Glenbow Alberta Institute, 1970.

MacEwan, John Walter Grant. *Between the Red and the Rockies*. Toronto: University of Toronto, 1952.

________. *Harvest of Bread*. Saskatoon: Western Producer, 1969.

MacGregor, James G. *Father Lacombe*. Edmonton: Hurtig, 1975.

Mackenzie Delta Task Force. "Report No. 2." Submitted to the Department of Indian Affairs and Northern Development, 1970. Mimeographed.

Madill, D.F.K. *Selected Annotated Bibliography of Métis History and Claims*. Ottawa: Indian and Northern Affairs Canada, 1983.

Malaspina, A. *Politico-Scientific Voyage Round the World by Corvettes Descubierta and Atrevida from 1789–94*. Translated by C. Robinson. Vancouver: University of British Columbia Press, 1934.

Malaurie, Jean. "Raids et esclavage dans les sociétés autochtones du détroit Behring." *Inter-Nord* 13/14, 1974.

Malaurie, Jean and Jacques Rousseau, eds. *Le Nouveau-Québec. Contribution à l'étude de l'occupation humaine.* Paris: Mouton, 1964.

Marchak, Pat, Neil Guppy and John L. McMullan, eds. *Uncommon Property: Fishing and Fish Processing Industries in British Columbia.* Toronto: Methuen, forthcoming.

Marchand, J.F. "Tribal Epidemics in the Yukon." *Journal of the American Medical Association* 123, 1943.

Marshall, Ingeborg. "Disease as a Factor in the Demise of the Beothuk Indians." *Culture*, vol. 1, no. 1, 1981.

Masson, L.R. ed. "Arrangements of the Proprietors, Clerks, Interpreters, etc. of the North-West Company in the Indian Departments, 1799 (the Old Company)." In *Les Bourgeois de la Compagnie du Nord-Ouest*, vol. 2. New York: Antiquarian Press, 1960.

________. "Liste des 'Bourgeois', Commis, Engagés, et 'Voyageurs', de la Compagnie du Nord-Ouest, aprés la Fusion de 1804." In *Les Bourgeois de la Compagnie du Nord-Ouest*, vol. 1. New York: Antiquarian Press, 1960.

Mather, Cotton. *Magnalia.* 1572.

Mather, Increase. *A Brief History of the War with the Indians of New England.* Plymouth, 1676.

Mayne, Richard Charles. *Four Years in British Columbia and Vancouver Island.* London: John Murray, 1862.

McDonald, James Andrew. "A History of the Traplines that have once been Registered by Kitsumkalums." Kitsumkalum Social History Research Project, Report No. 4, 1982.

________. "An Historic Event in the Political Economy of the Tsimshian: Information on the Ownership of the Zimacord District." *British Columbia Studies* 57, 1983.

________. "Trying to Make a Life: The Historic Political Economy of Kitsumkalum." Ph.D. diss., University of British Columbia, 1985.

McDonnell, John. "Some Account of the Red River (about 1797)." *Les Bourgeois de la Compagnie du Nord-Ouest*, edited by L.R. Masson, vol. 1. New York: Antiquarian Press, 1960.

McDougall, John. *Saddle, Sled and Snowshoe: Pioneering on the Saskatchewan in the Sixties.* Toronto: Wm. Briggs, 1896.

McGhee, R. *Beluga Hunters: An Archaeological Reconstruction of the Mackenzie Delta Kittegaryumiut.* St. John's: Memorial University of Newfoundland, Institute of Social and Economic Resources, 1974.

McIlwraith, T.F. *The Bella Coola Indians.* 2 volumes. Toronto: University of Toronto Press, 1948.

McLean, John. *John McLean's Notes of a Twenty-Five Years' Service in the Hudson's Bay Territory.* Toronto: Champlain Society, 1932.

Meares, J. *Voyages made in the Years 1788–89 from China to the Northwest Coast of America.* New York: Da Capo Press, 1967.

Meldrum, Sheila and Marion Helman. *Summary of the Statistical Data from the D.I.A.N.D. Northern Manpower Survey Program in the Yukon and Northwest Territories, 1969–1971.* Ottawa: Department of Indian and Northern Affairs, 1975.

Merriman, R.O. "The Bison and the Fur Trade." *Queen's Quarterly* 34, 1926.

Michigan Pioneer and Historical Collections. 40 volumes. Lansing: Thorpe & Godfrey, State Printers, 1888.

Mitchell, Donald and Leland Donald. "Some Economic Aspects of Tlingit, Haida, and Tsimshian Slavery." *Research in Economic Anthropology* 7, 1985.

Morantz, T. *An Ethnohistoric Study of Eastern James Bay Cree Social Organization, 1700–1850.* Ottawa: National Museum of Man, 1983.

Morgan, Lewis Henry. *The Indian Journals, 1859-62*. Edited with an Introduction by Leslie A. White. Ann Arbor: University of Michigan Press, 1959.

Morris, Alexander. *The Treaties of Canada with the Indians of Manitoba and the North-West Territories*. Toronto: Belfords, Clarke & Co., 1880.

Morrow, Justice W.G. "Reasons for Judgement of the Honourable Mr. Justice W.G. Morrow in the Matter of an Application by Chief François Paulette et al. to Lodge a Certain Caveat with the Registrar of Titles of the Land Titles Office for the Northwest Territories." Supreme Court of the Northwest Territories, Yellowknife, 1973. Mimeographed.

Morton, A.S. "The Place of the Red River Settlement in the Plans of the Hudson's Bay Company, 1812–1825." *Report of the Annual Meeting of the Canadian Historical Association*, 1930.

_________. *History of the Prairie Settlement*. Toronto: Macmillan, 1938.

_________. *A History of the Canadian West to 1870–71; Being a History of Rupert's Land (The Hudson's Bay Company's Territory), and of the North-West Territory (Including the Pacific Slope)*. London: Thomas Nelson and Sons, 1939.

_________. *A History of the Canadian West to 1870–71*. 2nd ed. Toronto: University of Toronto Press, 1973.

Morton, W.L. "Agriculture in the Red River Colony." *Canadian Historical Review* 30, 1949.

_________. *Manitoba: A History*. Toronto: University of Toronto Press, 1967.

_________. "A History of Plain and Parkland." *Alberta Historical Review*, vol. 17, no. 2, 1969.

Mourelle, F. "Voyage of the 'Sonora' in the Second Bucareli Expedition . . . The Journal Kept in 1775 on the 'Sonora' by Don Francisco Antonio Mourelle." In *Miscellanies* by Daines Barrington. London, 1781.

Murray, Stanley Norman. *The Valley Comes of Age: A History of Agriculture in the Valley of the Red River of the North, 1812–1920*. Fargo: North Dakota Institute for Regional Studies, 1967.

Nash, J. and M.P. Fernandez-Kelly, eds. *Women, Men, and the International Division of Labor*. Albany: State University of New York Press, 1983.

Neek, J.V., W.R. Centerwall, N.A. Chagnon, and H.L. Casey. "Notes on the Effect of Measles and Measles Vaccine in a Virgin-Soil Population of South American Indians." *American Journal of Epidemiology*, vol. 91, no. 4, 1970.

Nichols, R.L., ed. *The American Indian: Past and Present*. New York, 1986.

Nicks, Trudy. "Native Responses to the Early Fur Trade at Lesser Slave Lake." Paper presented at the 5th North American Fur Trade Conference, Montreal, Quebec, 30 May 1985.

Niebor, H.J. *Slavery as an Industrial System*. The Hague: Martinus Nijhoff, 1910.

Oberg, Kalervo. *The Social Economy of the Tlingit Indians*. Seattle: University of Washington Press, 1973.

O'Callaghan, F. *Documents Relating to the Colonial History of the State of New York*. Vol. I & II. Albany: Weed, Parsons & Co., 1849.

Olson, R.L. *Social Structure and Social Life of the Tlingit in Alaska*. University of California Anthropological Records 26. Berkeley, 1967.

Opening Up the West: being the Official Reports of the North-West Mounted Police from 1874–1881. Toronto: MacLean, Roger & Co., 1973.

Orvic, N. and K. Patterson. *The North in Transition*. Kingston: McGill-Queen's University Press, 1976.

Osborne, A.C., ed. "The Migration of Voyageurs from Drummond Island to Penatanguishene in 1818 and List of the Drummond Island Voyageurs." *Ontario Historical Society Papers and Records* 3, 1901.

Osgood, L. Basic *Kangiruarmiut Eskimo Dictionary*. Inuvik: Committee for the Original People's Entitlement, 1983.

Otterbein, K. "Why the Iroquois Won—An Analysis of Military Tactics." *Ethnohistory* 2, 1965.

Paine, R., ed. *The White Arctic: Anthropological Essays on Tutelage and Ethnicity*. Toronto: University of Toronto Press, 1977.

Palmer, William P. and H.W. Flournoy, eds. *Calendar of Virginia State Papers and Other Manuscripts*. 11 volumes. Richmond, 1875–93.

Pannekoek, Frits. "The Rev. Griffiths, Owen Corbett and the Red River Civil War of 1869–70." *Canadian Historical Review*, vol. 57, no. 2, 1976.

Paré, George. *The Catholic Church in Detroit, 1701–1888*. Detroit: Gabriel Richard Press, 1961.

Paré, George and Milo M. Quaife, eds. "The St. Joseph Baptismal Register." *The Mississippi Valley Historical Review* 13, June 1926.

Parkman, F. *The Jesuits in North America in the Seventeenth Century*. Boston: Little Brown & Co., 1867.

_________. *La Salle and the Discovery of the Great West*. Boston: Little Brown & Co., 1897.

Pastore, Ralphe. *Newfoundland Micmacs: A History of Their Traditional Life*. Newfoundland Historical Society Pamphlet, No. 5. St. John's, Newfoundland, 1978.

Patterson, E.P. *The Canadian Indian: A History Since 1500*. Don Mills, 1972.

Patterson, Orlando. *Slavery and Social Death: A Comparative Study*. Cambridge, MA: Harvard University Press, 1982.

Patterson, S. *Narrative of the Adventures and Sufferings of Samuel Patterson*. Washington: Galleon Press, 1967.

Payment, Diane. *Batoche (1870–1910)*. Winnipeg: Les Éditions du Blé, 1983.

Peterson, H.L. *Arms and Armour in Colonial America*. Harrisburg, PA: The Stackpole Co., 1956.

Peterson, Jacqueline. "Prelude to Red River: A Social Portrait of the Great Lakes Métis." *Ethnohistory*, vol. 25, no. 1, 1978.

_________. "The People in Between: Indian-White Marriage and the Genesis of a Métis Society and Culture in the Great Lakes Region, 1680–1830." Ph.D. diss., University of Illinois at Chicago Circle, 1981.

_________. "Ethnogenesis and the Growth of a 'New People'." *American Indian Culture and Research Journal*, vol. 6, no. 2, 1982.

Peterson, Jacqueline and Jennifer S.H. Brown. *The New Peoples: Being and Becoming Métis in North America*. Winnipeg: University of Manitoba Press, 1985.

Pimlott, D.H., K. Vincent, and C.E. McKnight. *Arctic Alternatives: A National Workshop on People, Resources on the Environment of '60*. Ottawa: Canadian Arctic Resources Committee, 1973.

Prattis, J.I. *The Structure of Resource Development in the Canadian North*. Carleton University, Department of Sociology and Anthropology, Working Paper 80-6. Ottawa, 1980.

_________. "The Political Economy of Native Land Claims in the Canadian North." Ottawa: Unpublished manuscript, 1983.

Prattis, J. and J.P. Chartrand. *System and Process: Inuktitut-English Bilingualism in the Northwest Territories of Canada*. Center for Research on Ethnic Minorities, Working Paper No. 5. Ottawa: Carleton University, Department of Sociology and Anthropology, 1985.

Price, John A. "An Overview of Recent Books and Graduate Theses in Canadian Native Studies." Paper presented at the Canadian Ethnology Society Meeting, University of Toronto, May 10–12, 1985.

Pritchard, John C. "Economic Development and the Disintegration of Traditional Culture Among the Harsla." Ph.D. diss., University of British Columbia, 1977.

Proceedings, XL Congresso Internatzionali degli Americanisti. Vol. 2. Geneva: Tilgher, 1974.

Proceedings of the Fifth Northern Development Conference, Edmonton. Edmonton: Northern Development Conference, 1970.

Québec. *The James Bay and Northern Québec Agreement*. Québec City: National Library, 1976.

Quimby, George. *Indian Cultures and Indian Trade Goods*. Madison: University of Wisconsin Press, 1966.

Rasporich, A.W., ed. *Western Canada Past and Present*. Calgary, 1975.

Ray, A.J. "Diffusion of Diseases in the Western Interior of Canada, 1830–1850." *Geographical Review*, vol. 66, no. 2 (n.d.).

________. *The Indian in the Fur Trade, 1660-1870*. Toronto, 1974.

Rea, K. *The Political Economy of Northern Development*. Ottawa: Science Council of Canada, 1976.

Reitz, J. *The Survival of Ethnic Groups*. Toronto: McGraw-Hill Ryerson Ltd., 1980.

"The Reminiscences of Peter Erasmus as told to Henry T. Thompson." Glenbow Alberta Institute. Calgary, Alberta.

Rich, E.E., ed. *London Correspondence Inward from Eden Colvile, 1849–1852*. London: Hudson's Bay Record Society, 1956.

________. *The History of the Hudson's Bay Company, 1670–1870*. Vol. I & II. London, 1958.

________. "Trade Habits and Economic Motivation among the Indians of North America." *Canadian Journal of Economics and Political Science* XXVI, 1960.

Ritchie, J.C. "Northern Fiction—Northern Homage." *Arctic*, vol. 31, no. 2, 1978.

Robinson, Elwyn B. *History of North Dakota*. Lincoln: University of Nebraska Press, 1966.

Robitaille, N. and R. Choinière. *An Overview of Demographic and Socio-Economic Conditions of the Inuit in Canada*. Ottawa: Department of Indian Affairs and Northern Development, 1985.

Roe, Frank Gilbert. *The North American Buffalo: A Critical Study of the Species in its Wild State*. Toronto: University of Toronto Press, 1951.

Rogers, Edward S. *The Hunting Group—Hunting Territory Complex among the Mistassini Indians*. Ottawa: National Museum of Canada, 1963.

Ronald, Grant and E.S. Wellhoffer. *Ethnonationalism, Multinational Corporations and the Modern State*. Monograph, Science and World Affairs, vol. 1, no. 15, bk. 4. Denver: University of Denver, 1979.

Roquefeuil, C. *A Voyage Round the World Between the Years 1816–19*. London, 1823.

Rosaldo, M. and L. Lamphere, eds. *Woman, Culture, and Society*. Palo Alto, CA: Stanford University Press, 1974.

Ross, Alexander. *The Red River Settlement: Its Rise, Progress, and Present State. With Some Account of the Native Races and its General History to the Present Day*. 1856. Reprint. Minneapolis: Ross and Haines, 1957.

Ross, Jeffrey and Anne Baker, eds. *The Mobilization of Collective Identity: Comparative Perspectives*. Lanham, MD: University Press of America, 1980.

Ross, W.M. *Salmon Cannery Pack Statistics on the Nass and Skeena Rivers of British Columbia*. Vancouver: University of British Columbia Press, n.d.

Russell, Carl H. *Guns on the Early Frontiers*. Berkeley: University of California Press, 1962.

Saffioti, H.I.B. *Women in Class Society*. Translated by Michael Vale. NewYork: Monthly Review Press, 1978.

Sahlins, Marshall David. *Social Stratification in Polynesia*. Seattle: University of Washington Press, 1958.

Sanday, P. "Toward a Theory of the Status of Women." *American Anthropologist* 75, 1973.

Saum, Lewis O. *The Fur Trader and the Indian*. Seattle: University of Washington Press, 1965.

Sawchuk, Joe. *The Métis of Manitoba: Reformulation of an Ethnic Identity*. Toronto: Peter Martin Associates, 1978.

_________. "The Métis, Non-Status Indians and the New Aboriginality: Government Influence on Native Political Alliances and Identity." *Canadian Ethnic Studies*, vol. 17, no. 2, 1985.

Schlesier, K. "Die Irokesenkriege und die Grosse Vertreibung, 1609-1656." *Zeitschrift für Ethnologie*, 1975.

Schoolcraft, Henry Rowe. *Personal Memoir of a Residence of Thirty Years with the Indian Tribes on the American Frontier with Brief Notices of Passing Events, Facts, and Opinions, A.D. 1812 to A.D. 1842*. Philadelphia: Lippincott, Grambo & Co., 1851.

_________. *Information Respecting the History, Condition and Prospects of the Indian Tribes of the United States*. Philadelphia: Lippincott, Grambo and Co., 1854.

_________. *Narrative Journal of Travels . . . to the Sources of the Mississippi River in the Year 1820*. 1921. Reprint. University Microfilms, 1966.

Scott, Colin. "Production and Exchange Among Wemindji Cree: Egalitarian Ideology and Economic Base." *Culture*, vol. 2, no. 3, 1982.

Service, F.R. *Primitive Social Organization, an Evolutionary Perspective*. New York: Random House, 1962.

Settlers and Rebels: Being the Official Reports to Parliament of the Activities of the North-West Mounted Police from 1882 to 1885 by the Commissioner of the NWMP. Toronto: MacLean, Roger & Co., 1973.

Shulman, Martin and Don McLean. "Lawrence Clarke: Architect of Revolt." *Canadian Journal of Native Studies*, vol. 3, no. 1, 1983.

Smith, D. *Native and Outsiders: Pluralism in the Mackenzie Delta*. Ottawa: Department of Indian Affairs and Northern Development, 1975.

_________. "Mackenzie Delta Eskimos." In *Handbook of North American Indians*, vol. 5. Edited by W.C. Sturtevant. Washington: Smithsonian Institute, 1984.

Speck, F.G. "The Family Hunting Band as the Basis of Algonquian Social Organization." *American Anthropologist* 17, 1915.

_________. "Social Structure of the Northern Algonkian." Publications of the American Sociological Society, 1917.

_________. *Beothuk and Micmac*. Indian Notes and Monographs. New York: Heye Foundation, 1922.

_________. "Mistassini Hunting Territories in the Labrador Penninsula." *American Anthropologist* 25, 1923.

_________. "Family Hunting Territories of the Lake St. John Montagnais and Neighboring Bands." *Anthropos* 22, 1927.

Sprague, D.N. "Government Lawlessness in the Administration of Manitoba Land Claims 1870–1887." *Manitoba Law Journal* 10, 1980.

Sprague, D.N. and R.P. Frye, comps. *The Geneology of the First Métis Nation*. Winnipeg: Pemmican Publications, 1983.

Stabler, J.C. "The Report of the Mackenzie Valley Pipeline Inquiry, Volume I: A Socio-Economic Critique." *Musk-ox* 20, 1977.

Stanley, George. *The Birth of Western Canada: A History of the Riel Rebellions*. Toronto: University of Toronto Press, 1960.

Statement Respecting the Earl of Selkirk's Settlement upon the Red River in North America; its Destruction in 1815 and 1816, and the Massacre of Governor Semple and his Party. 1817. Coles Facsimile Edition, 1970.

Stearne, E.W. and A.E. Stearne. *The Effects of Smallpox on the Destiny of the Amerindian*. Boston: Bruce Humphries, Inc., 1945.

Steegmann, A. Theodore, Jr., ed. *Boreal Forest Adaptations: The Northern Algonkians*. New York: Plenum Press, 1983.

Stone, Lyle M. and Donald Chaput. "History of the Upper Great Lakes Area." *Handbook of North American Indians*. Smithsonian Institution, vol. 15. Edited by Bruce Trigger. Washington, D.C., 1978.

Strange, J. *Journal and Narrative of the Commercial Expedition from Bombay to the Northwest Coast of America*. Madras, 1928.

Strong, W.D. "Cross-cousin Marriage and the Culture of the Northeastern Algonkian." *American Anthropologist* 31, 1929.

Swadesh, Morris. "Motivations in Nootka Warfare." *Southwestern Journal of Anthropology* 4, 1948.

Tanner, Adrian. "Existe-t-il des territoires de chasses?" *Récherches amerindiennes au Québec* 1, 1972.

———. *Bringing Home Animals: Mode of Production and Religious Ideology among the Mistassini Cree Hunters*. St. John's: The Institute of Social and Economic Research, 1979.

Taylor, I. and J. Knowelden. *Principles of Epidemiology*. London, 1964.

Taylor, J.F. "Sociocultural Effects of Epidemics on the Northern Plains: 1734–1850." *Western Canadian Journal of Anthropology*, vol. 7, no. 4 (n.d.)

Thompson, M., M. Garcia, and F. Kense, eds. *Status, Structure, and Stratification*. Proceedings of the Sixteenth Annual Conference, Archaeological Association of the University of Calgary, 1985.

Thwaites, R.G., ed. *The Jesuit Relations and Allied Documents: Travels and Explorations of the Jesuit Missionaries of New France, 1610–1791*. 71 volumes.

Tooker, E. "The Iroquois Defeat of the Huron: A Review of Causes." *Pennsylvania Archaeology* 33, 1963.

Tooker, E., ed. *The Development of Political Organization in Native North America*. 1979 Proceedings of the American Ethnological Society, 1983

Trealease, A.W. *Indian Affairs in Colonial New York: The Seventeenth Century*. Ithaca, New York: Cornell University Press, 1960.

Treaty Commissioners. *Treaty No. 11 and Adhesion, with Reports, etc.* Ottawa: Queen's Printer, 1926.

Trigger, B.G. *The Huron: Farmers of the North*. New York: Holt, Rinehart and Winston, Inc., 1969.

———. *The Impact of Europeans on Huronia*. Toronto: Copp, Clark, 1969.

———. *The Children of the Aataentsic: A History of the Huron People to 1660*. Montreal: McGill-Queen's University Press, 1976.

Tuchman, B.W. *A Distant Mirror*. New York: Alfred A. Knopf, 1979.

Turkki, Pat. *Burns Lake and District: A History Formal and Informal*. Burns Lake, B.C.: Burns Lake Historical Society, 1973.

Turner, D. and G. Smith, eds. *Challenging Anthropology*. Toronto: McGraw-Hill Ryerson, 1979.

Tyrrell, J.B., ed. *Journal of Samuel Hearne and Philip Turnor*. Toronto, 1934.

———. *David Thompson's Narrative of his Explorations in Western America, 1784–1812*. Toronto: The Champlain Society, 1968.

Upton, Leslie. "The Extermination of the Beothuks." *Canadian Historical Review*, vol. 57, no. 3, 1977.

U.S. Department of the Interior. *Final Environmental Impact Statement, Trans-Alaska Pipeline*. Vol. V. Washington, D.C.: U.S. Government Printing Office, 1972.

Usher, P.J. "Evaluating Country Food in the Northern Native Economy." *Arctic*, vo. 29, no. 2, 1976.

Valaskakis, G. "Communications and Control in the North: The Potential of Interactive Satellites." *Etudes Inuit Studies* 6, 1982.

Vancouver, G. *A Voyage of Discovery to the North Pacific Ocean and Around the World*. 3 volumes. London, 1798.

Van Kirk, Sylvia. *Many Ties: Women in Fur Trade Society*. Watson and Dwyer, 1980.

Van Laer. *New York Historical Manuscripts*. Albany: New York State Archives, 1908.

Vayda, A.P. and A. Leeds, eds. *Man, Culture and Animals*. American Association for the Advancement of Science, Publication 78. Washington, D.C., 1965.

Von Landsdorff, G. *Voyages and Travels in Various Parts of the World*. Vol. II. New York: Da Capo Press, 1968.

Wagner, H. *Spanish Explorations in the Strait of Juan de Fuca*. Santa Anna, California, 1933.

Wah-Shee, J. "Address to the Fifth International Congress of the Fondation Française d'Études Nordiques, LeHavre, May, 1973." *Northern Perspectives*, July-August 1973.

Walker, A. *An Account of a Voyage to the Northwest Coast of America in 1785 and 1786*. Edited by R. Fisher and J.M. Bumsted. Seattle: University of Washington Press, 1982.

Walker, James W. St. G. "The Indian in Canadian Historical Writing." *Historical Papers*. Canadian Historical Association, 1971.

Wallace, D. *The Long Labrador Trail*. New York: Outing Publishing Co., 1907.

Ward, H.M. *The United Colonies of New England*. New York: Vantage Press, 1961.

Warren, William W. *History of the Ojibway Nation*. 1885. Reprint. Minneapolis: Ross & Haines, 1957.

Watkins, M., ed. *Dene Nation: The Colony Within*. Toronto: University of Toronto Press, 1977.

Williams, Glydwr, ed. *Andrew Graham's Observations on Hudson's Bay, 1767-91*. London, 1969.

Wilson, Daniel. *Prehistoric Man: Researches into the Origin of Civilisation in the Old and the New World*. Vol. 2. London, 1876.

Winthrop, John. *Journal*. Edited by James K. Hosmer. Vol. 2. New York: Charles Scribner's Sons, 1908.

Wisconsin Historical Collections. 31 volumes. Madison: State Historical Society of Wisconsin, 1855–1931.

Wolforth, J.R. *The Mackenzie Delta—Its Economic Base and Development*. Ottawa: Northern Science Research Group, 1967.

Wright, J.V. "A Review: Children of Aataentsic, A History of the Huron People to 1660." *Canadian Journal of Archaeology* 1, 1977.

Wrong, G.M. *The Long Journey to the Country of the Hurons*. Toronto: The Champlain Society, 1939.

Yukon Native Brotherhood. "Together Today for Our Children Tomorrow: A Statement of Grievances and an Approach to Settlement by the Yukon Native People." Yukon Native Brotherhood, Whitehorse, 1973. Mimeographed.

Young, H. *Elementary English for the Eskimo*. Ottawa: Ministry of Resources and Development, 1950.